THE NEW BOOK
OF KNOWLEDGE

HOME AND SCHOOL
READING AND STUDY
GUIDES

GROLIER
INCORPORATED
DANBURY, CONN.

The editors of THE NEW BOOK OF KNOWLEDGE wish to acknowledge Educational Consultant Barbara Darga, whose experience as a teacher and whose research into current curriculum issues and trends guided the development and preparation of this edition of the HOME AND SCHOOL READING AND STUDY GUIDES.

The editors also wish to thank the teachers, librarians, and parents whose experiences, reviews, and suggestions help keep the information in these guides both useful and practical.

For the 1995 edition:
Editor: Whitney Pratt-Côté
Copy Editor: Sara Boak
Art Director: Nancy Hamlen
Production Manager: Teresa Kluk
Production Editor: Carolyn F. Reil

THE HOME AND SCHOOL READING GUIDE

THE HOME AND SCHOOL STUDY GUIDE

CONTENTS

PART I · THE READING GUIDE

PART II · THE STUDY GUIDE

PART I
THE READING GUIDE

INTRODUCTION

You have probably already discovered that THE NEW BOOK OF KNOWLEDGE is a valuable resource for finding information about a topic of special interest, beginning a school report or project, or answering a specific question. In pursuing your search for information, you may also have had the experience of wanting to know even more about a topic than what you found in its many articles. No single reference work—even one as comprehensive as THE NEW BOOK OF KNOWLEDGE—can contain everything known about a topic. It simply isn't possible to hold within the covers of 21 volumes the vast storehouse of knowledge that has been accumulated during thousands of years of discovery, experience, and research.

The HOME AND SCHOOL READING GUIDE has been compiled to help you expand the information in THE NEW BOOK OF KNOWLEDGE. The READING GUIDE is a unique listing of more than 5,000 quality books dealing with hundreds of different topics. These books represent the best of current fiction and nonfiction, as well as "old standards" and classics of juvenile and young adult literature. Almost every title in the list has been recommended by parent groups, teachers, librarians, literature specialists, or by young people themselves. Many of the books have also been cited by textbook publishers as recommended supplements to their science, social studies, or language arts series. Where can you find the books that may be of interest to you? The titles in the READING GUIDE should be readily available through your local bookstores or in your school or public library.

You will find the READING GUIDE a handy resource for building collections of books about many different subject areas for users at different ability levels. Because the READING GUIDE is updated each year, it will also help you keep such collections current and relevant to young people's school needs and extracurricular interests.

THE NEW BOOK OF KNOWLEDGE provides additional book listings in two of its articles: "Children's Book Awards" and "Children's Literature," both in Volume C.

Nancy Larrick, the Children's Literature Adviser for THE NEW BOOK OF KNOWLEDGE, helped establish the guidelines for the development of the READING GUIDE. The original READING GUIDE was prepared by John T. Gillespie and Christine B. Gilbert, co-editors of *Best Books for Children,* published by the R. R. Bowker Company.

To make it easy for you to use the READING GUIDE with THE NEW BOOK OF KNOWLEDGE, book titles are listed under alphabetically arranged topic headings that correspond directly to the titles of THE NEW BOOK OF KNOWLEDGE articles. Wherever possible, books on a topic cover a range of ability levels from primary to advanced.

Key to abbreviations used in the READING GUIDE:

(P)	primary (through 4th grade)	comp.	compiler; compiled
(I)	intermediate (5th through 8th grade)	ed.	editor; edition; edited
(A)	advanced (9th grade and up)	illus.	illustrator; illustrated
ad.	adapter; adapted	trans.	translator

The following book lists are among the sources used in the preparation of the READING GUIDE:

Adventuring with Books: A Booklist for Pre-K —Grade 6. 9th ed. National Council of Teachers of English, 1989.

Appraisal: Science Books for Young People. Published three times a year by the Children's Science Book Review Committee, sponsored by the Science and Mathematics Program of Boston University School of Education and the New England Roundtable of Children's Librarians.

Best Books for Children, by John T. Gillespie and Corrine J. Naden, R. R. Bowker, 1990 (4th ed.).

Best Books for Junior High Readers, by John T. Gillespie, R. R. Bowker, 1991.

Booklist. American Library Association.

Bulletin of the Center for Children's Books. University of Chicago.

Children's Books. New York Public Library. Published annually.

Children's Catalog. 15th ed. H. W. Wilson, 1986.

Children's Choices. October issues of *The Reading Teacher.*

The Elementary School Library Collection. 16th ed. Brodart, 1988.

The Horn Book Magazine. Horn Book, Inc.

Notable Children's Books, 1976–80. American Library Association, 1986.

Notable Children's Trade Books in the Field of Social Studies. April/May issues of *Social Education,* a professional journal of the National Council for the Social Studies.

Outstanding Science Trade Books for Children. March issues of *Science and Children,* a professional journal of the National Science Teachers Association.

School Library Journal. R. R. Bowker.

ABACUS. See COMPUTERS.

ABORIGINES, AUSTRALIAN

Browne, Rollo. *An Aboriginal Family.* Lerner, 1986. *(P)*
Reynolds, Jan. *Down Under: Vanishing Cultures.* HarBraceJ, 1992. *(P; I)*

ABRAHAM. See BIBLE AND BIBLE STORIES.

ACID RAIN

Baines, John. *Acid Rain.* Steck-Vaughn, 1990. *(I)*
Gay, Kathlyn. *Acid Rain.* Watts, 1983. *(I; A)*
Lucas, Eileen. *Acid Rain.* Childrens, 1991. *(I)*
Pringle, Laurence. *Rain of Troubles: The Science and Politics of Acid Rain.* Macmillan, 1988. *(A)*
Turck, Mary. *Acid Rain.* Crestwood, 1990. *(I)*

ADAMS, JOHN

Dwyer, Frank. *John Adams.* Chelsea House, 1989. *(I)*
Santrey, Laurence. *John Adams: Brave Patriot.* (Easy Biography Series) Troll, 1986. *(P; I)*
Stefoff, Rebecca. *John Adams: 2nd President of the United States.* Garrett Educational, 1988. *(A)*

ADAMS, JOHN QUINCY

Coelho, Tony. *John Quincy Adams.* Chelsea House, 1990. *(I; A)*
Kent, Zachary. *John Quincy Adams: Sixth President of the United States.* Childrens, 1987. *(I)*

ADAMS, SAMUEL

Fritz, Jean. *Why Don't You Get a Horse, Sam Adams?* Putnam, 1974. *(I)*

ADDAMS, JANE

Keller, Gail F. *Jane Addams.* Harper, 1971. *(P; I)*
Kittredge, Mary. *Jane Addams.* Chelsea House, 1988. *(I; A)*
Wheeler, Leslie A. *Jane Addams.* Silver Burdett, 1990. *(I)*

ADEN. See MIDDLE EAST.

ADOLESCENCE

Greenberg, Harvey R., M.D. *Hanging In: What You Should Know About Psychotherapy.* Scholastic, 1982. *(A)*
LeShan, Eda. *You and Your Feelings.* Macmillan, 1975; *What Makes Me Feel This Way? Growing Up with Human Emotions,* 1972. *(I)*
See also MENTAL HEALTH.

ADOPTION

Banish, Roslyn, and Jordan-Wong, Jennifer. *A Forever Family.* HarperCollins, 1992. *(P)*
Byars, Betsy. *The Pinballs.* Harper, 1977. (Fiction) *(I)*
Cohen, Shari. *Coping with Being Adopted.* Rosen, 1988. *(A)*
DuPrau, Jeanne. *Adoption: The Facts, Feelings and Issues of a Double Heritage.* Messner, 1990. *(I; A)*
Gravelle, Karen, and Fischer, Susan. *Where Are My Birth Parents? A Guide for Teenage Adoptees.* Walker, 1993. *(A)*
Hermes, Patricia. *Heads I Win.* Newsom, 1989. (Fiction) *(I; A)*
Hyde, Margaret O. *Foster Care and Adoption.* Watts, 1982. *(I; A)*
Krementz, Jill. *How It Feels to Be Adopted.* Knopf, 1982. *(I)*
Montgomery, L. M. *Anne of Green Gables.* Grosset, 1983 (1904). (Fiction) *(I; A)*
Nickman, Steven L. *The Adoption Experience.* Messner, 1985. *(A)*
Rosenberg, Maxine B. *Being Adopted.* Lothrop, 1984. *(P; I)*
Sobol, Harriet Langsam. *We Don't Look Like Our Mom and Dad.* Coward, 1984. *(P; I)*
Stewart, Gail B. *Adoption.* Crestwood, 1989. *(P; I)*

ADVENTURE*

Evslin, Bernard. *The Adventures of Ulysses.* Scholastic, 1969. *(I; A)*
London, Jack. *The Call of the Wild.* Dutton, 1968 (1903). (Fiction) *(I; A)*
Sperry, Armstrong. *Call It Courage.* Macmillan, 1968 (1940). (Fiction) *(P; I)*
Steinbeck, John. *Travels with Charley.* Penguin, 1986 (1962). *(I; A)*
Stevenson, Robert Louis. *Kidnapped.* Penguin, 1983 (1886). (Fiction) *(I; A); Treasure Island.* Penguin, 1981 (1883). (Fiction) *(I; A)*
Twain, Mark. *Adventures of Huckleberry Finn.* Penguin, 1986 (1888). (Fiction) *(I; A); Adventures of Tom Sawyer.* Penguin, 1983 (1876). (Fiction) *(I; A)*
Verne, Jules. *Around the World in Eighty Days.* Morrow, 1988 (1872). (Fiction) *(I; A); Twenty Thousand Leagues under the Sea.* Penguin, 1987 (1869). (Fiction) *(P; I)*

ADVERTISING

Greenberg, Jan. *Advertising Careers.* Holt, 1987. *(A)*

AENEID

Church, Alfred J. *The Aeneid for Boys and Girls.* Macmillan, 1962. *(I)*

AERODYNAMICS. See AVIATION.

---

*This is a popular theme with young readers. However, it is not a separate article in *The New Book of Knowledge.*

AFGHANISTAN

Afghanistan . . . in Pictures. Lerner, 1989. *(I; A)*

Clifford, Mary Louise. *The Land and People of Afghanistan*. Lippincott, 1989. (rev. ed.) *(I; A)*

Howarth, Michael. *Afghanistan*. Chelsea House, 1988. *(P)*

AFRICA

Botswana . . . in Pictures. Lerner, 1990. *(I; A)*

Morocco . . . in Pictures. Lerner, 1989. *(I; A)*

Tanzania . . . in Pictures. Lerner, 1988. *(I)*

Tunisia . . . in Pictures. Lerner, 1989. *(I)*

Anderson, Lydia. *Nigeria, Cameroon, and the Central African Republic*. Watts, 1981. *(I; A)*

Barker, Carol. *Kayode and His Village in Nigeria*. Merrimack, n.d. *(P; I)*

Baynham, Simon. *Africa; From 1945*. Watts, 1987. *(I; A)*

Bernheim, Marc, and Bernheim, Evelyne. *The Drums Speak: The Story of Kofi, a Boy of West Africa*. Harcourt, 1972. *(P); In Africa*. Atheneum, 1973. *(P)*

Blumberg, Rhoda. *Southern Africa: South Africa, Namibia, Swaziland, Lesotho, and Botswana*. Watts, 1981. *(I; A)*

Boyd, Herb. *The Former Portuguese Colonies: Angola, Mozambique, Guinea-Bissau, Cape Verde, São Tomé, and Príncipe*. Watts, 1981. *(I; A)*

Chiasson, John. *African Journey*. Bradbury, 1987. *(I; A)*

Conway, Jessica. *Swaziland*. Chelsea House, 1989. *(P; I)*

Davidson, Basil. *The Story of Africa*. Mitchell Beazley, 1984. *(I)*

Ellis, Veronica Freeman. *Afro-Bets First Book About Africa: An Introduction for Young Readers*. Just Us Books, 1990. *(P)*

Feelings, Muriel. *Jambo Means Hello: Swahili Alphabet Book*. Dial, 1981. *(P)*

Fichter, George S. *The Bulge of Africa: Senegal, Guinea, Ivory Coast, Togo, Benin, and Equatorial Guinea*. Watts, 1981. *(I; A)*

Foster, F. Blanche. *East Central Africa: Kenya, Uganda, Tanzania, Rwanda, and Burundi*. Watts, 1981. *(I; A)*

Gilfond, Henry. *Gambia, Ghana, Liberia, and Sierra Leone*. Watts, 1981. *(I; A)*

Godbeer, Deardre. *Somalia*. Chelsea House, 1988. *(P; I)*

Gould, D. E. *Namibia*. Chelsea House, 1988. *(P; I)*

Hathaway, Jim. *Cameroon . . . in Pictures*. Lerner, 1989. *(I)*

Hintz, Martin. (Enchantment of the World Series). Childrens, 1985. *(P;I)*

Holmes, Timothy. *Zambia*. Chelsea House, 1988. *(P; I)*

Hornburger. *African Countries and Cultures: A Concise Illustrated Dictionary*. McKay, 1981. *(I; A)*

Lawson, Don. *Morocco, Algeria, Tunisia, and Libya*. Watts, 1978. *(I; A); South Africa*. Watts, 1986. *(I)*

Margolies, Barbara A. *Rehema's Journey: A Visit in Tanzania*. Scholastic, 1990. *(P)*

McCulla, Patricia E. *Tanzania*. Chelsea House, 1988. *(I)*

McKown, Robin. *The Colonial Conquest of Africa*. Watts, 1971. *(I)*

Milsome, John. *Sierra Leone*. Chelsea House, 1988. *(P; I)*

Musgrove, Margaret. *Ashanti to Zulu: African Traditions*. Dial, 1980. *(P; I)*

Newman, Gerald. *Zaire, Gabon, and the Congo*. Watts, 1981. *(I; A)*

Pomeray, J. K. *Rwanda*. Chelsea House, 1988. *(I)*

Taylor, L. B., Jr. *South East Africa: Zimbabwe, Zambia, Malawi, Madagascar, Mauritius, and Réunion*. Watts, 1981. *(I; A)*

Tonsing-Carter, Betty. *Lesotho*. Chelsea House, 1988. *(P; I)*

Wolbers, Marian F. *Burundi*. Chelsea House, 1989. *(I)*

Woods, Harold, and Woods, Geraldine. *The Horn of Africa: Ethiopia, Sudan, Somalia, and Djibouti*. Watts, 1981. *(I; A)*

AFRICA, ART AND ARCHITECTURE OF

Kerina, Jane. *African Crafts*. Lion, 1970. *(P; I)*

Price, Christine. *Dancing Masks of Africa*. Scribner's, 1975. *(P; I)*

AFRICA, LITERATURE OF

Aardema, Verna. *Bringing the Rain to Kapiti Plain*. Dial, 1981; *Why Mosquitoes Buzz in People's Ears*, 1978. *(P)*

Abrahams, Roger. *African Folktales*. Pantheon, 1983 *(I)*

Courlander, Harold. *A Treasury of African Folktales*. Crown, 1975. *(P); The Crest and the Hide and Other African Stories*. Coward, 1982. *(I)*

Courlander, Harold, and Herzog, George, eds. *The Cow-Tail Switch and Other West African Stories*. Holt, 1975. *(I)*

Feelings, Muriel. *Jambo Means Hello: Swahili Alphabet Book*. Dial, 1981. *(P)*

Mathabane, Mark. *Kaffir Boy*. New American Library, 1987. *(I; A)*

McDermott, Gerald. *The Magic Tree: A Tale from the Congo*. Penguin, 1973. *(P)*

Parrinder, Geoffrey. *African Mythology*. Harper, 1986 (rev. ed.). *(A)*

AFRICAN AMERICANS

Adams, Russell L. *Great Negroes Past and Present*. Afro-Am Publishing, 1984. *(I)*

Altman, Susan. *Extraordinary Black Americans: From Colonial to Contemporary Times*. Childrens, 1989. *(I)*

Andrews, Bert. *In the Shadow of the Great White Way: Images from the Black Theatre*. Thunder's Mouth Press, 1989. *(I; A)*

Armstrong, William Howard. *Sounder*. Harper, 1969. (Fiction) *(I; A)*

Brodie, James Michael. *Created Equal: The Lives and Ideas of Black American Innovators*. Morrow, 1993. *(A)*

Cameron, Ann. *The Stories Julian Tells*. Pantheon, 1981. (Fiction) *(P; I)*

Du Bois, W. E. *The Souls of Black Folk*. Dodd, 1979. *(I; A)*

Everett, Gwen. *Li'l Sis and Uncle Willie*. Rizzoli, 1991. *(P; I)*

Evitts, William J. *Captive Bodies, Free Spirits: The Story of Southern Slavery*. Messner, 1985. *(I)*

Fields, Julia. *The Green Lion of Zion Street*. McElderry, 1988. (Fiction) *(I)*

Flournoy, Valerie. *The Patchwork Quilt*. Dutton, 1985. (Fiction) *(P)*

Greene, Bette. *Philip Hall Likes Me, I Reckon Maybe*. Dial, 1974. (Fiction) *(P; I)*

Greene, Carol. *Thurgood Marshall: First African-American Supreme Court Justice*. Childrens, 1991. *(P; I)*

Greenfield, Eloise. *Grandpa's Face*. Philomel, 1988. (Fiction) *(P); She Come Bringing Me That Little Baby Girl*. Lippincott, 1974. *(P)*

Hamilton, Virginia. *Anthony Burns: The Defeat and Triumph of a Fugitive Slave*. Knopf, 1988. *(I; A); Drylongso*. Harcourt, 1992. *(P; I); The People Could Fly: American Black Folktales*. Dillon, 1985. *(I); Sweet Whisper, Brother Rush*. Philomel, 1982. (Fiction) *(I; A); Zeely*. Macmillan, 1967. (Fiction) *(P; I)*

Hancock, Sibyl. *Famous Firsts of Black Americans*. Pelican, 1983. *(P; I)*

Haskins, Jim. *Outward Dreams: Black Inventors and Their Inventions*. Walker, 1991. *(I)*

Havill, Juanita. *Jamaica's Find*. Houghton, 1986. (Fiction) *(P)*

Hughes, Langston. *Not Without Laughter*. Macmillan, 1969. *(I; A)*

Igus, Toyomi, ed. *Great Women in the Struggle*. Just Us Books, 1991. *(P; I)*

Jackson, Florence. *The Black Man in America*. Watts, 1975. *(A)*

Johnson, James Weldon. *Lift Every Voice and Sing*. Walker, 1993. *(P; I; A)*

Johnston, Johanna. *A Special Bravery*. Dodd, 1967. *(I)*

Katz, William L. *Black People Who Made the Old West*. Harper, 1977. *(I; A)*

Klots, Steve. *Richard Allen: Religious Leader and Social Activist*. Chelsea House, 1991. *(I)*

Lawrence, Jacob. *The Great Migration: An American Story*. HarperCollins, 1994. *(I)*

Lester, Julius. *Long Journey Home: Stories from Black History*. Dial, 1972. *(I); Tales of Uncle Remus (and) The Adventures of Brer Rabbit*. Dial, 1987. *(P; I); This Strange New Feeling*. Dial, 1982. *(A)*

McKissack, Patricia. *Flossie and the Fox*. Dial, 1986. (Fiction) *(P); Mary McLeod Bethune: A Great American Educator*. Childrens, 1985. *(P; I); Mirandy and Brother Wind*. Knopf, 1988. (Fiction) *(P); Nettie Jo's Friends*. Knopf, 1989. (Fiction) *(P)*

McKissack, Patricia C., and McKissack, Fredrick, Jr. *Black Diamond: The Story of the Negro Baseball Leagues*. Scholastic, 1994. *(I)*

Mendez, Phil. *The Black Snowman*. Scholastic, 1989. (Fiction) *(P; I)*

Myers, Walter Dean. *The Mouse Rap*. Harper, 1990. (Fiction) *(I); Scorpions*. Harper, 1988. (Fiction) *(I; A); Now is Your Time: The African-American Struggle for Freedom*. HarperCollins, 1991. *(I; A)*

Parks, Rosa, with Haskins, Jim. *Rosa Parks: My Story*. Dial, 1992. *(I)*

Patterson, Lillie G. *Benjamin Banneker: Genius of Early America*. Abingdon, 1978. *(P; I)*

Potter, Joan, and Clayton, Constance. *African-American Firsts*. Pinto Press, 1994. *(A)*

Reef, Catherine. *Buffalo Soldiers*. 21st Century, 1993. *(I; A)*

Richardson, Ben. *Great Black Americans*. Crowell, 1976. *(I)*

Ringgold, Faith. *Tar Beach*. Crown, 1991. *(P; I)*

Roberts, Naurice. *Barbara Jordan: The Great Lady from Texas*. Childrens, 1984. *(I; A)*

Rummel, Jack. *Malcolm X: Militant Black Leader*. Chelsea House, 1989. *(I; A)*

San Souchi, Robert. *The Talking Eggs: A Folktale from the American South*. Dial, 1989. *(P)*

Spangler, Earl. *Blacks in America*. Lerner, 1980 (rev. ed.). *(I; A)*

Steptoe, John. *Stevie*. Lothrop, 1987 (1969). (Fiction) *(P)*

Sterling, Dorothy, ed. *The Trouble They Seen: Black People Tell the Story of Reconstruction*. Doubleday, 1976. *(A)*

Sullivan, Charles, ed. *Children of Promise: African-American Literature and Art for Young People*. Abrams, 1991. *(I; A)*

Taylor, Mildred. *The Gold Cadillac*. Dial, 1987. (Fiction) *(I); Roll of Thunder, Hear My Cry*. Dial, 1976. (Fiction) *(P; I)*

Thum, Marcella. *Exploring Black America: A History and Guide*. Atheneum, 1975. *(A)*

Williams-Garcia, Rita. *Fast Talk on a Slow Track*. Lodestar, 1991. (Fiction) *(A)*

Yates, Elizabeth. *Amos Fortune, Free Man*. Dutton, 1950. *(P; I)*

AGING

Ackerman, Karen. *Song and Dance Man*. Knopf, 1988. (Fiction) *(P)*

Broncato, Robin F. *Sweet Bells Jangled out of Tune*. Knopf, 1982. (Fiction) *(I; A)*

Cooney, Barbara. *Miss Rumphius*. Viking, 1982. (Fiction) *(I)*

Dychtwald, Ken, and Flower, Joe. *Age Wave: The Challenges and Opportunities of an Aging America*. Tarcher, 1989. *(A)*

Gelfand, Marilyn. *My Great-Grandpa Joe*. Four Winds, 1986. (Fiction) *(P)*

Landau, Elaine. *Growing Old in America*. Messner, 1985. *(I)*

Langone, John. *Growing Older: What Young People Should Know About Aging*. Little, 1990. *(I; A)*

LeShan, Eda. *Grandparents: A Special Kind of Love*. Macmillan, 1984. *(I)*

MacLachlan, Patricia. *Through Grandpa's Eyes*. Harper, 1980. (Fiction) *(P)*

Mathis, Sharon Bell. *The Hundred Penny Box*. Viking, 1975. (Fiction) *(I)*

Rylant, Cynthia. *An Angel for Solomon Singer*. Orchard Books, 1992. (Fiction) *(P; I); When I Was Young in the Mountains*. Dutton, 1982. (Fiction) *(P)*

Shecter, Ben. *Grandma Remembers*. Harper, 1989. (Fiction) *(P)*

Sobol, Harriet. *Grandpa: A Young Man Grown Old*. Coward, 1980. *(I)*

Worth, Richard. *You'll be Old Someday, Too*. Watts, 1986. *(A)*

Zolotow, Charlotte. *I Know a Lady*. Viking, 1989. (Fiction) *(P)*

AGRICULTURE

Bowman, Keith. *Agriculture*. Silver Burdett, 1987. *(I)*

Horwitz, Elinor L. *On the Land: The Evolution of American Agriculture*. Atheneum, 1980. *(I; A)*

Murphy, Wendy. *The Futureworld of Agriculture*. (An Epcot Center Book). Watts, 1985. *(I; A)*

White, William, C., and Collins, Donald N. *Opportunities in Agriculture Careers*. VGM Career Books, 1987. *(A)*

AIDS

Arrick, Fran. *What You Don't Know Can Kill You*. Bantam/Starfire, 1993. (Fiction) *(A)*

Cozic, Charles P., ed. *The AIDS Crisis*. Greenhaven, 1991. *(I; A)*

Eagles, Douglas A. *The Menace of AIDS: A Shadow on Our Land*. Watts, 1988. *(I)*

Girard, Linda Walvoord. *Alex, the Kid with Aids*. Albert Whitman, 1991. (Fiction) *(P)*

Hawkes, Nigel. *AIDS*. Watts, 1987. *(I)*

Hyde, Margaret O., and Forsyth, Elizabeth H. *AIDS: What Does It Mean to You?* Walker, 1990. (rev. ed.) *(I; A); Know About AIDS*. Walker, 1990. *(P; I)*

Kuklin, Susan. *Fighting Back: What Some People Are Doing About AIDS*. Putnam, 1989. *(A)*

Kurland, Morton L. *Coping with AIDS: Facts and Fears*. Rosen, 1988. *(A)*

Landau, Elaine. *We Have AIDS*. Watts, 1990. *(I; A)*

Madaras, Lynda. *Lynda Madaras Talks to Teens About AIDS: An Essential Guide for Parents, Teachers, and Young People*. Harper, 1988. *(A)*

Nourse, Alan E. *AIDS*. Watts, 1989. *(I; A)*

White, Ryan, and Cunningham, Ann Marie. *Ryan White: My Own Story*. Dial, 1991. *(I; A)*

Wilson, Jonnie. *AIDS*. Lucent Books, 1989. *(I; A)*

AIRPLANE MODELS

Berliner, Don. *Flying-Model Airplanes*. Lerner, 1982; *Scale-Model Airplanes*, 1982. *(P; I)*

Curry, Barbara A. *Model Aircraft*. Watts, 1979. *(I)*

Herda, O. J. *Model Historical Aircraft*. Watts, 1982. *(I; A)*

Monfort, Platt. *Styro-Flyers: How to Build Super Model Airplanes from Hamburger Boxes and Other Fast-Food Containers*. Random, 1981. *(I)*

Radlauer, Ed. *Model Fighter Planes*. Childrens, 1983. *(P; I)*

AIR POLLUTION. See POLLUTION.

ALABAMA

McNair, Sylvia. *Alabama*. Childrens, 1989. *(P; I)*

Thompson, Kathleen. *Alabama*. Raintree, 1988. *(P; I)*

ALASKA

Cheney, Cora. *Alaska: Indians, Eskimos, Russians, and the Rest*. Dodd, 1980. *(I)*

Lewin, Ted. *World Within a World—Pribilofs*. Dodd, 1980. *(I)*

Redding, Robert H. *Alaska Pipeline*. Childrens, 1980. *(I)*

Stefansson, Evelyn, and Yahn, Linda. *Here Is Alaska*, Scribner's, 1983 (4th ed.). *(I; A)*

Thompson, Kathleen. *Alaska*. Raintree, 1988. *(P; I)*

ALBANIA

Lear, Aaron E. *Albania*. Chelsea House, 1987. *(A)*

ALBERTA. See CANADA.

ALCOHOLISM

Claypool, Jane. *Alcohol and You*. Watts, 1988. (rev. ed.) *(I; A)*

Graeber, Laurel. *Are You Dying for a Drink?: Teenagers and Alcohol Abuse*. Messner, 1985. *(A)*

Nielsen, Nancy J. *Teen Alcoholism*. Lucent Books, 1990. *(I)*

O'Neill, Catherine. *Focus on Alcohol*. 21st Century Books, 1990. *(I)*

Rosenberg, Maxine B. *Not My Family: Sharing the Truth About Alcoholism*. Bradbury, 1988. *(I)*

Seixas, Judith S. *Living with a Parent Who Drinks Too Much*. Greenwillow, 1979. *(I)*

Silverstein; Herma. *Alcoholism*. Watts, 1990. *(I; A)*

ALCOTT, LOUISA MAY

Burke, Kathleen. *Louisa May Alcott*. Chelsea House, 1987. *(I; A)*

Greene, Carol. *Louisa May Alcott: Author, Nurse, Suffragette*. Childrens, 1984. *(I)*

Johnston, Norma. *Louisa May: The World and Works of Louisa May Alcott*. Four Winds, 1991. *(I; A)*

Meigs, Cornelia. *Invincible Louisa*. Little, 1968. *(A)*

Santrey, Laurence. *Louisa May Alcott: Young Writer*. (Easy Biography Series) Troll, 1986. *(P;I)*

ALEXANDER THE GREAT

Harris, Nathaniel. *Alexander the Great and the Greeks*. Bookwright, 1986. *(I)*

Krensky, Stephen. *Conqueror and Hero: The Search for Alexander*. Little, 1981. *(I)*

ALGAE

Daegling, Mary. *Monster Seaweeds: The Story of Giant Kelp*. Dillon, 1986. *(I)*

Kavaler, Lucy. *Green Magic: Algae Rediscovered*. Harper, 1983. *(I; A)*

ALGEBRA

Stallings, Pat. *Puzzling Your Way into Algebra*. Activity Resources, 1978 (new ed.). *(I; A)*

ALGERIA. See AFRICA.

ALLEN, ETHAN

Holbrook, Stewart. *America's Ethan Allen*. Houghton, n.d. *(I)*

Peck, Robert Newton. *Rabbits and Redcoats*. Walker, 1976. *(I)*

ALPHABET

Fisher, Leonard Everett. *Alphabet Art: Thirteen ABCs from Around the World*. Scholastic, 1978. *(P)*

Kaye, Cathryn Berger. *Word works: Why the Alphabet Is a Kid's Best Friend*. Little, 1985. *(I)*

Warburton, Lois. *The Beginning of Writing*. Lucent Books, 1990. *(I)*

ALPHABET BOOKS

Anno, Mitsumasa. *Anno's Alphabet: An Adventure in Imagination*. Harper, 1975. *(P)*

Baskin, Leonard, and others. *Hosie's Alphabet*. Viking, 1972. *(P)*

Berger, Terry. *Ben's ABC Day*. Lothrop, 1982. *(P)*

Boynton, Sandra. *A Is for Angry*. Workman, 1983. *(P)*

Brown, Marcia. *All Butterflies: An ABC*. Scribner's, 1974. *(P)*

Brunhoff, Laurent de. *Babar's ABC*. Random, 1983. *(P)*

Duvoisin, Roger. *A for the Ark*. Lothrop, 1952. *(P)*

Emberley, Edward R. *Ed Emberley's A B C*. Little, 1978. *(P)*

Gag, Wanda. *The ABC Bunny*. Putnam, 1978. *(P)*

Greenaway, Kate. *A Apple Pie*. Warne, 1987 (rev. ed.). *(P)*

Isadora, Rachel. *City Seen from A to Z*. Greenwillow, 1983. *(P)*

Jewell, Nancy. *ABC Cat*. Harper, 1983. *(P)*

Lear, Edward. *An Edward Lear Alphabet*. Lothrop, 1983. *(P)*

Oxenbury, Helen. *Helen Oxenbury's ABC of Things*. Delacorte, 1983. *(P)*

Rey, H. A. *Curious George Learns the Alphabet*. Houghton, 1963. *(P)*

Scarry, Richard. *Richard Scarry's Find Your ABC's*. Random, 1973. *(P)*

Seuss, Dr. *Dr. Seuss' ABC*. Random, 1963. *(P)*

Wildsmith, Brian. *Brian Wildsmith's ABC*. Watts, 1963. *(P)*

ALUMINUM. See METALS AND METALLURGY.

AMAZON RIVER

Cheney, Glenn Alan. *The Amazon*. Watts, 1984. *(I; A)*

Cousteau Society. *An Adventure in the Amazon*. Simon & Schuster, 1992. *(P; I)*

Lourie, Peter. *Amazon: A Young Reader's Look at the Last Frontier*. Caroline House: Boyds Mills Press, 1991. *(P; I)*

McConnell, Rosemary. *The Amazon*. Silver Burdett, 1978. *(I; A)*

AMERICAN LITERATURE. See UNITED STATES (ART, LITERATURE, AND MUSIC).

AMUSEMENT AND THEME PARKS. See PARKS AND PLAYGROUNDS.

ANCIENT CIVILIZATIONS

Board, Tessa. *Ancient Greece*. Watts, 1984 (rev. ed.). *(P; I)*

Burrell, Roy. *The Greeks*. Oxford University Press, 1990. *(I)*

Cohen, Daniel. *Ancient Egypt*. Doubleday, 1990. *(P; I)*

Connolly, Peter. *Pompeii*. Oxford University Press, 1990. *(I)*

Coolidge, Olivia E. *The Golden Days of Greece*. Harper, 1968; *The Trojan War*. Houghton, 1952. *(I; A)*

Corbishley, Mike. *The Roman World*. Watts, 1987. *(I; A)*

Defrates, Joanna. *What Do We Know About the Egyptians?* Peter Berick, 1991. *(I)*

Garber, Janet, ed. *The Concise Encyclopedia of Ancient Civilizations*. Watts, 1978. *(I; A)*

Goode, Ruth. *People of the First Cities*. Macmillan, 1977. *(I)*

Goor, Ron, and Goor, Nancy. *Pompeii*. Crowell, 1987. *(I)*

Harris, Geraldine. *Ancient Egypt*. Facts on File, 1990. *(I)*

Hart, George. *Ancient Egypt*. Knopf, 1990. *(I)*

Hodges, Henry. *Technology in the Ancient World*. Knopf, 1970. *(I)*

Hoobler, Dorothy, and Hoobler, Thomas. *Lost Civilizations*. Walker, 1992. *(P; I)*.

James, Simon. *Ancient Rome*. Knopf, 1990. *(I)*

Katan, Norma J., and Mints, Barbara. *Hieroglyphs: The Writing of Ancient Egypt*. Atheneum, 1981. *(P; I)*

Koenig, Viviane, and Ageorges, Veronique. *The Ancient Egyptians: Life in the Nile Valley*. Millbrook, 1992. *(I)*

Macaulay, David. *Pyramid*. Houghton, 1975. *(I; A)*

Macdonald, Fiona. *A Greek Temple*. Peter Bedrick, 1992. *(P; I)*

Millard, Anne. *Ancient Civilizations*. Watts, 1983. *(P; I)*

Pace, Mildred Mastin. *Pyramids: Tombs for Eternity*. McGraw, 1981

Pearson, Anne. *Ancient Greece*. Knopf, 1992. *(P; I; A)*

Perl, Lila. *Mummies, Tombs and Treasure: Secrets of Ancient Egypt*. Clarion, 1987. *(P)*

Purdy, Susan, and Sandak, Cass R. *Ancient Egypt; Ancient Greece* (Civilization Project Books). Watts, 1982. *(P; I)*

Reeves, Nicholas. *Into the Mummy's Tomb: The Real-Life Discovery of Tutankhamun's Treasures*. Scholastic, 1992. *(I)*

Robinson, Charles A., Jr. *First Book of Ancient Egypt; First Book of Ancient Greece*. Watts, 1984 (rev. by Lorna Greenberg). *(I; A)*

Rutland, Jonathan. *See Inside a Roman Town*. Kingfisher, 1986. *(I)*

Stolz, Mary. *Zekmet, the Stone Carver: A Tale of Ancient Egypt*. Harcourt, 1988. *(P; I)*

Tubb, Jonathan. *Bible Lands*. Knopf, 1991. *(I; A)*

Unstead, R. J. *See Inside an Egyptian Town*. Watts, 1978. *(I)*

See also ARCHAEOLOGY; ROME, ANCIENT.

ANDERSEN, HANS CHRISTIAN

Andersen, Hans Christian. *Hans Andersen's Fairy Tales*. Penguin, 1981; *Hans Christian Andersen's Favorite Fairy Tales*. Western, 1974; *Michael Hague's Favorite Hans Christian Andersen Fairy Tales*. Holt, 1981. *(I)*

ANDES. See SOUTH AMERICA.

ANGOLA. See AFRICA.

ANIMALS

Arnosky, Jim. *Secrets of a Wildlife Watcher*. Lothrop, 1983. *(I; A)*

Attenborough, David. *Discovering Life on Earth*. Little, 1982. *(P; I; A)*

Brooks, Bruce. *Making Sense: Animal Perception and Communication*. Farrar, 1993. *(I)*

Bruemmer, Fred. *Arctic Animals*. North Word, 1987. *(A)*

Burnford, Sheila. *The Incredible Journey*. Little, 1961. (Fiction) *(P; I)*

Cohen, Daniel. *Animal Rights: A Handbook for Young Adults*. Millbrook, 1993. *(I; A)*

Curtis, Patricia. *Aquatic Animals in the Wild and in Captivity*. Lodestar, 1992. *(I)*

Cutchins, Judy, and Johnston, Ginny. *Parenting Papas: Unusual Animal Fathers*. Morrow, 1994. *(I)*

Evans, Lisa Gollin. *An Elephant Never Forgets Its Snorkel: How Animals Survive Without Tools and Gadgets*. Crown, 1992. *(I)*

Facklam, Margery. *Bees Dance and Whales Sing*. Sierra, 1992. *(I)*

Freedman, Russell. *Animal Superstars: Biggest, Strongest, Fastest, Smartest*. Prentice Hall, 1981. *(I; A)*

Goble, Paul. *The Great Race of the Birds and Animals*. Bradbury, 1985. *(P)*

Gutfreund, Geraldine Marshall. *Animals Have Cousins Too: Five Surprising Relatives of Animals You Know*. Watts, 1990. *(P; I)*

Herbst, Judith. *Animal Amazing*. Atheneum, 1991. *(I)*

Herriot, James. *All Creatures Great and Small*. St. Martin's, 1972. *(I; A)*

Johnston, Ginny, and Cutchins, Judy. *Windows on Wildlife*. Morrow, 1990. *(P; I)*

Kitchen, Bert. *And So They Build*. Candlewick, 1993. *(P; I)*

Komori, Atsushi. *Animal Mothers*. Putnam, 1983. *(P)*

Lambert, David. *First Picture Book of Animals*. Watts, 1982. *(P); Animal Life*, 1982. *(P; I)*

Loewer, Peter. *The Inside-Out Stomach: An Introduction to Animals Without Backbones*. Atheneum, 1990. *(P; I)*

Matthews, Rupert. *Ice Age Animals*. Bookwright, dist. by Watts, 1990. *(P; I)*

National Geographic editors. *Secrets of Animal Survival*. National Geographic, 1983. *(I; A)*

Paladino, Catherine. *Our Vanishing Farm Animals: Saving America's Rare Breeds*. Joy Street, 1991. *(P; I)*

Parsons, Alexandra. *Amazing Poisonous Animals*. Knopf, 1989. *(P)*

Presnall, Judith. *Animals That Glow*. Watts, 1993. *(I)*

Pringle, Laurence. *Feral: Tame Animals Gone Wild*. Macmillan, 1983. *(I; A)*

Selsam, Millicent E., and Hunt, Joyce. *A First Look at Animals with Backbones*. Walker, 1978; *A First Look at Animals Without Backbones*, 1976. *(P)*

Shedd, Warner. *The Kids' Wildlife Book: Exploring Animal Worlds Through Indoor/Outdoor Experiences*. Williamson, 1994. *(P; I)*

Simon, Seymour. *Little Giants*. Morrow, 1983. *(P)*

Sowler, Sandie. *Amazing Animal Disguises*. Knopf, 1992. *(P); Amazing Armored Animals*. Knopf, 1992. *(P)*

Staple, Michele, and Gamlin, Linda. *The Random House Book of 1001 Questions and Answers about Animals*. Random, 1990. *(P; I; A)*

Taylor, Barbara. *The Animals Atlas*. Knopf, 1992. *(I; A)*

Taylor, David. *Nature's Creatures of the Dark*. Dial, 1993. *(P; I)*

Taylor, Kim. *Hidden by Darkness*. Delacorte, 1990. *(I); Hidden Inside*. Delacorte, 1990. *(I); Hidden Underneath*. Delacorte, 1990. *(I); Hidden Under Water*. Delacorte, 1990. *(I)*

Van Der Meer, Atie and Ron. *Amazing Animal Senses*. Joy Street, 1990. *(P; I)*

Yabuuchi, Masayuki. *Animals Sleeping*. Putnam, 1983. *(P)*

Zoehfeld, Kathleen Weidner. *What Lives in a Shell?* HarperCollins, 1994. *(P)*

ANIMATION

Scott, Elaine. *Look Alive: Behind the Scenes of an Animated Film*. Morrow, 1992. *(P; I; A)*

Thomas, Bob. *Disney's Art of Animation: From Mickey Mouse to Beauty and the Beast*. Hyperion, 1991. *(P; I; A)*

ANTARCTICA

Hackwell, W. John. *Desert of Ice: Life and Work in Antarctica*. Scribner's, 1991. *(I; A)*

Lye, Keith. *Take a Trip to Antarctica*. Watts, 1984. *(P; I)*

Pringle, Laurence. *Antarctica: Our Last Unspoiled Continent*. Simon & Schuster, 1992. *(I; A)*

Reader's Digest Press. *Antarctica*. Random, 1985. *(A)*

ANTHROPOLOGY

Asimov, Isaac. *Our Human Roots*. Walker, 1979. *(I)*

Bell, Neill. *Only Human: Why We Are the Way We Are*. Little, 1983. *(P; I)*

Branigan, Keith. *Prehistory*. Watts, 1984. *(I; A)*

Chapham, Frances, ed. *Our Human Ancestors*. Warwick, 1976. *(I)*

Cohen, Robert. *The Color of Man*. Random, 1968. *(I; A)*

Coville, Bruce. *Prehistoric People*. Doubleday, 1990. *(I)*

Fisher, Maxine P. *Recent Revolutions in Anthropology*. Watts, 1986. *(A)*

Jaspersohn, William. *How People First Lived*. Watts, 1985. *(P)*

Johanson, Donald C., and O'Farrell, Kevin. *Journey from the Dawn: Life with the World's First Family*. Villard, 1990. *(I; A)*

Lasky, Kathryn. *Traces of Life*. Morrow, 1989. *(I; A)*

Leakey, Richard E. *Human Origins*. Dutton, 1982. *(I; A)*

Leakey, Richard E., and Lewin, Roger. *People of the Lake*. Avon, 1983. *(I; A)*

Martell, Hazel Mary. *Over 6,000 Years Ago: in the Stone Age*. Macmillan, 1992. *(I)*

Merriman, Nick. *Early Humans*. Knopf, 1989. *(P; I; A)*

Milbauer, Barbara. *Suppose You Were a Netsilik: Teenagers in Other Societies*. Messner, 1981. *(A)*

Millard, Anne. *Early People*. Watts, 1982. *(I; A)*

Nance, John. *Lobo of the Tasaday: A Stone Age Boy Meets the Modern World*. Pantheon, 1982. *(A)*

Sattler, Helen Roney. *The Earliest Americans*. Clarion, 1993. *(I; A)*; *Hominids: A Look Back at Our Ancestors*. Lothrop, 1988. *(I; A)*

ANTIGUA AND BARBUDA. See CARIBBEAN SEA AND ISLANDS.

ANTS

Cook, David. *Small World of Ants*. Watts, 1981. *(P)*

Dorros, Arthur. *Ant Cities*. Crowell, 1987. *(P)*

Fischer-Nagel, Heiderose and Fischer-Nagel, Andrea. *An Ant Colony*. Carolrhoda, 1989. *(P; I)*

Overbeck, Cynthia. *Ants*. Lerner, 1982. *(P)*

Patent, Dorothy. *Looking at Ants*. Holiday, 1989. *(P; I)*

APES

Arnold, Caroline. *Orangutan*. Morrow, 1990. *(I)*

Bailey, Jill. *Gorilla Rescue*. Steck-Vaughn, 1990. *(P; I)*

Barrett, N. S. *Monkeys and Apes*. Watts, 1988. *(P; I)*

Fossey, Dian. *Gorillas in the Mist*. Houghton, 1983. *(A)*

Gelman, Rita Golden. *Monkeys and Apes of the World*. Watts, 1990. *(P)*

Goodall, Jane. *The Chimpanzee Family Book*. Picture Book Studio, 1989. *(P; I)*

Hunt, Patricia. *Gibbons*. Dodd, 1983. *(P; I)*

McDearmon, Kay. *Orangutans*. Dodd, 1983. *(P; I)*

Schlein, Miriam. *Gorillas*. Atheneum, 1990. *(I)*

AQUARIUMS

Braemer, Helga, and Scheurmann, Ines. *Tropical Fish*. Barron, 1983. *(I; A)*

Broekel, Ray. *Aquariums and Terrariums*. Childrens, 1982; *Tropical Fish*, 1983. *(P)*

Carrington, Neville. *A Fishkeeper's Guide to Maintaining a Healthy Aquarium*. Arco, 1986. *(A)*

Simon, Seymour. *Tropical Saltwater Aquariums: How to Set Them Up and Keep Them Going*. Viking, 1976. *(P; I)*

Watts, Barrie. *Keeping Minibeasts Series*. Watts, 1989. *(P)*

AQUINO, CORAZON

Chua-Eoan, Howard. *Corazon Aquino*. Chelsea House, 1987. *(A)*

Haskins, James. *Corazon Aquino: Leader of the Philippines*. Enslow, 1988. *(A)*

Siegel, Beatrice. *Cory: Corazon Aquino and the Philippines*. Lodestar, 1988. *(I)*

ARABS. See MIDDLE EAST.

ARCHAEOLOGY

Anderson, Joan. *From Map to Museum: Uncovering Mysteries of the Past*. Morrow, 1988. *(P)*

Arnold, Caroline. *Dinosaurs Down Under: And Other Fossils from Australia*. Clarion, 1989. *(P; I)*

Avi-Yonah, Michael. *Search for the Past*. Lerner, 1974. *(I)*

Braymer, Marjorie. *Atlantis: The Biography of a Legend*. Atheneum, 1983; *The Walls of Windy Troy: A Biography of Heinrich Schliemann*. Harcourt, 1966. *(I; A)*

Ford, Barbara, and Switzer, David C. *The Underwater Dig: The Excavation of a Revolutionary War Privateer*. Morrow, 1982. *(P; I)*

Goor, Ron. *Pompeii: Exploring a Roman Ghost Town*. Crowell, 1986. *(P; I)*

Hackwell, W. John. *Digging to the Past: Excavations in Ancient Lands*. Scribner's, 1986. *(I; A)*

Hoover, H. M. *The Lost Star*. Viking, 1979. (Fiction) *(I; A)*

James, Carollyn. *Digging Up the Past: The Story of an Archeological Adventure*. Watts, 1990. (Fiction) *(I)*

Kunhardt, Edith. *Pompeii: Buried Alive!* Random, 1987. *(I)*

Lasky, Kathryn. *Traces of Life: The Origins of Humankind*. Morrow, 1989. *(I; A)*

Le Guin, Ursula. *The Tombs of Atuan*. Atheneum, 1971. (Fiction) *(I; A)*

Lyttle, Richard B. *Waves Across the Past: Adventures in Underwater Archeology*. Atheneum, 1981. *(I; A)*

Marston, Elsa. *Mysteries in American Archeology*. Walker, 1986. *(A)*

Perl, Lila. *Mummies, Tombs, and Treasure*. Clarion, 1987. *(I)*

Rollin, Sue. *The Illustrated Atlas of Archaeology*. Watts, 1982. *(P; I)*

Snyder, Thomas F. *Archeology Search Book*. McGraw, 1982. *(P; I; A)*

Swinburne, Irene, and Swinburne, Lawrence. *Behind the Sealed Door: The Discovery of the Tomb and Treasures of Tutankhamen*. Sniffen Court, 1977. *(I; A)*

Tantillo, Joe. *Amazing Ancient Treasures*. Pantheon, 1983. *(P; I)*

Ventura, Piero, and Ceserani, Gian Paolo. *In Search of Ancient Crete*. Silver Burdett, 1985. *(I; A); In Search of Troy*, 1985. *(I; A); In Search of Tutankhamun*, 1985. *(I; A)*

Williams, Barbara. *Breakthrough: Women in Archaeology*. Walker, 1981. *(I; A)*

ARCHERY

Boy Scouts of America. *Archery*. Boy Scouts, 1978. *(I; A)*

Thomas, Art. *Archery Is for Me*. Lerner, 1981. *(P; I)*

ARCHITECTURE

Carter, Katherine. *Houses*. Childrens, 1982. *(P)*

Fagg, C. D. *How They Built Long Ago*. Watts, 1981. *(I; A)*

Gibbons, Gail. *Up Goes the Skyscraper*. Macmillan, 1986. *(P)*

Hoberman, Mary Ann. *A House is a House for Me*. Viking, 1978. (Fiction) *(P)*

MacCauley, David. *Unbuilding*. Houghton, 1980. *(P)*

MacGregor, Anne, and MacGregor, Scott. *Domes: A Project Book*. Lothrop, 1982; *Skyscrapers: A Project Book*, 1981. *(I)*

Morris, Ann. *Houses and Homes*. Lothrop, 1992. *(P)*

Van Zandt, Eleanor. *Architecture*. Steck-Vaughn, 1990. *(I; A)*

Weiss, Harvey. *Shelters: From Teepee to Igloo*. Crowell, 1988. *(I; A)*

ARCTIC

Dekkers, Midas. *Arctic Adventure*. Watts, 1987. *(A)*

Hiscock, Bruce. *Tundra: the Arctic Land*. Atheneum, 1986. *(P;I)*

Osborn, Kevin. *The Peoples of the Arctic*. Chelsea House, 1990. *(I; A)*

Pluckrose, Henry, ed. *Small World of Arctic Lands*. Watts, 1982. *(P)*

ARGENTINA

Fox, Geoffrey. *The Land and People of Argentina*. Lippincott, 1990. *(I; A)*

Huber, Alex. *We Live in Argentina*. Watts, 1984. *(I; A)*

Liebowitz, Sol. *Argentina*. Chelsea House, 1990. *(I; A)*

Lye, Keith. *Take a Trip to Argentina*. Watts, 1986. *(P)*

Peterson, Marge, and Peterson, Rob. *Argentina: A Wild West Heritage*. Dillon, 1990. *(I)*

ARITHMETIC

Allison, Linda, and Weston, Martha. *Eenie, Meenie, Miney Math! Math Play for You and Your Preschooler*. Little, 1993. *(P)*

Clement, Rod. *Counting on Frank*. Gareth Stevens, 1991. *(P; I)*

Hulme, Joy N. *Sea Squares*. Hyperion, 1991. *(P; I)*

ARIZONA

Filbin, Dan. *Arizona*. Lerner, 1991. *(I)*

Fradin, Dennis. *Arizona: In Words and Pictures*. Childrens, 1980. *(P; I)*

ARKANSAS

Fradin, Dennis. *Arkansas: In Words and Pictures*. Childrens, 1980. *(P; I)*

Heinrichs, Ann. *Arkansas*. Childrens, 1989. *(P; I)*

ARMOR

Mango, Karin. *Armor: Yesterday and Today*. Messner, 1980. *(I; A)*

Watts, Edith. *A Young Person's Guide to European Arms and Armor in the Metropolitan Museum of Art*. Metropolitan Museum of Art, 1982. *(I)*

Wilkinson, Frederick. *Arms and Armor*. Watts, 1984. *(P; I)*

ARNOLD, BENEDICT

Alderman, Clifford L. *The Dark Eagle: The Story of Benedict Arnold*. Macmillan, 1976. *(I; A)*

Fritz, Jean. *Traitor: The Case of Benedict Arnold*. Putnam, 1981. *(I; A)*

ART AND ARTISTS

Cummings, Pat, ed. *Talking With Artists*. Bradbury, 1992. *(P; I)*

DePaola, Tomie. *The Art Lesson*. Putnam, 1989. (Fiction) *(P)*

Greenberg, Jan, and Jordan, Sandra. *The Painter's Eye: Learning to Look at Contemporary Art*. Delacorte, 1991. *(I; A)*

Greenfeld, Howard. *Marc Chagall*. Abrams, 1990. *(I; A)*

Henderson, Kathy. *Market Guide for Young Artists & Photographers*. Betterway, 1990. *(I; A)*

Isaacson, Philip M. *A Short Walk Around the Pyramids & Through the World of Art*. Knopf, 1993. *(I; A)*

Janson, H. W., and Janson, Anthony F. *History of Art For Young People*. Abrams, 1987. *(A)*

Lionni, Leo. *Matthew's Dream*. Knopf, 1991. (Fiction) *(P)*

Lynton, Norbert. *A History of Art*. Watts, 1982. *(I; A)*

Powell, Jillian. *Painting and Sculpture*. Steck-Vaughn, 1990. *(I; A)*

Sills, Leslie. *Visions: Stories About Women Artists*. Albert Whitman, 1993. *(I)*

Smith, Dian G. *Careers in the Visual Arts*. Messner, 1980. *(I; A)*

Testa, Fulvio. *If You Take a Paintbrush: A Book of Colors*. Dial, 1983. *(P)*

Waterford, Giles. *Faces*. Atheneum, 1982. *(I)*

Woolf, Felicity. *Picture This: A First Introduction to Paintings*. Doubleday, 1990. *(I)*

Yenawine, Philip. *Colors*. Delacorte, 1991. *(P); Lines*. Delacorte, 1991. *(P); Shapes*. Delacorte, 1991. *(P)*

Zadrzynska, Ewa. *The Girl with a Watering Can*. Chameleon, 1990. *(P; I)*

ARTHUR, CHESTER ALAN

Stevens, Rita. *Chester A. Arthur: 21st President of the United States*. Garrett Educational, 1989. *(I)*

ARTHUR, KING

Hastings, Selina. *Sir Gawain and the Green Knight*. Lothrop, 1981. *(P; I)*

Malory, Thomas. *King Arthur and His Knights of the Round Table,* ed. by Sidney Lanier and Howard Pyle. Putnam, n.d. *(P; I)*

Pyle, Howard. *The Story of King Arthur and His Knights*. Scribner's, 1903. *(I; A)*

Riordan, James. *Tales of King Arthur*. Rand, 1982. *(I)*

Sutcliff, Rosemary. *The Light Beyond the Forest*. Dutton, 1980; *The Road to Camlann: The Death of King Arthur,* 1982. *The Sword and the Circle: King Arthur and Knights of the Round Table,* 1981. *(I; A)*

ASIA

Asian Cultural Center for UNESCO, ed. *Folk Tales from Asia for Children Everywhere: Bks. 1–6*. Weatherhill, 1975–1978. *(P; I)*

Franck, Irene M., and Brownstone, David M. *Across Asia by Land*. Facts on File, 1990. *(A)*

St. Tamara. *Asian Crafts*. Lion, 1972. *(P; I)*

See also individual countries.

ASTRONOMY

Apfel, Necia H. *Astronomy Projects for Young Scientists*. Arco, 1984. *(A)*

Asimov, Isaac. *Astronomy Today*. Gareth Stevens, 1990. *(P; I); How Did We Find Out About the Universe?* Walker, 1983; *How Was the Universe Born?* Gareth Stevens, 1989. *(P; I)*

Berger, Melvin. *Bright Stars, Red Giants, and White Dwarfs*. Putnam, 1983; *Star Gazing, Comet Tracking and Sky Mapping*. Putnam, 1985. *(I; A)*

Branley, Franklyn M. *Journey into a Black Hole*. Harper, 1988. *(P); The Sky Is Full of Stars*. Harper, 1983. *(P); Space Telescope*. Crowell, 1985. *(P; I); Venus: Magellan Explores Our Twin Planet*. Harper, 1994. *(I)*

Chaple, Glenn F. *Exploring with a Telescope*. Watts, 1988. *(I)*

Fisher, David E. *The Origin and Evolution of Our Own Particular Universe*. Atheneum, 1988. *(A)*

Fradin, Dennis B. *Astronomy*. Childrens, 1987. *(A)*

Gallant, Roy A. *Once Around the Galaxy*. Watts, 1983. *(I; A); The Macmillan Book of Astronomy*. Atheneum, 1986. *(P; I)*

Herbst, Judith. *Sky Above and Worlds Beyond*. Atheneum, 1983. *(I; A)*

Jastrow, Robert. *Red Giants and White Dwarfs*. Norton, 1990. *(I; A)*

Jespersen, James, and Fitz-Randolph, Jane. *Looking at the Invisible Universe*. Atheneum, 1990. *(A)*

Kelsey, Larry, and Hoff, Darrel. *Recent Revolutions in Astronomy*. Watts, 1987. *(I; A)*

Levinson, Riki. *Watch the Stars Come Out*. Dutton, 1985. *(P)*

Moeschl, Richard. *Exploring the Sky: 100 Projects for Beginning Astronomers*. Chicago Review Press, 1988. *(I; A)*

Moore, Patrick, ed. *International Encyclopedia of Astronomy*. Orion Books, 1987. *(A)*

Simon, Seymour. *Galaxies*. Morrow, 1988. *(P)*

Vbrova, Zuza. *Space and Astronomy*. Gloucester Press, 1990. *(I)*

ATHENS. See GREECE.

ATLANTA. See GEORGIA.

ATLANTIC OCEAN. See OCEANS AND OCEANOGRAPHY.

ATMOSPHERE

Branley, Franklyn. *Air Is All Around You*. Crowell, 1986. *(P)*

Gallant, Roy A. *Rainbows, Mirages, and Sun Dogs: The Sky As a Source of Wonder*. Macmillan, 1987. *(I)*

Jefferies, Lawrence. *Air, Air, Air*. Troll, 1983. *(P; I)*

Lloyd, David. *Air*. Dial, 1983. *(P)*

ATOMS

Ardley, Neil. *The World of the Atom*. Gloucester Press, 1989. *(I)*

Asimov, Isaac. *How Did We Find Out About Atoms*. Walker, 1976. *(I; A)*

Mebane, Robert C., and Rybolt, Thomas R. *Adventures with Atoms and Molecules, Book II; Chemistry Experiments for Young People*. Enslow, 1987. *(I; A)*

AUDUBON, JOHN JAMES

Brenner, Barbara. *On the Frontier with Mr. Audubon*. Putnam, 1977. *(I)*

AUSTRALIA

Arnold, Caroline. *Australia Today*. Watts, 1987. *(P; I)*

Australia. Gareth Stevens, 1988. *(P)*

Dolce, Laura. *Australia*. Chelsea House, 1990. *(I)*

Ellis, Ronnie. *We Live in Australia*. Watts, 1983. *(I; A)*

Kelly, Andrew. *Australia*. Bookwright, 1989. *(I)*

Parker, K. Langloh. *Australian Legendary Tales*. Merrimack, 1980. *(P; I)*

Schneck, S., ed. *Australian Animals*. Western, 1983. *(I; A)*

Stark, Al. *Australia: A Lucky Land*. Dillon, 1987. *(P; I)*

AUSTRIA

Wohlrabe, Raymond, and Krusch, Werner. *The Land and People of Austria*. Lippincott, 1972. *(I; A)*

AUTOMATION. See TECHNOLOGY.

AUTOMOBILE RACING

Harmer, Paul. *Racing Cars*. Rourke, 1988. *(P)*

Higdon, Hal. *Johnny Rutherford: Indy Champ*. Putnam, 1980. *(I; A)*

Knudson, Richard L. *Land Speed Record Breakers*. Lerner, 1981. *Racing Yesterday's Cars*, 1984. *(I; A)*

Sheffer, H. R. *Race Cars*. Crestwood, 1982. *(I; A)*

Wilkinson, Sylvia. *Stock Cars*. Childrens, 1981. *(I; A)*

AUTOMOBILES

Bendick, Jeanne. *The First Book of Automobiles*. Watts, 1984 (rev. ed.). *(I)*

Cole, Joanna. *Cars and How They Go*. Harper, 1983. *(P)*

Florian, Douglas. *An Auto Mechanic*. Greenwillow, 1991. *(P)*

Ford, Barbara. *The Automobile*. Walker, 1987. *(I)*

Gunning, Thomas G. *Dream Cars*. Dillon, 1990. *(P; I)*

Lord, Harvey G. *Car Care for Kids and Former Kids*. Atheneum, 1983. *(I; A)*

Lord, Trevor. *Amazing Cars*. Knopf, 1992. *(P)*

Sullivan, George. *Cars*. Doubleday, 1991. *(I)*

Sutton, Richard. *Car*. Knopf, 1990. *(I)*

Taylor, John. *How Cars Are Made*. Facts on File, 1987. *(I)*

Tessendorf, K. C. *Look Out! Here Comes the Stanley Steamer*. Atheneum, 1984. *(P; I)*

Young, Frank. *Automobile: From Prototype to Scrapyard*. Watts, 1982. *(I)*

AVIATION

Ardley, Neil. *Air and Flight*. Watts, 1984. *(I)*

Barton, Byron. *Airport*. Harper, 1982. *(P)*

Bellville, Cheryl Walsh. *The Airplane Book*. Carolrhoda, 1991. *(P; I)*

Bendick, Jeanne. *Airplanes*. Watts, 1982 (rev. ed.). *(I)*

Berliner, Don. *Before the Wright Brothers*. Lerner, 1990. *(I)*; *Personal Airplanes*. Lerner, 1982. *(I; A)*

Boyne, Walter J. *Flight*. Time-Life, 1990. *(A)*; *The Smithsonian Book of Flight for Young People*. Aladdin, 1988. *(I; A)*

Burleigh, Robert. *Flight: The Journey of Charles Lindbergh*. Philomel, 1991. *(P; I)*

Cave, Joyce, and Cave, Ronald, *Aircraft*. Watts, 1982. *(P)*

Dwiggins, Don. *Flying the Frontiers of Space*. Dodd, 1982. *(I; A)*

Freeman, Tony. *Aircraft That Work for Us*. Childrens, 1981. *(P; I)*

Hodgman, Ann, and Djabbaroff, Ruby. *Skystars: The History of Women in Aviation*. Atheneum, 1981. *(I; A)*

Jaspersohn, William. *A Week in the Life of an Airline Pilot*. Little, 1991. *(I)*

Kerrod, Robin. *Amazing Flying Machines*. Knopf, 1992. *(P)*

Langton, Jane. *The Fledgling*. Harper, 1980. (Fiction) *(P; I)*

Levinsonk, Nancy S. *Chuck Yeager: The Man Who Broke the Sound Barrier*. Walker, 1988. *(I; A)*

Lindblom, Steven. *Fly the Hot Ones*. Houghton, 1991. *(I; A)*

Maurer, Richard. *Airborne: The Search for the Secret of Flight*. Simon & Schuster, 1990. *(I)*

Maynard, Chris, and Paton, John. *The History of Aircraft*. Watts, 1982. *(I)*

Moulton, Robert R. *First to Fly*. Lerner, 1983. *(I; A)*

Nahum, Andrew. *Flying Machine*. Knopf, 1990. *(I)*

Provenson, Alice, and Provenson, Martin. *The Glorious Flight: Across the Channel with Louis Blériot*. Viking, 1983. *(P)*

Rosenblum, Richard. *The Golden Age of Aviation*. Atheneum, 1984. *(P; I)*

Sloate, Susan. *Amelia Earhart: Challenging the Skies.* Fawcett, 1990. *(I)*

Stacey, Tom. *Airplanes: The Lure of Flight.* Lucent Books, 1990. *(I)*

Tessendorf, K. C. *Barnstormers and Daredevils.* Atheneum, 1988. *(I; A)*

BABY

Banish, Roslyn. *I Want to Tell You About My Baby.* Wingbow, 1982. *(P)*

Harris, Robbie H., and Levy, Elizabeth. *Before You Were Three: How You Began to Walk, Talk, Explore and Have Feelings.* Delacorte, 1981. *(A)*

Ormerod, Jan. *101 Things to Do with a Baby.* Lothrop, 1984. *(P)*

Wilkes, Angela. *See How I Grow: A Photographic Record of a Baby's First Eighteen Months.* Dorling Kindersley, 1994. *(P)*

See also REPRODUCTION, HUMAN.

BACTERIA. See MICROBIOLOGY.

BADGERS. See OTTERS AND OTHER MUSTELIDS.

BADMINTON

Wright, Len. *Your Book of Badminton.* Transatlantic, 1972. *(I; A)*

BAHAMAS. See CARIBBEAN SEA AND ISLANDS.

BAHRAIN. See MIDDLE EAST.

BALKANS

Lear, Aaron E. *Albania.* Chelsea House, 1987. *(A)*

BALLADS. See FOLK MUSIC.

BALLET. See DANCE.

BALLOONS AND BALLOONING

Briggs, Carole S. *Ballooning.* Lerner, 1986. *(P; I)*

Coombs, Charles. *Hot-Air Ballooning.* Morrow, 1981. *(I)*

Scarry, Huck. *Balloon Trip: A Sketchbook.* Prentice Hall, 1983. *(I)*

BALTIMORE. See MARYLAND.

BANDS AND BAND MUSIC. See MUSIC AND MUSICIANS.

BANGKOK (KRUNG THEP). See SOUTHEAST ASIA.

BANGLADESH

Wright, R. E. *Bangladesh.* Chelsea House, 1988. *(P)*

BANKS AND BANKING

Cantwell, Lois. *Money and Banking.* Watts, 1984. *(I; A)*

Scott, Elaine. *The Banking Book.* Warne, 1981. *(I; A)*

BARBADOS. See CARIBBEAN SEA AND ISLANDS.

BAROMETER. See WEATHER.

BARTON, CLARA

Bains, Rae. *Clara Barton: Angel of the Battlefield.* Troll, 1982. *(P; I)*

Kraske, Robert. *Clara Barton.* Winston, 1980 (new ed.). *(P)*

Stevenson, Augusta. *Clara Barton: Founder of the American Red Cross.* Bobbs, 1983. *(P; I)*

BASEBALL

Aaseng, Nate. *Baseball: You Are the Manager.* Lerner, 1983. *(P; I)*

Arnow, Jan. *Louisville Slugger: The Making of a Baseball Bat.* Pantheon, 1984. *(P; I)*

Berler, Ron. *The Super Book of Baseball.* Sports Illustrated for Kids Books, 1991. *(I; A)*

Clark, Steve. *The Complete Book of Baseball Cards.* Putnam, 1982. *(P; I; A)*

Cluck, Bob. *The Winning Edge: Baserunning; The Winning Edge: Catching; The Winning Edge: Hitting; The Winning Edge: Shortstop.* Pantheon, 1987. *(I; A)*

Dolan, Edward F. *Great Moments in the World Series.* Watts, 1982. *(I)*

Earle, Vana. *The All-Star Book of Baseball Fun.* Macmillan, 1982. *(P; I)*

Frommer, Harvey. *A Hundred and Fiftieth Anniversary Album of Baseball.* Watts, 1988. *(I; A); Baseball's Hall of Fame.* Watts, 1985. *(P; I)*

Jaspersohn, William. *The Ballpark: One Day Behind the Scenes at a Major League Game.* Little, 1980. *(I; A); Bat, Ball, Glove: The Making of Major League Baseball Gear.* Little, 1989. *(I; A)*

Kreutzer, Peter, and Kerley, Ted. *Little League's Official How-to-Play Baseball Book.* Doubleday, 1990. *(I)*

Ritter, Lawrence S. *The Story of Baseball.* Morrow, 1983. *(I)*

Sandak, Cass R. *Baseball and Softball.* Watts, 1982. *(P)*

Solomon, Chuck. *Major-League Batboy.* Crown, 1992. *(P; I)*

Sullivan, George. *All About Baseball.* Putnam, 1989. *(P; I); The Art of Base-Stealing.* Dodd, 1982; *Better Baseball for Boys,* 1981 (rev. ed.). *(I); Baseball Backstage.* Holt, 1986. *(I)*

See also LITTLE LEAGUE BASEBALL.

BASKETBALL

Aaseng, Nate. *Basketball: You Are the Coach; Basketball's Playmakers; Basketball's Sharpshooters.* Lerner, 1983. *(I; A)*

Anderson, Dave. *The Story of Basketball.* Morrow, 1988. *(I; A)*

Beard, Butch and others. *Butch Beard's Basic Basketball.* Michael Kesend, 1985. *(A)*

Finney, Shan. *Basketball.* Watts, 1982. *(P)*

Lerner, Mark. *Careers in Basketball.* Lerner, 1983. *(P; I)*

Liss, Howard. *Strange but True Basketball Stories.* Random, 1983. *(I; A)*

Radlauer, Ruth, and Radlauer, Ed. *Some Basics About Women's Basketball.* Childrens, 1982. *(P; I; A)*

Rosenthal, Bert. *Basketball.* Childrens, 1983. *(P)*

Young, Faye, and Coffey, Wayne. *Winning Basketball for Girls.* Facts on File, 1984. *(I; A)*

BATS

Bash, Barbara. *Shadows of Night: The Hidden World of the Little Brown Bat.* Sierra Club Books, 1993. *(P)*

Cannon, Janell. *Stellaluna.* Harcourt, 1993. *(P)*

Greenaway, Frank. *Amazing Bats.* Knopf, 1991. *(P)*

Hopf, Alice L. *Bats.* Dodd, 1985. *(P; I)*

Johnson, Sylvia A. *Bats.* Lerner, 1985. *(P; I)*

Mulleneux, Jane. *Discovering Bats.* Bookwright, 1989. *(P)*

Pringle, Laurence. *Batman: Exploring the World of Bats.* Scribner's, 1991. *(P; I); Vampire Bats.* Morrow, 1982. *(I; A)*

Schlein, Miriam. *Billions of Bats.* Harper, 1982. *(I)*

Selsam, Millicent E., and Hunt, Joyce. *A First Look at Bats.* Walker, 1991. *(P)*

BATTERIES. See ELECTRICITY.

BEARS

Banks, Martin. *The Polar Bear on the Ice.* Gareth Stevens, 1990. *(I)*

Calabro, Marian. *Operation Grizzly Bear.* Four Winds, 1989. *(I)*

Harrison, Virginia. *The World of Polar Bears.* Gareth Stevens, 1990. *(P)*

Larsen, Thor. *The Polar Bear Family.* Picture Books Studio, 1990. *(P; I)*

Patent, Dorothy H. *Bears of the World.* Holiday, 1980. *(I; A)*

Schoenherr, John. *Bear.* Philomel, 1991. (Fiction) *(P)*

Weaver, John L. *Grizzly Bears.* Dodd, 1982. *(P; I)*

BEATLES, THE

Evans, Mike. *The Art of the Beatles.* Beech Tree Books, 1985. *(A)*

Harry, Bill. *The Book of Beatle Lists.* Javelin Books, 1985. *(A)*

Hoffmann, Dezo. *The Beatles Conquer America.* Avon, 1985. *(A)*

BEAVERS

Lane, Margaret. *The Beaver.* Dial, 1982. *(P)*

Nentl, Jerolyn. *Beaver.* Crestwood, 1983. *(P; I)*

Ryden, Hope. *The Beaver.* Putnam, 1987. *(I; A)*

BEES

Cook, David. *Small World of Bees and Wasps.* Watts, 1981. *(P)*

Fischer-Nagel, Heiderose, and Fischer-Nagel, Andreas. *Life of the Honeybee.* Carolrhoda, 1985. *(P)*

Migutsch, Ali. *From Blossom to Honey.* Carolrhoda, 1981. *(P)*

BEETHOVEN, LUDWIG VAN

Blackwood, Alan. *Beethoven.* Watts, 1987. *(I)*

Thompson, Wendy. *Ludwig van Beethoven.* Viking, 1991. *(I)*

BEETLES

Still, John. *Amazing Beetles.* Knopf, 1991. *(P)*

BEIJING. See CHINA.

BELGIUM

Hargrove, Jim. *Belgium.* Childrens, 1988. *(P; I)*

Lye, Keith. *Take A Trip to Belgium.* Watts, 1984. *(P; I)*

BELIZE. See CENTRAL AMERICA.

BELL, ALEXANDER GRAHAM

Quackenbush, Robert. *Ahoy! Ahoy! Are You There? A Story of Alexander Graham Bell.* Prentice Hall, 1981. *(P; I)*

Shippen, Katherine B. *Alexander Graham Bell Invents the Telephone.* Random, 1982. *(P; I)*

BELLS AND CARILLONS. See MUSICAL INSTRUMENTS.

BENIN. See AFRICA.

BEOWULF

Crossley-Holland, Kevin, tr. *Beowulf.* Oxford University Press, 1984. *(I; A)*

Hieatt, Constance B., ed. *Beowolf and Other Old English Poems.* Bantam, 1982. *(A)*

Nye, Robert. *Beowulf.* Dell, 1982. *(I; A)*

BERLIN. See GERMANY.

BERLIN, IRVING

Streissguth, Tom. *Say It With Music: A Story About Irving Berlin*. Carolrhoda, 1994. *(I)*

BERLIOZ, HECTOR. See MUSIC AND MUSICIANS.

BHUTAN

Foster, Leila Merrell. *Bhutan*. Childrens, 1989. *(I)*

BIBLE AND BIBLE STORIES

Holy Bible. *King James Version*. Holy Bible. *Rev. Standard Version (Catholic Edition)*. Many publishers.

Asimov, Isaac. *Animals of the Bible*. Doubleday, 1978. *(I); The Story of Ruth*. 1972. *(I)*

Chaikin, Miriam. *Esther*. Jewish Publication Society, 1987. *(I)*

Daniel, Rebecca. *Women of the Old Testament*. Good Apple, 1983. *(I; A)*

DePaola, Tomie. *Noah and the Ark*. Winston, 1983. *(P)*

Hutton, Warwick, ad. and illus. *Jonah and the Great Whale*. Atheneum, 1984. *(P)*

Leeton, Will C. *David and Goliath*. Dandelion, 1979. *(P; I)*

L'Engle, Madeleine. *The Glorious Impossible*. Simon & Schuster, 1990. *(I; A)*

Petersham, Maud, and Petersham, Miska. *The Christ Child*. Macmillan, 1931; 1980 (paper). *(P)*

Pilling, Ann. *Before I Go to Sleep: Bible Stories, Poems, and Prayers for Children*. Crown, 1990. *(P)*

Singer, Isaac Bashevis. *The Wicked City*. Farrar, 1972. *(I)*

Stoddard, Sandol. *Doubleday Illustrated Children's Bible*. Doubleday, 1983. *(P; I); Five Who Found the Kingdom: New Testament Stories*, 1981. *(I)*

Turner, Philip. *The Bible Story*. Merrimack, 1982. *(P; I)*

BICYCLING

Berto, Frank J. *Bicycling Magazine's Complete Guide to Upgrading Your Bike*. Rodale, 1988. *(A)*

Coombs, Charles. *BMX: A Guide to Bicycle Motocross*. Morrow, 1983. *(I)*

Eds. of *Bicycling*. *Bicycling's Complete Guide to Bicycle Maintenance and Repair*. Rodale, 1986. *(A)*

LeMond, Greg, and Gordis, Kent. *Greg LeMond's Complete Book of Bicycling*. Putnam, 1987. *(A)*

Monroe, Lynn. *The Old-Time Bicycle Book*. Carolrhoda, 1979. *(P)*

Murphy, Jim. *Two Hundred Years of Bicycles*. Lippincott, 1983. *(I)*

Olney, Ross. *Riding High: Bicycling for Young People*. Lothrop, 1981. *(I; A)*

Roth, Harold. *Bike Factory*. Pantheon, 1985. *(I)*

Scioscia, Mary. *Bicycle Rider*. Harper, 1983. *(P; I)*

Stine, Megan. *Wheels!: The Kids' Bike Book*. Sports Illustrated for Kids Books, 1990. *(P; I)*

BIOGRAPHIES

Blackwood, Alan. *Captain Cook*. Bookwright, 1987. *(I)*

Carpenter, Angelica Shirley, and Shirley, Jean. *L. Frank Baum: Royal Historian of Oz*. Lerner, 1991. *(I; A)*

Chaney, J. R. *Aleksandr Pushkin: Poet for the People*. Lerner, 1991. *(I; A)*

Collins, David R. *Pioneer Plowmaker: A Story About John Deere*. Carolrhoda, 1991. *(I)*

Cryan-Hicks, Kathryn T. *W. E. B. DuBois: Crusader for Peace*. Discovery, 1991. *(I)*

Faber, Doris. *Calamity Jane*. Houghton, 1992. *(I)*

Ferris, Jeri. *Arctic Explorer: The Story of Matthew Henson*. Carolrhoda, 1989. *(I)*

Finkelstein, Norman H. *Theodor Herzl: Architect of a Nation*. Lerner, 1991. *(I; A)*

Fritz, Jean. *Surprising Myself*. Richard C. Owen, 1992. *(P; I)*

Goldberg, Herbert S. *Hippocrates: Father of Medicine*. Watts, 1963. *(I)*

Green, Carl R., and Sanford, William R. *Belle Starr*. Enslow, 1992. *(I)*

Hamilton, Virginia. *Anthony Burns: The Defeat and Triumph of a Fugitive Slave*. Knopf, 1988. *(I; A)*

Haskins, Jim, and Benson, Kathleen. *Space Challenger: The Story of Guion Bluford*. Carolrhoda, 1984. *(I)*

Ipsen, D. C. *Archimedes: Greatest Scientist of the Ancient World*. Enslow, 1988. *(I; A)*

McKissack, Patricia, and McKissack, Frederick. *Carter G. Woodson: The Father of Black History*. Enslow, 1991. *(P)*

McPherson, Stephanie Sammartino. *Rooftop Astronomer: A Story About Maria Mitchell*. Carolrhoda, 1990. *(I)*

Phelan, Mary Kay. *Probing the Unknown: The Story of Dr. Florence Sabin*. Crowell, 1969. *(I; A)*

Pinkney, Andrea Davis. *Alvin Ailey*. Hyperion, 1993. *(P; I)*

Stanley, Diane, and Vennema, Peter. *Bard of Avon: The Story of William Shakespeare*. Morrow, 1992. *(I); Shaka, King of the Zulus*. Morrow, 1988. *(I)*

Stanley, Fay. *The Last Princess: The Story of Princess Ka'iulani of Hawai'i*. Four Winds, 1991. *(I)*

Stevens, Byrna. *Handel and the Famous Sword Swallower of Halle*. Philomel, 1990. *(P)*

Tarnes, Richard. *Alexander Fleming*. Watts, 1990. *(I)*

Tolan, Sally. *John Muir: Naturalist, Writer and Guardian of the North American Wilderness*. Gareth Stevens, 1990. *(I)*

Towle, Wendy. *The Real McCoy: The Life of an African-American Inventor*. Scholastic, 1993. *(P; I)*

Vare, Ethlie Ann. *Adventurous Spirit: A Story About Ellen Swallow Richards*. Carolrhoda, 1992. *(I)*

Wisniewski, David. *Sundiata, Lion King of Mali*. Clarion, 1992. *(P; I)*

BIOLOGY

Evans, Ifor. *Biology*. Watts, 1984. *(I)*

Silver, Donald M. *Life on Earth: Biology Today*. Random, 1983. *(A)*

Tocci, Salvatore. *Biology Projects for Young Scientists*. Watts, 1987. *(A)*

BIOLUMINESCENCE

Jacobs, Francine. *Nature's Light: The Story of Biolumi-nescence*. Morrow, 1974. *(P; I)*

BIRDS

Arnosky, Jim. *Crinkleroot's 25 Birds Every Child Should Know*. Bradbury, 1993. *(P)*; *Crinkleroot's Guide to Knowing the Birds*. Bradbury, 1992. *(P; I)*

Barrie, Anmarie. *A Step-by-Step Book About Canaries; A Step-by-Step Book About Cockatiels*. TFH Publications, 1988. *(I; A)*

Bash, Barbara. *Urban Roosts: Where Birds Nest in the City*. Sierra Club Books, 1990. *(P; I)*

Blassingame, Wyatt. *Wonders of Egrets, Bitterns, and Herons*. Dodd, 1982. *(I; A)*

Brown, Mary Barrett. *Wings Along the Waterway*. Orchard, 1992. *(P; I)*

Burnie, David. *Bird*. Knopf, 1988. *(I)*

Burton, Maurice. *Birds*. Facts on File, July, 1985. *(I)*

Cole, Joanna. *A Bird's Body*. Morrow, 1982. *(P)*

Fischer-Nagel, Heiderose, and Fischer-Negal, Andreas. *Season of the White Stork*. Carolrhoda, 1985. *(P; I)*

Fleischman, Paul. *Townsend's Warbler*. Harper, 1992. *(I)*

Freedman, Russell. *How Birds Fly*. Holiday, 1977. *(I)*

Goble, Paul. *The Great Race of the Birds and Animals*. Bradbury, 1985. *(P)*

Greenberg, Polly. *Birds of the World*. Putnam, 1983. *(P; I)*

Hume, Rob. *Birdwatching*. Random, 1993. *(I)*

Klein, Tom. *Loon Magic for Kids*. Gareth Stevens, 1990. *(P)*

Mansell, William C. *North American Birds of Prey*. Morrow, 1980. *(I; A)*

Matthews, Downs. *Skimmers*. Simon & Schuster, 1990. *(P; I)*

McCauley, Jane B. *Baby Birds and How They Grow*. National Geographic, 1984. *(P)*

Milkins, Colin S. *Discovering Songbirds*. Bookwright, 1990. *(P; I)*

Sattler, Helen Roney. *The Book of Eagles*. Lothrop, 1989. *(I)*

Selsam, Millicent, and Hunt, Joyce. *A First Look at Birds*. Walker, 1973. *(P)*

Sill, Cathryn. *About Birds: A Guide for Children*. Peachtree, 1991. *(P)*

Singer, Marilyn. *Exotic Birds*. Doubleday, 1991. *(P; I)*

Stone, Lynn M. *Birds of Prey*. Childrens, 1983. *(P)*

Taylor, Barbara. *The Bird Atlas*. Dorling Kindersley, 1993. *(P; I)*

Wharton, Anthony. *Discovering Ducks, Geese, and Swans*. Watts, 1987. *(P)*

Yolen, Jane. *Bird Watch*. Philomel, 1990. *(P)*

BIRTH CONTROL

Nourse, Alan E. *Birth Control*. Watts, 1988. *(A)*

BLACK AMERICANS. See AFRICAN AMERICANS.

BLACKWELL, ELIZABETH

Schleichert, Elizabeth. *The Life of Elizabeth Blackwell*. 21st Century Books, 1992. *(P; I)*

BLINDNESS

Arnold, Caroline. *A Guide Dog Puppy Grows Up*. Harcourt, 1991. *(P; I)*

Brighton, Catherine. *My Hands, My World*. Macmillan, 1984. *(P)*

Curtis, Patricia. *Greff, The Story of a Guide Dog*. Dutton, 1982. *(P; I; A)*

Davidson, Margaret. *Louis Braille: The Boy Who Invented Books for the Blind*. Hastings, 1972. *(I)*

Marcus, Rebecca B. *Being Blind*. Hastings, 1981. *(I)*

Weiss, Malcolm E. *Blindness*. Watts, 1980. *(P; I)*

BLOOD

Showers, Paul. *A Drop of Blood*. Harper, 1967. *(P)*

Ward, Brian R. *The Heart and Blood*. Watts, 1982. *(I)*

BLY, NELLIE

Quackenbush, Robert. *Stop the Presses, Nellie's Got a Scoop! A Story of Nellie*. Simon & Schuster, 1992. *(P)*

BOATS AND BOATING

Gelman, Rita G., and Buxbaum, Susan K. *Boats That Float*. Watts, 1981. *(P)*

Gibbons, Gail. *Boat Book*. Holiday, 1983. *(P)*

Kentley, Eric. *Boat*. Knopf, 1992. *(I; A)*

Rockwell, Anne. *Boats*. Dutton, 1982. *(I)*

See also SAILING.

BODY, HUMAN

Avraham, Regina. *The Circulatory System*. Chelsea House, 1989. *(I)*

Baldwin, Dorothy, and Lister, Claire. *How You Grow and Change*. Watts, 1984. *(P; I)*

Beckelman, Laurie. *The Fact About Transplants*. Crestwood, 1990. *(P; I)*

Berger, Gilda. *The Human Body*. Doubleday, 1989. *(P)*

Berger, Melvin. *Why I Cough, Sneeze, Shiver, Hiccup, and Yawn*. Harper, 1983. *(P)*

Branley, Franklyn M. *Shivers and Goose Bumps: How We Keep Warm*. Crowell, 1984. *(I; A)*

Brunn, Ruth Dowling, M.D., and Brunn, Bertel, M.D.

The Human Body: Your Body and How It Works. Random, 1982. *(I; A)*

Buxbaum, Susan Kovacs, and Gelman, Rita Golden. *Body Noises: Where They Come From, Why They Happen.* Knopf, 1983. *(P; I)*

Cole, Joanna. *Cuts, Breaks, Bruises, and Burns: How Your Body Heals.* Crowell, 1985. *(I); The Human Body: How We Evolved.* Morrow, 1987. *(P); The Magic School Bus Inside the Human Body.* Scholastic, 1989. *(P; I); Your Insides.* Putnam, 1992. *(P)*

Cosgrove, Margaret. *Your Muscles and Ways to Exercise Them.* Dodd, 1980. *(P; I)*

Day, Trevor. *The Random House Book of 1001 Questions and Answers About the Human Body.* Random, 1994. *(I)*

Epstein, Beryl, and Epstein, Samuel. *Doctor Beaumont and the Man with the Hole in His Stomach.* Coward, 1978. *(P; I)*

Facklam, Margery, and Facklam, Howard. *Spare Parts for People.* Harcourt, 1987. *(I; A)*

Fekete, Irene, and Ward, Peter D. *Your Body.* Facts on File, 1984. *(I)*

Gamlin, Linda. *The Human Body.* Watts, 1988. *(I; A)*

Goor, Ron, and Goor, Nancy. *All Kinds of Feet.* Crowell, 1984. *(P)*

Harris, Robie H. *It's Perfectly Normal: A Book About Changing Bodies, Growing Up, Sex, and Sexual Health.* Candlewick, 1994. *(I)*

Isberg, Emily. *Peak Performance: Sports, Science, and the Body in Action.* Simon & Schuster, 1989. *(P; I)*

Leinwand, Gerald. *Transplants: Today's Medical Miracles.* Watts, 1985. *(I; A)*

Machotka, Hana. *Breathtaking Noses.* Morrow, 1992. *(P)*

Metos, Thomas H. *Artificial Humans: Transplants and Bionics.* Messner, 1985. *(I)*

Miller, Jonathan. *The Human Body.* Viking, 1983 (a pop-up book). *(P; I; A)*

Parker, Steve. *Eating a Meal: How You Eat, Drink, and Digest.* Watts, 1991. *(P); Food and Digestion.* Watts, 1990. *(I); Human Body.* Dorling Kindersley, 1994. *(P; I)*

Pluckrose, Henry. *Feet.* Watts, 1988. *(P)*

Reader's Digest ABC's of the Human Body. Reader's Digest, 1987. *(I; A)*

Royston, Angela. *The Human Body and How It Works.* Random, 1991. *(P; I)*

Settel, Joanne, and Baggett, Nancy. *Why Does My Nose Run?: (and Other Questions Kids Ask About Their Bodies).* Atheneum, 1985. *(I; A)*

Silverstein, Alvin, and Silverstein, Virginia B. *The Story of Your Mouth.* Coward, 1984. *(I; A); The Story of Your Foot.* Putnam, 1987. *(I; A)*

Thomson, Ruth. *Hands.* Watts, 1988. *(P)*

Westheimer, Ruth. *Dr. Ruth Talks to Kids: Where You Came From, How Your Body Changes, and What Sex Is All About.* Macmillan, 1993. *(I; A)*

BODYBUILDING. See HEALTH AND PHYSICAL FITNESS.

BOLIVIA

Bolivia . . . In Pictures. Lerner, 1987. *(I; A)*

Blair, David Nelson. *The Land and People of Bolivia.* Lippincott, 1990. *(I)*

Morrison, Marion. *Bolivia.* Childrens, 1988. *(I)*

Schimmel, Karen. *Bolivia.* Chelsea House, 1990. *(I)*

BOOKS

Ahlstrom, Mark. *Books.* Crestwood, 1983. *(P; I)*

Aliki. *How a Book Is Made.* Crowell, 1986. *(P)*

Althea. *Making a Book.* Cambridge University Press, 1983. *(I; A)*

Greenfeld, Howard. *Books: From Writer to Reader.* Crown, 1989 (rev. ed.). *(A)*

Kehoe, Michael. *The Puzzle of Books.* Carolrhoda, 1982. *(P)*

BOONE, DANIEL

Brandt, Keith. *Daniel Boone: Frontier Adventures.* Troll, 1983. *(P; I)*

Lawlor, Laurie. *Daniel Boone.* Albert Whitman, 1989. *(I)*

Stevenson, Augusta. *Daniel Boone: Young Hunter and Tracker.* Bobbs, 1983. *(P; I)*

BORNEO. See SOUTHEAST ASIA.

BOSTON

Monke, Ingrid. *Boston.* Dillon, 1989. *(P; I)*

Vanderwarker, Peter. *Boston Then and Now: Sixty-Five Boston Sites Photographed in the Past and Present.* Dover, 1982. *(P; I)*

See also MASSACHUSETTS.

BOTANY. See PLANTS.

BOTSWANA. See AFRICA.

BOWLING

Holman, Marshall, and Nelson, Roy G. *Marshall Holman's Bowling Tips and Techniques.* Contemporary Books, 1985. *(A)*

Lerner, Mark. *Bowling Is for Me.* Lerner, 1981. *(P; I)*

BOXING

Edwards, Audrey, and Wohl, Gary. *Muhammed Ali, the People's Champ.* Little, 1977. *(I)*

Riciutti, Edward R. *How to Box: Boxing for Beginners.* Harper, 1982. *(P; I)*

BOY SCOUTS

Blassingame, Wyatt. *Story of the Boy Scouts.* Garrard, 1968. *(I)*

Boy Scouts of America. *Bear Cub Scoutbook.* Boy Scouts, 1973. *(I); Boy Scout Fieldbook.* Workman,

1967. *(A); Scout Handbook.* Boy Scouts, 1972. *(I); Wolf Cub Scoutbook.* 1986 (rev. ed.). *(I)*

BRAHMS, JOHANNES. See Music and Musicians.

BRAIN

Baldwin, Dorothy, and Lister, Claire. *Your Brain and Nervous System.* Watts, 1984. *(I; A)*

Berger, Melvin. *Exploring the Mind and Brain.* Harper, 1983. *(I; A)*

Parker, Steve. *The Brain and Nervous System.* Watts, 1990. *(I)*

Silverstein, Alvin, and Silverstein, Virginia. *World of the Brain.* Morrow, 1986. *(P; I)*

Stafford, Patricia. *Your Two Brains.* Macmillan, 1986. *(I)*

BRAZIL

Bennett, Olivia. *A Family in Brazil.* Lerner, 1986. *(P; I)*

Carpenter, Mark L. *Brazil: An Awakening Giant.* Dillon, 1987. *(P; I)*

Cross, Wilbur, and Cross, Susanna. *Brazil.* Childrens, 1984. *(I; A)*

Haverstock, Nathan A. *Brazil in Pictures.* Lerner, 1987. *(I)*

Lye, Keith. *Take a Trip to Brazil.* Watts, 1983. *(P; I)*

BREAD AND BAKING

Lucas, Angela. *A Loaf of Bread.* Watts, 1983. *(I)*

Mitgutsch, Ali. *From Grain to Bread.* Carolrhoda, 1981. *(P; I)*

Ogren, Sylvia. *Shape It and Bake It: Quick and Simple Ideas for Children from Frozen Bread Dough.* Dillon, 1981. *(I)*

Sumption, Lois L., and Ashbrook, Marguerite L. *Breads from Many Lands.* Dover, 1982. *(I)*

BRICKS AND MASONRY. See Building Construction.

BRIDGES

Ardley, Neil. *Bridges.* Garrett Educational, 1990. *(P; I)*

Carlisle, Norman, and Carlisle, Madelyn. *Bridges.* Childrens, 1983. *(P)*

Carter, Polly. *The Bridge Book.* Simon & Schuster, 1992. *(P; I)*

Mitgutsch, Ali. *From Cement to Bridge.* Carolrhoda, 1981. *(P)*

Pelta, Kathy. *Bridging the Golden Gate.* Lerner, 1987. *(P)*

Robbins, Ken. *Bridges.* Dial, 1991. *(P; I)*

St. George, Judith. *The Brooklyn Bridge: They Said It Couldn't Be Built.* Putnam, 1982. *(I; A)*

Sandak, Cass R. *Bridges.* Watts, 1983. *(P)*

BRITISH COLUMBIA. See Canada.

BRONTË SISTERS

Brontë, Charlotte. *Jane Eyre,* ad. by Diana Stewart. Raintree, 1983. (Fiction) *(I)*

Brontë, Emily. *Wuthering Heights,* ad. by Betty K. Wright. Raintree, 1983. (Fiction) *(I; A)*

Martin, Christopher. *The Brontës.* Rourke, 1989. *(I; A)*

Sarnoff, Jane. *That's Not Fair.* Scribner's, 1980. *(P)*

BRUNEI. See Southeast Asia.

BUCHANAN, JAMES

Brill, Marlene Targ. *James Buchanan.* Childrens, 1988. *(I)*

BUCK, PEARL

La Farge, Ann. *Pearl Buck.* Chelsea House, 1988. *(A)*

BUDDHA AND BUDDHISM. See Religions of the World.

BUFFALO AND BISON

Freedman, Russell. *Buffalo Hunt.* Holiday, 1988. *(P; I)*

Patent, Dorothy Hinshaw. *Buffalo: The American Bison Today.* Clarion, 1986. *(I)*

BUFFALO BILL

D'Aulaire, Ingri, and D'Aulaire, Edgar Parin. *Buffalo Bill.* Doubleday, 1952. *(I)*

BUILDING CONSTRUCTION

Barton, Byron. *Building a House.* Greenwillow, 1981. *(P)*

Darling, David. *Spiderwebs to Skyscrapers.* Dillon, 1991. *(I)*

Fagg, C. D. *How They Built Long Ago.* Watts, 1981. *(I)*

Florian, Douglas. *A Carpenter.* Greenwillow, 1991. *(P)*

Gibbons, Gail. *How a House Is Built.* Holiday, 1990. *(P)*

Horwitz, Elinor L. *How to Wreck a Building.* Pantheon, 1982. *(I)*

Jennings, Terry J. *Cranes, Dumptrucks, Bulldozers, and Other Building Machines.* Kingfisher, 1993. *(I)*

Robbins, Ken. *Building a House.* Four Winds, 1984. *(P; I)*

Royston, Angela. *Diggers and Dump Trucks.* Aladdin, 1991. *(P)*

Stephen, R. J. *Cranes.* Watts, 1987. *(P); Earthmovers,* 1987. *(P)*

BULGARIA. See Balkans.

BULLETIN BOARDS

Finton, Esther. *Bulletin Boards for Science and Health.* Good Apple, 1980; *Math Bulletin Boards,* 1981. *(P; I)*

Jenkins, Betty. *Bulletin Board Book No. 1*. Good Apple, 1977; *Bulletin Board Book No. 2*, 1979. *(P)*

BULLFIGHTING. See SPAIN.

BURBANK, LUTHER

Quakenbush, Robert. *Here a Plant, There a Plant, Everywhere a Plant, Plant! A Story of Luther Burbank.* Prentice Hall, 1982. *(P; I)*

BURMA. See SOUTHEAST ASIA.

BURR, AARON. See HAMILTON, ALEXANDER.

BURUNDI. See AFRICA.

BUSES AND BUS TRAVEL. See TRANSPORTATION.

BUSH, GEORGE

Schneiderman, Ron. *The Picture Life of George Bush.* Watts, 1989. *(I)*
Sufrin, Mark. *George Bush: The Story of the Forty-first President of the United States.* Dell, 1989. *(I)*

BUTTERFLIES AND MOTHS

Cook, David. *Small World of Butterflies and Moths.* Watts, 1981. *(P)*
Dallinger, Jane, and Overbeck, Cynthia. *Swallowtail Butterflies.* Lerner, 1983. *(P; I)*
Gibbons, Gail. *The Monarch Butterfly.* Holiday, 1989. *(P; I)*
Jourdan, Eveline. *Butterflies and Moths Around the World.* Lerner, 1981. *(I; A)*
McClung, Robert M. *Sphinx: The Story of a Caterpillar.* Morrow, 1981. *(P)*
Mitchell, Robert T., and Zim, Herbert S. *Butterflies and Moths: A Guide to the More Common American Species.* Western, 1964. *(I)*
Norsgaard, E. Jaediker. *How to Raise Butterflies.* Putnam, 1988. *(P)*
Penn, Linda. *Young Scientists Explore Butterflies and Moths.* Good Apple, 1983. *(P)*
Reidel, Marlene. *From Egg to Butterfly.* Carolrhoda, 1981. *(P)*
Ryder, Joanne. *Where Butterflies Grow.* Dutton, 1989. *(P)*
Tarrant, Graham. *Butterflies.* Putnam, 1983. *(P)*
Whalley, Paul. *Butterfly & Moth.* Knopf, 1988. *(P; I)*
Yoshi. *The Butterfly Hunt.* Picture Book Studio, 1990. (Fiction) *(I)*

CABOT, JOHN AND SEBASTIAN

Goodnough, David. *John Cabot and Son.* Troll, 1979 (new ed.). *(P; I)*

CACTUS

Holmes, Anita. *Cactus: The All-American Plant,* Scholastic, 1982; *The 100-Year-Old Cactus,* 1983. *(P; I)*
Overbeck, Cynthia. *Cactus.* Lerner, 1982. *(I)*

CAESAR, GAIUS JULIUS

Matthews, Rupert. *Julius Caesar.* Bookwright, 1989. *(P; I)*
Shakespeare, William. *Julius Caesar;* ad. by Diana Stewart. Raintree, 1983. *(I; A)*
See also ROME, ANCIENT.

CALENDAR

Apfel, Necia H. *Calendars.* Watts, 1985. *(I; A)*
Bolton, Carole. *The Good-Bye Year.* Lodestar, 1982, *(I; A)*
Hughes, Paul. *The Days of the Week: Stories, Songs, Traditions, Festivals, and Surprising Facts About the Days of the Week from All Over the World.* Garrett Educational, 1989. *(P; I); The Months of the Year: Stories, Songs, Traditions, Festivals, and Surprising Facts About the Months of the Year from All Over the World.* Garrett Educational, 1989. *(P; I)*
Perry, Susan. *How Did We Get Clocks and Calendars?* Creative Education, 1981. *(P; I)*
Watkins, Peter, and Hughes, Erica. *Here's the Year.* Watts, 1982. *(I; A)*

CALIFORNIA

Cash, Judy. *Kidding Around Los Angeles: A Young Person's Guide to the City.* John Muir, 1989. *(I; A)*
Haddock, Patricia. *San Francisco.* Dillon, 1988. *(P)*
Oliver, Rice D. *Student Atlas of California.* California Weekly, 1982. *(I; A)*
Pack, Janet. *California.* Watts, 1987. *(I; A)*
Stein, R. Conrad. *California.* Childrens, 1988. *(P)*

CAMBODIA. See SOUTHEAST ASIA.

CAMELS

Cloudsley-Thompson, John. *Camels.* Raintree, 1980. *(I; A)*
Wexo, John Bonnett. *Camels.* Creative Education, 1988. *(P)*

CAMEROON. See AFRICA.

CAMPING

Dolan, Edward. *Bicycle Camping and Touring.* Wanderer Books, 1982. *(I; A)*
Jay, Michael. *Camping and Orienteering.* Warwick Press, 1990. *(I)*
National Geographic Society. *Wilderness Challenge.* National Geographic, 1980. *(I; A)*

Neimark, Paul. *Camping and Ecology*. Childrens, 1981. *(I)*

Riviere, Bill. *Camper's Bible*. Doubleday, 1984 (3rd rev. ed.). *(I; A)*

Zeleznak, Shirley. *Camping*. Crestwood, 1980. *(P; I; A)*

See also HIKING AND BACKPACKING.

CANADA

Bercuson. *Opening the Canadian West*. Watts, 1980. *(I; A)*

Brickenden, Jack. *Canada*. Bookwright, 1989. *(I)*

Harrison, Ted. *O Canada*. Ticknor & Fields, 1993. *(I; A)*

Holbrook, Sabra. *Canada's Kids*. Atheneum, 1983. *(I)*

Kurelek, William. *A Prairie Boy's Summer*. Houghton, 1975. *(I); A Prairie Boy's Winter*, 1973. *(P)*

LeVert, Suzanne. *Ontario*. Chelsea House, 1990. *(I); Quebec*. Chelsea House, 1990. *(I)*

Lye, Keith. *Take a Trip to Canada*. Watts, 1983. *(P)*

Martin, Eva, ed. *Canadian Fairy Tales*. Douglas & McIntyre, 1984. *(P; I)*

Morton, Desmond. *New France and War*. Watts, 1984. *(I; A)*

Patterson, E. Palmer. *Inuit Peoples of Canada*. Watts, 1982. *(I; A)*

Shepherd, Jennifer. *Canada*. Childrens, 1988. *(P; I)*

Skeoch, Alan. *The United Empire Loyalists and the American Revolution*. Watts, 1983. *(I; A)*

Thompson, Wayne C. *Canada 1985*. Stryker-Post, 1985. *(A)*

CANALS

Boyer, Edward. *River and Canal*. Holiday, 1986. *(I)*

Hilts, Len. *Timmy O'Dowd and the Big Ditch: A Story of the Glory Days on the Old Erie Canal*. HarBraceJ, 1988. (Fiction) *(I)*

Sandak, Cass R. *Canals*. Watts, 1983. *(P)*

Scarry, Huck. *Life on a Barge: A Sketchbook*. Prentice Hall, 1982. *(I)*

Spier, Peter. *The Erie Canal*. Doubleday, 1970. (Fiction) *(P; I)*

St. George, Judith. *Panama Canal: Gateway to the World*. Putnam, 1989. *(I; A)*

CANCER

Burns, Sheila L. *Cancer: Understanding and Fighting It*. Messner, 1982. *(I; A)*

Fine, Judylaine. *Afraid to Ask: A Book About Cancer*. Kids Can Press, 1984. *(A)*

Gaes, Jason. *My Book for Kids with Cansur*. Melius & Peterson, 1988. *(P; I)*

Holleb, Arthur I., Ed. *The American Cancer Society Cancer Book*. Doubleday, 1986. *(A)*

Hyde, Margaret Oldroyd, and Hyde, Lawrence E. *Cancer in the Young: A Sense of Hope*. Westminster, 1985. *(A)*

Krisher, Trudy. *Kathy's Hats: A Story of Hope*. Marianist Press, 1991. *(P)*

Rodgers, Joann Ellison. *Cancer*. Chelsea House, 1990. *(I; A)*

Silverstein, Alvin and Virginia B. *Cancer: Can It Be Stopped?* Lippincott, 1987. *(A)*

Swenson, Judy Harris, and Kunz, Roxanne Brown. *Cancer: The Whispered Word*. Dillon, 1986. *(P; I)*

Trull, Patti. *On with My Life*. Putnam, 1983. *(I; A)*

CANDLES

Yonck, Barbara. *Candle Crafts*. Lion, 1981. *(P; I)*

CANDY. See RECIPES; FOOD AROUND THE WORLD.

CANOEING

Boy Scouts of America. *Canoeing*. Boy Scouts, 1977. *(I; A)*

Koon, Celeste A. *Canoeing*. Harvey, 1981. *(I; A)*

Moran, Tom. *Canoeing Is for Me*. Lerner, 1983. *(P; I)*

CAPITALISM. See ECONOMICS.

CARD GAMES

Belton, John, and Cramblit, Joella. *Card Games*. Raintree, 1976. *(P; I); Let's Play Cards*, 1975. *(P); Solitaire Games*, 1975. *(P; I)*

Perry, Susan. *How to Play Rummy Card Games*. Creative Education, 1980. *(P; I)*

Reisberg, Ken. *Card Games*. Watts, 1979. *(P; I); Card Tricks*, 1980. *(P)*

Sackson, Sid. *Playing Cards Around the World*. Prentice Hall, 1981. *(I; A)*

CAREERS. See VOCATIONS.

CARIBBEAN SEA AND ISLANDS

Bryan, Ashley, ed. *The Dancing Granny*. Atheneum, 1977. *(P)*

Carroll, Raymond. *The Caribbean: Issues in U.S. Relations*. Watts, 1984. *(I; A)*

Hubley, John, and Hubley, Penny. *A Family in Jamaica*. Lerner, 1986. *(P)*

Saunders, Dave. *Through the Year in the Caribbean*. David & Charles, 1981. *(I; A)*

Wolkstein, Diane, ed. *The Magic Orange Tree and Other Haitian Folktales*. Schocken, 1980. *(I)*

CARNIVALS. See FAIRS AND EXPOSITIONS.

CAROLS

Cope, Dawn, and Cope, Peter, eds. *Christmas Carols for Young Children*. Evergreen, 1981. *(P; I)*

Cusack, Margaret. *The Christmas Carol Sampler*. Harcourt, 1983. *(P; I; A)*

Mohr, Joseph. *Silent Night*. Dutton, 1984. *(P; I; A)*

Tennyson, Noel, illus. *Christmas Carols: A Treasury of Holiday Favorites with Words and Pictures*. Random, 1983. *(I; A)*

CARROLL, LEWIS

Carroll, Lewis. *Alice's Adventures in Wonderland* (many editions and publishers); *Through the Looking Glass and What Alice Found There*, illus. by Barry Moser. University of California Press, 1983. *(I; A)*

CARSON, KIT

McCall, Edith. *Hunters Blaze the Trails*. Childrens, 1980. *(P; I; A)*

CARSON, RACHEL

Goldberg, Jake. *Rachel Carson*. Chelsea House, 1991. *(P; I)*

Jezer, Marty. *Rachel Carson*. Chelsea House, 1988. *(A)*

Reef, Catherine. *Rachel Carson: A Wonder of Nature*. 21st Century Books, 1991. *(P; I)*

Stwertka, Eve. *Rachel Carson*. Watts, 1991. *(P; I)*

CARTER, JAMES EARL, JR.

Richman, Daniel A. *James E. Carter*. Garrett Educational, 1989. *(I)*

CARTIER, JACQUES

Averill, Esther. *Cartier Sails the St. Lawrence*. Harper, 1956. *(I)*

Syme, Ronald. *Cartier: Finder of the St. Lawrence*. Morrow, 1958. *(I)*

CARTOONS

Hoff, Syd. *How to Draw Cartoons*. Scholastic, 1975. *(P)*

Weiss, Harvey. *Cartoons and Cartooning*. Houghton, 1990. *(I; A)*

CARVER, GEORGE WASHINGTON

Coil, Suzanne M. *George Washington Carver*. Watts, 1990. *(P; I)*

Holt, Rackham. *George Washington Carver: An American Biography*. Doubleday, 1963. *(I; A)*

White, Anne Terry. *George Washington Carver: The Story of a Great American*. Random, 1953. *(I)*

CASSATT, MARY

Meyer, Susan E. *Mary Cassatt*. Abrams, 1990. *(I)*

Turner, Robyn Montana. *Mary Cassatt*. Little, 1992. *(P; I)*

CASTLES

Berenstain, Michael. *The Castle Book*. McKay, 1977. *(I)*

Davison, Brian. *Explore a Castle*. David & Charles, 1983. *(I)*

Macaulay, David. *Castle*. Houghton, 1982. *(I)*

Macdonald, Fiona. *A Medieval Castle*. Peter Bedrick, 1990. *(I)*

Monks, John. *Castles*. Rourke, 1988. *(P)*

Smith, Beth. *Castles*. Watts, 1988. *(I; A)*

Vaughan, Jennifer. *Castles*. Watts, 1984. *(P)*

CASTRO, FIDEL. See CUBA.

CATHEDRALS

Gallagher, Maureen. *The Cathedral Book*. Paulist Press, 1983. *(I; A)*

Macaulay, David. *Cathedral: The Story of Its Construction*. Houghton, 1973. *(A); Cathedral*. Houghton, 1981. *(I)*

Watson, Percy. *Building the Medieval Cathedrals*. Lerner, 1978. *(I; A)*

CATS

Barrett, N. S. *Big Cats*. Watts, 1988. *(P; I)*

Cajacob, Thomas. *Close to the Wild: Siberian Tigers in a Zoo*. Carolrhoda, 1985. *(P; I)*

Eaton, Randall L. *Cheetah: Nature's Fastest Racer*. Dodd, 1981. *(I; A)*

Gag, Wanda. *Millions of Cats*. Coward, 1977 (1928). (Fiction) *(P)*

Hamer, Martyn. *Cats*. Watts, 1983. *(P)*

Levitin, Sonia. *All the Cats in the World*. HarBraceJ, 1982. *(P)*

Parsons, Alexandra. *Amazing Cats*. Knopf, 1989. *(P)*

Ryden, Hope, *Bobcat*. Putnam, 1983. *(I; A)*

Simon, Seymour. *Big Cats*. Harper, 1991. *(P; I)*

Winston, Peggy D. *Wild Cats*. National Geographic, 1981. *(P)*

CATS, DOMESTIC

Cole, Joanna. *A Cat's Body*. Morrow, 1982. *(I)*

Fischer-Nagel, Heiderose, and Fischer-Nagel, Andreas. *A Kitten Is Born*. Putnam, 1983. *(P)*

Hess, Lilo. *A Cat's Nine Lives*. Scribner's, 1984; *Listen to Your Kitten Purr*, 1980. *(P; I)*

Selsam. Millicent E., and Hunt, Joyce. *A First Look at Cats*. Walker, 1981. *(P; I)*

Steneman, Shep. *Garfield: The Complete Cat Book*. Random, 1981. *(I; A)*

CATTLE. See COWBOYS.

CAVES AND CAVERNS

Dean, Anabel. *Going Underground: All About Caves and Caving*. Dillon, 1984. *(I)*

Gans, Roma. *Caves*. Harper, 1977. *(P)*
Kerbo, Ronal C. *Caves*. Childrens, 1981. *(P; I)*

CELLS

Balkwill, Dr. Fran. *Cells Are Us*. Carolrhoda, 1993. *(P; I)*
Fichter, George S. *Cells*. Watts, 1986. *(I; A)*
Young, John K. *Cells: Amazing Forms and Functions*. Watts, 1990. *(I; A)*

CELTS. See ENGLAND, HISTORY OF.

CENTIPEDES AND MILLIPEDES

Preston-Mafham, Ken. *Discovering Centipedes & Millipedes*. Bookwright, 1990. *(I)*

CENTRAL AFRICAN REPUBLIC. See AFRICA.

CENTRAL AMERICA

Central America. Greenhaven, 1990. *(A)*
Adams, Faith. *El Salvador: Beauty Among the Ashes*. Dillon, 1986. *(P; I)*
Castaneda, Omar S. *Among the Volcanoes*. Lodestar, 1991. (Fiction) *(I; A)*
Cheney, Glenn Alan. *El Salvador: Country in Crisis*. Watts, 1990. *(A)*
Hanmer, Trudy J. *Nicaragua*. Watts, 1986. *(I)*
Haverstock, Nathan A. *El Salvador in Pictures*. Lerner, 1987. *(I); Nicaragua . . . In Pictures*, 1987. *(I; A)*
Markun, Maloney P. *Panama Canal*. Watts, 1979 (rev. ed.). *(P; I)*
Markun, Patricia M. *Central America and Panama*. Watts, 1983 (rev. ed.). *(P; I)*
Perl, Lila. *Guatemala: Central America's Living Past*. Morrow, 1982. *(I; A)*
Visual Geography. *Costa Rica in Pictures*. Lerner, 1987. *(I); Guatemala in Pictures*, 1987. *(I)*

CERAMICS

Gilbreath, Alice. *Slab, Coil and Pinch: A Beginner's Pottery Book*. Morrow, 1977. *(P; I)*
Price, Christine. *Arts of Clay*. Scribner's, 1977. *(P; I)*
Weiss, Harvey. *Ceramics: From Clay to Kiln*. Addison-Wesley, 1982. *(I; A)*

CHAD. See AFRICA.

CHAMBER MUSIC. See MUSIC AND MUSICIANS.

CHAMPLAIN, SAMUEL DE

Grant, Matthew G. *Champlain*. Creative Education, 1974. *(I)*

CHAPLIN, CHARLIE. See MOTION PICTURES.

CHARLEMAGNE

Pyle, Katharine. *Charlemagne and His Knights*. Lippincott, 1932. *(I)*
Winston, Richard. *Charlemagne*. Harper, 1968. *(I; A)*

CHAUCER, GEOFFREY

Chaucer, Geoffrey. *Canterbury Tales*. Hyman, 1988. *(P; I; A); The Canterbury Tales*. adapt. by Geraldine McCaughrean. Rand, 1985. *(I; A)*
Cohen, Barbara. *Canterbury Tales*. Lothrop, 1988. *(P; I; A)*

CHEMISTRY

Cobb, Vicki. *Chemically Active! Experiments You Can Do at Home*. Lippincott, 1985. *(A)*
Conway, Lorraine. *Chemistry Concepts*. Good Apple, 1983. *(I; A)*
Corrick, James A. *Recent Revolutions in Chemistry*. Watts, 1986. *(I)*
Mebane, Robert C., and Rybolt, Thomas R. *Adventures with Atoms and Molecules, Book II: Chemistry Experiments for Young People*. Enslow, 1987. *(P; I)*
Pimentel, George C., and Coonrod, Janice A. *Opportunities in Chemistry, Today and Tomorrow*. National Academy Press, 1987. *(I; A)*
Walters, Derek. *Chemistry*. Watts, 1983. *(I; A)*
See also EXPERIMENTS AND OTHER SCIENCE ACTIVITIES.

CHESS

Kidder, Harvey. *The Kids' Book of Chess*. Workman, 1990. *(I)*
Marsh, Carole. *Go Queen Go! Chess for Kids*. Gallopade, 1983. *(P; I)*
Pandolfini, Bruce. *Let's Play Chess: A Step-by-Step Guide for Beginners*. Messner, 1980. *(I; A)*
Reinfeld, Fred. *Chess for Children*. Sterling, 1980 (rev. ed.). *(P; I; A)*

CHIANG KAI-SHEK. See CHINA.

CHICAGO. See ILLINOIS.

CHILD ABUSE

Benedict, Helen. *Safe, Strong and Streetwise*. Joy Street, Feb. 1987. *(A)*
Dolan, Edward F., Jr. *Child Abuse*. Watts, 1984. *(A)*
Hall, Lynn. *The Boy in the Off-White Hat*. Scribner's, 1984. *(I; A)*
Hyde, Margaret O. *Cry Softly! The Story of Child Abuse*. Westminster, 1986 (rev. ed.). *(I; A); Sexual Abuse: Let's Talk About It*. 1984. *(A)*
Irwin, Hadley. *Abby, My Love*. Atheneum, 1985. *(A)*
Landau, Elaine. *Child Abuse: An American Epidemic*. Messner, 1990 (rev. ed.). *(A)*

Morgan, Marcia. *My Feelings*. Equal Justice (Eugene, OR 97405), 1984. *(P; I)*

Mufson, Susan, and Kranz, Rachel. *Straight Talk About Child Abuse*. Facts on File, 1990. *(I; A)*

Newman, Susan. *Never Say Yes to a Stranger*. Putnam, 1985. *(I; A)*

Stanek, Muriel. *Don't Hurt Me, Mama*. Albert Whitman, 1983. *(P)*

Terkel, Susan N., and Rench, Janice E. *Feeling Safe, Feeling Strong: How to Avoid Sexual Abuse and What to Do if it Happens to You*. Lerner, 1984. *(P; I; A)*

Wachter, Oralee. *No More Secrets for Me*. Little, 1983. *(P)*

CHILDREN'S LITERATURE

Lipson, Eden Ross. *The New York Times Parent's Guide to the Best Books for Children*. Times Books, 1991. *(A)*

CHILE

Galvin, Irene Flum. *Chile: Land of Poets and Patriots*. Dillon, 1990. *(I)*

Haverstock, Nathan A. *Chile in Pictures*. Lerner, 1988. *(I; A)*

Huber, Alex. *We Live in Chile*. Bookwright, 1986. *(P; I)*

CHINA

Bell, William. *Forbidden City*. Bantam, 1990. (Fiction) *(I; A)*

Bradley, John. *China: A New Revolution?* Gloucester Press, 1990. *(I; A)*

Buck, Pearl. *Chinese Story Teller*. Harper, 1971. *(P)*

Chaves, Jonathan, tr. Poems by Yang Wan-Li from *Heaven My Blanket, Earth My Pillow*. Weatherhill, 1976. *(I)*

Feinstein, Stephen C. *China . . . in Pictures*. Lerner, 1989. *(I)*

Fisher, Leonard. *The Great Wall of China*. Macmillan, 1986. *(P)*

Fritz, Jean. *China Homecoming*. Putnam, 1985. *(I); China's Long March: 6,000 Miles of Danger*. Putnam, 1988. *(I; A)*

Fyson, Nance Lui, and Greenhill, Richard. *A Family in China*. Lerner, 1986. *(P)*

Hacker, Jeffrey H. *The New China*. Watts, 1986. *(A)*

Keeler, Stephen. *Passport to China*. Watts, 1987. *(I; A)*

Lewis, Elizabeth. *Young Fu of the Upper Yangtze*. Holt, 1963. (Fiction) *(I)*

Major, John S. *The Land and People of China*. Lippincott, 1989. *(I; A)*

McLenighan, Valjean. *China: A History to 1949*. Childrens, 1983. *(I)*

Merton, Anna, and Kan, Shio-yun. *China: The Land and Its People*. Silver Burdett, 1987. *(P; I)*

Murphey, Rhoads, ed. *China*. Gateway Press, 1988. *(I; A)*

Neville, Emily Cheney. *The China Year*. Harper, 1991. (Fiction) *(I)*

Ross, Stewart. *China Since 1945*. Bookwright, 1989. *(I; A)*

Sadler, Catherine. *Heaven's Reward: Fairy Tales from China*. Macmillan, 1985. *(I); Two Chinese Families*. Atheneum, 1981. *(P; I)*

Sherwood, Rhoda, with Sally Tolan. *China*. Gareth Stevens, 1988. *(P)*

Steele, Philip. *China*. Steck-Vaughn, 1989. *(I)*

Tate, Joan, tr. *Children of the Yangtze River*. Salem House, 1985. (Fiction) *(P)*

Tsow, Ming. *A Day with Ling*. Hamish Hamilton, 1983. *(P)*

Wallace, Ian. *Chin Chiang and the Dragon's Dance*. Atheneum, 1984. (Fiction) *(P)*

Yee, Paul. *Tales from Gold Mountain*. Macmillan, 1989. *(I; A)*

Yep, Lawrence. *The Rainbow People*. Harper, 1989. *(I; A); The Serpent's Children*. Harper, 1984. *(I)*

Yin Lien C Chin et al, eds. *Traditional Chinese Folktales*. M.E. Sharpe, 1989. *(I)*

Young, Ed. *Lon Po Po: A Red-Riding Hood Story from China*. Philomel, 1989. *(P)*

CHOCOLATE

Ammon, Richard. *The Kids' Book of Chocolate*. Atheneum, 1987. *(P; I)*

CHOPIN, FRÉDERIC. See MUSIC AND MUSICIANS.

CHORAL MUSIC. See MUSIC AND MUSICIANS.

CHRISTMAS

Anderson, Joan. *Christmas on the Prairie*. Clarion, 1985. *(P)*

Barth, Edna. *Holly, Reindeer, and Colored Lights: The Story of the Christmas Symbols*. Houghton, 1981. *(P; I)*

Daniel, Mark. *A Child's Christmas Treasury*. Dial, 1988. *(P)*

Hunt, Roderick. *The Oxford Christmas Book for Children*. Merrimack, 1983. *(P; I)*

Kelly, Emily. *Christmas Around the World*. Carolrhoda, 1986. *(P)*

Patent, Dorothy Hinshaw. *Christmas Trees*. Dodd, 1987. *(P)*

Purdy, Susan. *Christmas Cooking Around the World*. Watts, 1983. *(I; A)*

Sawyer, Ruth. *Joy to the World: Christmas Legends*. Little, 1966. *(P; I)*

Thomas, Dylan. *A Child's Christmas in Wales*. Holiday, 1985. *(P; I)*

CHURCHILL, SIR WINSTON

Driemen, J. E. *Winston Churchill: An Unbreakable Spirit*. Dillon, 1990. *(I)*

Finlayson, Iain. *Winston Churchill*. David & Charles, 1981. *(P; I)*

CIRCUS

Cross, Helen Reeder. *The Real Tom Thumb*. Scholastic, 1980. *(P; I)*

Cushman, Kathleen, and Miller, Montana. *Circus Dreams*. Joy Street, 1990. *(I)*

Fenton, Don, and Fenton, Barb. *Behind the Circus Scene*. Crestwood, 1980. *(P; I)*

Harmer, Mabel. *Circus*. Childrens, 1981. *(P)*

Machotka, Hana. *The Magic Ring: A Year with the Big Apple Circus*. Morrow, 1988. *(P; I; A)*

CITIES

Asch, Frank. *City Sandwich*. Greenwillow, 1978. *(P)*

Beekman, Daniel. *Forest, Village, Town, City*. Har-Row, 1982. *(P; I)*

Boxxo, Maxine Zohn. *Toby in the Country, Toby in the City*. Greenwillow, 1982. (Fiction) *(P)*

Carey, Helen. *How to Use Your Community as a Resource*. Watts, 1983. *(I; A)*

Florian, Douglas. *The City*. Crowell, 1982. *(P)*

Hanmer, Trudy. *The Growth of Cities*. Watts, 1985. *(A)*

Isadora, Rachael. *City Seen from A to Z*. Greenwillow, 1983. *(P)*

Macaulay, David. *City*. Houghton, 1983. *(I); Underground*. Houghton, 1976. *(P; I; A)*

Maestro, Betsy. *Taxi: A Book of City Words*. Clarion, 1989. *(P)*

Provensen, Alice, and Provensen, Martin. *Town and Country*. Crown, 1985. *(P)*

Rice, Eve. *City Night*. Greenwillow, 1987. *(P)*

CITIZENSHIP

Abel, Sally. *How to Become a U.S. Citizen*. Nolo Pr, 1983. *(I; A)*

Burt, Olive W. *I Am an American*. Har-Row, 1968. *(I)*

CIVIL RIGHTS

Adler, David A. *A Picture Book of Martin Luther King, Jr.* Holiday, 1989. *(P)*

Adoff, Arnold. *Today We Are Brother and Sister*. Lothrop, 1981. *(P)*

Anders, Rebecca. *A Look at Prejudice and Understanding*. Lerner, 1976. *(P; I)*

Bach, Julie S., ed. *Civil Liberties*. Greenhaven Press, 1988. *(A)*

Bolton, Carole. *Never Jam Today*. Atheneum, 1971. *(I; A)*

Bradley, John. *Human Rights*. Gloucester Press, 1987. *(I)*

Conta, Marcia Maher. *Women for Human Rights*. Raintree, 1979. *(I)*

Cook, Fred J. *The Ku Klux Klan: America's Recurring Nightmare*. Messner, 1980. *(A)*

Evans, J. Edward. *Freedom of Religion*. Lerner, 1990. *(I; A); Freedom of Speech*. Lerner, 1990. *(I; A)*

Hampton, Henry, and Fayer, Steve. *Voices of Freedom*. Bantam, 1990. *(I)*

Hanley, Sally A. *Philip Randolph*. Chelsea House, 1989. *(I)*

Jacobs, William. *Mother, Aunt Susan, and Me: The First Fight for Women's Rights*. Coward, 1979. (Fiction) *(I)*

Lapping, Brian. *Apartheid: A History*. Braziller, 1987. *(A)*

McKissack, Patricia, and McKissack, Frederick. *The Civil Rights Movement in America From 1865 to the Present*. Childrens, 1991. (Revised) *(I; A)*

Meltzer, Milton. *The Bill of Rights: How We Got It and What It Means*. Crowell, 1990. *(A)*

Morrison, Dorothy Nafus. *Chief Sarah: Sarah Winnemucca's Fight for Indian Rights*. Atheneum, 1980. *(I)*

Pascoe, Elaine. *Racial Prejudice*. Watts, 1985. *(I; A)*

Price, Janet R., and others. *The Rights of Students; the Basic ACLU Guide to a Student's Rights*. Southern Illinois University, 1988. *(A)*

Rochelle, Belinda. *Witnesses to Freedom: Young People Who Fought for Civil Rights*. Lodestar, 1993. *(I; A)*

Selby, David. *Human Rights*. Cambridge University Press, 1987. *(I; A)*

Tilley, Glennette. *Take a Walk in Their Shoes*. Cobblehill, 1989. *(P; I)*

Watson, James. *Talking in Whispers*. Knopf, 1984. (Fiction) *(I; A)*

CIVIL WAR, UNITED STATES

Alcott, Louisa May. *Little Women*. Little, 1968 (1868). (Fiction) *(I; A)*

Blos, Joan W. *A Gathering of Days: A New England Girl's Journal*. Scribner's, 1979. (Fiction) *(P; I)*

Burchard, Peter. *Jed: The Story of a Yankee Soldier and a Southern Boy*. Coward, 1960. (Fiction) *(I)*

Crane, Stephen. *Red Badge of Courage*. Macmillan, 1962. (Fiction) *(I; A)*

Fritz, Jean. *Stonewall*. Putnam, 1979. *(I; A)*

Gauch, Patricia. *Thunder at Gettysburg*. Putnam, 1990. (Fiction) *(I)*

Goldston, Robert. *The Coming of the Civil War*. Macmillan, 1972. *(I; A)*

Hamilton, Virginia. *The House of Dies Drear*. Macmillan, 1968. (Fiction) *(I; A)*

Hunt, Irene. *Across Five Aprils*. Ace Bks, 1982. (Fiction) *(A)*

Kent, Zachary. *The Story of Sherman's March to the Sea*. Childrens, 1987. *(I); The Story of the Surrender at Appomattox Courthouse*. Childrens, 1987. *(I)*

Koch, Robert. *The Deserter*. Herald Press, 1990. (Fiction) *(I; A)*

Lyon, George Ella. *Cecil's Story*. Orchard Books, 1991. (Fiction) *(P)*

Meltzer, Milton, ed. *Voices from the Civil War: A Documentary History of the Great American Conflict*. Crowell, 1989. *(I; A)*

Monjo, F. N. *The Drinking Gourd*. Harper, 1983. (Fiction) *(P; I); Me and Willie and Pa*. Simon & Schuster, 1973. *(P; I)*

Murphy, Jim. *The Boys' War: Confederate and Union Soldiers Talk About the Civil War*. Clarion, 1990. *(I; A)*

Perez, Norah. *The Slopes of War: A Novel of Gettysburg*. Houghton, 1984. (Fiction) *(I)*

Ray, Delia. *Behind the Blue and the Gray: The Soldier's Life in the Civil War*. Lodestar, 1991. *(I; A)*

Reeder, Carolyn. *Shades of Gray*. Macmillan, 1989. (Fiction) *(P; I)*

Reit, Seymour. *Behind Rebel Lines: The Incredible Story of Emma Edmonds, Civil War Spy*. Harcourt, 1988. *(P; I)*

Richards, Kenneth. *The Story of the Gettysburg Address*. Childrens, 1969. *(I)*

Robertson, James I., Jr. *Civil War! America Becomes One Nation*. Knopf, 1992. *(I; A)*

Stein, R. Conrad. *The Story of the Monitor and the Merimack*. Childrens, 1983. *(P; I)*

Windrow, Martin. *The Civil War Rifleman*. Watts, 1985. *(I)*

CLAY, HENRY

Kelly, Regina Z. *Henry Clay: Statesman and Patriot*. Houghton, 1960. *(I)*

CLEMENS, SAMUEL. See TWAIN, MARK.

CLEVELAND, GROVER

Collins, David R. *Grover Cleveland: 22nd and 24th President of the United States*. Garrett Educational, 1988. *(A)*

Kent, Zachary. *Grover Cleveland: Twenty-second and Twenty-fourth President of the United States*. Childrens, 1988. *(P; I)*

See also PRESIDENCY OF THE UNITED STATES.

CLIMATE

Lye, Keith. *Weather and Climate*. Silver Burdett, 1984. *(P)*

Peters, Lisza. *The Sun, the Wind, and the Rain*. Holt, 1988. *(P)*

Pringle, Laurence. *Frost Hollows and Other Microclimates*. Morrow, 1981. *(I)*

Updegraffe, Imelda, and Updegraffe, Robert. *Continents and Climates*. Penguin, 1983. *(I; A)*

See also WEATHER.

CLINTON, WILLIAM

Cwiklik, Robert. *Bill Clinton: Our 42nd President*. Millbrook, 1993. *(I)*

Gallen, David. *Bill Clinton as They Know Him*. Gallen, 1994. *(A)*

Martin, Gene L., and Boyd, Aaron. *Bill Clinton: President from Arkansas*. Tudor, 1993. *(I; A)*

CLOTHING

Cooke, Jean. *Costumes and Clothes*. Watts, 1987. *(P)*

Moss, Miriam. *Fashion Designer*. Crestwood, 1991. *(I)*

Perl, Lila. *From Top Hats to Baseball Caps, From Bustles to Blue Jeans: Why We Dress the Way We Do*. Clarion, 1990. *(I)*

Rowland-Warne, L. *Costume*. Knopf, 1992. *(I; A)*

Weil, Lisl. *New Clothes: What People Wore—From Cavemen to Astronauts*. Atheneum, 1988. *(I)*

Wilson, K. *Costumes and Uniforms*. Starlog, 1980. *(I; A)*

CLOUDS. See WEATHER; CLIMATE.

CLOWNS

Fife, Bruce, and others. *Creative Clowning*. Java Publishing, 1988. *(A)*

COAL AND COAL MINING

Asimov, Isaac. *How Did We Find Out About Coal?* Walker, 1980. *(I; A)*

Davis, Bertha, and Whitfield, Susan. *The Coal Question*. Watts, 1982. *(I; A)*

Hendershot, Judy. *In Coal Country*. Knopf, 1987. (Fiction) *(P)*

Kraft, Betsy. *Coal*. Watts, 1982 (rev. ed.). *(P; I)*

CODES AND CIPHERS

Baker, Eugene. *Secret Writing—Codes and Messages*. Childrens, 1980. *(P; I)*

Brandreth, Gyles. *Writing Secret Codes and Sending Hidden Messages*. Sterling, 1984. *(I)*

Fletcher, Helen J. *Secret Codes*. Watts, 1980. *(P)*

Grant, E. A. *The Kids' Book of Secret Codes, Signals, and Ciphers*. Running Press, 1989. *(P; I)*

Janeczko, Paul B. *Loads of Codes and Secret Ciphers*. Macmillan, 1984. *(I)*

Mango, Karin N. *Codes, Ciphers and Other Secrets*. Watts, 1988. *(P; I)*

COINS AND COIN COLLECTING

Boy Scouts of America. *Coin Collecting*. Boy Scouts, 1975. *(I; A)*

Hobson, Burton H. *Coin Collecting as a Hobby*. Sterling, 1982 (rev. ed.). *(I; A)*

Reinfeld, Fred, and Hobson, Burton H. *How to Build a Coin Collection*. Sterling, 1977. *(P; I; A)*

Reisberg, Ken. *Coin Fun*. Watts, 1981. *(P)*

COLLAGE

Beaney, Jan. *Fun with Collage.* Sportshelf, 1980. *(P; I)*

COLOMBIA

Jacobsen, Peter O., and Kristensen, Preben S. *A Family in Colombia.* Bookwright, 1986. *(P)*
Visual Geography. *Colombia in Pictures.* Lerner, 1987. *(I; A)*

COLONIAL LIFE IN AMERICA. See THIRTEEN AMERICAN COLONIES.

COLOR

Ardley, Neil. *The Science Book of Color.* Gulliver Books, 1991. *(P; I)*

COLORADO

Kent, Deborah. *Colorado.* Childrens, 1989. *(P; I)*
Spies, Karen. *Denver.* Dillon, 1988. *(P)*

COLUMBUS, CHRISTOPHER

Adler, David A. *A Picture Book of Christopher Columbus.* Holiday, 1991. *(P)*
Batherman, Muriel. *Before Columbus.* Houghton, 1981. *(P)*
Brenner, Barbara. *If You Were There in 1492.* Bradbury, 1991. *(I)*
Columbus, Christopher. *The Log of Christopher Columbus' First Voyage to America in the Year 1492: As Copied out in Brief by Bartholomew Las Casas.* Linnet Books, 1989. *(P; I)*
D'Aulaire, Ingri, and D'Aulaire, Edgar P. *Columbus.* Doubleday, n.d. *(P)*
Dodge, Stephen C. *Christopher Columbus and the First Voyages to the New World.* Chelsea House, 1990. *(A)*
Fritz, Jean. *Where Do You Think You're Going, Christopher Columbus?* Putnam, 1980. *(I)*
Hodges, C. Walter. *Columbus Sails.* Coward, 1939. *(I)*
Levinson, Nancy Smiler. *Christopher Columbus.* Lodestar, 1990. *(I; A)*
Meltzer, Milton. *Columbus and the World Around Him.* Watts, 1990. *(I; A)*
Roop, Peter, and Roop, Connie, eds. *I, Columbus: My Journal—1492–3.* Walker, 1990. *(I)*
Sis, Peter. *Follow the Dream: The Story of Christopher Columbus.* Knopf, 1991. *(P)*
Ventura, Pietro. *Christopher Columbus.* Random, 1978. *(P; I)*
Weil, Lisl. *I, Christopher Columbus.* Atheneum, 1983. *(A)*

COMETS, METEORITES, AND ASTEROIDS

Asimov, Isaac. *Comets and Meteors.* Gareth Stevens, 1990. *(P; I); Asimov's Guide to Halley's Comet.* 1985. *(I; A)*

Berger, Melvin. *Comets, Meteors, and Asteroids.* Putnam, 1981. *(A)*
Branley, Franklyn M. *Comets.* Harper, 1984. *(P); Halley: Comet 1986.* Lodestar, 1983. *(I; A)*
Darling, David J. *Comets, Meteors, and Asteroids: Rocks in Space.* Dillon, 1984. *(P)*
Hamer, Martyn. *Comets.* Watts, 1984. *(P; I)*
Krupp, Edwin C. *The Comet and You.* Macmillan, 1985. *(P)*
Simon, Seymour. *Comets, Meteors, and Asteroids.* Morrow, 1994. *(P; I); The Long Journey from Space.* Crown, 1982. *(P)*
Vogt, Gregory. *Halley's Comet: What We've Learned.* Watts, 1987. *(I)*

COMIC BOOKS

Rovin, Jeff. *The Encyclopedia of Superheroes.* Facts on File, 1985. *(A)*

COMMUNICATION

Fisher, Trevor. *Communications.* David & Charles, 1985. *(I; A)*
Graham, Ian. *Communications.* Watts, 1989. *(P; I)*
Herda, D. J. *Communication Satellites.* Watts, 1988. *(I; A)*
Jespersen, James, and Fitz-Randolph, Jane. *Mercury's Web: The Story of Telecommunications.* Atheneum, 1981. *(I; A)*
Schefter, James L. *Telecommunications Careers.* Watts, 1988. *(A)*
Storrs, Graham. *The Telecommunications Revolution.* Bookwright, 1985. *(I; A)*
Sullivan, George. *How Do We Communicate?* Watts, 1983. *(P)*
Wolverton, Ruth, and Wolverton, Mike. *The News Media.* Watts, 1981. *(I; A)*
See also SATELLITES; TELEPHONE AND TELEGRAPH.

COMMUNISM

Forman, James D. *Communism.* Watts, 1979 (2nd ed.). *(I; A)*

COMPUTERS

Asimov, Isaac. *How Did We Find Out About Computers?* Walker, 1984. *(I)*
Ault, Rosalie S. *BASIC Programming for Kids.* HM, 1983. *(I; A)*
Berger, Melvin. *Computer Talk.* Messner, 1984. *(I); Computers in Your Life.* Crowell, 1984. *(I; A)*
Bly, Robert W. *A Dictionary of Computer Words.* Dell, 1983. *(I; A)*
Howard, Penny. *Looking at Computers; Looking at Computer Programming; Looking at LOGO.* Watts, 1984. *(P)*
Lampton, Christopher. *Advanced BASIC for Beginners; BASIC for Beginners; COBOL for Beginners; FOR-*

TRAN for Beginners; The Micro Dictionary; PASCAL for Beginners; PILOT for Beginners. Watts, 1984. *(I; A); Super-Conductors.* Enslow, 1989. *(I; A)*

Lipson, Shelley. *It's BASIC: The ABC's of Computer Programming.* Holt, 1982. *(P; I)*

Norback, Judith. *The Complete Computer Career Guide.* TAB Books, 1987. *(A)*

Petty, Kate. *Computers.* Watts, 1984. *(P)*

Sullivan, George. *Computer Kids.* Dodd, 1984. *(I; A)*

CONFEDERATE STATES OF AMERICA. See CIVIL WAR.

CONGO. See AFRICA.

CONGO RIVER

Lauber, Patricia. *The Congo: River into Central Africa.* Garrard, 1964. *(I)*

CONNECTICUT

Carpenter, Allan. *Connecticut.* Childrens, 1979. *(P; I)*

Fradin, Dennis. *Connecticut: In Words and Pictures.* Childrens, 1980. *(P; I)*

CONSERVATION. See ENVIRONMENT.

CONSTELLATIONS. See STARS.

CONSUMERISM

Arnold, Caroline. *What Will We Buy?* Watts, 1983. *(P)*

Berger, Melvin. *Consumer Protection Labs.* Harper, 1975. *(A)*

Kelly, Brendan. *Consumer Math.* EDC Publishing, 1981. *(I)*

Walz, Michael K. *The Law and Economics: Your Rights as a Consumer.* Lerner, 1990. *(I; A)*

COOKING

Betty Crocker's Cookbook for Boys and Girls. Western, 1984. *(P; I)*

Bjork, Christina. *Elliot's Extraordinary Cookbook.* R & S Books, 1991. *(P; I)*

Cooper, Terry T., and Ratner, Marilyn. *Many Friends Cooking: An International Cookbook for Boys and Girls.* Putnam, 1980. *(P; I)*

Coronado, Rosa. *Cooking the Mexican Way.* Lerner, 1982. *(I; A)*

Delmar, Charles. *The Essential Cook: Everything You Really Need to Know About Foods and Cooking Except the Recipes.* Hill House, 1989. *(I; A)*

Drew, Helen. *My First Baking Book.* Knopf, 1991. *(P; I)*

Goldstein, Helen H. *Kid's Cuisine.* News & Observer, 1983. *(P; I)*

Greene, Karen. *Once Upon a Recipe: Delicious, Healthy Foods for Kids of All Ages.* New Hope Press, 1988. *(P; I)*

John, Sue. *The Special Days Cookbook.* Putnam, 1982. *(P; I)*

Moore, Carolyn E., and others. *Young Chef's Nutrition Guide and Cookbook.* Barron, 1990. *(I)*

Pfommer, Marian. *On the Range: Cooking Western Style.* Atheneum, 1981. *(P; I)*

Sanderson, Marie C., and Schroeder, Rosella J. *It's Not Really Magic: Microwave Cooking for Young People.* Dillon, 1981. *(I; A)*

COOLIDGE, CALVIN

Kent, Zachary. *Calvin Coolidge: Thirtieth President of the United States.* Childrens, 1988. *(P; I)*

COPLAND, AARON. See MUSIC AND MUSICIANS.

COPPER. See METALS AND METALLURGY.

CORALS

Bender, Lionel. *Life on a Coral Reef.* Gloucester Press, 1989. *(P; I)*

Cousteau Society. *Corals: The Sea's Great Builders.* Simon & Schuster, 1992. *(P; I)*

Jacobson, Morris K., and Franz, David R. *Wonders of Coral Reefs.* Dodd, 1979. *(I; A)*

Reese, Bob. *Coral Reef.* Childrens, 1983. *(P)*

Sargent, William. *Night Reef: Dusk to Dawn on a Coral Reef.* Watts, 1991. *(P; I)*

Segaloff, Nat, and Erickson, Paul. *A Reef Comes to Life: Creating an Undersea Exhibit.* Watts, 1991. *(I)*

CORN

Aliki. *Corn Is Maize: The Gift of the Indians.* Harper, 1976. *(P)*

Selsam, Millicent E. *Popcorn.* Morrow, 1976. *(P; I)*

CORTES, HERNANDO

Marrin, Albert. *Aztecs and Spaniards: Cortes and the Conquest of Mexico.* Atheneum, 1986. *(A)*

Wilkes, John. *Hernan Cortes: Conquistador in Mexico.* Lerner, 1977. *(I; A)*

COSMIC RAYS. See NUCLEAR ENERGY.

COSTA RICA. See CENTRAL AMERICA.

COTTON

Miles, Lewis. *Cotton.* (Spotlight on Resources) Rourke Enterprises, 1987. *(P; I)*

Mitgutsch, Ali. *From Cotton to Pants.* Carolrhoda, 1981. *(P)*

Selsam, Millicent E. *Cotton.* Morrow, 1982. *(P; I)*

See also TEXTILES.

COUNTRY MUSIC

Harris, Stacy, and Krishef, Robert K. *The Carter Family: Country Music's First Family*. Lerner, 1978. *(I; A)*

Krishef, Robert K. *The Grand Ole Opry*. Lerner, 1978; *Introducing Country Music*, 1979. *(I; A)*

Lomax, John. *Nashville: Music City USA*. Abrams, 1985. *(A)*

COURTS. See LAW AND LAW ENFORCEMENT; SUPREME COURT OF THE UNITED STATES.

COWBOYS

Traditional. *Cowboy Songs*. Macmillan, 1938. *(I)*

Dean, Frank. *Cowboy Fun*. Sterling, 1980. *(I)*

Freedman, Russell. *Cowboys of the Wild West*. Clarion, 1985. *(A)*

Gorsline, Marie, and Gorsline, Douglas. *Cowboys*. Random, 1980. *(P)*

Helberg, Kristin. *Cowboys*. Troubador, 1982. *(I; A)*

Ling, Mary. *Calf*. Dorling Kindersley, 1993. *(P)*

Malone, Margaret G. *Cowboys and Computers: Life on a Modern Ranch*. Messner, 1982. *(P; I)*

Patent, Dorothy Hinshaw. *The Sheep Book*. Dodd, 1985. *(I)*

CRABS

Bailey, Jill. *Discovering Crabs and Lobsters*. Watts, 1987. *(P)*

Johnson, Sylvia A. *Crabs*. Lerner, 1982. *(P; I; A)*

CRANE, STEPHEN

Sufrin, Mark. *Stephen Crane*. Atheneum, 1992. *(I; A)*

CRIME AND CRIMINOLOGY. See JUVENILE CRIME; LAW AND LAW ENFORCEMENT; POLICE.

CROCKETT, DAVY

McCall, Edith. *Hunters Blaze the Trails*. Childrens, 1980. *(P; I; A)*

Santrey, Laurence. *Davy Crockett: Young Pioneer*. Troll, 1983. *(P; I)*

Townsend, Tom. *Davy Crockett: An American Hero*. Eakin Press, 1987. *(I)*

CROCODILES AND ALLIGATORS

Alligators and Crocodiles. Facts on File, 1990. *(I)*

Arnosky, Jim. *All About Alligators*. Scholastic, 1994. *(P)*

Bare, Colleen Stanley. *Never Kiss an Alligator!* Cobblehill, 1989. *(P)*

Bender, Lionel. *Crocodiles and Alligators*. Gloucester Press, 1988. *(I)*

Harris, Susan. *Crocodiles and Alligators*. Watts, 1980. *(P)*

Scott, Jack Denton. *Alligators*. Putnam, 1984. *(P; I; A)*

CRUSADES

Williams, Ann. *The Crusades*. Longman, 1975. *(I; A)*

Williams, Jay. *Knights of the Crusades*. Harper, 1962. *(I; A)*

CRYSTALS

Gans, Roma. *Millions and Millions of Crystals*. Crowell, 1973. *(P)*

CUBA

Cowan, Rachel. *Growing Up Yanqui*. Viking, 1975. *(I; A)*

Dolan, Edward D., and Scariano, Margaret M. *Cuba and the United States*. Watts, 1987. *(A)*

Haverstock, Nathan. *Cuba . . . In Pictures*. Lerner, 1987. *(I; A)*

Lindon, Edmund. *Cuba*. Watts, 1980. *(P; I)*

Vazquez, Ana Maria, and Casas, Rosa E. *Cuba*. Childrens, 1988. *(P; I)*

CURIE, MARIE AND PIERRE

Birch, Beverley. *Marie Curie: The Polish Scientist Who Discovered Radium and Its Life-Saving Properties*. Gareth Stevens, 1988. *(I)*

Brandt, Keith. *Marie Curie: Brave Scientist*. Troll, 1983. *(I)*

Conner, Edwina. *Marie Curie*. Watts, 1987. *(I)*

Keller, Mollie. *Marie Curie*. Watts, 1982. *(I; A)*

Tarnes, Richard. *Marie Curie*. Watts, n.d. *(I)*

CZECHOSLOVAKIA

Hall, Elvajean. *The Land and People of Czechoslovakia*. Harper, 1972 (rev. ed.). *(I; A)*

Ish-Kishor, S. *A Boy of Old Prague*. Scholastic, 1980. *(P; I)*

Lye, Keith. *Take a Trip to Czechoslovakia*. Watts, 1986. *(P)*

DAIRYING AND DAIRY PRODUCTS

Dineen, Jacqueline. *Food from Dairy and Farming*. Enslow, 1988. *(P; I)*

Gibbons, Gail. *The Milk Makers*. Macmillan, 1985. *(P)*

Moon, Cliff. *Dairy Cows on the Farm; Pigs on the Farm; Poultry on the Farm; Sheep on the Farm*. Watts, 1983. *(P)*

Patterson, Geoffrey. *Dairy Farming*. Andre Deutsch, 1984. *(P)*

Scuro, Vincent. *Wonders of Dairy Cattle*. Dodd, 1986. *(P; I)*

DALLAS. See TEXAS.

DAMS

Ardley, Neil. *Dams*. Garrett Educational, 1990. *(P; I)*

Sandak, Cass R. *Dams*. Watts. 1983. *(P)*

DANCE

Ancona, George. *Dancing Is*. Dutton, 1981. *(P)*

Barboza, Steven. *I Feel Like Dancing: A Year With Jacques D'Amboise and the National Dance Institute*. Crown, 1992. *(P; I)*

Brown, LouLou, ed. *Ballet Class*. Arco, 1985. *(I)*

Collard, Alexandra. *Two Young Dancers: Their World of Ballet*. Messner, 1984. *(I; A)*

Finney, Shan. *Dance*. Watts, 1983. *(I; A)*

Haney, Lynn. *I Am a Dancer*. Putnam, 1981. *(I; A)*

Haskins, James. *Black Dance in America: A History Through Its People*. Crowell, 1990. *(I; A)*

Isadora, Rachel. *Opening Night*. Greenwillow, 1984. *(P)*

Kuklin, Susan. *Reaching for Dreams: A Ballet From Rehearsal to Opening Night*. Lothrop, 1987. *(I; A)*

Rosenberg, Jane. *Dance Me a Story*. Norton, 1985. *(I; A)*

Royal Academy of Dancing. *Ballet Class*. Arco, 1985. *(P; I)*

Sinibaldi, Thomas. *Tap Dancing Step by Step*. Sterling, 1981. *(I; A)*

Sorine, D. *Imagine That! It's Modern Dance; At Every Turn: It's Ballet*. Knopf, 1981. *(P)*

Switzer, Ellen E. *Dancers!* Atheneum, 1982. *(I; A)*

DARWIN, CHARLES ROBERT

Karp, Walter. *Charles Darwin and the Origin of Species*. Harper, 1968. *(I; A)*

Parker, Steve. *Charles Darwin and Evolution*. Harper, 1992. *(I)*

Shapiro, Irwin. *Darwin and the Enchanted Isles*. Coward, 1977. *(I)*

Skelton, Renee. *Charles Darwin and the Theory of Natural Selection*. Barron, 1987. *(P; I)*

Ward, Peter. *The Adventures of Charles Darwin: A Story of the Beagle Voyage*. Cambridge University Press, 1982. *(A)*

DAVIS, JEFFERSON. See CIVIL WAR, UNITED STATES.

DEAFNESS

Aseltine, Lorraine and others. *I'm Deaf and It's Okay*. Albert Whitman, 1986. *(P)*

Charlip, Remy, and others. *Handtalk: An ABC of Finger Spelling and Sign Language*. Scholastic, 1974. *(P; I)*

Curtis, Patricia. *Cindy: A Hearing Ear Dog*. Dutton, 1981. *(P; I)*

Hlibok, Bruce. *Silent Dancer*. Messner, 1981. *(I)*

LaMore, Gregory S. *Now I Understand: A Book About Hearing Impairment*. Gallaudet College Press, 1986. *(P; I)*

Neimark, Anne E. *A Deaf Child Listened: Thomas Gallaudet, Pioneer in American Education*. Morrow, 1983. *(I; A)*

Walker, Lou Ann. *Amy: The Story of a Deaf Child*. Lodestar, 1985. *(P; I)*

DEATH

Alexander, Sue. *Nadia the Willful*. Pantheon, 1983. *(P)*

Anson, Robert Sam. *Best Intentions—The Education and Killing of Edmund Perry*. Vintage, 1987. *(I; A)*

Bode, Janet. *Death Is Hard to Live With: Teenagers and How They Cope With Death*. Delacorte, 1993. *(A)*

Clardy, Andrea Fleck. *Dusty Was My Friend: Coming to Terms with Loss*. Human Sciences Press, 1984. *(P; I)*

Donnelley, Elfie. *So Long, Grandpa*; tr. from the German by Anthea Bell. Crown, 1981. *(P; I)*

Douglas, Eileen. *Rachel and the Upside Down Heart*. Price Stern, 1990. (Fiction) *(P)*

Goble, Paul. *Beyond the Ridge*. Bradbury, 1989. (Fiction) *(P; I)*

Heegaard, Marge Eaton. *Coping with Death and Grief*. Lerner, 1990. *(I)*

Hermes, Patricia. *Who Will Take Care of Me?* Harcourt, 1983. *(P; I)*

Jukes, Mavis. *Blackberries in the Dark*. Knopf, 1985. (Fiction) *(P; I)*

Krementz, Jill. *How It Feels When a Parent Dies*. Knopf, 1981. *(I)*

Lanton, Sandy. *Daddy's Chair*. Kar-Ben, 1991. (Fiction) *(P)*

Mazer, Norma Fox, and Mazer, Harry. *Heartbeat*. Bantam, 1989. (Fiction) *(I; A)*

Mazer, Norma. *After the Rain*. Avon, 1988. (Fiction) *(I; A)*

McDaniel, Lurlene. *Too Young to Die*. Bantam, 1989. (Fiction) *(I; A)*

Miles, Miska. *Annie and the Old One*. Little, 1971. *(P)*

Morris, Jeanne. *Brian Piccolo: A Short Season*. Dell, 1971. *(I; A)*

Paterson, Katherine. *Bridge to Terabithia*. Crowell, 1977. (Fiction) *(P; I)*

Patterson, Francine. *Koko's Kitten*. Scholastic, 1985. (Fiction) *(P; I)*

Paulsen, Gary. *Tracker*. Bradbury, 1984. (Fiction) *(I; A)*

Peck, Robert Newton. *A Day No Pigs Would Die*. Knopf, 1982 (1972). (Fiction) *(I; A)*

Rofes, Eric E., ed. *The Kids' Book About Death and Dying: By and For Kids*. Little, 1985. *(I; A)*

Rohr, Janelle. *Death and Dying*. Greenhaven Press, 1987. *(A)*

Zolotow, Charlotte. *My Grandson Lew*. Harper, 1974. (Fiction) *(P)*

DEBATES AND DISCUSSIONS

Dunbar, Robert E. *How to Debate*. Watts, 1994. *(A)*

DECLARATION OF INDEPENDENCE

Commager, Henry Steele. *The Great Declaration*. Bobbs, 1958. *(I; A)*

Dalgliesh, Alice. *The Fourth of July Story*. Scribner's, 1956. *(P; I)*

Fradin, Dennis B. *The Declaration of Independence.* Childrens, 1988. *(P)*

Giblin, James C. *Fireworks, Picnics, and Flags: The Story of the Fourth of July.* Houghton, 1983. *(I)*

See also REVOLUTIONARY WAR; UNITED STATES (HISTORY AND GOVERNMENT).

DÉCOUPAGE

Gilbreath, Alice Thompson. *Simple Decoupage: Having Fun with Cutouts.* Morrow, 1978. *(I)*

Linsley, Leslie. *Decoupage for Young Crafters.* Dutton, 1977. *(I)*

DEER

Ahlstrom, Mark. *The Whitetail.* Crestwood, 1983. *(P; I)*

Bailey, Jill. *Discovering Deer.* Watts, 1988. *(P)*

McClung, Robert M. *White Tail.* Morrow, 1987. *(P; I)*

Rawlings, M. K. *The Yearling.* Scribner's, 1939. (Fiction) *(I; A)*

DE GAULLE, CHARLES. See FRANCE.

DELAWARE

Carpenter, Allan. *Delaware.* Childrens, 1979. *(I)*

Fradin, Dennis. *Delaware: In Words and Pictures.* Childrens, 1980. *(P; I)*

DELHI. See INDIA.

DEMOCRACY

Chute, Marchette. *The Green Tree of Democracy.* Dutton, 1971. *(I)*

Crout, George. *The Seven Lives of Johnny B. Free.* Denison, n.d. *(P; I)*

DENMARK

Andersen, Ulla. *We Live in Denmark.* Watts, 1984. *(P; I)*

Anderson, Madelyn Klein. *Greenland: Island at the Top of the World.* Dodd, 1983. *(I; A)*

Haugaard, Erik C. *Leif the Unlucky.* Houghton, 1982. *(I)*

Lepthien, Emilie U. *Greenland.* Childrens, 1989. *(I)*

Mussari, Mark. *The Danish Americans.* Chelsea House, 1988. *(I; A)*

DENTISTRY

Berenstain, Stan, and Berenstain, Jan. *The Berenstain Bears Visit the Dentist.* Random, 1981. (Fiction) *(P)*

Betancourt, Jeanne. *Smile: How to Cope with Braces.* Knopf, 1982. *(I; A)*

Krauss, Ronnie. *Mickey Visits the Dentist.* Putnam, 1980. *(P)*

Marsoli, Lisa Ann. *Things to Know Before Going to the Dentist.* Silver Burdett, 1985. *(I)*

Ward, Brian R. *Dental Care.* Watts, 1986. *(I; A)*

See also TEETH.

DENVER. See COLORADO.

DEPARTMENT STORES. See RETAIL STORES.

DESERTS

Baylor, Byrd. *The Desert Is Theirs.* Macmillan, 1975. (Fiction) *(P)*; *Desert Voices.* Scribner's, 1981. (Fiction) *(P)*

Bramwell, Martyn. *Deserts.* Watts, 1988. *(I)*

Dewey, Jennifer Owings. *A Night and Day in the Desert.* Little, 1991. *(P; I)*

Dixon, Dougal. *Deserts and Wastelands.* Watts, 1985. *(I)*

George, Jean Craighead. *One Day in the Desert.* Harper, 1983. *(P; I)*

Goetz, Delia. *Deserts.* Morrow, 1956. *(P)*

Lye, Keith. *Deserts.* Silver Burdett, 1987. *(P)*

Moore, Randy, and Vodopich, Darrell S. *The Living Desert.* Enslow, 1991. *(I)*

Pringle, Laurence. *The Gentle Desert: Exploring an Ecosystem.* Macmillan, 1977. *(P; I)*

Simon, Seymour. *Deserts.* Morrow, 1990. *(P; I)*

Twist, Clint. *Deserts.* Dillon: Macmillan, 1991. *(P; I)*

Watson, Jane W. *Deserts of the World; Future Threat or Promise?* Putnam, 1981. *(A)*

Watts, Barie. *24 Hours in a Desert.* Watts, 1991. *(P; I)*

Wiewandt, Thomas. *The Hidden Life of the Desert.* Crown, 1990. *(I)*

DESIGN

Branley, Franklyn M. *Color: From Rainbows to Lasers.* Harper, 1978. *(A)*

Hoban, Tana. *Is It Red? Is It Yellow? Is It Blue? An Adventure in Color.* Greenwillow, 1978. *(P)*

O'Neill, Mary. *Hailstones and Halibut Bones.* Doubleday, 1961. *(P; I; A)*

DE SOTO, HERNANDO. See EXPLORATION AND DISCOVERY.

DETROIT. See MICHIGAN.

DIAMONDS

Campbell, Archie. *Diamonds in the Dirt.* Childrens, 1978. *(P; I)*

Rickard, Graham. *Spotlight on Diamonds.* Rourke, 1988. *(P; I)*

DICKENS, CHARLES

Collins, David R. *Tales for Hard Times: A Story About Charles Dickens.* Carolrhoda, 1990. *(I)*

Dickens, Charles. *A Tale of Two Cities.* Pendulum Press, 1978. (Fiction) *(I; A)*; *American Notes.* Penguin, 1974. *(I; A)*; *Hard Times.* New American Library, 1961. (Fiction) *(I; A)*; *The Magic Fishbone.* Retold by Hans J. Schmidt. Coach House, 1961. *(P; I)*

DICKINSON, EMILY

Barth, Edna. *I'm Nobody! Who Are You? The Story of Emily Dickinson*. Houghton, 1971. *(I)*

Dickinson, Emily. *Poems for Youth*. Little, 1934. *(I; A)*

Longsworth, Polly. *Emily Dickinson: Her Letter to the World*. Harper, 1965. *(I; A)*

DICTIONARIES

Karske, Robert. *The Story of the Dictionary*. Harcourt, 1975. *(I; A)*

DIESEL ENGINES. See ENGINES.

DINOSAURS

Aliki. *Digging Up Dinosaurs*. Harper, 1981. *(P); My Visit to the Dinosaurs*, 1985. *(P)*

Bates, Robin, and Simon, Cheryl. *The Dinosaurs and the Dark Star*. Macmillan, 1985. *(I)*

Booth, Jerry. *The Big Beast Book: Dinosaurs and How They Got That Way*. Little, 1988. *(P; I)*

Brown, Marc. *Dinosaurs Beware!* Little, 1982. *(P)*

Butterworth, Oliver. *The Enormous Egg*. Little, 1956. (Fiction) *(P; I)*

Cohen, Daniel. *Dinosaurs*. Doubleday, 1987. *(P; I)*

Cohen, Daniel, and Cohen, Susan. *Where to Find Dinosaurs Today*. Dutton/Cobblehill, 1992. *(I)*

Davis, Susan. *The Dinosaur Who Lived in My Backyard*. Viking, 1988. (Fiction) *(P)*

Dixon, Dougal. *Be a Dinosaur Detective*. Lerner, 1988. *(I)*

Eldredge, Niles, and others. *The Fossil Factory: A Kid's Guide to Digging Up Dinosaurs, Exploring Evolution, and Finding Fossils*. Addison-Wesley, 1990. *(I)*

Farlow, James O. *On the Tracks of Dinosaurs: A Study of Dinosaur Footprints*. Watts, 1991. *(I)*

Freedman, Russell. *Dinosaurs and Their Young*. Holiday, 1983. *(P)*

Funston, Sylvia. *The Dinosaur Question and Answer Book: Everything Kids Want to Know About Dinosaurs, Fossils and Paleontology*. Joy Street/Little, 1992. *(P; I)*

Gay, Tanner Ottley. *Dinosaurs and Their Relatives in Action*. Aladdin, 1990. *(P)*

Horner, John R., and Gorman, James. *Maia: A Dinosaur Grows Up*. Courage Books, 1987. *(P)*

Jacobs, Francine. *Supersaurus*. Putnam, 1982. *(P)*

Lasky, Kathryn. *Dinosaur Dig*. Morrow, 1990. *(P; I)*

Lauber, Patricia. *Dinosaurs Walked Here: and Other Stories Fossils Tell*. Bradbury, 1987. *(P); Living with Dinosaurs*. Bradbury, 1991. *(P; I); The News About Dinosaurs*. Bradbury, 1989. *(I)*

Mannetti, William. *Dinosaurs in Your Backyard*. Atheneum, 1982. *(P; I)*

Moseley, Keith. *Dinosaurs: A Lost World*. Putnam, 1984. *(P; I)*

Most, Bernard. *The Littlest Dinosaurs*. Harcourt, 1989. (Fiction) *(P)*

Murphy, Jim. *The Last Dinosaur*. Scholastic, 1988. (Fiction) *(P; I)*

Norman, David, and Milner, Angela. *Dinosaur*. Knopf, 1989. *(I)*

Parker, Steve. *Dinosaurs and Their World*. Grosset, 1988. *(P; I)*

Sattler, Helen Roney. *Dinosaurs of North America*. Lothrop, 1981. *(P; I; A); The Illustrated Dinosaur Dictionary*, 1983. *(P; I); Pterosaurs, the Flying Reptiles*. Lothrop, 1985. *(P;I)*

Simon, Seymour. *The Largest Dinosaurs*. Macmillan, 1986. *(P; I); New Questions and Answers About Dinosaurs*. Morrow, 1990. *(P; I)*

Wilford, John Noble. *The Riddle of the Dinosaur*. Knopf, 1986. *(I; A)*

Zalinger, Peter. *Dinosaurs and Other Archosaurs*. Random, 1986. *(P; I)*

DISABLED PEOPLE

Aaseng, Nathan. *Cerebral Palsy*. Watts, 1991. *(I; A)*

Alexander, Sally Hobart. *Mom Can't See Me*. Macmillan, 1990. *(P)*

Allen, Anne. *Sports for the Handicapped*. Walker, 1981. *(I; A)*

Almonte, Paul, and Desmond, Theresa. *Learning Disabilities*. Crestwood House, 1992. *(P; I)*

Bergman, Thomas. *Going Places: Children Living with Cerebral Palsy*. Gareth Stevens, 1991. *(P; I)*

Bernstein, Joanne E., and Fireside, Bryna J. *Special Parents, Special Children*. Albert Whitman, 1991. *(P; I)*

Boy Scouts of America. *Handicapped Awareness*. Boy Scouts, 1981. *(I; A)*

Bridgers, Sue Ellen. *All Together Now*. Knopf, 1979. (Fiction) *(I; A)*

Broncato, Robin F. *Winning*. Knopf, 1977. (Fiction) *(I; A)*

Brown, Tricia. *Someone Special: Just Like You*. Holt, 1984. *(P)*

Byars, Betsy. *The Summer of the Swans*. Viking, 1970. (Fiction) *(P; I)*

Cattoche, Robert J. *Computers For the Disabled*. Watts, 1987. *(I)*

Charlip, Remy, and Charlip, Mary Beth. *Handtalk: An ABC of Finger Spelling and Sign Language*. Parents, 1974. *(P; I)*

Cunningham, Julia. *The Silent Voice*. Dutton, 1981. (Fiction) *(I; A)*

DeAngelie, Marguerite. *The Door in the Wall*. Doubleday, 1949. (Fiction) *(P; I)*

Dunn, Kathryn Boesel, and Boesel, Allison. *Trouble With School: A Family Story About Learning Disabilities*. Woodbine, 1992. *(P)*

Gilson, Jamie. *Do Bananas Chew Gum?* Lothrop 1980. (Fiction) *(P; I)*

Landau, Elaine. *Dyslexia*. Watts, 1991. *(P; I)*

Levinson, Harold N., and Sanders, Addie. *The Upside-Down Kids: Helping Dyslexic Children Understand Themselves and Their Disorder*. Evans, 1991. *(P; I)*

Martin, Bill, Jr., and Archambault, John. *Knots on a Counting Rope*. Holt, 1987. (Fiction) *(P)*

Mitchell, Joyce S. *See Me More Clearly: Career and Life Planning for Teens with Physical Disabilities*. Harcourt, 1980. *(I; A)*

Nardo, Don. *The Physically Challenged*. Chelsea House, 1994. *(I; A)*

Peterson, Jeanne Whitehouse. *I Have a Sister, My Sister Is Deaf*. Harper, 1977. *(P)*

Rosenberg, Maxine B. *My Friend Leslie: The Story of a Handicapped Child*. Lothrop, 1983. *(P; I)*

Roy, Ron. *Move Over, Wheelchairs Coming Through!* Clarion, 1985. *(I)*

Weiss, Malcolm. *Blindness*. Watts, 1980. *(I; A)*

See also Blindness; Deafness.

DISEASES

Anderson, Madelyn Klein. *Environmental Diseases*. Watts, 1987. *(A)*

Arnold, Caroline. *Heart Disease*. Watts, 1990. *(I; A)*

Bahr, Mary. *The Memory Box*. Albert Whitman, 1992. (Fiction) *(P)*

Brown, Fern G. *Hereditary Diseases*. Watts, 1987. *(A)*

Check, William A. *Alzheimer's Disease*. Chelsea House, 1989. *(A)*

Eagles, Douglas A. *Nutritional Diseases*. Watts, 1987. *(A)*

Edelson, Edward. *Allergies*. Chelsea House, 1989. *(I; A)*

Fekete, Irene, and Ward, Peter Dorrington. *Disease and Medicine*. World of Science Series, 1985. *(A)*

Frank, Julia. *Alzheimer's Disease: The Silent Epidemic*. Lerner, 1985. *(I; A)*

Getz, David. *Thin Air*. Holt, 1990. (Fiction) *(I)*

Hughes, Barbara. *Drug Related Diseases*. Watts, 1987. *(A)*

Jacobs, Francine. *Breakthrough—the True Story of Penicillin*. Dodd, 1985. *(I)*

Klein, Aaron E. *The Parasites We Humans Harbor*. Elsevier-Nelson, 1981. *(A)*

Kubersky, Rachel. *Everything You Need to Know About Eating Disorders*. Rosen, 1992. *(I; A)*

Landau, Elaine. *Alzheimer's Disease*. Watts, 1987; *Rabies*. Lodestar, 1993. *(I)*; *Why Are They Starving Themselves? Understanding Anorexia Nervosa and Bulimia*. Messner, 1983. *(I; A)*; *Weight: A Teenage Concern*. Lodestar, 1991. *(I; A)*

Metos, Thomas A. *Communicable Diseases*. Watts, 1987. *(A)*

Patent, Dorothy Hinshaw. *Germs!* Holiday, 1983. *(I)*

Seixas, Judith S. *Allergies: What They Are, What They Do*. Greenwillow, 1991. *(P)*

Silverstein, Alvin, Silverstein, Virginia, and Silverstein, Robert. *Cystic Fibrosis*. Watts, 1994. *(I; A)*; *Overcoming Acne: The How and Why of Healthy Skin Care*. Morrow, 1990. *(I; A)*; *So You Think You're Fat?* Harper, 1991. *(I; A)*

Tiger, Steven. *Diabetes*. Messner, 1987. *(P; I)*

DISNEY, WALT

Fisher, Maxine R. *Walt Disney*. Watts, 1988. *(I)*

Ford, Barbara. *Walt Disney*. Walker, 1989. *(I; A)*

DIVING. See Swimming and Diving.

DIVORCE

Blume, Judy. *It's Not the End of the World*. Bantam, 1977. (Fiction) *(P; I)*

Coleman, William L. *What Children Need to Know When Parents Get Divorced*. Bethany, 1983. *(P; I)*

Craven, Linda. *Stepfamilies: New Patterns of Harmony*. Messner, 1982. *(I; A)*

Krementz, Jill. *How It Feels When Parents Divorce*. Knopf, 1984. *(I)*

Lazo, Caroline Evensen. *Divorce*. Crestwood, 1989. *(P; I)*

Ourth, John. *Help! for Children of Divorce at Home and School*. Good Apple, 1983. *(I; A)*

DIX, DOROTHEA

Schleichert, Elizabeth. *The Life of Dorothea Dix*. 21st Century Books, 1992. *(P; I)*

DOCTORS

Bluestone, Naomi. *So You Want to Be a Doctor: The Realities of Pursuing Medicine as a Career*. Lothrop, 1981. *(I; A)*

Forsey, Chris. *At the Doctor*. Watts, 1984. *(P)*

Oxenbury, Helen. *The Checkup*. Dutton, 1983. *(P)*

See also Medicine.

DOGS

Benjamin, Carol Lea. *Dog Training for Kids*. Howell, 1988. *(I)*

Casey, Brigid, and Haugh, Wendy. *Sled Dogs*. Dodd, 1983. *(I)*

Cole, Joanna. *My Puppy Is Born*. Morrow, 1973. *(P)*; *A Dog's Body*, 1987. *(P)*

Hart, Angela. *Dogs*. Watts, 1982. *(P)*

Patent, Dorothy Hinshaw. *Hugger to the Rescue*. Cobblehill, 1994. *(P)*

Rinard, Judith E. *Puppies*. National Geographic, 1982. *(P)*

Schoder, Judith. *Canine Careers: Dogs at Work*. Messner, 1981. *(P; I)*

Silverstein, Alvin, and Silverstein, Virginia. *Dogs: All About Them*. Lothrop, 1986. *(I; A)*

DOLLS AND DOLLHOUSES

Boulton, Vivienne. *The Dollhouse Decorator*. Dorling Kindersley, 1992. *(I; A)*

Glubok, Shirley. *Doll's Houses: Life in Miniature*. Harper, 1984. *(I; A)*

Horwitz, Joshua. *Doll Hospital*. Pantheon, 1983. *(I)*

Nicklaus, Carol. *Making Dolls*. Watts, 1981. *(P)*

Radlauer, Ruth. *Dolls*. Childrens, 1980. *(P; I)*

Roche, P. K. *Dollhouse Magic: How to Make and Find Simple Dollhouse Furniture*. Dial, 1977. *(P; I)*

Schnurnberger, Lynn Edelman. *A World of Dolls That You Can Make*. Harper, 1982. *(P; I)*

DOLPHINS AND PORPOISES

Dolphins and Porpoises. Facts on File, 1990. *(I)*

Grover, Wayne. *Dolphin Adventure: A True Story*. Greenwillow, 1990. *(P)*

Jacka, Martin. *Waiting for Billy*. Orchard Books, 1991. *(P)*

Leatherwood, Stephen, and Reeves, Randall. *The Sea World Book of Dolphins*. Harcourt, 1987. *(P; I)*

Patent, Dorothy Hinshaw. *Dolphins and Porpoises*. Holiday, 1988. *(I); Looking at Dolphins and Porpoises*. Holiday, 1989. *(P; I)*

Reed, Don C. *The Dolphins and Me*. Sierra Club Books, 1989. *(I)*

Smith, Elizabeth Simpson. *A Dolphin Goes to School: The Story of Squirt, a Trained Dolphin*. Morrow, 1986. *(P)*

Torgersen, Don. *Killer Whales and Dolphin Play*. Childrens, 1982. *(P; I)*

DOMINICA. See CARIBBEAN SEA AND ISLANDS.

DOMINICAN REPUBLIC

Creed, Alexander. *Dominican Republic*. Chelsea House, 1987. *(A)*

Haverstock, Nathan A. *Dominican Republic in Pictures*. Lerner, 1988. *(P; I)*

DOUGLASS, FREDERICK

Davis, Ossie. *Escape to Freedom: The Story of Young Frederick Douglass*. Viking, 1978. *(A)*

Douglass, Frederick. *Narrative of the Life of Frederick Douglass, an American Slave*. New American Library, 1968. *(I; A)*

Miller, Douglas T. *Frederick Douglass and the Fight For Freedom*. Facts on File, 1988. *(A)*

Russell, Sharman. *Frederick Douglass and the Fight for Freedom*. Chelsea House, 1989. *(I; A)*

DOYLE, SIR ARTHUR CONAN

Doyle, Arthur Conan. *The Adventures of Sherlock Holmes, Books One–Four*. Adapted by Catherine E.

Sadler. Avon, 1981. *(P; I); Sherlock Holmes*, adapted by Diana Stewart. Raintree, 1983. *(P; I; A)*

DRAKE, SIR FRANCIS

Goodnough, Davis. *Francis Drake*. Troll, 1979 (new ed.). *(P; I)*

DRAMA. See THEATER.

DRAWING

Ames, Lee J. *Draw Fifty Airplanes, Aircraft, and Spacecraft*. Doubleday, 1977; *Draw Fifty Dogs*, 1981; *Draw Fifty Monsters, Creepy Creatures, Superheroes*, 1983; and other titles. *(P; I; A)*

Arnosky, Jim. *Drawing Life in Motion*. Lothrop, 1984. *(I; A); Drawing from Nature*. Lothrop, 1982. *(P; I)*

Bolognese, Don. *Drawing Dinosaurs and Other Prehistoric Animals*. Watts, 1982; *Drawing Spaceships and Other Spacecraft*, 1982. *(P; I)*

Emberley, Ed. *Ed Emberley's Big Green Drawing Book*, Little, 1979; *Big Purple Drawing Book*, 1981; *Little Drawing Book of Birds*, 1973; and other titles. *(P; I; A)*

Ivenbaum, Elliott. *Drawing People*. Watts, 1980. *(P; I; A)*

Nicklaus, Carol. *Drawing Pets; Drawing Your Family and Friends*. Watts, 1980. *(P)*

Witty, Ken. *A Day in the Life of an Illustrator*. Troll, 1981. *(I; A)*

DREAMING

Stafford, Patricia A. *Dreaming and Dreams*. Atheneum, 1992. *(I)*

DREYFUS, ALFRED

Schechter, Betty. *The Dreyfus Affair: A National Scandal*. Houghton, 1965. *(I; A)*

DRUGS AND DRUG ABUSE

Chemical Dependency. Greenhaven, 1991. *(I; A)*

Berger, Gilda. *Addiction: Its Causes, Problems and Treatment*. Watts, 1982. *(I; A); Crack: The New Drug Epidemic!; Drug Abuse: The Impact on Society*. Watts, 1988. *(A); Drug Testing*. Watts, 1987. *(A); Meg's Story: Straight Talk About Drugs*. Millbrook, 1992. *(I; A); Patty's Story: Straight Talk About Drugs*. Millbrook, 1991. *(I; A)*

Childress, Alice. *A Hero Ain't Nothin' But a Sandwich*. Putnam, 1973. (Fiction) *(I; A)*

Clayton, Lawrence. *Coping With a Drug Abusing Parent*. Rosen, 1991. *(I; A)*

DeStefano, Susan. *Drugs and the Family*. 21st Century Books, 1991. *(I)*

Friedman, David. *Focus on Drugs and the Brain*. 21st Century Books, 1990. *(P; I)*

Johnson, Joan J. *America's War on Drugs*. Watts, 1990. *(A)*

Kendall, Sarita. *Cocaine*. Steck-Vaughn, 1992. *(I; A)*

Madison, Arnold. *Drugs and You*. Messner, 1990 (rev. ed.). *(I)*

Nardo, Don. *Drugs and Sports*. Lucent Books, 1990. *(I)*

Perry, Robert. *Focus on Nicotine and Caffeine*. 21st Century Books, 1990. *(P; I)*

Pownall, Mark. *Heroin*. Steck-Vaughn, 1992. *(I; A)*

Rosenberg, Maxine B. *On the Mend: Getting Away from Drugs*. Bradbury, 1991. *(I; A)*

Shulman, Jeffrey. *The Drug-Alert Dictionary and Resource Guide*. 21st Century Books, 1991. *(I); Drugs and Crime*. 21st Century Books, 1991. *(I); Focus on Cocaine and Crack*. 21st Century Books, 1990. *(P; I); Focus on Hallucinogens*. 21st Century Books, 1991. *(I)*

Stewart, Gail B. *Drug Trafficking*. Lucent Books, 1990. *(I; A)*

Super, Gretchen. *Drugs and Our World*. 21st Century Books, 1990. *(P); What Are Drugs?* 21st Century Books, 1990. *(P); You Can Say "No" to Drugs!* 21st Century Books, 1990. *(P)*

Talmadge, Katherine S. *Drugs and Sports*. 21st Century Books, 1991. *(I); Focus on Steroids*. 21st Century Books, 1991. *(I)*

Terkel, Susan Neiburg. *Should Drugs Be Legalized?* Watts, 1990. *(I; A)*

Washton, Arnold M., and Boundy, Donna. *Cocaine and Crack: What You Need to Know*. Enslow, 1989. *(I; A)*

Yoslow, Mark. *Drugs in the Body*. Watts, 1992. *(A)*

Zeller, Paul Klevan. *Focus on Marijuana*. 21st Century Books, 1990. *(P; I)*

DRUM. See MUSICAL INSTRUMENTS.

DUCKS, GEESE, AND SWANS

Burton, Jane. *Dabble the Duckling*. Gareth Stevens, 1989. *(P)*

Freschet, Berniece. *Wood Duck Baby*. Putnam, 1983. *(P)*

Wharton, Anthony. *Discovering Ducks, Geese, and Swans*. Watts, 1987. *(P)*

DUNBAR, PAUL LAURENCE

McKissack, Patricia. *Paul Laurence Dunbar: A Poet to Remember*. Childrens, 1984. *(I)*

EAGLES

McConoughey, Jane. *Bald Eagle*. Crestwood, 1983. *(P; I)*

Melville, Herman. *Catskill Eagle*. Philomel, 1991. (Fiction) *(P; I; A)*

Patent, Dorothy Hinshaw. *Where the Bald Eagles Gather*. Houghton, 1984. *(P; I)*

Ryden, Hope. *America's Bald Eagle*. Putnam, 1985. *(I; A)*

Sattler, Helen Roney. *The Book of Eagles*. Lothrop, 1989. *(P; I)*

Van Wormer, Joe. *Eagles*. Lodestar, 1985. *(P; I)*

Wildlife Education Staff. *Eagles*. Wildlife Education, 1983. *(I; A)*

EAR

Showers, Paul. *Ears Are for Hearing*. Crowell, 1990. *(P)*

EARHART, AMELIA

Sloate, Susan. *Amelia Earhart: Challenging the Skies*. Fawcett, 1990. *(I)*

EARTH

Asimov, Isaac. *Earth: Our Home Base*. Gareth Stevens, 1989. *(P; I)*

Bain, Iain. *Mountains and Earth Movements*. Bookwright, 1984. *(I)*

Ballard, Robert D. *Exploring Our Living Planet*. National Geographic, 1983. *(I; A)*

Bennett, David. *Earth*. Bantam, 1988. *(P)*

Berger, Melvin. *As Old as the Hills*. Watts, 1989. *(P; I)*

Cole, Joanna. *The Magic Schoolbus Inside the Earth*. Scholastic, 1987. *(I)*

Darling, David. *Could You Ever Dig a Hole to China?* Dillon, 1990. *(I)*

Durell, Ann; Paterson, Katherine, and Craighead George, Jean, eds. *The Big Book for Our Planet*. Dutton, 1993. *(P; I)*

Farndon, John. *How the Earth Works*. Reader's Digest, 1992. *(I)*

Fradin, Dennis. *Continents*. Childrens, 1986. *(P); Earth*. Childrens, 1989. *(P)*

George, Jean C. *The Talking Earth*. Harper, 1983. *(I; A)*

Lambert, David. *The Active Earth*. Lothrop, 1982. *(P; I); Planet Earth*. Watts, 1983. *(I; A)*

Lampton, Christopher. *Planet Earth*. Watts, 1982. *(I)*

Lauber, Patricia. *Seeing Earth From Space*. Orchard Books, 1990. *(I)*

Livingston, Myra Cohn. *Earth Songs*. Holiday, 1986. *(P)*

Markle, Sandra. *Digging Deeper: Investigations into Rocks, Shocks, Quakes, and Other Earthly Matters*. Lothrop, 1987. *(I); Earth Alive!* Lothrop, 1990. *(I)*

Scarry, Huck. *Our Earth*. Messner, 1984. *(I)*

Silver, Donald M. *Earth: The Ever-Changing Planet*. Random, 1989. *(I)*

Simon, Seymour. *Earth: Our Planet in Space*. Scholastic, 1984. *(P)*

Van Rose, Susanna. *Earth*. Dorling Kindersley, 1994. *(I; A)*

Whitfield, Philip. *Why Do Volcanoes Erupt?* Viking, 1990. *(I)*

See also GEOLOGY.

EARTHQUAKES

Asimov, Isaac. *How Did We Find Out About Earthquakes?* Walker, 1978. *(I)*

Dudman, John. *The San Francisco Earthquake*. Bookwright, 1988. *(P; I)*

Fradin, Dennis Brindell. *Disaster! Earthquakes*. Childrens, 1982. *(P; I)*

Golden, Frederic. *The Trembling Earth: Probing and Predicting Earthquakes*. Scribner's, 1983. *(I; A)*

Lambert, David. *Earthquakes*. Watts, 1982. *(P)*

Levine, Ellen. *If You Lived at the Time of the Great San Francisco Earthquake*. Scholastic, 1987. *(P)*

Paananen, Eloise. *Tremor! Earthquake Technology in the Space Age*. Messner, 1982. *(A)*

Simon, Seymour. *Earthquakes*. Morrow, 1991. *(P; I)*

Vogt, Gregory. *Predicting Earthquakes*. Watts, 1989. *(I)*

EASTER

Barth, Edna. *Lillies, Rabbits, and Painted Eggs: The Story of the Easter Symbols*. HM, 1970. *(P; I)*

Berger, Gilda. *Easter and Other Spring Holidays*. Watts, 1983. *(P; I; A)*

Milhous, Katherine. *The Egg Tree*. Scribner's, n.d. *(P)*

Sandak, Cass R. *Easter*. Watts, 1980. *(P)*

EASTMAN, GEORGE

Mitchell, Barbara. *Click! A Story About George Eastman*. Carolrhoda, 1987. *(I)*

ECLIPSES. See MOON; SUN.

ECOLOGY

Hughey, Pat. *Scavengers and Decomposers: The Cleanup Crew*. Atheneum, 1984. *(I)*

Parnall, Peter. *Woodpile*. Macmillan, 1990. *(P)*

Patent, Dorothy Hinshaw. *Places of Refuge: Our National Wildlife Refuge System*. Clarion, 1992. *(I)*

Pringle, Laurence. *Living Treasures: Saving Earth's Threatened Biodiversity*. Morrow, 1991. *(I)*

Sabin, Francene. *Ecosystems and Food Chains*. Troll, 1985. *(I)*

ECONOMICS

Abels, Harriette S. *Future Business*. Crestwood, 1980. *(I; A)*

Adler, David A. *Prices Go Up, Prices Go Down: The Law of Supply and Demand*. Watts, 1984. *(P)*

Armstrong, Louise. *How to Turn Lemons into Money: A Child's Guide to Economics*. Harcourt, 1976; *How to Turn Up into Down into Up: A Child's Guide to Inflation, Depression, and Economic Recovery*, 1978. *(P; I)*

Kalman, Bobbie. *Early Stores and Markets*. Crabtree, 1981. *(I)*

Killen, M. Barbara. *Economics and the Consumer*. Lerner, 1990. *(I; A)*

Klevin, Jill. *The Turtle Street Trading Company*. Delacorte, 1982. *(P)*

Marsh, Carole. *The Teddy Bear Company: Easy Economics for Kids; The Teddy Bear's Annual Report: Tomorrow's Books*. Gallopade, 1983. *(P; I)*

O'Toole, Thomas. *Global Economics*. Lerner, 1991. *(A)*

Schmitt, Lois. *Smart Spending: A Young Consumer's Guide*. Scribners, 1989. *(I; A)*

Shanaman, Fred, and Malnig, Anita. *The First Official Money Making Book for Kids*. Bantam, 1983. *(I)*

ECUADOR

Sterling Editors, ed. *Ecuador in Pictures*. Sterling, 1973. *(I)*

EDISON, THOMAS A.

Adler, David. *Thomas Alva Edison: Great Inventor*. Holiday, 1990. *(P)*

Buranelli, Vincent. *Thomas Alva Edison*. Silver Burdett, 1989. *(I)*

Cousins, Margaret. *The Story of Thomas Alva Edison*. Random, 1981. *(I)*

Greene, Carol. *Thomas Alva Edison: Bringer of Light*. Childrens, 1985. *(I)*

Guthridge, Sue. *Thomas A. Edison: Young Inventor*. Bobbs, 1983. *(P; I)*

Lampton, Christopher. *Thomas Alva Edison*. Watts, 1988. *(P; I)*

Mintz, Penny. *Thomas Edison: Inventing the Future*. Fawcett, 1990. *(I)*

Quackenbush, Robert. *What Has Wild Tom Done Now?* Prentice Hall, 1981. *(P)*

EDUCATION

Fisher, Leonard. *Schoolmasters*. Godine, 1986. *(I)*; *The Schools*. Holiday, 1983. *(I)*

Hand, Phyllis. *The Name of the Game Is . . . Learning*. Good Apple, 1983. *(P; I)*

Kalman, Bobbie. *Early Schools*. Crabtree, 1981. *(I)*

Lenski, Lois. *Prairie School*. Dell, 1967. *(I)*

Loeper, John J. *Going to School in 1776*. Atheneum, 1984. *(I)*

Marshall, Edward. *Fox at School*. Dial, 1983. (Fiction) *(P)*

McCully, Emily. *School*. Harper, 1987. (Fiction) *(P)*

Sloane, Eric. *The Little Red Schoolhouse*. Doubleday, 1973. *(I)*

EELS

Friedman, Judi. *The Eels' Strange Journey*. Harper, 1976. *(P)*

Halton, Cheryl Mays. *Those Amazing Eels*. Dillon, 1990. *(I)*

EGGS AND EMBRYOS

Burton, Robert. *Eggs: Nature's Perfect Package*. Facts on File, 1987. *(I; A)*

Johnson, Sylvia A. *Inside an Egg*. Lerner, 1982. *(I)*

McClung, Robert M. *The Amazing Egg*. Dutton, 1980. *(I)*

Selsam, Millicent E. *Egg to Chick*. Harper, 1970. *(P)*

EGYPT

Egypt . . . in Pictures. Lerner, 1988. *(I)*

Cross, Wilbur. *Egypt*. Childrens, 1982. *(I; A)*

Kristensen, Preben, and Cameron, Fiona. *We Live in Egypt*. Bookwright, 1987. *(P)*

Lye, Keith. *Take a Trip to Egypt*. Watts, 1983. *(P)*

Mozley, Charles. *Tales of Ancient Egypt*. Watts, 1960. *(I)*

Sullivan, George. *Sadat: The Man Who Changed Mid-East History*. Walker, 1981. *(I; A)*

See also ANCIENT CIVILIZATIONS.

EGYPTIAN ART AND ARCHITECTURE. See EGYPT; ANCIENT CIVILIZATIONS.

EINSTEIN, ALBERT

Apfel, Necia H. *It's All Relative: Einstein's Theory of Relativity*. Lothrop, 1981. *(I; A)*

Dank, Milton. *Albert Einstein*. Watts, 1983. *(I; A)*

Hunter, Nigel. *Einstein*. Bookwright, 1987. *(P; I)*

EISENHOWER, DWIGHT D.

Cannon, Marian G. *Dwight David Eisenhower: War Hero and President*. Watts, 1990. *(I; A)*

Ellis, Rafaela. *Dwight D. Eisenhower: 34th President of the United States*. Garrett Educational, 1989. *(I)*

Hargrove, Jim. *Dwight D. Eisenhower: Thirty-fourth President of the United States*. Childrens, 1987. *(P; I)*

See also PRESIDENCY OF THE UNITED STATES.

ELECTIONS

Archer, Jules. *Winners and Losers: How Elections Work in America*. HarBraceJ, 1984. *(I; A)*

Fradin, Dennis. *Voting and Elections*. Childrens, 1985. *(P)*

Hargrove, Jim. *The Story of Presidential Elections*. Childrens, 1988. *(I)*

Lindrop, Edmund. *The First Book of Elections*. Watts, 1972. *(I)*

Modl, Thomas, ed. *America's Elections*. Greenhaven Press, 1988. *(A)*

Phelan, M. K. *Election Day*. Crowell, 1967. *(I)*

Priestly, E. J. *Finding Out About Elections*. David & Charles, 1983. *(I; A)*

Samuels, Cynthia. *It's a Free Country: A Young Person's Guide to Politics and Elections*. Atheneum, 1988. *(I; A)*

Scher, Linda. *The Vote: Making Your Voice Heard*. Raintree, 1993. *(I)*

Sullivan, George. *Campaigns and Elections*. Silver Burdett, 1991. *(I; A)*

ELECTRICITY

Ardley, Neil. *Electricity*. New Discovery, 1992. *(I)*

Berger, Melvin. *Switch On, Switch Off*. Crowell, 1989. *(P)*

Grossman, Peter Z. *In Came the Darkness: The Story of Blackouts*. Scholastic, 1981. *(I; A)*

Keating, Joni. *Watt's Happening?* Good Apple, 1981. *(P; I)*

Markle, Sandra. *Power Up: Experiments, Puzzles, and Games Using Electricity*. Macmillan, 1989. *(I)*

Math, Irwin. *More Wires and Watts: Understanding and Using Electricity*. Scribner's, 1988. *(I; A); Wires and Watts: Understanding and Using Electricity*. Scribner's, 1981. *(I; A)*

Parker, Steve. *Electricity*. Dorling Kindersley, 1992. *(P; I; A)*

Stwertka, Eve, and Stwertka, Albert. *Heat, Lights, and Action!* Messner, 1991. *(I)*

Vogt, Gregory. *Electricity and Magnetism*. Watts, 1985. *(I); Generating Electricity*. Watts, 1986. *(I)*

Zubrowski, Bernie. *Blinkers and Buzzers*. Morrow, 1991. *(I)*

ELECTRIC MOTORS. See TECHNOLOGY.

ELECTRONICS

Billings, Charlene W., *Microchip: Small Wonder*. Dodd, 1984. *(I)*

Gutnik, Martin J. *Simple Electrical Devices*. Watts, 1986. *(I)*

Laron, Carl. *Electronics Basics*. Prentice Hall, 1984. *(I; A)*

Tatchess, J., and Cutter, N. *Practical Things to Do*. EDC, 1983. *(I; A)*

ELEMENTS, CHEMICAL

Asimov, Isaac. *Building Blocks of the Universe*. Abelard, 1974 (rev. ed.). *(I; A)*

ELEPHANTS

Aliki. *Wild and Wooly Mammoths*. Har-Row, 1983. *(P)*

Bare, Colleen Stanley. *Elephants on the Beach*. Cobblehill, 1989. *(P)*

Barrett, N. S. *Elephants*. Watts, 1988. *(P; I)*

Bright, Michael. *Elephants*. Gloucester Press, 1990. *(P; I)*

Douglas-Hamilton, Oria. *The Elephant Family Book*. Picture Book Studio, 1990. *(P; I)*

Hintz, Martin. *Tons of Fun: Training Elephants*. Messner, 1982. *(P; I)*

Patent, Dorothy Hinshaw. *African Elephants: Giants of the Land*. Holiday, 1991. *(P; I)*

Payne, Katharine. *Elephants Calling*. Crown, 1992. *(I)*

Petty, Kate. *Elephants*. Gloucester Press, 1990. *(P; I)*

Schlein, Miriam. *Elephants*. Atheneum, 1990. *(I)*

Stewart, John. *Elephant School*. Pantheon, 1982. *(I; A)*

Torgersen, Dan. *Elephant Herds and Rhino Horns*. Childrens, 1982. *(I; A)*

Yoshida, Toshi. *Elephant Crossing*. Philomel, 1990. *(P)*

ELIZABETH I

Greene, Carol. *Elizabeth the First: Queen of England*. Childrens, 1990. *(P)*

Stanley, Diane, and Vennema, Peter. *Good Queen Bess: The Story of Elizabeth I of England*. Four Winds, 1990. *(I)*

Turner, Dorothy. *Queen Elizabeth I*. Watts, 1987. *(I)*

Zamoyska, Betka. *Queen Elizabeth I*. McGraw, 1981. *(I; A)*

ELIZABETH II

Lacey, Robert. *Elizabeth II: The Work of the Queen*. Viking, 1977. *(I; A)*

Turner, Dorothy. *Queen Elizabeth II*. Bookwright, 1985. *(I)*

EL SALVADOR. See CENTRAL AMERICA.

EMANCIPATION PROCLAMATION. See SLAVERY; LINCOLN, ABRAHAM; CIVIL WAR, UNITED STATES.

EMBROIDERY. See SEWING AND NEEDLECRAFT.

ENDANGERED SPECIES

Arnold, Caroline. *On the Brink of Extinction: The California Condor*. Harcourt, 1993. *(I); Saving the Peregrine Falcon*. Carolrhoda, 1985. *(I)*

Banks, Martin. *Endangered Wildlife*. Rourke, 1988. *(I)*

Bloyd, Sunni. *Endangered Species*. Lucent Books, 1989. *(I; A)*

Burton, John. *Close to Extinction*. Gloucester Press, 1988. *(I)*

Hendrich, Paula. *Saving America's Birds*. Lothrop, 1982. *(I; A)*

Lampton, Christopher. *Endangered Species*. Watts, 1988. *(A)*

Maynard, Thane. *Endangered Animal Babies*. Watts, 1993. *(I)*

Pringle, Laurence. *Saving Our Wildlife*. Enslow, 1990. *(I; A)*

Schlein, Miriam. *Project Panda Watch*. Atheneum, 1984. *(I; A)*

Schorsch, Nancy T. *Saving the Condor*. Watts, 1991. *(P; I)*

Stone, Lynn. *Endangered Animals*. Childrens, 1984. *(P)*

Wolkomir, Joyce Rogers, and Wolkomir, Richard. *Junkyard Bandicoots & Other Tales of the World's Endangered Species*. Wiley, 1992. *(P; I)*

See also BIRDS.

ENERGY

Energy. Raintree, 1988. *(I)*

Adler, David. *Wonders of Energy*. Troll, 1983. *(P; I)*

Asimov, Isaac. *How Did We Find Out About Energy?* Avon, 1981. *(I)*

Berger, Melvin. *Energy*. Watts, 1983. *(P; I)*

Carey, Helen H. *Producing Energy*. Watts, 1984. *(I; A)*

Fogel, Barbara R. *Energy Choices for the Future*. Watts, 1985. *(A)*

Gardiner, Brian. *Energy Demands*. Gloucester Press, 1990. *(I)*

Kaplan, Sheila. *Solar Energy*. Raintree, 1985. *(I)*

McKie, Robin. *Energy*. Watts, 1989. *(P; I)*

Millard, Reed, and Editors of Science Book Associates. *Energy: New Shapes/New Careers*. Messner, 1982. *(I; A)*

Pringle, Laurence. *Nuclear Energy: Troubled Past, Uncertain Future*. Macmillan, 1989. *(I)*

Rice, Dale. *Energy from Fossil Fuels*. Raintree, 1983. *(P; I)*

Tuggle, Catherine, and Weir, Gary E. *The Department of Energy*. Chelsea House, 1989. *(I)*

See also COAL AND COAL MINING; NUCLEAR ENERGY; PETROLEUM; SOLAR ENERGY.

ENGINEERING. See TECHNOLOGY.

ENGINES

Olney, Ross R. *The Internal Combustion Machine*. Harper, 1982. *(I; A)*

Weiss, Harvey. *Motors and Engines and How They Work*. Harper, 1969. *(I)*

ENGLAND

Fairclough, Christ. *Take a Trip to England*. Watts, 1982. *(P)*

Ferguson, Sheila. *Village and Town Life*. David & Charles, 1983. *(I; A)*

Greene, Carol. *England*. Childrens, 1982. *(I; A)*

James, Ian. *Inside Great Britain*. Watts, 1988. *(P; I)*

Mitsumasa, Anno. *Anno's Britain*. Philomel, 1986. *(I)*

Pyle, Howard. *The Merry Adventures of Robin Hood*. Macmillan, 1977. *(I)*

Rutherford, Edward. *Sarum*. Crown, 1987. (Fiction) *(I)*

Sproule, Anna. *Great Britain*. Bookwright, 1988. *(P); Living in London*. Silver Burdett, 1987. *(P)*

St. John, Jetty. *A Family in England*. Lerner, 1988. *(P)*

ENGLAND, HISTORY OF

Barber, Richard. *A Strong Land and a Sturdy: Life in Medieval England*. Houghton, 1976. *(I)*

Brooks, Polly Schoyer. *Queen Eleanor: Independent Spirit of the Medieval World: A Biography of Eleanor of Aquitaine*. Lippincott, 1983. *(I; A)*

Clarke, Amanda. *Growing Up in Ancient Britain*. David

& Charles, 1981; *Growing Up in Puritan Times,* 1980. *(I; A)*

Corbishley, Mike. *The Romans.* Warwick, 1984. *(I)*

Fyson, Nance L. *Growing Up in Edwardian Britain.* David & Charles, 1980. *(I; A)*

Goodall, John S. *The Story of an English Village.* Atheneum, 1979. *(I)*

Jones, Madeline. *Growing Up in Regency England.* David & Charles, 1980; *Growing Up in Stuart Times,* 1979. *(I; A)*

Lane, Peter. *Elizabethan England,* David & Charles, 1981; *Norman England,* 1980. *(I; A)*

Wilkins, Frances. *Growing Up During the Norman Conquest.* David & Charles, 1980. *(I; A)*

ENVIRONMENT

Anderson, Madelyn Klein. *Oil Spills.* Watts, 1990. *(I)*

Bailey, Donna. *What We Can Do About Litter.* Watts, 1991. *(P)*

Banks, Martin. *Conserving Rain Forests.* Steck-Vaughn, 1990. *(I)*

Bash, Barbara. *Desert Giant.* Little, 1989. *(P; I)*

Bellamy, David. *How Green Are You?* Clarkson Potter, 1991. *(P)*

Cherry, Lynne. *A River Ran Wild.* HarBraceJ/Gulliver, 1992. *(P); The Great Kapok Tree: A Tale of the Amazon Rain Forest.* Harcourt, 1990. *(P; I)*

Elkington, John, and others. *Going Green: A Kid's Handbook to Saving the Planet.* Viking, 1990. *(I)*

Foster, Joanna. *Cartons, Cans and Orange Peels: Where Does Your Garbage Go?* Clarion, 1991. *(I)*

George, Jean Craighead. *One Day in the Tropical Rain Forest.* Crowell, 1990. *(P; I)*

Hadingham, Evan, and Hadingham, Janet. *Garbage! Where It Comes From, Where It Goes.* Simon & Schuster, 1990. *(I; A)*

Herda, D. J. *Environmental America: The North Central States.* Millbrook, 1991. *(I; A); Environmental America: The Northeastern States.* Millbrook, 1991; *(I; A); Environmental America: The Northwestern States.* Millbrook, 1991. *(I; A); Environmental America: The South Central States.* Millbrook, 1991. *(I; A); Environmental America: The Southeastern States.* Millbrook, 1991. *(I; A); Environmental America: The Southwestern States.* Millbrook, 1991. *(I; A)*

Johnson, Rebecca. *The Greenhouse Effect: Life on a Warmer Planet.* Lerner, 1990. *(I)*

Kouhoupt, Rudy, and Marti, Donald B. *How on Earth Do We Recycle Metal?* Millbrook, 1992. *(I)*

Landau, Elaine. *Tropical Rain Forests Around the World.* Watts, 1990. *(P)*

Lee, Sally. *The Throwaway Society.* Watts, 1990. *(I; A)*

Lowery, Linda. *Earth Day.* Lerner, 1991. *(P)*

Miles, Betty. *Save the Earth: An Action Handbook for Kids.* Knopf, 1991. *(I; A)*

Milne, Margery, and Milne, Lorus J. *Dreams of a Perfect Earth.* Atheneum, 1982. *(I; A)*

Pringle, Laurence. *Global Warming: Assessing the Greenhouse Threat.* Arcade, 1990. *(I); Lives At Stake: The Science and Politics of Environmental Health.* Macmillan, 1980. *(I); Our Hungry Earth.* Macmillan, 1976. *(I); Restoring Our Earth.* Enslow, 1987. *(P); What Shall We Do with the Land?* Harper, 1981. *(I)*

Taylor, Paula. *The Kids' Whole Future Catalog: A Book About Your Future.* Random, 1982. *(I; A)*

Vandivert, Rita. *To the Rescue: Seven Heroes of Conservation.* Warne, 1982. *(I; A)*

Walker, Jane. *The Ozone Hole.* Gloucester, 1993. *(I; A)*

Wild, Russell, Ed. *The Earth Care Annual 1990.* National Wildlife Federation: Rodale, 1990. *(I; A)*

EQUATORIAL GUINEA. See AFRICA.

ERICSON, LEIF

Humble, Richard. *The Age of Leif Eriksson.* Watts, 1989. *(I)*

Jensen, Malcolm C. *Leif Erikson the Lucky.* Watts, 1979. *(A)*

Simon, Charnan. *Leif Eriksson and the Vikings.* Childrens, 1991. *(I)*

ERIE CANAL. See CANALS.

ESKIMOS (INUIT)

Alexander, Bryan, and Alexander, Cherry. *An Eskimo Family.* Lerner, 1985. *(P)*

Ekoomiak, Normee. *Arctic Memories.* Holt, 1988. *(P; I)*

Hughes, Jill. *Eskimos.* Watts, 1984 (rev. ed.). *(P; I)*

Kendall, Russ. *Eskimo Boy: Life in an Inupiaq Eskimo Village.* Scholastic, 1992. *(I; A)*

Patterson, E. Palmer. *Inuit Peoples of Canada.* Watts, 1982. *(I; A)*

Pluckrose, ed. *Small World of Eskimos.* Watts, 1980. *(P)*

Rogers, Jean. *Goodbye, My Island.* Greenwillow, 1983. *(I)*

ETHICS

Dronenwetter, Michael. *Journalism Ethics.* Watts, 1988. *(A)*

Finn, Jeffrey, and Marshall, Eliot L. *Medical Ethics.* Chelsea House, 1990. *(I; A)*

Hyde, Margaret O., and Forsyth, Elizabeth H. *Medical Dilemmas.* Putnam, 1990. *(I; A)*

Jussim, Daniel. *Medical Ethics.* Silver Burdett, 1990. *(I; A)*

Terkel, Susan Neiburg. *Ethics.* Lodestar, 1992. *(I; A)*

ETHIOPIA

Abebe, Daniel. *Ethiopia in Pictures.* Lerner, 1988. *(I)*

Fradin, Dennis Brindell. *Ethiopia.* Childrens, 1988. *(I)*

Kleeberg, Irene Cumming. *Ethiopia*. Watts, 1986. *(I; A)*

Laird, Elizabeth. *The Miracle Child: A Story from Ethiopia*. Holt, 1985. *(P)*

Lye, Keith. *Take a Trip to Ethiopia*. Watts, 1986. *(P)*

ETIQUETTE

Adamson, Elizabeth C. *Mind Your Manners*. Good Apple, 1981. *(P)*

Aliki. *Manners*. Greenwillow, 1990. *(P)*

Brown, Fern G. *Etiquette*. Watts, 1985. *(I)*

Brown, Marc, and Krensky, Stephen. *Perfect Pigs: An Introduction to Manners*. Atlantic, 1983. *(P)*

Howe, James. *The Muppet Guide to Magnificent Manners*. Random, 1984. *(P)*

Scarry, Richard. *Richard Scarry's Please and Thank You Book*. Random, 1978. *(P)*

Zeldis, Yona. *Coping with Social Situations: A Handbook of Correct Behavior*. Rosen, 1988. *(A)*

EUROPE

Bradley, John. *Eastern Europe: The Road to Democracy*. Gloucester Press, 1990. *(I; A)*

Cairns, Trevor. *Europe Around the World*. Lerner, 1982. *(I; A)*

Kronenwetter, Michael. *The New Eastern Europe*. Watts, 1991. *(I; A)*

Roberts, Elizabeth. *Europe 1992: The United States of Europe?* Gloucester Press, 1990. *(I; A)*

EVEREST, MOUNT. See MOUNTAINS AND MOUNTAIN CLIMBING.

EVOLUTION

Asimov, Isaac. *How Did We Find Out About the Beginning of Life?* Walker, 1982. *(I)*

Attenborough, David. *Life on Earth: A Natural History*. Little, 1981. *(I)*

British Museum of Natural History. *Origin of Species*. Cambridge University Press, 1982. *(A)*

Gallant, Roy A. *Before the Sun Dies: The Story of Evolution*. Macmillan, 1989. *(A)*

Gamlin, Linda. *Origins of Life*. Watts, 1988. *(I; A)*

Matthews, Rupert. *How Life Began*. Bookwright, 1989. *(P; I)*

Peters, David. *From the Beginning: The Story of Human Evolution*. Morrow, 1991. *(I; A)*

Savage, R., and Long, M. *Mammal Evolution: An Illustrated Guide*. Facts on File, 1986. *(I)*

Stein, Sara B. *The Evolution Book*. Workman, 1986. *(I)*

EXPERIMENTS AND OTHER SCIENCE ACTIVITIES

Food and the Kitchen: Step-by-Step Science Activity Projects from the Smithsonian Institution. Gareth Stevens, 1993. *(I)*

Apfel, Necia H. *Astronomy Projects for Young Scientists*. Arco, 1984. *(A)*

Cash, Terry, and Taylor, Barbara. *175 More Science Experiments to Amuse and Amaze Your Friends*. Random, 1991. *(I)*

Challand, Helen J. *Science Projects and Activities*. Childrens, 1985. *(I)*

Cobb, Vicki. *Chemically Active! Experiments You Can Do at Home*. Lippincott, 1985. *(A)*. *Lots of Rot*, 1981. *(P); The Secret Life of Hardware: A Science Experiment Book*. 1982. *(I; A); The Secret Life of School Supplies*. 1981. *(I)*

Cobb, Vicki, and Darling, Kathy. *Bet You Can't! Science Impossibilities to Fool You*. Lothrop, 1980. *(I)*

Dekkers, Midas. *The Nature Book*. Macmillan, 1988. *(I)*

Filson, Brent. *Famous Experiments and How to Repeat Them*. Messner, 1986. *(P;I)*

Gardner, Robert. *Kitchen Chemistry: Science Experiments to Do at Home*. Messner, 1982. *(I); Experimenting with Light*. Watts, 1991. *(A); Famous Experiments You Can Do*. Watts, 1990. *(A)*

Gold, Carol. *Science Express: 50 Scientific Stunts from the Ontario Science Centre*. Addison-Wesley, 1991. *(P; I)*

Markle, Sandra. *The Kids' Earth Handbook*. Atheneum, 1991. *(P; I)*

Mebane, Robert C., and Rybolt, Thomas R. *Adventures with Atoms and Molecules*. Enslow, 1991. *(I; A)*

Orii, Eiji and Masako. *Simple Science Experiments with Circles; Simple Science Experiments with Marbles; Simple Science Experiments with Ping-Pong Balls; Simple Science Experiments with Water*. Gareth Stevens, 1989. *(P)*

Richards, Roy. *101 Science Surprises: Exciting Experiments with Everyday Materials*. Sterling, 1993. *(P; I)*

Scienceworks: An Ontario Science Centre Book of Experiments. Kids Can Press, 1984. *(I)*

VanCleave, Janice. *Janice VanCleave's Earth Science for Every Kid: 101 Easy Experiments That Really Work*. John Wiley, 1991. *(P; I); Janice VanCleave's Physics for Every Kid*. John Wiley, 1991. *(I)*

Walpole, Brenda. *175 Science Experiments to Amuse and Amaze Your Friends*. Random, 1988. *(P; I)*

Wellnitz, William K. *Be a Kid Physicist*. TAB Books, 1993. *(I)*

White, Laurence B., and Broekel, Ray. *Shazam! Simple Science Magic*. Albert Whitman, 1991. *(P; I)*

Willow, Daine, and Curran, Emily. *Science Sensations*. Addison-Wesley, 1989. *(P; I)*

Wood, Robert W. *Physics for Kids: 49 Easy Experiments with Electricity and Magnetism*. TAB Books, 1990. *(I)*

Zubrowski, Bernie. *Balloons: Building and Experimenting with Inflatable Toys*. Morrow, 1990. *(P; I); Messing Around with Baking Chemistry: A Children's Museum Activity Book*. Little, 1981. *(P; I)*

EXPLORATION AND DISCOVERY

Barden, Renardo. *The Discovery of America*. Greenhaven, 1990. *(I; A)*

Beattie, Owen, and Geiger, John. *Buried in Ice: The Mystery of a Lost Arctic Expedition.* Scholastic, 1992. *(I; A)*

Brosse, Jacques. *Great Voyages of Discovery.* Facts On File, 1985. *(A)*

Ceserani, Gian Paolo. *Marco Polo.* Putnam, 1982. *(P; I)*

Ferris, Jeri. *Arctic Explorer: The Story of Matthew Henson.* Carolrhoda, 1988. *(P; I)*

Fisher, Leonard Everett. *Prince Henry the Navigator.* Macmillan, 1990. *(P; I)*

Fradin, Dennis B. *Explorers.* Childrens, 1984. *(P)*

Gaffney, Timothy. *Edmund Hillary: First to Climb Mt. Everest.* Childrens, 1990. *(I; A)*

Grosseck, Joyce. *Great Explorers.* Fideler, 1981 (rev. ed.). *(I; A)*

Lomask, Milton. *Great Lives: Exploration.* Scribner's, 1988. *(I; A)*

Maestro, Betsy. *The Discovery of the Americas.* Lothrop, 1991. *(P)*

Matthews, Rupert. *Explorer.* Knopf, 1991. *(I; A)*

Miguel, Pierre. *The Age of Discovery.* Silver Burdett, 1980. *(I)*

Poole, Frederick. *Early Exploration of North America.* Watts, 1989. *(P; I)*

Sandak, Cass R. *Explorers and Discovery.* Watts, 1983. *(I; A)*

Walsh, Richard, ed. *The Adventures of Marco Polo.* John Day, 1948. *(I)*

See also FUR TRADE IN NORTH AMERICA; VIKINGS; WESTWARD MOVEMENT AND PIONEER LIFE; and individual explorers.

EXPLOSIVES

Anderson, Norman D., and Brown, Walter R. *Fireworks! Pyrotechnics on Display.* Dodd, 1983. *(P; I)*

Gleasner, Diana C. *Dynamite.* Walker, 1982. *(I; A)*

EXTRASENSORY PERCEPTION

Akins, William R. *ESP: Your Psychic Powers and How to Test Them.* Watts, 1980. *(P; I; A)*

Cohen, Daniel. *How to Test Your ESP.* Dutton. 1982. *(A)*

Deem, James M. *How to Read Your Mother's Mind.* Houghton, 1994. *(P; I)*

EYE

Parker, Steve. *The Eye and Seeing.* Watts, 1989. *(P; I)*

Thomson, Ruth. *Eyes.* Watts, 1988. *(P)*

FABLES

Aesop. *Aesop's Fables;* illus. by Heidi Holder. Viking, 1981. *(I)*

Caldecott, Randolph. *The Caldecott Aesop—Twenty Fables.* Doubleday, 1978. *(I)*

Michie, James. *LaFontaine: Selected Fables.* Viking, 1979. *(P; I)*

Winter, Milo. *The Aesop for Children.* Rand, 1984. *(P; I)*

FAIRS AND EXPOSITIONS

Bial, Raymond. *County Fair.* Houghton, 1992. *(P; I)*

Pierce, Jack. *The State Fair Book.* Carolrhoda, 1980. *(P)*

Marsh, Carole. *A Fun Book of World's Fairs.* Gallopade, 1982. *(P; I)*

FAIRY TALES. See FOLKLORE AND FAIRY TALES.

FAMILY

Brown, Laurene Krasny. *Dinosaurs Divorce: A Guide for Changing Families.* Atlantic, 1986, *(P)*

Brown, Margaret Wise. *The Runaway Bunny.* Harper, 1970. (Fiction) *(P)*

Burningham, John. *Granpa.* Crown, 1992. (Fiction) *(P)*

Burns, Olive Ann. *Cold Sassy Tree.* Ticknor, 1984. (Fiction) *(I; A)*

Cannon, Ann. *My Home Has One Parent.* Broadman, 1983. *(I; A)*

Cleary, Beverly. *Ramona Forever.* Morrow, 1984. (Fiction) *(P; I)*

Dragonwagon, Crescent. *Home Place.* Macmillan, 1990. (Fiction) *(P; I)*

Friedman, Ina. *How My Parents Learned to Eat.* Houghton, 1987. *(P)*

Gackenback, Dick. *With Love from Gran.* Clarion, 1989. (Fiction) *(P)*

Gelfand, Marilyn. *My Great Grandpa Joe.* Four Winds, 1985. (Fiction) *(P)*

Gilbert, Sara. *How to Live with a Single Parent.* Morrow, 1982. *(I)*

Goffstein, M. B. *Family Scrapbook.* Farrar, 1978. (Fiction) *(P)*

Greenfield, Eloise. *Grandmama's Joy.* Philomel, 1980. (Fiction) *(P)*

Grove, Vicki. *Good-bye, My Wishing Star.* Putnam, 1988. (Fiction) *(P; I)*

Hautizig, Esther. *A Gift for Mama.* Viking, 1981. (Fiction) *(I)*

Jenness, Aylette. *Families: A Celebration of Diversity, Commitment, and Love.* Houghton, 1990. *(P; I)*

Jukes, Mavis. *Like Jake and Me.* Knopf, 1984. (Fiction) *(P; I)*

Keats, Ezra Jack. *Peter's Chair.* Harper, 1967. (Fiction) *(P)*

Klein, Norma. *Mom, the Wolfman and Me.* Pantheon, 1972. (Fiction) *(I; A)*

LeShan, Eda. *Grandparents: A Special Kind of Love.* Macmillan, 1984. *(P; I)*

Levinson, Riki. *I Go with My Family to Grandma's.* Dutton, 1986. (Fiction) *(P)*

Locker, Thomas. *Family Farm.* Dial, 1988. *(P; I)*

MacLachlan, Patricia. *Three Names.* Harper, 1991. (Fiction) *(P; I); Through Grandpa's Eyes.* Harper, 1980. (Fiction) *(P)*

McDonald, Megan. *The Potato Man.* Orchard Books, 1991. (Fiction) *(P)*

Melmering, Doris. *I Have Two Families.* Abingdon, 1981. (Fiction) *(P)*

Paterson, Katherine. *Jacob Have I Loved.* Avon, 1980. (Fiction) *(I; A)*

Porte, Barbara Ann. *Harry's Mom.* Greenwillow, 1985. (Fiction) *(P)*

Rench, Janice. *Family Violence: How to Recognize and Survive It.* Lerner, 1992. *(I; A)*

Rodgers, Mary. *Freaky Friday.* Harper, 1972. (Fiction) *(I; A)*

Rylant, Cynthia. *The Relatives Came.* Bradbury, 1985. (Fiction) *(P); When I Was Young in the Mountains.* Dutton, 1982. (Fiction) *(P)*

Salus, Naomi Panush. *My Daddy's Mustache.* Doubleday, 1979. (Fiction) *(P)*

Scott, Ann Herbert. *On Mother's Lap.* McGraw, 1972. (Fiction) *(P)*

Sendak, Philip. *In Grandpa's House.* Harper, 1986. (Fiction) *(I)*

Simon, Norma. *All Kinds of Families.* Albert Whitman, 1976. *(P)*

Smith, Robert Kimmel. *The War with Grandpa.* Delacorte, 1984. (Fiction) *(P; I)*

Streich, Corrine. *Grandparents' Houses: Poems About Grandparents.* Greenwillow, 1984. *(I)*

Thomas, Jane. *Saying Goodbye to Grandma.* Clarion, 1988. (Fiction) *(P)*

Viorst, Judith. *Alexander and the Terrible, Horrible, No Good, Very Bad Day.* Atheneum, 1984. (Fiction) *(P)*

Williams, Vera B. *A Chair for My Mother.* Greenwillow, 1982. (Fiction) *(P)*

Worth, Richard, *The American Family.* Watts, 1984. *(I; A)*

FANTASY*

Adams, Richard. *Watership Down.* Macmillan, 1974. (Fiction) *(I; A)*

Alexander, Lloyd. *The Book of Three.* Holt, 1964. (Fiction) *(I; A); The Fortune-Tellers.* Dutton, 1992. (Fiction) *(P); The High King.* Holt, 1968. (Fiction) *(P; I)*

Babbitt, Natalie. *Tuck Everlasting.* Farrar, 1975. (Fiction) *(P; I)*

Brown, Margaret Wise. *Goodnight Moon.* Harper, 1947. (Fiction) *(P)*

Carroll, Lewis. *Alice in Wonderland and Through the Looking Glass.* Grossett, 1984 (1865). (Fiction) *(I; A)*

Cole, Joanna. *Bony-Legs.* Four Winds, 1983. (Fiction) *(P)*

Conrad, Pam. *Stonewords.* Harper, 1990. (Fiction) *(I; A)*

Dahl, Roald. *Charlie and the Chocolate Factory.* Knopf, 1964. (Fiction) *(P; I)*

Le Guin, Ursula K. *Catwings.* Orchard Books, 1988. (Fiction) *(P; I)*

Lewis, C. S. *The Lion, the Witch and the Wardrobe.* Macmillan, 1950. (Fiction) *(P; I)*

Lindgren, Astrid. *Pippi Longstocking.* Viking, 1977 (1950). (Fiction) *(P; I)*

MacDonald, George. *The Princess and the Goblin.* Morrow, 1986. (Fiction) *(P; I)*

Mayer, Mercer. *There's a Nightmare in My Closet.* Dial, 1968. (Fiction) *(P)*

Milne, A. A. *Winnie the Pooh.* Dutton, 1961 (1926). (Fiction) *(P)*

Norton, Mary. *The Borrowers.* Harcourt, 1953. (Fiction) *(P; I)*

O'Brien, Robert C. *Mrs. Frisby and the Rats of NIMH.* Atheneum, 1971. (Fiction) *(P; I)*

Osborne, Mary Pope. *American Tall Tales.* Knopf, 1991. (Fiction) *(P; I)*

Place, Francois. *The Last Giants.* Godine, 1993. (Fiction) *(I; A)*

Seuss, Dr. *Green Eggs and Ham.* Random, 1960. (Fiction) *(P)*

Sis, Peter. *A Small Tall Tale from the Far Far North.* Knopf, 1993. (Fiction) *(P; I)*

Snyder, Zilpha Keatley. *Below the Root.* Atheneum, 1975. (Fiction) *(I; A)*

Tolkien, J. R. R. *The Hobbit.* Houghton, 1984 (1938). (Fiction) *(I; A)*

Wiesner, David. *June 29, 1999.* Clarion, 1992. (Fiction) *(P; I)*

FARMS AND FARMING

Ancona, George, and Anderson, Joan. *The American Family Farm.* Harcourt, 1989. *(I)*

Bellville, Charyl Walsh. *Farming Today Yesterday's Way.* Carolrhoda, 1984. *(P)*

Bushey, Jerry. *Farming the Land: Modern Farmers and Their Machines.* Carolrhoda, 1987. *(P; I)*

Gibbons, Gail. *Farming.* Holiday, 1988. *(P)*

Gorman, Carol. *America's Farm Crisis.* Watts, 1987. *(A)*

Graff, Nancy Price. *The Strength of the Hills: A Portrait of a Family Farm.* Little, 1989. *(P; I; A)*

Jeffries, Tony, and Hindley, Judy. *Farm Animals.* Watts, 1982. *(P)*

Kushner, Jill Menkes. *The Farming Industry.* Watts, 1984. *(I; A)*

Lambert, Mark. *Farming Technology.* Bookwright, 1990. *(I)*

Marston, Hope I. *Machines on the Farm.* Dodd, 1982. *(P; I)*

Murphy, Jim. *Tractors: From Yesterday's Steam Wagons to Today's Turbocharged Giants.* Lippincott, 1984. *(P; I)*

Patent, Dorothy Hinshaw. *Farm Animals.* Holiday, 1984. *(P; I)*

Provensen, Alice, and Provensen, Martin. *The Year at Maple Hill Farm.* Macmillan, 1988. *(P)*

Smith, E. Boyd. *The Farm Book.* Houghton, 1982. *(P)*

Stephen, R. J. *Farm Machinery.* Watts, 1987. *(P)*

Wilder, Laura Ingalls. *Farmer Boy.* Harper, 1953. (Fiction) *(I)*

---

*This is a popular theme with young readers. However, it is not a separate article in *The New Book of Knowledge.*

FARRAGUT, DAVID

Latham, Jean Lee. *Anchor's Aweigh: The Story of David Glasgow Farragut*. Harper, 1968. *(I)*

FASCISM. See HITLER, ADOLF; MUSSOLINI, BENITO.

FEET AND HANDS. See BODY, HUMAN.

FERDINAND AND ISABELLA. See SPAIN.

FERNS

Shuttleworth, Floyd S., and Zim, Herbert. *Non-Flowering Plants*. Western, 1967. *(I)*

Wexler, Jerome. *From Spore to Spore: Ferns and How They Grow*. Dodd, 1985. *(I)*

FEUDALISM. See MIDDLE AGES.

FIBERS. See TEXTILES.

FIELD HOCKEY

Preston-Mauks, Susan. *Field Hockey Is for Me*. Lerner, 1983. *(P; I)*

Sullivan, George. *Better Field Hockey for Girls*. Dodd, 1981. *(I; A)*

FILLMORE, MILLARD

Casey, Jane Clark. *Millard Fillmore: Thirteenth President of the United States*. Childrens, 1988. *(P; I)*

See also PRESIDENCY OF THE UNITED STATES.

FINLAND

Hentz, Martin. *Finland*. Childrens, 1983. *(I; A)*

Lander, Patricia, and Charbonneau, Claudette. *The Land and People of Finland*. Lippincott, 1990. *(I; A)*

FIRE AND COMBUSTION

Fradin, Dennis B. *Disaster! Fires*. Childrens, 1982. *(I)*

Gibbons, Gail. *Fire! Fire!* Crowell, 1982. *(P)*

Satchwell, John. *Fire*. Dial, 1983. *(P)*

FIRE AND EARLY PEOPLE. See ANTHROPOLOGY.

FIRE FIGHTING AND PREVENTION

Broekel, Ray. *Fire Fighters*. Childrens, 1981. *(P)*

Bundt, Nancy. *The Fire Station Book*. Carolrhoda, 1981. *(P)*

Fichter, George. *Disastrous Fires*. Watts, 1981. *(I)*

Lee, Mary Price, and Lee, Richard S. *Careers in Firefighting*. Rosen, 1993. *(I; A)*

Loeper, John. *By Hook and Ladder*. Atheneum, 1981. *(I)*

Poynter, Margaret. *Wildland Fire Fighting*. Atheneum, 1982. *(I; A)*

Stephen, R. J. *Fire Engines*. Watts, 1987. *(P)*

Wolf, Bernard. *Firehouses*. Morrow, 1983. *(I)*

FIREWORKS. See EXPLOSIVES.

FIRST AID

Boelts, Maribeth, and Boelts, Darwin. *Kids to the Rescue! First Aid Techniques for Kids*. Parenting Press, 1992. *(P; I)*

Boy Scouts of America. *First Aid*. Boy Scouts, 1981. *(I; A)*

Freeman, Lory. *What Would You Do If? A Children's Guide to First Aid*. Parenting Press, 1983. *(P)*

Nourse, Alan. *Fractures, Dislocations and Sprains*. Watts, 1978. *(I)*

FIRST LADIES

Boller, Paul F. *Presidential Wives*. Oxford University Press, 1988. *(I; A)*

Butwin, Miriam, and Chaffin, Lillie. *America's First Ladies*. (2 volumes). Lerner, n.d. *(I; A)*

Caroli, Betty Boyd. *First Ladies*. Oxford University Press, 1987. *(A)*

Healy, Diana Dixon. *America's First Ladies*. Atheneum, 1988. *(I; A)*

See also PRESIDENCY OF THE UNITED STATES.

FISH

Broekel, Ray. *Dangerous Fish*. Childrens, 1982. *(P)*

Freedman, Russell. *Killer Fish*. Holiday, 1982. *(P)*

Graham-Barber, Lynda. *Round Fish, Flatfish, and Other Animal Changes*. Crown, 1982. *(I)*

Harris, Jack C. *A Step-by-Step Book About Goldfish*. TFH Publications, 1988. *(I; A)*

Henrie, Fiona. *Fish*. Watts, 1981. *(P; I)*

Lane, Margaret. *The Fish: The Story of the Stickleback*. Dial, 1982. *(P)*

FISHING

Arnosky, Jim. *Flies in the Water, Fish in the Air: A Personal Introduction to Fly Fishing*. Lothrop, 1986. *(I; A); Freshwater Fish and Fishing*. Four Winds, 1982. *(P; I)*

Evanoff, Vlad. *A Complete Guide to Fishing*. Harper, 1981 (rev. ed.). *(I; A)*

Fabian, John. *Fishing for Beginners*. Atheneum, 1980. *(P; I)*

Randolph, John. *Fishing Basics*. Prentice Hall, 1981. *(P; I)*

Roberts, Charles P., and Roberts, George F. *Fishing for Fun: A Freshwater Guide*. Dillon, 1984. *(I)*

FISHING INDUSTRY

Ferrell, Nancy Warren. *The Fishing Industry*. Watts, 1984. *(I; A)*

Scarry, Huck. *Life on a Fishing Boat: A Sketchbook*. Prentice Hall, 1983. *(I; A)*

FLAGS

Crampton, William. *Flag*. Knopf, 1989. *(I)*
Langton, Jane. *Fragile Flag*. Harper, 1984. *(I)*
Spier, Peter. *The Star-Spangled Banner*. Doubleday, 1973. *(P)*
Swanson, June. *I Pledge Allegiance*. Carolrhoda, 1990. *(P)*
White, David. *Flags*. Rourke, 1988. *(P)*

FLORENCE. See ITALY.

FLORIDA

Coil, Suzanne M. *Florida*. Watts, 1987. *(P; I)*
Fradin, Dennis. *Florida: In Words and Pictures*. Childrens, 1980. *(P; I)*
Stone, Lynn M. *Florida*. Childrens, 1988. *(P; I)*

FLOWERS AND SEEDS

Allen, Sarah, ed. *Wildflowers: Eastern Edition; Western Edition*. Little, 1981. *(I; A)*
Crowell, Robert L. *The Lore and Legend of Flowers*. Harper, 1982. *(I; A)*
Dowden, Anne Ophelia. *The Clover & the Bee: A Book of Pollination*. Crowell, 1990. *(I; A)*
Kuchalla, Susan. *All About Seeds*. Troll, 1982. *(P)*
Lauber, Patricia. *From Flower to Flower: Animals and Pollination*. Crown, 1987. *(I)*
Lerner, Carol. *Plant Families*. Morrow, 1989. *(P; I)*
Overbeck, Cynthia. *How Seeds Travel*. Lerner, 1982; *Sunflowers*. Lerner, 1981. *(I; A)*
Patent, Dorothy Hinshaw. *Flowers for Everyone*. Cobblehill, 1990. *(I)*
Selsam, Millicent E., and Wexler, Jerome. *Eat the Fruit, Plant the Seed*. Morrow, 1980. *(P)*

FOG AND SMOG. See POLLUTION; WEATHER.

FOLK ART

Fowler, Virginia. *Folk Arts Around the World: And How to Make Them*. Prentice Hall, 1981. *(I; A)*
Horwitz, Elinor L. *Contemporary American Folk Artists*. Harper, 1975. *(I; A)*

FOLKLORE AND FAIRY TALES

Aardema, Verna. *Oh Kojo! How Could You?: An Ashanti Tale*. Dial, 1984. *(P)*; *Traveling to Tondo: A Tale of the Nkundo of Zaire*. Knopf, 1991. (Fiction) *(P)*
Benet, Rosemary, and Vincent, Steven. "Johnny Appleseed" from *A Book of Americans*. Holt, 1984. *(P)*
Briggs, Raymond. *The Fairy Tale Treasury*. Dell, 1980. *(P; I)*
Chase, Richard, ed. *The Jack Tales*. Houghton, 1971. *(P; I)*

Climo, Shirley. *The Egyptian Cinderella*. Crowell, 1989. *(P; I)*
Colwell, Eileen, ed. *The Magic Umbrella and Other Stories for Telling*. Merrimack, 1977. *(P; I)*
Corrin, Sara, ed. *The Faber Book of Modern Fairy Tales*. Faber, 1981. *(I)*
Crouch, Marcus. *The Whole World Storybook*. Oxford University Press, 1983. *(I)*
Cummings, E. E. *Fairy Tales*. Harcourt, 1975. *(P)*
DePaola, Tomie. *The Legend of Old Befana*. Harcourt, 1980. *(P)*; *The Legend of the Indian Paintbrush*. Putnam, 1988. *(P)*
Dixon, Ann. *How Raven Brought Light to People*. McElderry, 1993. *(P; I)*
Goble, Paul. *Buffalo Woman*. Bradbury, 1984. *(P; I)*
Goode, Diane. *Book of American Folktales and Songs*. Dutton, 1989. *(P; I)*
Grifalconi, Ann. *The Village of Round and Square Houses*. Little, 1986. *(P)*
Hamilton, Virginia. *The People Could Fly: American Black Folktales*. Knopf, 1985. *(I; A)*
Hong, Lily Toy, retel. *How the Ox Star Fell from Heaven*. Albert Whitman, 1991. *(P; I)*
Keats, Ezra. *John Henry: An American Legend*. Knopf, 1987. *(P)*
Kipling, Rudyard. *The Elephant's Child*. Harcourt, 1983. *(P; I)*
Lanes, Selma, ed. *A Child's First Book of Nursery Tales*. Western, 1983. *(P)*
Lang, Andrew. *Blue Fairy Book*. Viking, 1978; *Green Fairy Book*, Airmont, 1969 (and other Lang Fairy Books). *(I)*
Leach, Maria, ed. *Whistle in the Graveyard: Folktales to Chill Your Bones*. Penguin, 1982. *(P; I)*
Lester, Julius. *The Tales of Uncle Remus: The Adventure of Brer Rabbit*. Dial, 1987. *(I; A)*
Luenn, Nancy. *Song for the Ancient Forest*. Atheneum, 1993. *(P; I)*
MacDonald, George. *The Complete Fairy Tales of George MacDonald*. Schocken, 1979. *(P; I; A)*
Marshall, James. *Hansel and Gretel*. Dial, 1990. *(P)*
Mayer, Marianna. *Beauty and the Beast*. Four Winds, 1978. *(P; I)*
McDermott, Gerald. *Raven*. Harcourt, 1993. *(P)*
Newton, Pam. *The Stonecutter: An Indian Folktale*. Putnam, 1990. *(P)*
Oughton, Jerrie. *How the Stars Fell into the Sky: A Navajo Legend*. Houghton, 1992. *(P; I)*
Perrault, Charles. *Perrault's Complete Fairy Tales*, tr. by A. E. Johnson. Dodd, 1982. *(P; I)*
Philip, Neil, ed. *Fairy Tales of Eastern Europe*. Clarion, 1991. *(I)*
Pyle, Howard. *The Wonder Clock: Of Four and Twenty Marvelous Tales*. Dover, n.d. *(P)*
Rackham, Arthur, ed. *The Arthur Rackham Fairy Book*. Harper, 1950. *(I)*

Rohmer, Harriet. *The Invisible Hunters: A Legend from the Miskito Indians of Nicaragua*. Childrens, 1987. *(P; I)*; *Uncle Nacho's Hat*, Childrens, 1989. *(P; I)*

Sanfield, Steve. *The Adventures of High John the Conqueror*. Watts, 1989. *(I; A)*

San Souci, Robert. *Cut from the Same Cloth: American Women of Myth, Legend and Tall Tale*. Philomel, 1993. *(I; A)*; *The Talking Eggs*. Dial, 1989. *(P; I)*

Scieszka, Jon. *The Frog Prince Continued*. Viking, 1991. *(P)*

Shetterly, Susan Hand. *The Dwarf-Wizard of Uxmal*. Atheneum, 1990. *(I)*

Steptoe, John. *Mufaro's Beautiful Daughters: An African Tale*. Lothrop, 1987. *(P)*

Stevens, Janet, ed. *Coyote Steals the Blanket: A Ute Tale*. Holiday, 1993. *(P)*

Tudor, Tasha. *Tasha Tudor Book of Fairy Tales*. Platt, 1961. *(P)*

Winthrop, Elizabeth. *Vasilissa the Beautiful*. Harper, 1991. *(P; I)*

Wolf, A. *The True Story of the Three Little Pigs*. Puffin, 1989. *(P)*

Wright, Blanche Fisher. *The Real Mother Goose*. Rand, 1916. *(P)*

Zelinsky, Paul O. *Rumpelstiltskin*. Greenwillow, 1988. *(P)*

Zemach, Harve. *Duffy and the Devil*. Farrar, 1973. *(P)*

See also ANDERSEN, HANS CHRISTIAN; GRIMM, JACOB AND WILHELM.

FOLK MUSIC

Berger, Melvin. *The Story of Folk Music*. S. G. Phillips, 1976. *(I; A)*

Fox, Dan, ed. *Go In and Out the Window: An Illustrated Songbook for Young People*. Holt, 1987. *(P; I; A)*

Glazer, Tom. *Eye Winker, Tom Tinker, Chin Chopper*. Doubleday, 1978. *(P)*

Seeger, Ruth C. *American Folk Songs for Children*. Doubleday, 1980. *(P; I)*

Yolen, Jane, ed. *The Lullaby Songbook*. Harcourt, 1986. *(P; I)*

FOOD AROUND THE WORLD

Cooper, Terry, and Ratner, Marilyn. *Many Friends Cookbook: An International Cookbook for Boys and Girls*. Putnam, 1980. *(P; I)*

Hayward, Ruth Ann, and Warner, Margaret Brink. *What's Cooking: Favorite Recipes from Around the World*. Little, 1981. *(I; A)*

Pizer, Vernon. *Eat the Grapes Downward: An Uninhibited Romp Through the Surprising World of Food*. Dodd, 1983. *(I; A)*

Van der Linde, Polly, and Van der Linde, Tasha. *Around the World in Eighty Dishes*. Scroll, n.d. *(P; I)*

FOOD SHOPPING. See CONSUMERISM.

FOOD SUPPLY

Blumberg, Rhoda. *Famine*. Watts, 1978. *(A)*

Bonner, James. *The World's People and the World's Food Supply*. Carolina Biological, 1980. *(A)*

McCoy, J. J. *How Safe Is Our Food Supply?* Watts, 1990. *(A)*

Patent, Dorothy Hinshaw. *Where Food Comes From*. Holiday, 1991. *(P)*

FOOTBALL

Aaseng, Nate. *Football: You Are the Coach*. Lerner, 1983. *(I; A)*

Anderson, Dave. *The Story of Football*. Morrow, 1985. *(I; A)*

Barrett, Norman. *Football*. Watts, 1989. *(P)*

Berger, Melvin. *The Photo Dictionary of Football*. Methuen, 1980. *(P; I)*

Broekel, Ray. *Football*. Childrens, 1982. *(P)*

Madden, John. *The First Book of Football*. Crown, 1988. *(I; A)*

Miller, J. David. *The Super Book of Football*. Sports Illustrated for Kids Books, 1990. *(I)*

Namath, Joe. *Football for Young Players and Parents*. Simon & Schuster, 1986. *(I)*

Potts, Steve. *San Francisco 49ers*. Creative Education, 1991. *(I)*

Rambeck, Richard. *Detroit Lions* *(I)*; *New England Patriots*. Creative Education, 1991. *(I)*

Sandak, Cass R. *Football*. Watts, 1982. *(P)*

Sullivan, George. *All About Football*. Dodd, 1987. *(P)*

FORD, GERALD R. See PRESIDENCY OF THE UNITED STATES.

FORESTS AND FORESTRY

Aldis, Rodney. *Rainforests*. Dillon: Macmillan, 1991. *(P; I)*

Batten, Mary. *The Tropical Forest*. Crowell, 1973. *(P)*

Bellamy, David. *The Forest*. Clarkson Potter, 1988. *(P)*

Challand, Helen J. *Vanishing Forests*. Childrens, 1991. *(I)*

Cowcher, Helen. *Rain Forest*. Farrar, 1989. *(P)*

Dixon, Dougal. *Forests*. Watts, 1984. *(P; I)* (Atlas format)

George, Jean. *One Day in the Woods*. Crowell, 1988. *(P)*

Newton, James. *A Forest Is Reborn*. Harper, 1982. *(P)*

Taylor, Mildred. *Song of the Trees*. Bantam, 1975. (Fiction) *(P)*

Vogt, Gregory. *Forests on Fire: The Fight to Save Our Trees*. Watts, 1990. *(A)*

FORTS AND FORTIFICATION

Peterson, Harold L. *Forts in America*. Scribner's, 1964. *(I)*

Stiles, David. *The Kids' Fort Book*. Avon, 1982. *(P; I)*

FOSSEY, DIAN

Jerome, Leah. *Dian Fossey*. Bantam, 1991. *(I)*

FOSSILS

Aliki. *Fossils Tell of Long Ago*. Crowell, 1990 (rev. ed.). *(P)*

Arnold, Caroline. *Dinosaur Mountain*. Clarion, 1989. *(I); Trapped in Tar: Fossils from the Ice Age*. Clarion, 1987. *(P)*

Baylor, Byrd. *If You Are a Hunter of Fossils*. Scribner's, 1980. *(P)*

Curtis, Neil. *Fossils*. Watts, 1984. *(P; I)*

Eldredge, Niles. *The Fossil Factory*. Addison-Wesley, 1989. *(I)*

Gallant, Roy A. *Fossils*. Watts, 1985. *(P)*

Lambert, David, and the Diagram Group. *The Field Guide to Prehistoric Life*. Facts on File, 1985. *(I; A)*

Lasky, Kathryn. *The Bone Wars*. Morrow, 1988. (Fiction) *(I); Dinosaur Dig*. Morrow, 1990. *(I)*

Lauber, Patricia. *Dinosaurs Walked Here (And Other Stories Fossils Tell)*. Bradbury, 1987. *(I; A)*

Taylor, Paul D. *Fossil*. Knopf, 1990. *(I; A)*

FOSTER CARE. See ADOPTION.

FOUNDERS OF THE UNITED STATES

Benchley, Nathaniel. *Sam the Minuteman*. Harper, 1969. *(P)*

Bennett, Wayne, ed. *Founding Fathers*. Garrard, 1975. *(I; A)*

Bliven, Bruce, Jr. *The American Revolution, 1760–1783*. Random, 1981. *(I)*

Coolidge, Olivia E. *Tom Paine, Revolutionary*. Scribner's, 1969. *(I)*

De Pauw, Linda G. *Founding Mothers: Women of America in the Revolutionary Era*. Houghton, 1975. *(I; A)*

FOXES

Ahlstrom, Mark. *The Foxes*. Crestwood, 1983. *(P; I)*

Burton, Jane. *Trill the Fox Cub*. Gareth Stevens, 1989. *(P)*

Lane, Margaret. *The Fox*. Dial, 1982. *(P)*

Mason, Cherie. *Wild Fox: A True Story*. Down East Books, 1993. *(P; I: A)*

McDearmon, Kay. *Foxes*. Dodd, 1981. *(P; I)*

FRACTIONS. See MATHEMATICS.

FRANCE

Balderdi, Susan. *France: The Crossroads of Europe*. Dillon, 1983. *(I; A)*

Blackwood, Alan, and Chosson, Brigitte. *France*. Bookwright, 1988. *(P)*

Harris, Jonathan. *The Land and People of France*. Lippincott, 1989. *(I; A)*

Jacobsen, Peter O., and Kristensen, Preben S. *A Family in France*. Watts, 1984. *(P; I)*

James, Ian. *France*. Watts, 1989. *(P; I)*

Morrice, Polly. *The French Americans*. Chelsea House, 1988. *(I; A)*

Moss, Peter, and Palmer, Thelma. *France*. Childrens, 1986. *(P)*

Rutland, Jonathan. *Take a Trip to France*. Watts, 1981. *(P)*

Tomlins, James. *We Live in France*. Watts, 1983. *(I; A)*

FRANKLIN, BENJAMIN

Adler, David A. *A Picture Book of Benjamin Franklin*. Holiday, 1990. *(P)*

D'Aulaire, Ingri, and D'Aulaire, Edgar P. *Benjamin Franklin*. Doubleday, 1950. *(P)*

Franklin, Benjamin. *The Autobiography of Benjamin Franklin*. Airmont, n.d. *(A); Poor Richard*. Peter Pauper, n.d. *(I; A)*

Fritz, Jean. *What's the Big Idea, Ben Franklin?* Putnam, 1982. *(I)*

Greene, Carol. *Benjamin Franklin: A Man With Many Jobs*. Childrens, 1988. *(P)*

Looby, Chris. *Benjamin Franklin*. Chelsea House, 1990. *(I; A)*

Meltzer, Milton. *Benjamin Franklin: The New American*. Watts, 1988. *(I; A)*

Sandak, Cass R. *Benjamin Franklin*. Watts, 1986. *(P; I)*

Santrey, Laurence. *Young Ben Franklin*. Troll, 1982. *(P; I)*

Stevens, Byrna. *Ben Franklin's Glass Armonica*. Carolrhoda, 1983. *(P)*

FREEDOM OF RELIGION, SPEECH, AND PRESS. See CIVIL LIBERTIES AND CIVIL RIGHTS.

FRENCH AND INDIAN WAR. See UNITED STATES (HISTORY AND GOVERNMENT).

FRENCH REVOLUTION

Cairns, Trevor. *Power for the People*. Cambridge University Press, 1978. *(A)*

Dickens, Charles. *A Tale of Two Cities*. Putnam, 1982. (Fiction) *(I; A)*

Lacey, Robert. *The French Revolution*. Viking, 1977. *(I; A)*

Powers, Elizabeth. *The Journal of Madame Royale*. Walker, 1976. *(I; A)*

FREUD, SIGMUND

Lager, Marilyn. *Sigmund Freud: Doctor of the Mind*. Enslow, 1986. *(A)*

FRIENDSHIP*

Bulla, Clyde Robert. *Shoeshine Girl*. Crowell, 1975. (Fiction) *(P; I)*

---

*This is a popular theme with young readers. However, it is not a separate article in *The New Book of Knowledge*.

Freeman, Don. *Corduroy*. Viking, 1976 (1968). (Fiction) *(P)*

Keats, Ezra Jack. *Jennie's Hat*. Harper, 1966. (Fiction) *(P)*

Lobel, Arnold. *Frog and Toad Are Friends*. Harper, 1970. (Fiction) *(P)*

Marshall, James. *George and Martha*. Houghton, 1972. (Fiction) *(P)*

Sachar, Louis. *There's a Boy in the Girls' Bathroom*. Knopf, 1987. (Fiction) *(P; I)*

Selden, George. *A Cricket in Times Square*. Farrar, 1960. (Fiction) *(P; I)* White, E. B. *Charlotte's Web*. Harper, 1952. (Fiction) *(P; I)*

White, E. B. *Charlotte's Web*. Harper, 1952. (Fiction) *(P; I)*

FROGS AND TOADS

Clarke, Barry. *Amazing Frogs and Toads*. Knopf, 1990. *(P; I)*

Cole, Joanna. *A Frog's Body*. Morrow, 1980. *(P)*

Dallinger, Jane, and Johnson, Sylvia A. *Frogs and Toads*. Lerner, 1982. *(I; A)*

Lacey, Elizabeth A. *The Complete Frog: A Guide for the Very Young Naturalist*. Lothrop, 1989. *(I)*

Lavies, Bianca. *Lily Pad Pond*. Dutton, 1989. *(P)*

Modiki, Masuda. *Tree Frogs*. Lerner, 1986. *(I)*

Tarrant, Graham. *Frogs*. Putnam, 1983. *(P)*

FROST, ROBERT

Bober, Natalie S. *A Restless Spirit: The Story of Robert Frost*. Holt, 1991 (rev. ed.). *(I; A)*

Frost, Robert. *The Road Not Taken: An Introduction to Robert Frost*. Holt, 1951. *(A)*

FRUITGROWING

Ancona, George. *Bananas: From Manolo to Margie*. Clarion, 1982. *(P; I)*

Jaspersohn, William. *Cranberries*. Houghton, 1991. *(P; I)*

Johnson, Sylvia A. *Apple Trees*. Lerner, 1983. *(P; I; A)*

Jukes, Mavis. *Blackberries in the Dark*. Knopf, 1985. (Fiction) *(P)*

Mitgutsch, Ali. *From Lemon to Lemonade*. Carolrhoda, 1986. *(P)*; *From Seed to Pear*, Carolrhoda, 1981. *(P)*

Potter, Marian. *A Chance Wild Apple*. Morrow, 1982. *(P; I)*

Williams, Vera B. *Cherries and Cherry Pits*. Greenwillow, 1986. (Fiction) *(P)*

FUELS. See ENERGY.

FULTON, ROBERT

Philip, Cynthia. *Robert Fulton: A Biography*. Watts, 1985. *(A)*

Quackenbush, Robert. *Watt Got You Started, Mr. Fulton?* Prentice Hall, 1982. *(P; I)*

FUNGI

Johnson, Sylvia A. *Mushrooms*. Lerner, 1982. *(I; A)*

Selsam, Millicent E. *Mushrooms*. Morrow, 1986. *(I)*

FUR TRADE IN NORTH AMERICA

Siegel, Beatrice. *Fur Trappers and Traders; The Indians, the Pilgrims, and the Beaver*. Walker, 1981. *(P; I)*

GABON. See AFRICA.

GALILEO. See ASTRONOMY.

GAMA, VASCO DA

Knight, David. *Vasco Da Gama*. Troll, 1979 (new ed.). *(P; I)*

GAMBIA, THE. See AFRICA.

GAMES

Bernarde, Anita. *Games from Many Lands*. Lion, 1971. *(P; I)*

Cline, Dallas, and Tornborg, Pat. *How to Play Almost Everything*. Putnam, 1982. *(P; I)*

D'Amato, Alex, and D'Amato, Janet. *Galaxy Games*. Doubleday, 1981. *(P; I)*

Ferretti, Fred. *The Great American Book of Sidewalk, Stoop, Dirt, Curb, and Alley Games*. Workman, 1975. *(P; I)*

Gould, Marilyn. *Playground Sports: A Book of Ball Games*. Lothrop, 1978. *(I)*

Hass, E. A. *Come Quick! I'm Sick*. Atheneum, 1982. *(P)*

McToots, Rudi. *Best-Ever Book of Indoor Games*. Arco, 1985. *(I; A)*

GANDHI, MOHANDAS KARAMCHAND

Cheney, Glenn A. *Mohandas Gandhi*. Watts, 1983. *(I; A)*

Rawding, F. W. *Gandhi*. Cambridge University Press, 1980. *(I)*; *Gandhi and the Struggle for India's Independence*. Lerner, 1982. *(I; A)*

GANGES RIVER. See INDIA.

GARDENS AND GARDENING

Bjork, Christina. *Linnea's Windowsill Garden*. R & S Books, 1988. (Fiction) *(I)*

Brown, Marc. *Your First Garden Book*. Little, 1981. *(P)*

Creasy, Rosalind. *Blue Potatoes, Orange Tomatoes: How to Grow a Rainbow Garden*. Sierra, 1994. *(P; I)*

Krementz, Jill. *A Very Young Gardener*. Dial, 1991. *(P)*

Markmann, Erika. *Grow It! An Indoor/Outdoor Gardening Guide for Kids*. Random, 1991. *(P; I)*

Murphy, Louise. *My Garden: A Journal for Gardening Around the Year*. Scribner's, 1980. *(P; I)*

Rangecroft, Derek, and Rangecroft, Sandra. *Nasturtiums*. Dell, 1993. *(P; I)*; *Pumpkins*. Dell, 1993. *(P; I)*;

Sunflowers. Dell, 1993. *(P; I)*; *Tomatoes*. Dell, 1993. *(P; I)*

Vogel, Antje, illus. *The Big Book for Little Gardeners*. Green Tiger, 1983. *(P)*

Waters, Marjorie. *The Victory Garden Kid's Book*. Houghton, 1988. *(P; I)*

Wilkes, Angela. *My First Garden Book*. Knopf, 1992. *(P; I)*

GARFIELD, JAMES A.

Lillegard, Dee. *James A. Garfield*. Childrens, 1988. *(P; I)*

See also PRESIDENCY OF THE UNITED STATES.

GARIBALDI, GIUSEPPE. See ITALY.

GASES

Griffin, Frank. *Industrial Gases*. Sportshelf, n.d. *(I; A)*

Pechey, Roger. *Gas*. (Spotlight on Resources) Rourke, 1987. *(P; I)*

GASOLINE. See PETROLEUM.

GEMSTONES. See ROCKS.

GENEALOGY

Cooper, Kay. *Where Did You Get Those Eyes? A Guide to Discovering Your Family History*. Walker, 1988. *(I)*

Stryker-Rodda, Harriet. *How to Climb Your Family Tree: Genealogy for Beginners*. Harper, 1977. *(I; A)*

Wubben, Pamela G. *Genealogy for Children*. One Percent, 1981. *(P; I)*

GENETICS AND GENETIC ENGINEERING

Arnold, Caroline. *Genetics: From Mendel to Gene Splicing*. Watts, 1986. *(I; A)*

Asimov, Isaac. *How Did We Find Out About Our Genes?* Walker, 1983. *(I)*

Bornstein, Sandy, and Bornstein, Jerry. *New Frontiers in Genetics*. Simon & Schuster, 1984 *(A); What Makes You What You Are: A First Look at Genetics*. Messner, 1989. *(I)*

Edelson, Edward. *Genetics and Heredity*. Chelsea House, 1990. *(I; A)*

Gutnik, Martin J. *Genetics: Projects for Young Scientists*. Watts, 1985. *(I)*

Hyde, Margaret O., and Hyde, Lawrence E. *Cloning and the New Genetics*. Enslow, 1984. *(A)*

Patent, Dorothy H. *Grandfather's Nose: Why We Look Alike or Different*. Watts, 1989. *(P)*

Snyder, Gerald S. *Test Tube Life: Scientific Advance and Moral Dilemma*. Messner, 1982. *(I; A)*

Stwertka, Eve, and Stwertka, Albert. *Genetic Engineering*. Watts, 1982. *(I; A)*

GEOGRAPHY

Bell, Neill. *The Book of Where or How to Be Naturally Geographic*. Little, 1982. *(I; A)*

Grolier Incorporated. *Lands and Peoples* (6 volumes). Grolier, 1995. *(I)*

Knowlton, Jack. *Geography From A to Z*. Crowell, 1988. *(P)*

National Geographic Society. *Nature's World of Wonders*. National Geographic, 1983. *(I; A)*

GEOLOGY

Boy Scouts of America. *Geology*. BSA, 1981. *(I; A)*

Dixon, Dougal. *Geology*. Watts, 1983. *(I; A); The Practical Geologist*. Simon and Schuster, 1992. *(I; A)*

Jacobs, Linda. *Letting Off Steam: The Story of Geothermal Energy*. Carolrhoda, 1989. *(I; A)*

Lambert, David, and the Diagram Group. *The Field Guide to Geology*. Facts on File, 1988. *(A)*

Markle, Sandra. *Digging Deeper: Investigations into Rocks, Shocks, Quakes, and Other Earthly Matters*. Lothrop, 1987. *(I)*

Rossbacher, Lisa A. *Recent Revolutions In Geology*. Watts, 1986. *(I; A)*

See also EARTH.

GEOMETRY AND GEOMETRIC FORMS

Froman, Robert. *Angles Are Easy as Pie*. Harper, 1976. *(P)*

Hoban, Tana. *Circles, Triangles, and Squares*. Macmillan, 1974. *(P)*

Phillips, Jo. *Exploring Triangles: Paper-Folding Geometry*. Harper, 1975. *(P); Right Angles: Paper-Folding Geometry*, 1972. *(P)*

Srivastava, Jane J. *Spaces, Shapes, and Sizes*. Harper, 1980. *(P)*

GEORGIA

Blackburn, Joyce. *James Edward Oglethorpe*. Dodd, 1983. *(I; A)*

Hepburn, Lawrence R. *The Georgia History Book*. University of Georgia, 1982. *(I; A)*

Kent, Zachary A. *Georgia*. Childrens, 1988. *(P; I)*

LaDoux, Rita C. *Georgia*. Lerner, 1991. *(I)*

Pedersen, Anne. *Kidding Around Atlanta: A Young Person's Guide to the City*. John Muir, 1989. *(I; A)*

Snow, Pegeen. *Atlanta*. Dillon, 1989. *(P; I)*

GERMANY

Bradley, Catherine, and Bradley, John. *Germany: The Reunification of a Nation*. Gloucester Press, dist. by Watts, 1991. *(I)*

Epler, Doris M. *The Berlin Wall: How It Rose and Why It Fell*. Millbrook, 1992. *(I; A)*

Flint, David. *Germany*. Steck-Vaughn, 1994. *(I)*

Goldston, Robert. *Sinister Touches: The Secret War Against Hitler*. Dial, 1982. *(I; A)*
Spencer, William. *Germany Then and Now*. Watts, 1994. *(A)*

GERONIMO

Wilson, Charles M. *Geronimo*. Dillon, 1973. *(I; A)*

GERSHWIN, GEORGE. See MUSIC AND MUSICIANS.

GETTYSBURG ADDRESS. See LINCOLN, ABRAHAM.

GEYSERS AND HOT SPRINGS

Lauber, Patricia. *Tapping Earth's Heat*. Garrard, 1978. *(P; I)*

GHANA

Ghana . . . in Pictures. Lerner, 1988. *(P; I)*
Barnett, Jeanie M. *Ghana*. Chelsea House, 1988. *(I)*

GHOSTS

Cohen, Daniel. *Great Ghosts*. Dutton, 1990. *(P; I)*
Hill, Susan. *The Random House Book of Ghost Stories*. Random, 1992. (Fiction) *(I)*
Mahy, Margaret. *Dangerous Spaces*. Viking, 1991. (Fiction) *(I)*

GIOTTO DI BONDONE. See ART AND ARTISTS.

GIRAFFES

Arnold, Caroline. *Giraffe*. Morrow, 1987. *(P; I)*
Bush, John. *This Is a Book About Giraffes*. Watts, 1983. *(P)*
Lavine, Sigmund A. *Wonders of Giraffes*. Dodd, 1986. *(I; A)*
Sattler, Helen Roney. *Giraffes, the Sentinels of the Savannahs*. Lothrop, 1990. *(I)*
Torgersen, Don. *Giraffe Hooves and Antelope Horns*. Childrens, 1982. *(P; I)*

GIRL SCOUTS

Girl Scouts of the United States of America. *Daisy Low of the Girl Scouts: The Story of Juliette Gordon Low, Founder of the Girl Scouts of America*. Girl Scouts, 1975 (rev. ed.). *(I; A); Wide World of Girl Guiding and Girl Scouting*. 1980. *(P; I); Worlds to Explore for Brownie and Junior Girl Scouts*. 1977. *(P; I)*
World Association of Girl Guides and Girl Scouts. *The Story of the Four World Centres: For Girls and Leaders*. Girl Scouts, 1982 (rev. ed.). *(P; I); Trefoil Round the World*. 1978. *(P; I; A)*

GLACIER NATIONAL PARK. See NATIONAL PARK SYSTEM.

GLACIERS

Nixon, Hershell H., and Nixon, Joan L. *Glaciers: Nature's Frozen Rivers*. Dodd, 1980. *(P; I)*
Robin, Gordon De Q. *Glaciers and Ice Sheets*. Watts, 1984. *(I)*
Simon, Seymour. *Icebergs and Glaciers*. Morrow, 1987. *(P; I)*
Walker, Sally M. *Glaciers: Ice on the Move*. Carolrhoda, 1990. *(I)*

GLASS

Cackett, Susan. *Glass*. Gloucester Press, 1988. *(P; I)*
Corning Museum of Glass. *Masterpieces of Glass from the Corning Museum*. Dover, 1983. *(I; A)*
Giblin, James Cross. *Let There Be Light*. Crowell, 1988. *(A)*
Kolb, Kenneth E. and Doris K. *Glass: Its Many Facets*. Enslow, 1988. *(I; A)*
Mitgutsch, Ali. *From Sand to Glass*. Carolrhoda, 1981. *(P)*
Paterson, Alan J. *How Glass Is Made*. Facts on File, 1985. *(P;I)*

GLIDERS

Penzler, Otto. *Hang Gliding*. Troll, 1976. *(I; A)*
Schmetz, Dorothy C. *Hang Gliding*. Crestwood, 1978. *(P)*

GOLD. See METALS AND METALLURGY.

GOLD, DISCOVERIES OF

Blumberg, Rhoda. *The Great American Gold Rush*. Bradbury, 1989. *(I)*
Cooper, Michael. *Klondike Fever: The Famous Gold Rush of 1898*. Clarion, 1989. *(I; A)*
Gough, Barry. *Gold Rush!* Watts, 1983. *(I; A) (Canada)*
McCall, Edith. *Gold Rush Adventures*. Childrens, 1980. *(P; I; A)*
Stein, R. Conrad. *The Story of the Gold at Sutter's Mill*. Childrens, 1981. *(P; I)*

GOLF

Golf Digest Editors. *Better Golf*. Sportshelf, n.d. *(I; A)*
Merrins, Eddie, and McTeigue, Michael. *Golf for the Young*. Atheneum, 1983. *(I; A)*

GOODALL, JANE

Lucas, Eileen. *Jane Goodall, Friend of the Chimps*. Millbrook, 1992. *(I)*

GORBACHEV, MIKHAIL

Caulkins, Janet. *The Picture Life of Mikhail Gorbachev*. Watts, 1989 (rev. ed.). *(P)*

Oleksy, Walter. *Mikhail Gorbachev: A Leader for Soviet Change*. Childrens, 1989. *(P; I)*

Sullivan, George. *Mikhail Gorbachev*. Messner, 1988. *(I)*

GOTHIC ART AND ARCHITECTURE

Gallagher, Maureen. *The Cathedral Book*. Paulist Press, 1983. *(P; I)*

Macaulay, David. *Castle*. Houghton, 1977. *(P; I; A); Cathedral: The Story of Its Construction*. 1973. *(P; I)*

Watson, Percy. *Building the Medieval Cathedrals*. Lerner, 1978. *(I; A)*

GOYA, FRANCISCO. See ART AND ARTISTS.

GRAIN AND GRAIN PRODUCTS

Blackwood, Alan. *Grain*. (Spotlight on Resources) Rourke, 1987. *(P; I)*

Johnson, Sylvia A. *Wheat*. Lerner, 1990. *(P; I)*

Mitgutsch, Ali. *From Grain to Bread*. Carolrhoda, 1981. *(P)*

Patent, Dorothy Hinshaw. *Wheat: The Golden Harvest*. Putnam, 1987. *(P; I)*

GRANT, ULYSSES S.

Falkof, Lucille. *Ulysses S. Grant: 18th President of the United States*. Garrett Educational, 1988. *(A)*

Kent, Zachary. *Ulysses S. Grant*. Childrens, 1989. *(P; I)*

O'Brien, Steven. *Ulysses S. Grant*. Chelsea House, 1990. *(I; A)*

See also PRESIDENCY OF THE UNITED STATES.

GRAPES AND BERRIES. See FRUITGROWING.

GRAPHS

Fry, Edward B. *Graphical Comprehension: How to Read and Make Graphs*. Jamestown, 1981. *(I; A)*

Stwertka, Eve, and Stwertka, Albert. *Make It Graphic!: Drawing Graphs for Science and Social Studies Projects*. Messner, 1985. *(A)*

GRASSES

Catchpole, Clive. *Grasslands*. Dial, 1984. *(I)*

Horton, Casey. *Grasslands*. Watts, 1985. *(I)*

GRAVITY AND GRAVITATION

Branley, Franklyn M. *Gravity Is a Mystery*. Harper, 1970; *Weight and Weightlessness*. 1972. *(P)*

Cobb, Vicki. *Why Doesn't the Earth Fall Up?* Dutton, 1988. *(I)*

Haines, Gail Kay. *Which Way Is Up?* Atheneum, 1987. *(I)*

Smith, Howard E., Jr. *Balance It!* Scholastic, 1982. *(I; A)*

GREAT LAKES

Henderson, Kathy. *The Great Lakes*. Childrens, 1989. *(P)*

GREECE

Elliott, Drossoula V., and Elliott, Sloane. *We Live in Greece*. Watts, 1984. *(I; A)*

Lye, Keith. *Take a Trip to Greece*. Watts, 1983. *(P)*

Monos, Dimitris. *The Greek Americans*. Chelsea House, 1988. *(I; A)*

Stein, R. Conrad. *Greece*. Childrens, 1988, *(P; I)*

See also ANCIENT CIVILIZATIONS.

GREEK MYTHOLOGY

Billout, Guy. *Thunderbolt and Rainbow: A Look at Greek Mythology*. Prentice Hall, 1981. *(P; I)*

Colum, Padraic. *The Children's Homer: Adventures of Odysseus and the Tale of Troy*. Macmillan, 1982. *(I); Golden Fleece and the Heroes Who Lived Before Achilles*. Macmillan, 1983. *(I)*

Coolidge, Olivia. *Greek Myths*. Houghton, 1949. *(I; A)*

D'Aulaire, Ingri, and D'Aulaire, Edgar. *D'Aulaires' Book of Greek Myths*. Doubleday, 1962. *(I)*

Evslin, Bernard. *Greeks Bearing Gifts*. Four Winds, 1971. *(I)*

Fisher, Leonard Everett. *The Olympians: Great Gods and Goddesses of Ancient Greece*. Holiday, 1984. *(P; I)*

Gates, Doris. *A Fair Wind for Troy*. Viking, 1976. *(I); Mightiest of Mortals: Hercules*. Viking, 1975. *(I)*

Green, Roger L. *Tales of Greek Heroes*. Penguin, 1974. *(I)*

Homer. *The Odyssey*. Random, 1990. *(I; A); The Voyage of Odysseus*. Troll, 1984. *(P; I)*

Low, Alice. *Greek Gods and Heroes*. Macmillan, 1985. *(P)*

Wise, William. *Monster Myths of Ancient Greece*. Putnam, 1981. *(I; A)*

GREENAWAY, KATE

Greenaway, Kate. *A—Apple Pie*. Warne, 1987 (rev. ed.); *The Language of Flowers*, 1977; *Mother Goose: Or, the Old Nursery Rhymes*, 1882. *(P; I)*

GREENLAND. See DENMARK.

GRENADA. See CARIBBEAN SEA AND ISLANDS.

GRIMM, JACOB AND WILHELM

Grimm's Fairy Tales. Simon & Schuster, 1989. *(P; I)*

Grimm Brothers. *The Best of Grimms' Fairy Tales*. Larousse, 1980. *(P)*

Manheim, Ralph, ed. *Grimms' Tales for Young and Old: The Complete Stories*. Doubleday, 1977. *(P; I; A)*

GUATEMALA. See CENTRAL AMERICA.

GUIANA. See SOUTH AMERICA.

GUINEA. See AFRICA.

GUINEA PIGS, HAMSTERS, AND GERBILS

Barrie, Anmarie. *A Step-by-Step Book About Guinea Pigs; A Step-by-Step Book About Hamsters.* TFH Publications, 1988. *(I; A)*

Burton, Jane. *Dazy the Guinea Pig.* Gareth Stevens, 1989. *(P)*

Henrie, Fiona. *Gerbils.* Watts, 1980; *Guinea Pigs,* 1981; *Hamsters,* 1981. *(P; I)*

Hess, Lilo. *Making Friends with Guinea Pigs.* Scribner's, 1983. *(P; I)*

Rubins, Harriett. *Guinea Pigs: An Owner's Guide to Choosing, Raising, Breeding, and Showing.* Lothrop, 1982. *(I; A)*

GUYANA

Guyana in Pictures. Lerner, 1988. *(P; I)*

GYMNASTICS

Barrett, Norman. *Gymnastics.* Watts, 1989. *(P)*

Berke, Art. *Gymnastics.* Watts, 1988. *(P; I)*

Dolan, Edward. *The Complete Beginners Guide to Gymnastics.* Doubleday, 1980. *(I)*

Gribble, McPhee. *Body Tricks: To Teach Yourself.* Penguin, 1982. *(I; A)*

Krementz, Jill. *A Very Young Gymnast.* Knopf, 1978. *(I)*

Kuklin, Susan. *Going to My Gymnastics Class.* Bradbury, 1991. *(P)*

Murdock, Tony, and Nik, Stuart. *Gymnastics.* Watts, 1985. *(I)*

Whitlock, Steve. *Gymnastics for Girls.* Sports Illustrated for Kids, 1991. *(I; A)*

HAIR AND HAIRSTYLING

Blakely, Pat. *Why Do We Have Hair?* Creative Education, 1982. *(P; I; A)*

Bozic, Patricia, and Lee, Pola. *Cutting Hair at Home.* New American Library, 1986. *(A)*

Tether, Graham. *The Hair Book.* Random, 1979. *(P)*

HAITI

Hanmer, Trudy J. *Haiti.* Watts, 1988. *(I; A)*

Temple, Frances. *Taste of Salt.* Orchard, 1992. (Fiction) *(I; A)*

HALE, NATHAN

Poole, Susan. *Nathan Hale.* Dandelion, 1979. *(P)*

HALLOWEEN

Corwin, Judith Hoffman. *Halloween Fun.* Messner, 1983. *(I)*

Gibbons, Gail. *Halloween.* Holiday, 1984. *(P)*

Herda, D. J. *Halloween.* Watts, 1983. *(P; I)*

Hopkins, Lee Bennett, ed. *Hey-How for Halloween!* Harcourt, 1974. *(P)*

HAMILTON, ALEXANDER

Kurland, Gerald. *Alexander Hamilton: Architect of American Nationalism.* SamHar Press, 1972. *(I; A)*

HANCOCK, JOHN

Fritz, Jean. *Will You Sign Here, John Hancock?* Putnam, 1976. *(I)*

HANDWRITING

Gourdie, Tom. *Handwriting.* Merry Thoughts, n.d. *(P; I)*

Sassoon, Rosemary. *A Practical Guide to Children's Handwriting.* Thames & Hudson, 1983. *(P; I)*

Steinberg, Margery A. *Handwriting.* Putnam, 1979. *(P; I)*

HANNIBAL

Hirsh, Marilyn. *Hannibal and His 37 Elephants.* Holiday, 1977. *(P)*

HANOI. See SOUTHEAST ASIA.

HANUKKAH

Adler, David A. *Hanukkah Game Book: Games, Riddles, Puzzles, and More.* Hebrew Publishing, 1978. *(P; I); A Picture Book of Hanukkah.* Holiday, 1982. *(P)*

Aleichem, Sholem. *Hanukkah Money.* Greenwillow, 1978. *(P)*

Becker, Joyce. *Hanukkah Crafts.* Hebrew Publishing, 1978. *(P; I)*

Behrens, June. *Hanukkah.* Childrens, 1983. *(P; I)*

Chaikin, Miriam. *Light Another Candle: The Story and Meaning of Hanukkah.* Houghton, 1981. *(P; I)*

Drucker, Malka. *Hanukkah: Eight Nights, Eight Lights.* Holiday, 1980. *(I; A)*

Hirsh, Marilyn. *The Hanukkah Story.* Hebrew Publishing, 1977. *(P; I); I Love Hanukkah,* Holiday, 1984. *(P)*

Levoy, Myron. *The Hanukkah of Great-Uncle Otto.* Jewish Publication Society, 1984. *(P)*

Singer, Isaac B. *The Power of Light: Eight Stories for Hanukkah.* Farrar, 1980. *(P; I; A)*

HARDING, WARREN G.

Wade, Linda R. *Warren G. Harding.* Childrens, 1989. *(P; I)*

HARP. See MUSICAL INSTRUMENTS.

HARRISON, BENJAMIN. See PRESIDENCY OF THE UNITED STATES.

HARRISON, WILLIAM HENRY

Fitz-Gerald, Christine Maloney. *William Henry Harrison.* Childrens, 1988. *(P; I)*
See also PRESIDENCY OF THE UNITED STATES.

HAWAII

Bauer, Helen. *Hawaii: The Aloha State.* Bess Press, 1982 (new ed.). *(I)*
Dunford, Elizabeth P. *The Hawaiians of Old.* Bess Press, 1980. *(P; I)*
Fradin, Dennis. *Hawaii: In Words and Pictures.* Childrens, 1980. *(P; I)*
Jacobsen, Peter O., and Kristensen, Preben S. *A Family in Hawaii.* Bookwright, 1987. *(P)*
Potter, Norris, and Kasdon, Lawrence. *The Hawaiian Monarchy.* Bess Press, 1982. *(I)*
Rizzuto, Shirley O. *Hawaii's Pathfinders.* Bess Press, 1983. *(I)*
Rublowsky, John. *Born in Fire: A Geological History of Hawaii.* Harper, 1981. *(I)*
Stanley, Fay. *The Last Princess: The Story of Princess Ka'iulani of Hawai'i.* Four Winds, 1991. *(P; I)*
Williams, Jay. *The Surprising Things Maui Did.* Scholastic, 1979. *(P)*

HAWTHORNE, NATHANIEL

Gaeddert, LouAnn. *A New England Love Story: Nathaniel Hawthorne and Sophia Peabody.* Dial, 1980. *(I; A)*
Wood, James P. *Unpardonable Sin: A Life of Nathaniel Hawthorne.* Pantheon, 1970. *(I; A)*
See also UNITED STATES (ART, LITERATURE, AND MUSIC).

HAYDN, JOSEPH. See MUSIC AND MUSICIANS.

HAYES, RUTHERFORD B.

Kent, Zachary. *Rutherford B. Hayes.* Childrens, 1989. *(P; I)*.

HAZARDOUS WASTES. See POLLUTION.

HEALTH AND PHYSICAL FITNESS

Berger, Melvin. *Ouch! A Book About Cuts, Scratches, and Scrapes.* Lodestar, 1991. *(P)*
Feder, R. F., and Taylor, G. J. *Junior Body Building.* Sterling, 1982. *(I; A)*
Heron, Jackie. *Careers in Health and Fitness.* Rosen, 1988. *(A)*
Lindquist, Marie. *Body Makeovers.* Pinnacle, 1985. *(A)*
Lyttle, Richard B. *The New Physical Fitness: Something for Everyone.* Watts, 1981. *(I; A)*
Trier, Carola S. *Exercise: What It Is, What It Does.* Greenwillow, 1982. *(P)*
Ward, Brian. *Health and Hygiene.* Watts, 1988. *(I)*

HEALTH FOODS. See NUTRITION.

HEART

Gaskin, John. *The Heart.* Watts, 1985. *(P; I)*
McGowan, Tom. *The Circulatory System: From Harvey to the Artificial Heart.* Watts, 1988. *(I)*
Silverstein, Alvin, and Silverstein, Virginia B. *Heartbeats: Your Body, Your Heart.* Harper, 1983. *(I); Heart Disease: America's #1 Killer.* Lippincott, 1985. *(A)*
Ward, Brian. *The Heart and Blood.* Watts, 1982. *(I)*

HEAT

Ardley, Neil. *Hot and Cold.* Watts, 1983. *(P)*
Darling, David. *Between Fire and Ice: The Science of Heat.* Dillon, 1992. *(I)*
Santrey, Laurence. *Heat.* Troll, 1985. *(I)*
Whyman, Kathryn. *Heat and Energy.* Gloucester Press, 1986. *(I)*

HELICOPTERS

Berliner, Don. *Helicopters.* Lerner, 1983. *(I; A)*
Delear, Frank J. *Airplanes and Helicopters of the U.S. Navy.* Dodd, 1982. *(I; A)*
Petersen, David. *Helicopters.* Childrens, 1983. *(P)*
White, David. *Helicopters.* Rourke, 1988. *(P)*

HENRY, PATRICK

Fritz, Jean. *Where Was Patrick Henry on the 29th of May?* Putnam, 1975. *(P; I)*
Reische, Diana. *Patrick Henry.* Watts, 1987. *(P)*
Sabin, Louis. *Patrick Henry: Voice of the American Revolution.* Troll, 1982. *(P; I)*

HERALDRY. See MIDDLE AGES.

HERBS, SPICES, AND CONDIMENTS

Barker, Albert. *The Spice Adventure.* Messner, 1980. *(P; I)*
Gabriel, Ingrid. *Herb Identifier and Handbook.* Sterling, 1975. *(I; A)*

HEREDITY. See GENETICS AND GENETIC ENGINEERING.

HIBERNATION

Brimner, Larry Dane. *Animals That Hibernate.* Watts, 1991. *(P; I)*
Busch, Phyllis. *The Seven Sleepers: The Story of Hibernation.* Macmillan, 1985. *(I)*
Facklam, Margery. *Do Not Disturb: The Mysteries of Animal Hibernation and Sleep.* Sierra Club Books, 1989. *(P; I)*
Ward, Andrew. *Baby Bear and the Long Sleep.* Little, 1980. *(P)*

HIKING AND BACKPACKING

Larson, Randy. *Illustrated Backpacking and Hiking Dictionary for Young People.* Prentice Hall, 1981. *(P; I; A)*

Peterson, P. J. *Nobody Else Can Walk It for You.* Delacorte, 1982. *(I; A)*

Randolph, John. *Backpacking Basics.* Prentice Hall, 1982. *(P; I)*

Thomas, Art. *Backpacking Is for Me.* Lerner, 1980. *(P; I)*

HIMALAYAS. See ASIA; INDIA; MOUNTAINS AND MOUNTAIN CLIMBING.

HINDUISM. See RELIGIONS OF THE WORLD.

HIPPOPOTAMUSES

Arnold, Caroline. *Hippo.* Morrow, 1989. *(P; I)*

HISPANIC AMERICANS

Catalano, Julie. *The Mexican Americans.* Chelsea House, 1988. *(P; I)*

Larsen, Ronald J. *The Puerto Ricans in America.* Lerner, 1989. *(I)*

Maynes, J. O. Hispanic Heroes of the U.S.A. (English version, 4 bks.): Bk. 1, *Raul H. Castro, Tony Nunez, and Vikki Carr;* Bk. 2, *Henry Gonzalez, Trini Lopez, and Edward Roybal;* Bk. 3, *Carmen R. Maymi, Roberto Clemente, and Jose Feliciano;* Bk. 4, *Tony Perez, Lee Trevino, and Jim Plunkett.* EMC Publishing, 1975. *(P; I; A)*

Meltzer, Milton. *The Hispanic Americans.* Harper, 1982. *(I; A)*

Morey, Janet, and Dunn, Wendy. *Famous Mexican Americans.* Cobblehill, 1989. *(I)*

Pinchot, Jane. *The Mexicans in America.* Lerner, 1989. *(I)*

Raintree Hispanic Stories. (Written in both English and Spanish) *Simon Bolivar; Hernando De Soto; David Farragut; Miguel Hildago Y Costilla; Jose Marti; Luis Munoz Marin; Diego Rivera; Junipero Serra; Luis W. Alvarez; Juana Ines De La Cruz; Carlos Finlay; Bernardo De Galvez; Queen Isabella I; Benito Juarez; Vilma Martinez; Pedro Menendez De Aviles.* Raintree, 1989–90. *(P; I)*

HISTORY

Chisholm. *First Guide to History.* EDC Publishing, 1983. *(I; A)*

Foster, Genevieve. *Birthdays of Freedom: From Early Egypt to July 4, 1776.* Scribner's, 1974. *(I)*

Van Loon, Hendrik W. *The Story of Mankind.* Liveright, 1972. *(A)*

HITLER, ADOLF

Dolan, Edward F., Jr. *Adolph Hitler: A Portrait in Tyranny.* Dodd, 1981. *(I; A)*

Gray, Ronald. *Hitler and the Germans.* Lerner, 1983. *(I; A)*

HOBBIES

Bottomly, Jim. *Paper Projects for Creative Kids of All Ages.* Little, 1983. *(P; I; A)*

Churchill, E. Richard. *Building with Paper.* Sterling, 1990. *(I)*

Fletcher, Helen. *Carton Crafts.* Lion, 1981. *(P; I)*

Greene, Peggy R. *Things to Make.* Random, 1981. *(P)*

Jackson, Paul. *Festive Folding: Decorative Origami for Parties and Celebrations.* North Light Books, 1991. *(P; I)*

Lewis, Shari. *The Do-It-Better Book; Things Kids Collect.* Holt, 1981. *(P; I)*

Lohf, Sabine. *Nature Crafts.* Childrens, 1990. *(P; I)*

McGill, Ormond. *Paper Magic: Creating Fantasies and Performing Tricks with Paper.* Millbrook, 1992. *(P; I)*

Scarry, Richard. *Richard Scarry's Best Make-It Book Ever.* Random, 1977. *(P)*

Schulz, Charles M. *Charlie Brown's Super Book of Things to Do and Collect.* Random, 1975. *(P; I)*

Supraner, Robyn. *Fun-to-Make Nature Crafts.* Troll, 1981. *(P; I)*

Volpe, Nancee. *Good Apple and Seasonal Arts and Crafts.* Good Apple, 1982. *(P; I)*

HO CHI MINH CITY (SAIGON). See SOUTHEAST ASIA.

HOCKEY. See FIELD HOCKEY; ICE HOCKEY.

HOISTING AND LOADING MACHINERY. See TECHNOLOGY.

HOLIDAYS

Behrens, June. *Gung Hay Fat Choy: Happy New Year.* Childrens, 1982. *(P)*

Berger, Gilda. *Easter and Other Spring Holidays.* Watts, 1983. *(I)*

Brown, Marc. *Arthur's April Fool.* Little, 1983. (Fiction) *(P); Arthur's Valentine.* Little, 1980. (Fiction) *(P)*

Cheng, Hou-Tien. *The Chinese New Year.* Holt, 1976. *(P)*

Chocolate, Deborah M. Newton. *Kwanzaa.* Childrens, 1990. *(P; I)*

Dickens, Charles. *A Christmas Carol.* Holiday, 1983 (1843). (Fiction) *(I; A)*

Grigoli, Valorie. *Patriotic Holidays and Celebrations.* Watts, 1985. *(P; I)*

Hautzig, Esther. *Make It Special: Cards, Decorations, and Party Favors for Holidays and Other Celebrations.* Macmillan, 1986. *(P)*

Hopkins, Lee Bennett. *Beat the Drum, Independence Day Has Come.* Harcourt, 1977. *(P)*

Keller, Holly. *Harry's Fourth of July*. Greenwillow, 1985. (Fiction) *(P)*

Livingston, Myra Cohn. *Celebrations*. Holiday, 1985. *(I; A)*

Nordqvist, Sven. *Merry Christmas, Festus and Mercury*. Carolrhoda, 1989. (Fiction) *(P)*

Perl, Lila, and Ada, Alma F. *Pinatas and Paper Flowers (Pinatas y Flores de Papel): Holidays of the Americas in English and Spanish*. Houghton, 1983. *(P; I)*

Pienkowski, Jan. *Christmas*. Knopf, 1991. *(P; I)*

Pinkney, Andrea Davis. *Seven Candles for Kwanzaa*. Dial, 1993. *(P)*

Quackenbush, Robert, ed. *The Holiday Song Book*. Lothrop, 1977. *(I)*

Rosen, Mike. *Autumn Festivals*. Bookwright, 1990. *(I)*; *Winter Festivals*. Bookwright, 1990. *(I)*

Scott, Geoffrey. *Memorial Day*. Carolrhoda, 1983. *(P)*

Van Allsburg, Chris. *The Polar Express*. Houghton, 1985. (Fiction) *(P)*

Van Straalen, Alice. *The Book of Holidays Around The World*. Dutton, 1987. *(A)*

Wells, Rosemary. *Max's Chocolate Chicken*. Dial, 1989. (Fiction) *(P)*

Zalben, Jane B. *Happy Passover, Rosie*. Holt, 1990. *(P)*

See also DECLARATION OF INDEPENDENCE (Fourth of July holiday) and names of other well-known holidays.

HOLLAND. See NETHERLANDS.

HOLOCAUST

Abells, Chana Byers. *The Childen We Remember*. Greenwillow, 1986. *(I)*

Bernbaum, Israel. *My Brother's Keeper*. Putnam, 1985. *(I; A)*

Chaikin, Miriam. *A Nightmare in History: The Holocaust*. Clarion, 1987. *(P; I)*

Finkelstein, Norman H. *Remember Not to Forget: A Memory of the Holocaust*. Watts, 1985. *(P)*

Frank, Anne. *Anne Frank: Diary of a Young Girl*. Doubleday, 1967. *(I; A)*

Friedman, Ina R. *The Other Victims: First Person Stories of Non-Jews Persecuted by the Nazis*. Houghton, 1990. *(I)*

Games, Sonia. *Escape into Darkness*. Shapolsky, 1991. *(A)*

Greenfield, Howard. *The Hidden Children*. Ticknor & Fields, 1993. *(I)*

Handler, Andrew, and Meschel, Susan V., comp. and ed. *Young People Speak: Surviving the Holocaust in Hungary*. Watts, 1993. *(A)*

Meltzer, Milton. *Never to Forget: The Jews of the Holocaust*. Harper, 1976. *(I; A)*

Orlev, Uri. *The Island on Bird Street*, tr. by Hillel Halkin. Houghton, 1984. *(I)*

Patterson, Charles. *Anti-Semitism: The Road to the Holocaust and Beyond*. Walker, 1982. *(I; A)*

Rogasky, Barbara. *Smoke and Ashes: The Story of the Holocaust*. Holiday, 1988. *(A)*

Rossel, Seymour. *The Holocaust: The Fire that Raged*. Watts, 1989. *(I; A)*

Toll, Nelly S. *Behind the Secret Window: A Memoir of a Hidden Childhood During World War Two*. Dial, 1993. *(I; A)*

Wild, Margaret. *Let the Celebrations Begin!* Orchard Books, 1991. (Fiction) *(I)*

HOMER, WINSLOW

Goldstein, Ernest. *Winslow Homer: The Gulf Stream*. New American Library, 1983. *(I; A)*

Hyman, Linda. *Winslow Homer: America's Old Master*. Doubleday, 1973. *(I; A)*

HOMES. See ARCHITECTURE; BUILDING CONSTRUCTION.

HOMING AND MIGRATION. See BIRDS.

HONDURAS. See CENTRAL AMERICA.

HONG KONG

Fairclough, Chris. *We Live in Hong Kong*. Bookwright, 1986. *(P; I)*

Lye, Keith. *Take a Trip to Hong Kong*. Watts, 1984. *(P; I)*

McKenna, Nancy Durrell. *A Family in Hong Kong*. Lerner, 1987. *(P)*

HOOVER, HERBERT

Clinton, Susan. *Herbert Hoover; Thirty-first President of the United States*. Childrens, 1988. *(P; I)*

See also PRESIDENCY OF THE UNITED STATES.

HORSEBACK RIDING

Dumas, Philippe. *The Lippizaners: And the Spanish Riding School*. Prentice Hall, 1981. *(P; I)*

Haney, Lynn. *Show Rider*. Putnam, 1982. *(I; A)*

Krementz, Jill. *A Very Young Rider*. Knopf, 1977. *(I)*

Reimer, Dianne, and Lee, Carol. *Horsebackriding Basics*. Prentice Hall, 1980. *(I; A)*

Rodenas, Paula. *The Random House Book of Horses and Horsemanship*. Random, 1991. *(I; A)*

Van Steenwyck, Elizabeth. *Illustrated Riding Dictionary for Young People*. Harvey, 1981. *(I; A)*

Wheatley, George. *The Young Rider's Companion*. Lerner, 1981. *(P; I)*

HORSES AND THEIR RELATIVES

Clutton-Brock, Juliet. *Horse*. Knopf, 1992. *(I; A)*

Cole, Joanna. *A Horse's Body*. Morrow, 1981. *(P)*

Freedman, Russell. *Getting Born*. Holiday, 1978. *(I)*

Lavine, Sigmund A., and Casey, Brigid. *Wonders of Draft Horses*. Dodd, 1983. *(P; I)*

Lavine, Sigmund A. and Scuro, Vincent. *Wonders of Donkeys*. Dodd, 1979; *Wonders of Mules*. 1982. *(P; I)*

Patent, Dorothy. *Arabian Horses*. Holiday, 1982; *Horses and Their Wild Relatives*, 1981; *Horses of America*, 1981; *Picture Book of Ponies*, 1983. *(P; I); Thoroughbred Horses*, 1985. *(A)*

Philp, Candace T. *Rodeo Horses*. Crestwood, 1983. *(P; I)*

Popescu, Charlotte. *Horses at Work*. David & Charles, 1983. *(P)*

Shub, Elizabeth. *The White Stallion*. Bantam, 1982. (Fiction) *(P)*

HOSPITALS

Elliott, Ingrid G. *Hospital Roadmap: A Book to Help Explain the Hospital Experience to Young Children*. Resources for Children in Hospitals, 1982. *(P)*

Holmes, Burnham. *Early Morning Rounds: A Portrait of a Hospital*. Scholastic, 1981. *(I; A)*

Howe, James. *The Hospital Book*. Crown, 1981. *(P)*

Rockwell, Anne F. *Emergency Room*. Macmillan, 1985. *(P)*

Rogers, Fred. *Going to the Hospital*. Putnam, 1988. *(P)*

Wolfe, Bob, and Wolfe, Diane. *Emergency Room*. Carolrhoda, 1983. *(I)*

HOUSEPLANTS. See PLANTS.

HOUSTON, SAMUEL. See MEXICAN WAR; TEXAS.

HUDSON, HENRY

Harley, Ruth. *Henry Hudson*. Troll, 1979 (new ed.). *(P; I)*

HUGHES, LANGSTON

Hughes, Langston. *Don't You Turn Back: Poems Selected by Lee Bennett Hopkins*. Knopf, 1969. *(P; I); Selected Poems of Langston Hughes*. Knopf, 1926, 1943. *(I; A)*

Larson, Norita D. *Langston Hughes, Poet of Harlem*. Creative Education, 1981. *(I; A)*

Walker, Alice. *Langston Hughes, American Poet*. Harper, 1974. *(P; I)*

HUMOR

Allard, Harry, and Marshall, James. *Miss Nelson Is Missing*. Houghton, 1977. (Fiction) *(P)*

Blume, Judy. *Otherwise Known as Sheila the Great*. Dutton, 1972. (Fiction) *(P; I); Tales of a Fourth Grade Nothing*. Dutton, 1972. (Fiction) *(P; I)*

Bond, Michael. *A Bear Called Paddington*. Houghton, 1960. (Fiction) *(P; I)*

Cameron, Ann. *More Stories Julian Tells*. Knopf, 1986. (Fiction) *(P; I)*

Ciardi, John. *Fast and Slow: Poems for Advanced Children and Beginning Parents*. Houghton, 1978. *(P)*

Cole, Joanna, and Calmenson, Stephanie. *The Laugh Book*. Doubleday, 1987. *(I; A)*

Corbett, Scott. *Jokes to Tell Your Worst Enemy*. Dutton, 1984. *(P; I)*

DeRegniers, Beatrice Schenk. *May I Bring a Friend?* Atheneum, 1964. (Fiction) *(P)*

Fleischman, Albert Sidney. *McBroom's Almanac*. Little, 1984. *(P; I)*

Hurwitz, Johanna. *The Hot and Cold Summer*. Scholastic, 1984. (Fiction) *(P; I)*

Klein, Norma. *The Cheerleader*. Juniper, 1985. (Fiction) *(I; A)*

Korman, Gordon. *Son of Interflux*. Scholastic, 1986. (Fiction) *(I; A)*

Lear, Edward. *Complete Nonsense Book*. Dodd, n. d. *(P; I)*

Leonard, Marcia, and Cricket Magazine Editors. *Cricket's Jokes, Riddles, and Other Stuff*. Random, 1977. *(P; I)*

Lobel, Arnold. *Fables*. Harper, 1980. (Fiction) *(P)*

Maestro, Giulio. *A Raft of Riddles*. Dutton, 1982. *(P; I); Riddle Romp*. Houghton, 1983. *(P)*

McCloskey, Robert. *Homer Price*. Viking, 1968. (Fiction) *(P; I)*

Park, Barbara. *Beanpole*. Knopf, 1983. (Fiction) *(I; A)*

Prelutsky, Jack, sel. *For Laughing Out Loud: Poems to Tickle Your Funnybone*. Knopf, 1991. *(P; I)*

Schwartz, Alvin. *Flapdoodle: Pure Nonsense from American Folklore*. Harper, 1980. *(I; A); Unriddling: All Sorts of Riddles to Puzzle Your Guessery*, 1983. *(P; I)*

Walton, Rick, and Walton, Ann. *Fossil Follies! Jokes About Dinosaurs*. Lerner, 1989. *(P)*

Ward, Lynd. *The Biggest Bear*. Houghton, 1980 (1952). (Fiction) *(P)*

Wood, Audrey, and Wood, Don. *The Napping House*. Harcourt, 1984. (Fiction) *(P)*

HUNGARY

Esbenshade, Richard S. *Hungary*. Marshall Cavendish, 1994. *(I; A)*

Hintz, Martin. *Hungary*. Childrens, 1988. *(I)*

Siegal, Aranka. *Upon the Head of a Goat: A Childhood in Hungary*. Farrar, 1981. *(I; A)*

St. John, Jetty. *A Family in Hungary*. Lerner, 1988. *(P)*

HURRICANES

Alth, Max, and Alth, Charlotte. *Disastrous Hurricanes and Tornadoes*. Watts, 1981. *(P; I)*

Fradin, Dennis Brindel. *Disaster! Hurricanes*. Childrens, 1982. *(I)*

McNulty, Faith. *Hurricane*. Harper, 1983. *(P; I)*

Simon, Seymour. *Storms*. Morrow, 1989. *(P)*

HYMNS AND SPIRITUALS

Bryan, Ashley. *I'm Going to Sing: Black American Spirituals,* Vol II. Atheneum, 1982; *Walk Together, Children.* 1974. *(P; I)*

Konkel, Wilbur. *Living Hymn Stories.* Bethany, 1982. *(P; I)*

Krull, Kathleen, collector and arranger. *Songs of Praise.* Harcourt, 1988. *(P)*

HYPNOSIS

Kirby, Vivian. *Hypnotism: Hocus Pocus or Science?* Messner, 1985. *(I; A)*

ICE AGES

Cole, Joanna. *Saber-Toothed Tiger and Other Ice-Age Mammals.* Enslow, 1981. *(P; I)*

Fodor, R. V. *Frozen Earth: Explaining the Ice Ages.* Enslow, 1981. *(I; A)*

ICEBERGS

Greenberg, Jan. *The Iceberg and Its Shadow.* Dell, 1982. *(I; A)*

Robin, Gordon De Q. *Glaciers and Ice Sheets.* Watts, 1984. *(I)*

Simon, Seymour. *Icebergs and Glaciers.* Morrow, 1987. *(P; I)*

ICE CREAM

Jaspersohn, William. *Ice Cream.* Macmillan, 1988. *(P)*

ICE HOCKEY

Aaseng, Nathan. *Hockey's Fearless Goalies; Hockey's Super Scores.* Lerner, 1983. *(P; I)*

MacLean, Norman. *Hockey Basics.* Prentice Hall, 1983. *(P; I)*

Olney, Ross R. *Winners! Super-Champions of Ice Hockey.* Houghton, 1982. *(I; A)*

Paulsen, Gary. *Facing Off, Checking, and Goaltending—Perhaps.* Raintree, 1979. *(P; I)*

ICELAND

Lepthien, Emilie U. *Iceland (Enchantment of the World).* Childrens, 1987. *(P; I)*

ICE-SKATING

Fox, Mary V. *The Skating Heidens.* Enslow, 1981. *(I; A)*

Haney, Lynn. *Skaters: Profile of a Pair.* Putnam, 1983. *(I; A)*

Kalb, Jonah, and Kalb, Laura. *The Easy Ice Skating Book.* Houghton, 1981. *(P; I)*

Krementz, Jill. *A Very Young Skater.* Knopf, 1979. *(P; I)*

MacLean, Norman. *Ice Skating Basics.* Prentice Hall, 1984. *(P; I)*

Ryan, Margaret. *Figure Skating.* Watts, 1987. *(P)*

Wood, Tim. *Ice Skating.* Watts, 1990. *(P; I)*

IDAHO

Fradin, Dennis. *Idaho: In Words and Pictures.* Childrens, 1980. *(P; I)*

Kent, Zachary. *Idaho.* Childrens, 1990. *(I; A)*

ILIAD

Homer. *The Iliad.* Norton, 1958. *(I; A)*

Picard, Barbara L., ed. *The Iliad of Homer.* Oxford University Press, 1980. *(I)*

ILLINOIS

Carter, Alden R. *Illinois.* Watts, 1987. *(P; I)*

Pfeiffer, Christine. *Chicago.* Dillon, 1989. *(P; I)*

Sandburg, Carl. "Chicago" from *Chicago Poems.* Buccaneer, 1986. *(I; A)*

IMAGINATION*

Barrett, Judi. *Cloudy with a Chance of Meatballs.* Atheneum, 1978. (Fiction) *(P)*

Barrie, J. M. *Peter Pan.* Holt, 1987 (1904). (Fiction) *(P; I)*

Jonas, Ann. *Round Trip.* Greenwillow, 1983. (Fiction) *(P)*

Ness, Evaline. *Sam, Bangs and Moonshine.* Holt, 1966. (Fiction) *(P)*

Sendak, Maurice. *Where the Wild Things Are.* Harper, 1963. (Fiction) *(P)*

Van Allsburg, Chris. *Jumanji.* Houghton, 1981. (Fiction) *(P; I)*

IMMIGRATION

Anderson, Kelly C. *Immigration.* Lucent, 1993. *(I; A)*

Ashabranner, Brent. *Still a Nation of Immigrants.* Cobblehill: Dutton, 1993. *(I; A)*

Blumenthal, Shirley. *Coming to America: Immigrants from Eastern Europe.* Delacorte, 1981. *(I; A)*

Bohner, Charles. *Bold Journey.* Houghton, 1985. *(I)*

Bouvier, Leon F. *Immigration: Diversity in the U.S.* Walker, 1988. *(A)*

Bunting, Eve. *How Many Days to America?* Clarion, 1988. (Fiction) *(P)*

Caroli, Betty Boyd. *Immigrants Who Returned Home.* Chelsea House, 1990. *(A)*

Dixon, Edward H., and Galan, Mark A. *The Immigration and Naturalization Service.* Chelsea House, 1990. *(I; A)*

Dudley, William, ed. *Immigration.* Greenhaven, 1990. *(I; A)*

Fisher, Leonard. *Ellis Island: Gateway to the New World.* Holiday, 1986. *(I)*

Garver, Susan, and McGuire, Paula. *Coming to North America: From Mexico, Cuba, and Puerto Rico.* Delacorte, 1981. *(I; A)*

*This is a popular theme with young readers. However, it is not a separate article in *The New Book of Knowledge.*

Hoobler, Dorothy, and Hoobler, Thomas. *The Chinese American Family Album*. Oxford University Press, 1994. *(I; A)*

Kennedy, John F. *A Nation of Immigrants*. Harper, 1964 (rev. ed.). *(A)*

Kurelek, William. *They Sought a New World: The Story of European Immigration to North America*. Tundra Books, 1985. *(I; A)*

Mayerson, Evelyn Wilde. *The Cat Who Escaped from Steerage*. Scribner's, 1990. (Fiction) *(P; I)*

Meltzer, Milton. *The Chinese Americans*. Crowell, 1980. *(I; A)*

Perrin, Linda. *Coming to America: Immigrants from the Far East*. Delacorte, 1980. *(A)*

Reimers, David M. *The Immigrant Experience*. Chelsea House, 1989. *(I; A)*

Rips, Gladys N. *Coming to America: Immigrants from Southern Europe*. Dell, 1981. *(A)*

Robbins, Albert. *Coming to America: Immigrants from Northern Europe*. Dell, 1982. *(A)*

Sandin, Joan. *The Long Way to a New Land*. Harper, 1981. (Fiction) *(P)*

INCOME TAX. See TAXATION.

INDIA

India . . . in Pictures. Lerner, 1989. *(I)*

Jacobsen, Peter O., and Kristensen, Preben S. *A Family in India*. Watts, 1984. *(P; I)*

Karan, P. P., ed. *India*. Gateway Press, 1988. *(I; A)*

Lamb, Harold. *Babur the Tiger: First of the Great Moguls*. Doubleday, 1961. *(I)*

Lye, Keith. *Take a Trip to India*. Watts, 1982. *(P)*

McNair, Sylvia. *India*. Childrens, 1990. *(I)*

Ogle, Carol, and Ogle, John. *Through the Year in India*. David & Charles, 1983. *(I; A)*

Sandal, Veenu. *We Live in India*. Watts, 1984. *(I)*

Sarin, Amitra Vohra. *India: An Ancient Land, a New Nation*. Dillon, 1984. *(I)*

Tames, Richard. *India and Pakistan in the Twentieth Century*. David & Charles, 1981. *(I; A)*

Tigwell, Tony. *A Family in India*. Lerner, 1985. *(P)*

Traub, James. *India: The Challenge of Change*. Messner, 1985 (rev. ed.). *(I; A)*

INDIANA

Carpenter, Allan. *Indiana*. Childrens, 1979. *(I)*

Fradin, Dennis. *Indiana: In Words and Pictures*. Childrens, 1980. *(P; I)*

INDIANS, AMERICAN

Ancona, George. *Powwow*. Harcourt, 1993. *(P; I)*

Ashabranner, Brent. *To Live in Two Worlds: American Indian Youth Today*. Dodd, 1984. *(I; A)*

Avery, Susan, and Skinner, Linda. *Extraordinary American Indians*. Childrens, 1992. *(I; A)*

Ayer, Eleanor H. *The Anasazi*. Walker, 1993. *(I)*

Banks, Lynne Reid. *The Indian in the Cupboard*. Doubleday, 1980. (Fiction) *(P; I)*

Beck, Barbara L. *The Ancient Mayas; The Incas*, both books rev. by Lorna Greenberg. Watts, 1983. *(I; A); The Aztecs*, rev. by Lorna Greenberg. Watts, 1983. *(I)*

Bierhorst, John. *Doctor Coyote: A Native American Aesop's Fables*. Macmillan, 1987. *(I); The Woman Who Fell from the Sky*. Morrow, 1993. *(P; I)*

Bierhorst, John, ed. *The Girl Who Married a Ghost and Other Tales from the North American Indians*. Scholastic, 1978. *(I; A); The Hungry Woman: Myths and Legends of the Aztecs*. Morrow, 1984. *(I; A); The Mythology of Mexico and Central America*. Morrow, 1990. *(A); Sacred Paths: Spells, Prayers and Power Songs of the American Indians*. Morrow, 1983. *(I; A)*

Blood, Charles. *American Indian Games and Crafts*. Watts, 1981. *(P)*

Bruchac, Joseph. *Stone Giants and Flying Heads: Adventure Stories of the Iroquois*. Crossing Press, 1979. *(I)*

Connolly, James. *Why the Possum's Tail is Bare and Other North American Indian Native Tales*. Stemmer House, 1985. *(P)*

Courlander, Harold. *People of the Short Blue Corn: Tales and Legends of the Hopi Indians*. Harcourt, 1970. *(I)*

Cwiklik, Robert. *Sequoyah and the Cherokee Alphabet*. Silver Burdett, 1989. *(I)*

DeArmond, Dale. *Berry Woman's Children*. Greenwillow, 1985. *(P)*

DePaola, Tomie. *The Legend of the Bluebonnet: An Old Tale of Texas*. Putnam, 1983. *(P); The Legend of the Indian Paintbrush*. Putnam, 1988. *(P)*

Fixico, Donald L. *Urban Indians*. Chelsea House, 1991. *(I; A)*

Freedman, Russell. *An Indian Winter*. Holiday, 1992. *(A); Indian Chiefs*. Holiday, 1987. *(I; A)*

Garbarino, Merwyn S. *The Seminole*. Chelsea House, 1988. *(A)*

Gardiner, John R. *Stone Fox*. Crowell, 1980. (Fiction) *(P; I)*

George, Jean Craighead. *Water Sky*. Harper, 1987. (Fiction) *(I; A)*

Glassman, Bruce. *Wilma Mankiller: Chief of the Cherokee Nation*. Blackbirch Press: Rosen, 1992. *(I)*

Goble, Paul. *Beyond the Ridge*. Bradbury, 1990. *(I; A); Buffalo Woman*. Bradbury, 1984. *(P); Her Seven Brothers*. Bradbury, 1988. *(P; I); Iktomi and the Boulder: A Plains Indian Story*. Orchard Press, 1988. *(P)*

Graymont, Barbara. *The Iroquois*. Chelsea House, 1988. *(A)*

Green, Rayna. *Women in American Indian Society*. Chelsea House, 1992. *(I; A)*

Highwater, Jamake. *Eyes of Darkness*. Lothrop, 1985. *(I; A)*

Hirschfelder, Arlene. *Happily May I Walk: American In-*

dians and Alaska Natives Today. Scribner's, 1986. *(I; A)*

Hirschfelder, Arlene B., and Singer, Beverly R., eds. *Rising Voices: Writings of Young Native Americans.* Scribner's, 1992. *(I; A)*

Hoyt-Goldsmith, Diane. *Totem Pole.* Holiday, 1990. *(P)*

Jacobson, Daniel. *Indians of North America.* Watts, 1983. *(I; A)*

Jones, Jayne Clark. *The American Indians in America.* Lerner, 1991. *(I; A)*

Keegan, Marcia. *Pueblo Boy: Growing Up in Two Worlds.* Cobblehill, 1991. *(P; I)*

Kelly, Lawrence C. *Federal Indian Policy.* Chelsea House, 1989. *(I; A)*

Koslow, Philip. *The Seminole Indians.* Chelsea, 1994. *(I)*

Levitt, Paul, and Guralnick, Elissa. *The Stolen Appaloosa and Other Indian Stories.* Bookmakers Guild, 1988. *(P)*

McClard, Megan, and Ypsilantis, George. *Hiawatha and the Iroquois League.* Silver Burdett, 1989. *(I)*

McDermott, Gerald. *Arrow to the Sun: A Pueblo Indian Tale.* Viking, 1974. *(P)*

Millard, Anne. *The Incas.* Warwick, 1980. *(I)*

Monroe, Jean Guard, and Williamson, Ray A. *First Houses: Native American Homes and Sacred Structures.* Houghton, 1993. *(I; A)*

Morris, Neil, and Morris, Ting. *Featherboy and the Buffalo.* Hodder & Stoughton, 1984. (Fiction) *(P)*

O'Dell, Scott. *Sing Down the Moon.* Houghton, 1970. (Fiction) *(P; I); Streams to the River, River to the Sea: Novel of Sacajawea.* Houghton, 1986. (Fiction) *(I)*

Osinski, Alice. *The Sioux.* Childrens, 1984. *(P)*

Parish, Peggy. *Good Hunting, Blue Sky.* Harper, 1988. (Fiction) *(P)*

Paterson, E. Palmer. *Indian Peoples of Canada.* Watts, 1982. *(I; A)*

Poatgieter, Hermina. *Indian Legacy: Native American Influences on World Life and Culture.* Messner, 1981. *(I; A)*

Robinson, Gail. *Raven the Trickster: Legends of North American Indians.* Atheneum, 1982. *(I)*

Ruoff, A. Lavonne Brown. *Literature of the American Indian.* Chelsea House, 1991. (Fiction) *(I; A)*

Sewall, Marcia. *People of the Breaking Day.* Atheneum, 1990. *(P)*

Seymour, Tryntje Van Ness. *The Gift of Changing Woman.* Holt, 1993. *(I; A)*

Shorto, Russell. *Tecumseh and the Dream of an American Indian Nation.* Silver Burdett, 1989. *(I)*

Sneve, Virginia Driving Hawk. *Dancing Teepees: Poems of American Indian Youth.* Holiday, 1989. *(P; I; A)*

Speare, Elizabeth George. *The Sign of the Beaver.* Houghton, 1983. (Fiction) *(P; I)*

Steptoe, John. *Story of Jumpimg Mouse: A Native American Legend.* Lothrop, 1984. *(P; I)*

Weinstein-Farson, Laurie. *The Wampanoag.* Chelsea House, 1988. *(A)*

Weiss, Malcolm E. *Sky Watchers of Ages Past.* Houghton, 1982. *(I; A)*

Wheeler, M. J. *First Came the Indians.* Atheneum, 1983. *(P; I)*

Wilson, Terry P. *The Osage.* Chelsea House, 1988. *(A)*

Wood, Ted, and Wanbli Numpa Afraid of Hawk. *A Boy Becomes a Man at Wounded Knee.* Walker, 1992. *(P; I)*

Yue, Charlotte. *The Tipi: A Center of Native American Life.* Knopf, 1984. *(I)*

INDIAN WARS OF NORTH AMERICA

Bachrach, Deborah. *Custer's Last Stand.* Greenhaven, 1990. *(I; A)*

Brown, Dee. *Wounded Knee: An Indian History of the American West.* Holt, 1974. *(I; A)*

Halliburton, Warren J. *The Tragedy of Little Bighorn.* Watts, 1989. *(P; I)*

Marrin, Albert. *War Clouds in the West: Indians & Cavalrymen 1860-1890.* Atheneum, 1984. *(A)*

McGaw, Jessie B. *Chief Red Horse Tells About Custer.* Lodestar, 1981. *(P; I)*

Mitchell, Barbara. *Tomahawks and Trombones.* Carolrhoda, 1982. *(P)*

Morris, Richard B. *The Indian Wars.* Lerner, 1986 (rev. ed.). *(I; A)*

Wills, Charles. *The Battle of the Little Bighorn.* Silver Burdett, 1990. *(I)*

INDONESIA. See SOUTHEAST ASIA.

INDUSTRY

Allan, Mabel. *The Mills Down Below.* Dodd, 1981. *(I)*

Burne, Gordon. *Tools and Manufacturing.* Watts, 1984. *(I)*

Claypool, Jane. *Manufacturing.* Watts, 1984. *(I; A)*

Grant, Neil. *The Industrial Revolution.* Watts, 1983. *(I)*

Grigoli, Valorie. *Service Industries.* Watts, 1984. *(I)*

Macaulay, David. *Mill.* Houghton, 1983. *(I)*

Sherwood, Martin. *Industry.* Watts, 1984. *(I)*

Vialls, Christine. *The Industrial Revolution Begins.* Lerner, 1982. *(I; A)*

INSECTS

The World In Your Backyard: And Other Stories of Insects and Spiders. Zaner-Bloser, 1989. *(P; I)*

Brinckloe, Julie. *Fireflies!* Macmillan, 1985. *(P)*

Cole, Joanna. *An Insect's Body.* Morrow, 1984. *(P)*

dos Santos, Joyce A. *Giants of Smaller Worlds Drawn in Their Natural Sizes.* Dodd, 1983. *(P)*

Goor, Ron, and Goor, Nancy. *Insect Metamorphosis: From Egg to Adult.* Atheneum, 1990. *(P)*

Johnson, Sylvia. *Water Insects.* Lerner, 1989. *(P; I)*

Lavies, Bianca. *Backyard Hunter: The Praying Mantis.* Dutton, 1990. *(I)*

Milne, Lorus J., and Milne, Margery. *Nature's Clean-Up Crew: The Burying Beetles*. Dodd, 1982. *(I; A)*

Podendorf, Illa. *Insects*. Childrens, 1981. *(P)*

Selsam, Millicent E. *Where Do They Go? Insects in Winter*. Scholastic, 1982. *(P)*

Selsam, Millicent E., and Goor, Ronald. *Backyard Insects*. Scholastic, 1983. *(P)*

Shepherd, Elizabeth. *No Bones: A Key to Bugs & Slugs, Worms & Ticks, Spiders & Centipedes, & Other Creepy Crawlies*. Collier, 1988. *(P; I)*

INTERIOR DECORATING

Greer, Michael. *Your Future in Interior Design*. Rosen, 1980. *(I; A)*

James, Elizabeth, and Barkin, Carol. *A Place of Your Own*. Dutton, 1981. *(A)*

INTERNATIONAL RELATIONS

Goode, Stephen. *The Foreign Policy Debate: Human Rights in American Foreign Policy*. Watts, 1984. *(I; A)*

Hart, William B. *The United States and World Trade*. Watts, 1985. *(A)*

Wibberley, Leonard. *The Mouse That Roared*. Bantam, 1971. *(I; A)* (Fiction)

Woody, D. W. *The Kids of Mischief Island*. Carlton, 1981. *(I; A)* (Fiction)

INVENTIONS

Aaseng, Nathan. *Better Mousetraps*. Lerner, 1990. *(I); The Unsung Heroes: Unheralded People Who Invented Famous Products*. Lerner, 1989. *(I)*

Aliki. *A Weed Is a Flower: The Life of George Washington Carver*. Prentice-Hall, 1965. *(P; I)*

Bender, Lionel. *Invention*. Knopf, 1991. *(I)*

Caney, Steven. *Steven Caney's Invention Book*. Workman, 1985. *(P; I)*

DuBois, William. *The Twenty-One Balloons*. Viking, 1975 (1947). (Fiction) *(P; I)*

Haskins, Jim. *Outward Dreams: Black Inventors and Their Inventions*. Walker, 1991. *(I; A)*

Klein, Aaron E., and Klein, Cynthia L. *The Better Mousetrap: A Miscellany of Gadgets, Labor-Saving Devices, and Inventions That Intrigue*. Beaufort Books NY, 1983. *(I; A)*

Provensen, Alice. *The Glorious Flight Across the Channel with Louis Bleriot*. Viking, 1983. *(P; I)*

Richards, Norman. *Dreamers and Doers: Inventors Who Changed the World*. Atheneum, 1984. *(I; A)*

Vare, Ethlie Ann, and Ptacek, Greg. *Mothers of Invention: From the Bra to the Bomb, Forgotten Women and Their Unforgettable Ideas*. Morrow, 1988. *(I; A)*

IOWA

Carpenter, Allan. *Iowa*. Childrens, 1979. *(I)*

Fradin, Dennis. *Iowa: In Words and Pictures*. Childrens, 1980. *(P; I)*

IRAN

Iran . . . in Pictures. Lerner, 1989. *(I; A)*

Mannetti, Lisa. *Iran and Iraq: Nations at War*. Watts, 1986. *(I; A)*

Sanders, Renfield. *Iran*. Chelsea House, 1990. *(I; A)*

IRAQ

Docherty, J. P. *Iraq*. Chelsea House, 1988. *(P)*

Mannetti, Lisa. *Iran and Iraq: Nations at War*. Watts, 1986. *(I; A)*

IRELAND

James, Ian. *Take a Trip to Ireland*. Watts, 1984. *(P)*

Langford, Sondra G. *Red Bird of Ireland*. Atheneum, 1983. (Fiction) *(I; A)*

Meyer, Kathleen A. *Ireland: Land of Mist and Magic*. Dillon, 1983. *(I; A)*

Ryan, Joan, and Snell, Gordon, eds. *Land of Tales: Stories of Ireland for Children*. Dufour, 1983. *(P; I)*

IRON AND STEEL

Cherry, Mike. *Steel Beams and Iron Men*. Scholastic, 1980. *(I; A)*

Harter, Walter. *Steel: The Metal with Muscle*. Messner, 1981. *(P; I)*

Lambert, Mark. *Spotlight on Iron and Steel*. Rourke, 1988. *(P; I)*

IRRIGATION. See DAMS.

IRVING, WASHINGTON

Irving, Washington. *The Complete Tales of Washington Irving*. Doubleday, 1975. (Fiction) *(I; A); Knickerbocker's History of New York*. Sleepy Hollow, 1981. *(I; A); Rip Van Winkle, the Legend of Sleepy Hollow, and Other Tales*. Putnam, n.d. (Fiction) *(I; A)*

ISLAM. See RELIGIONS OF THE WORLD.

ISLANDS

Rydell, Wendy. *All About Islands*. Troll, 1984. *(P; I)*

See also CARIBBEAN SEA AND ISLANDS; PACIFIC OCEAN AND ISLANDS.

ISRAEL

Ashabranner, Brent. *Gavriel and Jemal: Two Boys of Jerusalem*. Dodd, 1984. *(I)*

Burstein, Chaya M. *A Kid's Catalog of Israel*. Jewish Publication Society, 1988. *(I; A)*

Davidson, Margaret. *The Golda Meir Story*. Scribner's, 1976. *(I)*

Feinstein, Steve. *Israel . . . in Pictures*. Lerner, 1988. *(P; I)*

Haskins, Jim. *Count Your Way Through Israel*. Carolrhoda, 1990. *(P)*

Jones, Helen Hinckley. *Israel*. Childrens, 1986. *(P)*

Kuskin, Karla. *Jerusalem, Shining Still*. Harper, 1987. *(P)*

Lawton, Clive A. *Israel*. Watts, 1988. *(P; I)*

Levine, Gemma. *We Live in Israel*. Watts, 1984. *(I; A)*

Mills, Dorothy. *The People of Ancient Israel*. Scribner's, 1960. *(I)*

Taitz, Emily, and Henry, Sondra. *Israel: A Sacred Land*. Dillon, 1987. *(P; I)*

Taylor, Allegra. *A Kibbutz in Israel*. Lerner, 1987. *(P)*

Williams, Lorna, and Bergman, Denise. *Through the Year in Israel*. David & Charles, 1983. *(I; A)*

Worth, Richard. *Israel and the Arab States*. Watts, 1983. *(I; A)*

Zagoren, Ruby. *Chaim Weizmann: First President of Israel*. Garrard, 1972. *(I; A)*

ITALY

de Zulueta, Tana. *We Live in Italy*. Watts, 1984. *(I; A)*

DiFranco, Anthony. *Italy: Balanced on the Edge of Time*. Dillon, 1983. *(I; A)*

Fairclough, Chris. *Take a Trip to Italy*. Watts, 1981. *(P)*

James, Ian. *Inside Italy*. Watts, 1988. *(P; I)*

Mariella, Cinzia. *Passport to Italy*. Watts, 1986. *(P)*

Powell. *Renaissance Italy*. Watts, 1980. *(I; A)*

Stein, R. Conrad. *Italy*. Childrens, 1984. *(I; A)*

Ventura, Piero. *Venice: Birth of a City*. Putnam, 1988. *(I; A)*

IVES, CHARLES

Sive, Helen R. *Music's Connecticut Yankee: An Introduction to the Life and Music of Charles Ives*. Atheneum, 1977. *(I; A)*

IVORY

Havill, Juanita. *Sato and the Elephants*. Lothrop, 1993. *(P; I; A)*

IVORY COAST

Cote d'Ivoire . . . in Pictures. Lerner, 1988. *(I; A)*

JACKSON, ANDREW

Osinski, Alice. *Andrew Jackson: Seventh President of the United States*. Childrens, 1987. *(I)*

Stefoff, Rebecca. *Andrew Jackson, 7th President of the United States*. Garrett Educational, 1988. *(A)*

See also PRESIDENCY OF THE UNITED STATES.

JACKSON, JESSE

Haskins, James. *I Am Somebody!: A Biography of Jesse Jackson*. Enslow, 1992. *(A)*

Otfinoski, Steven. *Jesse Jackson: A Voice for Change*. Fawcett, 1990. *(I)*

Wilkinson, Brenda. *Jesse Jackson: Still Fighting for the Dream*. Silver Burdett, 1990. *(I; A)*

JACKSON, THOMAS JONATHAN (STONEWALL)

Fritz, Jean. *Stonewall*. Putnam, 1979. *(I; A)*

Harrison, and others. *Stonewall Jackson*. Dormac, 1981. *(P; I; A)*

JAMAICA. See CARIBBEAN SEA AND ISLANDS.

JAMESTOWN. See THIRTEEN AMERICAN COLONIES.

JAPAN

Japan . . . in Pictures. Lerner, 1989. *(I)*

Blumberg, Rhoda. *Commodore Perry in the Land of the Shogun*. Lothrop, 1985. *(I)*

Cobb, Vicki. *This Place is Crowded: Japan*. Walker, 1992. *(P)*

Coerr, Eleanor. *Sadako and the Thousand Paper Cranes*. Putnam, 1977. *(I)*

Davidson, Judith. *Japan: Where East Meets West*. Dillon, 1983. *(I)*

Dolan, Edward F., Jr., and Finney, Shan. *The New Japan*. Harper, 1983. *(A)*

Greene, Carol. *Japan*. Childrens, 1983. *(I)*

Haugaard, Erik. *The Samurai's Tale*. Houghton, 1984. (Fiction) *(I)*

Hersey, John. *Hiroshima*. Bantam, 1986. *(I; A)*

Kawamata, Kazuhide. *We Live in Japan*. Watts, 1984. *(I; A)*

Keene, Donald, ed. *Anthology of Japanese Literature*. Grove Press, 1955. (Fiction) *(A)*

Meyer, Carolyn. *A Voice From Japan: An Outsider Looks In*. Gulliver Books, 1988. *(I; A)*

Pitts, Forrest R. *Japan*. Gateway Press, 1988. *(I; A)*

Robertson, John R. *From Shogun to Sony*. Atheneum, 1985. *(A)*

Shikibu, Murasaki. *Tale of Genji*. Modern Library, 1960. *(A)*

Spry-Leverton, Peter, and Kornicki, Peter. *Japan*. Facts On File, 1987. *(A)*

Stefoff, Rebecca. *Japan*. Chelsea House, 1988. *(P; I)*

Tames, Richard. *Passport to Japan*. Watts, 1988. *(I)*

JAZZ

Griffin, Clive D. *Jazz*. Batsford, dist. by David & Charles, 1989. *(I; A)*

Hughes, Langston. *The First Book of Jazz*. Watts, 1982 (rev. ed.). *(I)*

Jones, Max. *Talking Jazz*. Norton, 1988. *(A)*

Kliment, Bud. *Ella Fitzgerald*. Chelsea House, 1988. *(A)*

Montgomery, Elizabeth R. *Duke Ellington: King of Jazz*. Garrard, 1972. *(P; I)*

Tanenhaus, Sam. *Louis Armstrong*. Chelsea House, 1989. *(P; I)*

Terkel, Studs. *Giants of Jazz*. Harper, 1975 (rev. ed.). *(I; A)*

JEFFERSON, THOMAS

Adler, David A. *A Picture Book of Thomas Jefferson*. Holiday, 1990. *(P)*; *Thomas Jefferson: Father of Our Democracy*. Holiday House, 1987. *(P)*

Bober, Natalie S. *Thomas Jefferson: Man on a Mountain*. Atheneum, 1988. *(A)*

Fisher, Leonard Everett. *Monticello*. Holiday, 1988. *(I)*

Hargrove, Jim. *Thomas Jefferson: Third President of the United States*. (Encyclopedia of Presidents) Childrens, 1986. *(P; I)*

Milton, Joyce. *The Story of Thomas Jefferson: Prophet of Liberty*. Dell, 1990. *(I; A)*

Sabin, Francene. *Young Thomas Jefferson*. (Easy Biography Series) Troll, 1986. *(P; I)*

See also PRESIDENCY OF THE UNITED STATES; DECLARATION OF INDEPENDENCE; FOUNDERS OF THE UNITED STATES.

JELLYFISHES AND OTHER COELENTERATES

Gowell, Elizabeth Tayntor. *Sea Jellies: Rainbows in the Sea*. Watts, 1993. *(I)*

MacQuitty, Miranda. *Discovering Jellyfish*. Bookwright, 1989. *(P)*

JENNER, EDWARD. See DISEASES.

JERUSALEM. See ISRAEL.

JESUS CHRIST

Bierhorst, John. *Spirit Child: A Story of the Nativity*. Morrow, 1984. *(P)*

Collins, David R. *The Wonderful Story of Jesus*. Concordia Publishing, 1980. *(P; I)*

Nystrom, Carolyn. *Jesus Is No Secret*. Moody, 1983. *(P; I)*; *Who Is Jesus?* 1980. *(P)*

Petersham, Maud, and Petersham, Miska. *Christ Child*. Doubleday, 1931. *(P; I)*

Sherlock, Connie. *Life of Jesus*. Standard, 1983. *(P; I)*

Storr, Catherine, and Lindvall, Ella K. *The Birth of Jesus*. Moody Press, 1983 (rev. ed.); *Jesus Begins His Work,* 1983 (rev. ed.). *(P; I)*

JET PROPULSION

Moxon, Julian. *How Jet Engines Are Made*. Facts on File, 1985. *(P; I)*

JEWS. See JUDAISM.

JOAN OF ARC, SAINT

Boutet de Monvel, Maurice. *Joan of Arc*. Viking, 1980. *(I)*

Brooks, Polly Schoyer. *Beyond the Myth: The Story of Joan of Arc*. Lippincott, 1990. *(A)*

Ready, Dolores. *Joan, the Brave Soldier: Joan of Arc*. Winston, 1977. *(P; I)*

JOGGING AND RUNNING. See TRACK AND FIELD.

JOHNSON, ANDREW

Kent, Zachary. *Andrew Johnson*. Childrens, 1989. *(P; I)*

Stevens, Rita. *Andrew Johnson: 17th President of the United States*. Garrett Educational, 1989. *(I)*

See also PRESIDENCY OF THE UNITED STATES.

JOHNSON, JAMES WELDON

Egypt, Ophelia Settle. *James Weldon Johnson*. Harper, 1974. *(P)*

JOHNSON, LYNDON BAINES

Devaney, John. *Lyndon Baines Johnson, President*. Walker, 1986. *(I; A)*

Falkof, Lucille. *Lyndon B. Johnson: 36th President of the United States*. Garrett Educational, 1989. *(I)*

Hargrove, Jim. *Lyndon B. Johnson*. Childrens, 1988. *(P; I)*

Kaye, Tony. *Lyndon B. Johnson*. Chelsea House, 1988. *(I; A)*

See also PRESIDENCY OF THE UNITED STATES.

JOKES AND RIDDLES. See HUMOR.

JOLLIET, LOUIS, AND MARQUETTE, JACQUES

Stein, R. Conrad. *The Story of Marquette and Jolliet*. Childrens, 1981. *(P; I)*

JORDAN

Jordan . . . in Pictures. Lerner, 1988. *(I)*

Whitehead, Susan. *Jordan*. Chelsea House, 1988. *(P)*

JOURNALISM

Jaspersohn, William. *A Day in the Life of a Television News Reporter*. Little, 1981. *(I; A)*

See also NEWSPAPERS.

JUDAISM

Brownstone, David M. *The Jewish-American Heritage*. Facts on File, 1988. *(I; A)*

Chaikin, Miriam. *Menorahs, Mezuzas, and Other Jewish Symbols*. Clarion, 1990. *(I)*; *Sound the Shofar: The Story and Meaning of Rosh Hashanah and Yom Kippur*. Clarion, 1986. *(I; A)*

Costabel, Eva D. *The Jews of New Amsterdam*. Atheneum, 1988. *(P; I)*

Domnitz, Myer. *Judaism*. Bookwright, 1987. *(I; A)*

Finkelstein, Norman A. *The Other 1492: Jewish Settlement in the New World*. Scribner's, 1989. *(I; A)*

Freeman, Joan G., and Freeman, Grace R. *Inside the Synagogue*. UAHC, 1984. *(P)*

Greenberg, Judith E., and Carey, Helen H. *Jewish Holidays*. Watts, 1985. *(P; I)*

Klaperman, Gilbert, and Klaperman, Libby. *The Story of the Jewish People,* 4 vols. Behrman House, 1974. *(I; A)*

Meltzer, Milton. *Taking Root: Jewish Immigrants in America*. Farrar, 1976. *(I; A)*

Metter, Bert. *Bar Mitzvah, Bat Mitzvah: How Jewish Boys and Girls Come of Age*. Houghton, 1984. *(I)*

Muggamin, Howard. *The Jewish Americans*. Chelsea House, 1988. *(I; A)*

Sanders, James. *Torah and Cannon*. Augsberg Fortress, 1972. *(I)*

Shamir, Ilana, and Shavit, Shlomo. *The Young Reader's Encyclopedia of Jewish History*. Viking, 1987. *(P; I)*

Strom, Yale. *A Tree Still Stands: Jewish Youth in Eastern Europe Today*. Philomel, 1990. *(I; A)*

Suhl, Yuri. *The Purim Goat*. Four Winds, 1980. (Fiction) *(I)*

Swartz, Sarah Silberstein. *Bar Mitzvah*. Doubleday, 1985. *(I; A)*

Turner, Reuben. *Jewish Festivals*. Rourke, 1987. *(P; I)*

See also HANUKKAH; HOLOCAUST; PASSOVER; PURIM.

JUDO AND KARATE

Brimner, Larry Dane. *Karate*. Watts, 1988. *(P; I)*

Parulski, George R., Jr. *Karate Power!: Learning the Art of the Empty Hand*. Contemporary Bks., 1985. *(P)*

Queen, J. Allen. *Karate to Win*. Sterling, 1988. *(I; A)*

Wood, Tim. *Judo*. Watts, 1990. *(P; I)*

JUNGLES

Batten, Mary. *The Tropical Forest*. Crowell, 1973. *(P)*

Cowcher, Helen. *Rain Forest*. Farrar, 1989. *(P)*

Forsyth, Andrian. *Journey Through a Tropical Jungle*. Simon & Schuster, 1989. *(P; I)*

Gibbons, Gail. *Nature's Green Umbrella: Tropical Rain Forests*. Morrow, 1994. *(P)*

Kipling, Rudyard. *The Jungle Book*. Viking, 1987. (Fiction) *(I; A)*

Mutel, Cornelia F., and Rodgers, Mary M. *Tropical Rain Forests*. Lerner, 1991. *(I)*

Norden, Carroll R. *The Jungle*. Raintree, 1978. *(P)*

Pepe, Joyce. *A Closer Look at Jungles*. Watts, 1978. *(I)*

Rowland-Entwistle, Theodore. *Jungles and Rain Forests*. Silver Burdett, 1987. *(P)*

JUPITER

Dunbar, Robert E. *Into Jupiter's World*. Watts, 1981. *(I; A)*

Petersen, Carolyn Collins. *Jupiter*. Facts on File, 1990. *(P; I)*

Simon, Seymour. *Jupiter*. Morrow, 1985. *(I; A)*

JURY. See LAW AND LAW ENFORCEMENT.

JUVENILE CRIME

Dolan, Edward F., Jr., and Finney, Shan. *Youth Gangs*. Messner, 1984. *(I; A)*

Hyde, Margaret O. *Juvenile Justice and Injustice*. Watts, 1983 (rev. ed.). *(I; A)*

LeShan, Eda. *The Roots of Crime: What You Need to Know About Crime and What You Can Do About It*. Scholastic, 1981. *(I; A)*

LeVert, Marianne. *Crime in America*. Facts on File, 1991. *(I; A)*

Riekes, Linda, and Ackerly, Sally M. *Juvenile Problems and Law*. West Publishing, 1980 (2nd ed.). *(P; I)*

Shanks, Ann Z. *Busted Lives: Dialogues with Kids in Jail*. Delacorte, 1982. *(I; A)*

KANGAROOS

Arnold, Caroline. *Kangaroo*. Morrow, 1987. *(P)*

Eugene, Toni. *Koalas and Kangaroos: Strange Animals of Australia*. National Geographic, 1981. *(P)*

Glendenning, Sally. *Little Blue and Rusty: Red Kangaroos*. Garrard, 1980. *(P)*

KANSAS

Carpenter, Allan. *Kansas*. Childrens, 1979. *(I)*

Desmond, J. *Kansas Boy*. Roush Books, 1979. *(I; A)*

Fradin, Dennis. *Kansas: In Words and Pictures*. Childrens, 1980. *(P; I)*

Wilder, Laura Ingalls. *Little House on the Prairie*. Harper, 1953. (Fiction) *(I)*

KARATE. See JUDO AND KARATE.

KARTING

Fichter, George S. *Karts and Karting*. Watts, 1982. *(P; I; A)*

Leonard, Jerry. *Kart Racing*. Messner, 1980. *(I; A)*

Radlauer, Ed. *Karting Winners*. Childrens, 1982. *(P; I)*

KASHMIR. See INDIA.

KELLER, HELEN

Adler, David A. *A Picture Book of Helen Keller*. Holiday, 1990. *(P)*

Keller, Helen. *The Story of My Life*. Scholastic, 1973. *(I; A)*

Sabin, Francene. *The Courage of Helen Keller*. Troll, 1982. *(P; I)*

Wepman, Dennis. *Helen Keller*. (American Women of Achievement) Chelsea House, 1987. *(I; A)*

Wilkie, Katherine E. *Helen Keller: From Tragedy to Triumph*. Bobbs, 1983. *(P; I)*

KENNEDY, JOHN F.

Adler, David A. *A Picture Book of John F. Kennedy.* Holiday, 1991. *(P)*

Anderson, Catherine Corley. *John F. Kennedy: Young People's President.* Lerner, 1991. *(I; A)*

Denenberg, Barry. *John Fitzgerald Kennedy: America's 35th President.* Scholastic, 1988. *(I)*

Donnelly, Judy. *Who Shot the President? The Death of John F. Kennedy.* Random, 1988. *(P)*

Falkof, Lucille. *John F. Kennedy: 35th President of the United States.* Garrett Educational, 1988. *(A)*

Frisbee, Lucy P. *John F. Kennedy: America's Youngest President.* Bobbs, 1983. *(P; I)*

Kent, Zachary. *John F. Kennedy: Thirty-fifth President of the United States.* Childrens, 1987. *(P; I)*

Mills, Judie. *John F. Kennedy.* Watts, 1988. *(A)*

Waggoner, Jeffrey. *The Assassination of President Kennedy.* Greenhaven, 1990. *(I; A)*

See also Presidency of the United States.

KENTUCKY

Fradin, Dennis. *Kentucky: In Words and Pictures.* Childrens, 1981. *(P; I)*

McNair, Sylvia. *Kentucky.* Childrens, 1988. *(P; I)*

Stuart, Jesse. *The Thread That Runs So True.* Scribner's, 1958. *(I; A)*

KENYA

Kenya . . . in Pictures. Lerner, 1988. *(I; A)*

Khalfan, Zulf M., and Amin, Mohamed. *We Live in Kenya.* Watts, 1984. *(I; A)*

Maren, Michael. *The Land and People of Kenya.* Lippincott, 1989. *(I; A)*

Winslow, Zachary. *Kenya.* Chelsea House, 1987. *(A)*

KEYBOARD INSTRUMENTS. See Musical Instruments.

KIDD, CAPTAIN WILLIAM. See Pirates and Piracy.

KING, MARTIN LUTHER, JR.

Adler, David A. *Martin Luther King, Jr.: Free at Last.* Holiday, 1987. *(P; I)*

Clayton, Edward. *Martin Luther King: The Peaceful Warrior.* Prentice Hall, 1968. *(P; I)*

Darby, Jean. *Martin Luther King, Jr.* Lerner, 1990. *(I; A)*

Faber, Doris, and Faber, Harold. *Martin Luther King, Jr.* Messner, 1986. *(P; I)*

Hakim, Rita. *Martin Luther King, Jr. and the March Toward Freedom.* Millbrook, 1991. *(P; I)*

Harris, Jacqueline. *Martin Luther King, Jr.* Watts, 1983. *(I; A)*

King, Martin Luther, Jr. *Why We Can't Wait.* Harper, 1964. *(A)*

Marzollo, Jean. *Happy Birthday, Martin Luther King.* Scholastic, 1993. *(P)*

McKissack, Patricia. *Martin Luther King, Jr.: A Man to Remember.* Childrens, 1984. *(I)*

Patterson, Lillie. *Martin Luther King, Jr. and the Freedom Movement.* Facts on File, 1989. *(I; A)*

Quayle, Louise. *Martin Luther King, Jr.: Dreams for a Nation.* Fawcett, 1990. *(I)*

Richardson, Nigel. *Martin Luther King, Jr.* David & Charles, 1983. *(P; I)*

Rowland, Della. *Martin Luther King, Jr.* Silver Burdett, 1989. *(I)*

Schloredt, Valerie. *Martin Luther King, Jr.: America's Great Nonviolent Leader in the Struggle for Human Rights.* Gareth Stevens, 1988. *(I)*

Thompson, Marguerite. *Martin Luther King, Jr.: A Story for Children.* Theo Gaus, 1983. *(P; I)*

KIPLING, RUDYARD

Kamen, Gloria. *Kipling: Storyteller of East and West.* Atheneum, 1985. *(P; I)*

Kipling, Rudyard. *The Jungle Book.* Doubleday, 1981. *(I); Just So Stories.* Rand, 1982. *(P; I)* (Other publishers of both books and of other Kipling titles)

KIRIBATI. See Pacific Ocean and Islands.

KITES

Marks, Burton, and Marks, Rita. *Kites for Kids.* Lothrop, 1980. *(P; I)*

Moran, Tom. *Kite Flying Is for Me.* Lerner, 1983. *(P; I)*

Newnham, Jack. *Kites to Make and Fly.* Penguin, 1982. *(P; I)*

Nicklaus, Carol. *Flying, Gliding, and Whirling: Making Things That Fly.* Watts, 1981. *(P)*

KNIGHTS, KNIGHTHOOD, AND CHIVALRY

Barber, Richard. *The Reign of Chivalry.* St. Martin's, 1980. *(I)*

Gibson, Michael, and Pike, Tricia. *All About Knights.* EMC Publishing, 1982. *(P; I; A)*

Lasker, Joe. *A Tournament of Knights.* Crowell, 1986. *(I)*

Pyle, Howard. *Men of Iron.* Harper, 1930. *(A)*

See also Middle Ages.

KNITTING AND CROCHETING. See Sewing and Needlecraft.

KOALAS

Eugene, Toni. *Koalas and Kangaroos: Strange Animals of Australia.* National Geographic, 1981. *(P)*

KOREA

Ashby, Gwynneth. *A Family in South Korea.* Lerner, 1987. *(P)*

Farley, Carol. *Korea: A Land Divided.* Dillon, 1983. *(I; A)*

Shepheard, Patricia. *South Korea*. Chelsea House, 1988. *(P)*

Solberg, S. E. *The Land and People of Korea*. Harper, 1991. *(I)*

So-un, Kim. *The Story Bag: A Collection of Korean Folk Tales*. Tuttle, 1955. *(I)*

KOREAN WAR

Fincher, E. B. *The War in Korea*. Watts, 1981. *(I; A)*

Smith, Carter. *The Korean War*. Silver Burdett, 1990. *(I)*

Sorensen, Virginia. *Miracles on Maple Hill*. Harcourt, 1988. *(P; I)*

KURDS

King, John. *Kurds*. Thomson Learning, 1994. *(I; A)*

KUWAIT. See MIDDLE EAST.

KYOTO. See JAPAN.

LABOR–MANAGEMENT RELATIONS

Claypool, Jane. *The Worker in America*. Watts, 1985. *(A)*

Fisher, Leonard. *The Unions*. Holiday, 1982. *(I)*

Lens, Sidney. *Strikemakers & Strikebreakers*. Lodestar, 1985. *(A)*

Meltzer, Milton. *Bread and Roses: The Struggle of American Labor, 1865–1915*. Facts on File, 1990. *(I; A)*

Morton, Desmond. *Labour in Canada*. Watts, 1982. *(I; A)*

Pelham, Molly. *People at Work*. Dillon, 1986. *(P)*

LAFAYETTE, MARQUIS DE. See REVOLUTIONARY WAR.

LAFITTE, JEAN. See LOUISIANA; PIRATES AND PIRACY.

LAKES

Hoff, Mary, and Rodgers, Mary M. *Rivers and Lakes*. Lerner, 1991. *(I)*

Mulherin, Jenny. *Rivers and Lakes*. Watts, 1984. *(P; I)* (Atlas format)

Rowland-Entwistle, Theodore. *Rivers and Lakes*. Silver Burdett, 1987. *(P; I)*

Updegraffe, Imelda, and Updegraffe, Robert. *Rivers and Lakes*. Penguin, 1983. *(I; A)*

LANGUAGES (Origin, History, and Usage)

Ashton, Christian. *Words Can Tell: A Book About Our Language*. Messner, 1989. *(P; I; A)*

Heller, Ruth. *Merry-Go-Round: A Book About Nouns*. Grosset, 1990. *(P)*

LANGUAGES (Foreign Language Studies)

Colyer, Penrose. *I Can Read French*. Watts, 1981; *I Can Read Italian*, 1983; *I Can Read Spanish*, 1981. *(P; I)*

Hautzig, Esther. *At Home: A Visit in Four Languages*. Macmillan, 1968. *(P)*

Woff, Diane. *Chinese Writing: An Introduction*. Holt, 1975. *(I)*

LAOS. See SOUTHEAST ASIA.

LAPLAND

Hagbrink, Bodil. *Children of Lapland*. Tundra Books, 1979. *(P; I)*

LA SALLE, ROBERT CAVELIER, SIEUR DE. See JOLLIET, LOUIS, AND MARQUETTE, JACQUES; MISSISSIPPI RIVER.

LASERS

Asimov, Isaac. *How Did We Find Out About Lasers?* Walker, 1990. *(I)*

Bender, Lionel. *Lasers in Action*. Bookwright, 1985. *(I; A)*

De Vere, Charles. *Lasers*. Watts, 1984. *(P; I)*

Filson, Brent. *Exploring with Lasers*. Messner, 1984. *(I; A)*

French, P. M. W., and Taylor, J. W. *How Lasers Are Made*. Facts on File, 1987. *(A)*

Nardo, Don. *Lasers: Humanity's Magic Light*. Lucent Books, 1990. *(I; A)*

LATIN AMERICA

Pascoe, Elaine. *Neighbors at Odds: U.S. Policy in Latin America*. Watts, 1990. *(I; A)*

See also individual countries.

LAVOISIER, ANTOINE LAURENT

Grey, Vivian. *The Chemist Who Lost His Head: The Story of Antoine Laurent Lavoisier*. Putnam, 1982. *(I)*

LAW AND LAW ENFORCEMENT

Arnold, Caroline. *Why Do We Have Rules?* Watts, 1983. *(P)*

Atkinson, Linda. *Your Legal Rights*. Watts, 1982. *(I; A)*

Ehrenfreund, Norbert, and Treat, Lawrence. *You're the Jury*. Holt, 1992. *(A)*

Epstein, Sam, and Epstein, Beryl. *Kids in Court*. Four Winds, 1982. *(I)*

Fincher, E. B. *The American Legal System*. Watts, 1980. *(I; A)*

Hyde, Margaret O. *The Rights of the Victim*. Watts, 1983. *(I; A)*

Smith, Elizabeth Simpson. *Breakthrough: Women in Law Enforcement*. Walker, 1982. *(I; A)*

Stern, Ron. *Law Enforcement Careers: A Complete Guide from Application to Employment*. Lawman Press, 1988. *(A)*

Weiss, Ann E. *The Supreme Court*. Enslow, 1986. *(A)*

Zerman, Melvyn B. *Beyond a Reasonable Doubt: Inside the American Jury System*. Harper, 1981. *(I; A)*
See also POLICE.

LAWYERS

Fry, William R., and Hoopes, Roy. *Legal Careers and the Legal System*. Enslow, 1988. *(A)*
Heath, Charles D. *Your Future as a Legal Assistant*. Rosen, 1982 (rev. ed.). *(I; A)*
Hewett, Joan. *Public Defender: Lawyer for the People*. Lodestar, 1991. *(I; A)*

LEAKEY FAMILY

Willis, Delta. *The Leakey Family*. Facts on File, 1992. *(I; A)*

LEAVES

Johnson, Sylvia A. *How Leaves Change*. Lerner, 1986. *(I)*
Kirkpatrick, Rena K. *Look at Leaves*. Raintree, 1978. *(P)*
Selsam, Millicent E., and Hunt, Joyce, eds. *A First Look at Leaves*. Walker, 1972. *(P)*
Testa, Fulvio. *Leaves*. Peter Bedrick, 1983. *(I)*

LEBANON

Lebanon . . . in Pictures. Lerner, 1988. *(I)*
Shapiro, William. *Lebanon*. Watts, 1984. *(I; A)*

LEE, ROBERT E.

Aaseng, Nathan. *Robert E. Lee*. Lerner, 1991. *(I)*
Commager, Henry Steele, and Ward, Lynd. *America's Robert E. Lee*. Houghton, n.d. *(I)*
Monsell, Helen A. *Robert E. Lee: Young Confederate*. Bobbs, 1983. *(P; I)*
Weidhorn, Manfred. *Robert E. Lee*. Atheneum, 1988. *(I; A)*
See also CIVIL WAR, UNITED STATES.

LEGENDS. See FOLKLORE AND FAIRY TALES.

LENIN

Rawcliffe, Michael. *Lenin*. Batsford, 1989. *(I; A)*
Resnick, Abraham. *Lenin: Founder of the Soviet Union*. Childrens, 1988. *(I)*
Topalian, Elyse. *V. I. Lenin*. Watts, 1983. *(I; A)*
See also UNION OF SOVIET SOCIALIST REPUBLICS.

LENSES

Aust, Siegfried. *Lenses! Take a Closer Look*. Lerner, 1991. *(I)*
Brindze, Ruth. *Look How Many People Wear Glasses: The Magic of Lenses*. Atheneum, 1975. *(I)*
Goodsell, Jane. *Katie's Magic Glasses*. Houghton, 1978. *(P)*

LEONARDO DA VINCI

Cooper, Margaret. *The Inventions of Leonardo da Vinci*. Macmillan, 1968. *(I)*
Konigsburg, E. L. *The Second Mrs. Giaconda*. Atheneum, 1975. (Fiction) *(I)*
McLanathan, Richard. *Leonardo da Vinci*. Abrams, 1990. *(I; A)*
Raboff, Ernest. *Leonardo da Vinci*. Lippincott, 1987. *(P; I)*
Sachs, Marianne. *Leonardo and His World*. Silver Burdett, 1979. *(I)*

LESOTHO. See AFRICA.

LETTER WRITING

Dettmer, M. L. *Bag of Letters*. Western, 1977. *(I; A)*
Leedy, Loreen. *Messages in the Mailbox: How to Write a Letter*. Holiday, 1991. *(P)*
Mischel, Florence D. *How to Write a Letter*. Watts, 1988. *(I)*

LEWIS AND CLARK EXPEDITION

Blumberg, Rhoda. *The Incredible Journey of Lewis & Clark*. Lothrop, 1987. *(P; I)*
Fitz-Gerald, Christine A. *Meriwether Lewis and William Clark*. Childrens, 1991. *(I)*
Kroll, Steven. *Lewis and Clark: Explorers of the American West*. Holiday, 1994. *(P)*
McGrath, Patrick. *The Lewis and Clark Expedition*. Silver Burdett, 1985. *(I; A)*
O'Dell, Scott. *Streams to the River, River to the Sea: Novel of Sacajawea*. Houghton, 1986. (Fiction) *(I)*

LIBERIA

Hope, Constance Morris. *Liberia*. Chelsea House, 1987. *(A)*
Sullivan, Jo M. *Liberia . . . in Pictures*. Lerner, 1988. *(P; I)*

LIBERTY, STATUE OF

Burchard, Sue. *The Statue of Liberty: Birth to Rebirth*. Harcourt, 1985. *(I)*
Fisher, Leonard Everett. *The Statue of Liberty*. Holiday, 1985. *(P; I)*
Haskins, James. *The Statue of Liberty: America's Proud Lady*. Lerner, 1986. *(P)*
Maestro, Betty. *The Story of the Statue of Liberty*. Morrow, 1986. *(P)*
Shapiro, Mary J. *How They Built the Statue of Liberty*. Random House, 1985. *(I)*

LIBERTY BELL

Boland, Charles M. *Ring in the Jubilee: The Story of America's Liberty Bell*. Chatham, 1973. *(I; A)*

LIBRARIES

Cleary, Florence D. *Discovering Books and Libraries*. Wilson, 1977 (2nd ed.). *(I; A)*

Hardendorff, Jeanne B. *Libraries and How to Use Them*. Watts, 1979. *(P; I; A)*

McInerney, Claire Fleischman. *Find It! The Inside Story of Your Library*. Lerner, 1989. *(I)*

Schurr, Sandra. *Library Lingo*. Incentive Publications, 1981. *(P; I)*

Shapiro, Lillian L. *Teaching Yourself in Libraries*. Wilson, 1978. *(I; A)*

LIBYA

Brill, Marlene Targ. *Libya*. Childrens, 1988. *(P; I)*

Sanders, Renfield. *Libya*. Chelsea House, 1987. *(A)*

LIES

Bawden, Nina. *Kept in the Dark*. Lothrop, 1982. *(I)*

Elliot, Dan. *Ernie's Little Lie*. Random, 1983. *(P)*

Moncure, Jane B. *Honesty*. Child's World, 1981 (rev. ed.); *John's Choice*, 1983. *(P; I)*

Ruby, Lois. *Two Truths in My Pocket*. Viking, 1982. *(I; A)*

Yep, Laurence. *Liar, Liar*. Morrow, 1983. *(I; A)*

LIFE

Berger, Melvin. *How Life Began*. Doubleday, 1991. *(P; I)*

Burnie, David. *Life*. Dorling Kindersley, 1994. *(I; A)*

LIGHT

Ardley, Neil. *The Science Book of Light*. Gulliver Books, 1991. *(P; I)*

Billings, Charlene W. *Fiber Optics: Bright New Way to Communicate*. Dodd, 1986. *(I)*

Burkig, Valerie. *Photonics: The New Science of Light*. Enslow, 1986. *(A)*

Crews, Donald. *Light*. Greenwillow, 1981. *(P; I)*

Darling, David. *Making Light Work: The Science of Optics*. Dillon, 1991. *(I)*

Friedhofer, Robert. *Light*. Watts, 1992. *(I)*

Goor, Ron, and Goor, Nancy. *Shadows: Here, There, and Everywhere*. Harper, 1981. *(I)*

Hecht, Jeff. *Optics: Light for a New Age*. Scribner's, 1988. *(A)*

Stuart, Gene S. *Hidden Worlds*. National Geographic, 1981. *(P; I)*

Taylor, Barbara. *Bouncing and Bending Light*. Watts, 1990. *(P; I); Seeing Is Not Believing! The Science of Shadow and Light*. Random, 1991. *(P; I)*

Ward, Alan. *Experimenting with Light and Illusions*. Batsford, 1985. *(I)*

Watson, Philip. *Light Fantastic*. Lothrop, 1983. *(P; I)*

White, Jack R. *The Invisible World of the Infrared*. Dodd, 1984. *(I)*

LIMA. See PERU.

LINCOLN, ABRAHAM

Adler, David A. *A Picture Book of Abraham Lincoln*. Holiday, 1989. *(P)*

Brandt, Keith. *Abe Lincoln: The Young Years*. Troll, 1982. *(P; I)*

Coolidge, Olivia. *The Apprenticeship of Abraham Lincoln*. Scribner's, 1974. *(I; A)*

D'Aulaire, Ingri, and D'Aulaire, Edgar P. *Abraham Lincoln*. Doubleday, 1957 (rev. ed.). *(P)*

Freedman, Russell. *Lincoln, A Photobiography*. Clarion, 1987. *(P; I; A)*

Gross, Ruth Belov. *True Stories About Abraham Lincoln*. Lothrop, 1990. *(P)*

Hargrove, Jim. *Abraham Lincoln*. Childrens, 1988. *(I)*

Sandburg, Carl. *Abe Lincoln Grows Up*. Harcourt, 1975. *(I)*

Shorto, Russell. *Abraham Lincoln and the End of Slavery*. Millbrook, 1991. *(P; I)*

Stevenson, Augusta. *Abraham Lincoln: The Great Emancipator*. Bobbs, 1983. *(P; I)*

See also PRESIDENCY OF THE UNITED STATES.

LINCOLN-DOUGLAS DEBATES. See LINCOLN, ABRAHAM.

LINDBERGH, CHARLES

Burleigh, Robert. *Flight: The Journey of Charles Lindbergh*. Philomel, 1991. *(P; I)*

Lindbergh, Charles A. *The Spirit of St. Louis*. Scribner's, 1956. *(A)*

Randolph, Blythe. *Charles Lindbergh*. Watts, 1990. *(I; A)*

LIONS AND TIGERS

Adamson, Joy. *Born Free*. Pantheon, 1960. *(A); Living Free*. Harcourt, 1961. *(A)*

Ashby, Ruth. *Tigers*. Atheneum, 1990. *(I)*

Lewin, Ted. *Tiger Trek*. Macmillan, 1990. *(P)*

McClung, Robert M. *Rajpur: Last of the Bengal Tigers*. Morrow, 1982. *(P; I)*

Overbeck, Cynthia. *Lions*. Lerner, 1981. *(P; I; A)*

Torgersen, Don. *Lion Prides and Tiger Marks*. Childrens, 1982. *(P; I)*

Yoshida, Toshi. *Young Lions*. Philomel, 1989. *(P)*

LIQUIDS. See MATTER.

LITTLE LEAGUE BASEBALL

Hale, Creighton H. *Official Little League Baseball Rules in Pictures*. Putnam, 1981. *(P; I)*

Remmers, Mary. *Ducks on the Pond: A Lexicon of Little League Lingo*. Shoal Creek, 1981. *(P; I)*

Sullivan, George. *Baseball Kids*. Dutton, 1990. *(P; I)*

LIVESTOCK. See RANCH LIFE.

LIZARDS AND CHAMELEONS

Chace, G. Earl. *The World of Lizards.* Dodd, 1982. *(I; A)*
Schnieper, Claudia. *Chameleons.* Carolrhoda, 1989. *(P; I)*
Smith, Trevor. *Amazing Lizards.* Knopf, 1990. *(P; I)*

LOBSTERS

Bailey, Jill. *Discovering Crabs and Lobsters.* Watts, 1987. *(P)*

LOCKS AND KEYS

Gibbons, Gail. *Locks and Keys.* Harper, 1980. *(P)*

LOCOMOTIVES. See RAILROADS.

LONDON. See ENGLAND.

LONDON, JACK

Schroeder, Alan. *Jack London.* Chelsea House, 1991. *(I; A)*

LONGFELLOW, HENRY WADSWORTH

Holberg, Ruth L. *American Bard: The Story of Henry Wadsworth Longfellow.* Harper, 1963. *(I; A)*
Longfellow, Henry Wadsworth. *The Children's Own Longfellow.* Houghton, n.d. *(P; I)*; *Hiawatha.* Dial, 1983. *(P)*

LOS ANGELES. See CALIFORNIA.

LOUISIANA

Fradin, Dennis. *Louisiana: In Words and Pictures.* Childrens, 1981. *(P; I)*
Kent, Deborah. *Louisiana.* Childrens, 1988. *(P; I)*

LOUISIANA PURCHASE

Phelan, Mary K. *The Story of the Louisiana Purchase.* Harper, 1979. *(P; I)*

LUMBER AND LUMBERING

Abrams, Kathleen, and Abrams, Lawrence. *Logging and Lumbering.* Messner, 1980. *(P; I)*
Langley, Andres. *Timber.* (Spotlight on Resources) Rourke, 1987. *(P; I)*
Newton, James R. *Forest Log.* Harper, 1980. *(P; I)*
See also FORESTS AND FORESTRY.

LUTHER, MARTIN

Fehlauer, Adolph. *The Life and Faith of Martin Luther.* Northwest, 1981. *(I; A)*
O'Neill, Judith. *Martin Luther.* Lerner, 1978. *(I; A)*

MACKENZIE, SIR ALEXANDER. See EXPLORATION AND DISCOVERY.

MACRAMÉ

Bress, Helene. *The Craft of Macramé.* Scribner's, 1977. *(I; A)*
Creative Educational Society Editors. *How to Have Fun with Macramé.* Creative Education, 1973. *(P; I)*

MADAGASCAR

Madagascar . . . in Pictures. Lerner, 1988. *(I)*
Stevens, Rita. *Madagascar.* Chelsea House, 1987. *(P; I)*

MADISON, JAMES

Leavell, J. Perry. *James Madison.* Chelsea House, 1988. *(A)*
See also PRESIDENCY OF THE UNITED STATES.

MAGELLAN, FERDINAND

Hargrove, Jim. *Ferdinand Magellan.* Childrens, 1990. *(I)*
Harley, Ruth. *Ferdinand Magellan.* Troll, 1979 (new ed.). *(P; I)*

MAGIC

Bellairs, John. *The House with a Clock in Its Walls.* Dial, 1973. (Fiction) *(I; A)*
Bernstein, Bob. *Monday Morning Magic.* Good Apple, 1982. *(P; I)*
Boyar, Jay. *Be a Magician! How to Put On a Magic Show and Mystify Your Friends.* Messner, 1981. *(I; A)*
Brittain, Bill. *The Wish Giver: Three Tales of Coven Tree.* Harper, 1983. (Fiction) *(I; A)*
Charnas, Suzy McGee. *The Golden Thread.* Bantam, 1989. (Fiction) *(I; A)*
Cobb, Vicki, and Darling, Kathy. *Bet You Can!* Lothrop, 1983. *(P; I)*
Cohen, Daniel. *Real Magic.* Dodd, 1982. *(P; I)*
DePaola, Tomie. *Strega Nona.* Prentice-Hall, 1975. (Fiction) *(P)*
Fortman, Jan. *Houdini and Other Masters of Magic.* Raintree, 1977. *(P; I)*
Hall, Lynn. *Dagmar Schultz and the Powers of Darkness.* Scribner's, 1989. (Fiction) *(I; A)*
Lewis, Shari. *Abracadabra: Magic and Other Tricks.* Ballantine, 1984. *(P; I)*
McKinley, Robin. *The Hero and the Crown.* Greenwillow, 1984. (Fiction) *(I; A)*
Nesbit, E. *The Story of the Treasure Seekers.* Scholastic, 1988. *(I; A)*
Roberts, Willo Davis. *The Magic Book.* Atheneum, 1986. (Fiction) *(I; A)*
Severin, Bill. *Magic with Rope, Ribbon, and String.* McKay, 1981. *(I; A)*
Shalit, Nathan. *Science Magic Tricks: Over 50 Fun Tricks That Mystify and Dazzle.* Holt, 1981. *(P; I)*
Steig, William. *Sylvester and the Magic Pebble.* Simon and Schuster, 1970. (Fiction) *(P; I)*
Stoddard, Edward. *Magic.* Watts, 1983 (rev. ed.). *(I; A)*

Travers, P. L. *Mary Poppins*. Harcourt, 1961. (Fiction) *(P; I)*

White, Laurence B., Jr., and Broekel, Ray. *Math-a-Magic: Number Tricks for Magicians*. Albert Whitman, 1990. *(P; I)*

MAGNA CARTA. See ENGLAND, HISTORY OF.

MAGNETS AND MAGNETISM

Adler, David. *Amazing Magnets*. Troll, 1983. *(P; I)*

Ardley, Neil. *Exploring Magnetism*. Watts, 1984. *(I)*

Catherall, Ed. *Exploring Magnets*. Steck-Vaughn, 1990. *(I)*

Hogan, Paula. *Compass*. Walker, 1982. *(I)*

Lampton, Christopher. *Superconductors*. Enslow, 1989. *(I; A)*

Satrey, Laurence. *Magnets*. Troll, 1985. *(I)*

MAINE

Engfer, LeeAnne. *Maine*. Lerner, 1991. *(I)*

Harrington, Ty. *Maine*. Childrens, 1989. *(P; I)*

MALAWI

Malawi . . . in Pictures. Lerner, 1988. *(I)*

Sanders, Renfield. *Malawi*. Chelsea House, 1987. *(P; I)*

MALAYSIA. See SOUTHEAST ASIA.

MALCOLM X

Myers, Walter Dean. *Malcolm X: By Any Means Necessary*. Scholastic, 1993. *(A)*

Stine, Megan. *The Story of Malcolm X, Civil Rights Leader*. Dell, 1994. *(I)*

MALI. See AFRICA.

MAMMALS

Anderson, Lucia. *Mammals and Their Milk*. Dodd, 1986. *(I)*

Board, Tessa. *Mammals*. Watts, 1983. *(P; I)*

Crump, Donald J., ed. *Giants from the Past*. National Geographic, 1983. *(P; I)*

Parker, Steve. *Mammal*. Knopf, 1989. *(I)*

Selsam, Millicent E., and Hunt, Joyce. *A First Look at Mammals*. Scholastic, 1976. *(P)*

MANITOBA. See CANADA.

MAO TSE-TUNG. See CHINA.

MAPLE SYRUP AND MAPLE SUGAR

Gokay, Nancy H. *Sugarbush: Making Maple Syrup*. Hillsdale, 1980. *(P)*

Lasky, Kathryn. *Sugaring Time*. Macmillan, 1983. *(I)*

Metcalf, Rosamund S. *The Sugar Maple*. Phoenix Publishing, 1982. *(P; I)*

MAPS AND GLOBES

Arnold, Caroline. *Maps and Globes: Fun, Facts, and Activities*. Watts, 1984. *(P)*

Baynes, John. *How Maps Are Made*. Facts on File, 1987. *(I)*

Carey, Helen. *How to Use Maps and Globes*. Watts, 1983. *(I; A)*

Cartwright, Sally. *What's in a Map?* Coward, 1976. *(P)*

Knowlton, Jack. *Geography from A to Z*. Crowell, 1988. *(P)*; *Maps and Globes*. Crowell, 1985. *(P; I)*

Madden, James F. *The Wonderful World of Maps*. Hammond, 1982. *(I; A)*

Mango, Karin. *Mapmaking*. Messner, 1984. *(P)*

Weiss, Harvey. *Maps: Getting from Here to There*. Houghton, 1991. *(I)*

MARIE ANTOINETTE. See FRENCH REVOLUTION.

MARS

Berger, Melvin. *If You Lived on Mars*. Lodestar, 1988. *(P; I)*

Cattermole, Peter. *Mars*. Facts on File, 1990. *(P; I)*

Simon, Seymour. *Mars*. Morrow, 1987. *(P)*

Vogt, Gregory. *Mars and the Inner Planets*. Watts, 1982. *(I; A)*

MARSUPIALS

Lavine, Sigmund A. *Wonders of Marsupials*. Dodd, 1979. *(I)*

Sherman, Geraldine. *Animals with Pouches: The Marsupials*. Holiday, 1978. *(P)*

See also KANGAROOS; KOALAS.

MARYLAND

Fradin, Dennis. *Maryland: In Words and Pictures*. Childrens, 1980. *(P; I)*

Rollo, Vera F. *A Geography of Maryland: Ask Me!* Maryland Historical Press, 1981. *(P; I)*

Schaun, George, and Schaun, Virginia. *Everyday Life in Colonial Maryland*. Maryland Historical Press, 1981. *(P; I; A)*

Seiden, Art. *Michael Shows Off Baltimore*. Outdoor Books, 1982. *(P; I)*

MASSACHUSETTS

Fradin, Dennis. *Massachusetts: In Words and Pictures*. Childrens, 1981. *(P; I)*

Kent, Deborah. *Massachusetts*. Childrens, 1988. *(P; I)*

MATERIALS SCIENCE

Bortz, Fred. *Superstuff!: Materials That Have Changed Our Lives*. Watts, 1990. *(I; A)*

MATHEMATICS

Adler, Irving. *Mathematics*. Doubleday, 1990. *(I; A)*

Anno, Mitsumasa. *All in a Day*. Putnam, 1990. *(P); Anno's Math Games II*. Philomel, 1989. *(P); Anno's Math Games III*. Philomel, 1991. (P; I); *Anno's Mysterious Multiplying Jar*. Philomel, 1983. *(P)*

Bendick, Jeanne. *Mathematics Illustrated Dictionary*. Watts, 1989. *(I; A)*

Birch, David. *The King's Chessboard*. Dial, 1988. (Fiction) *(P; I)*

Blocksma, Mary. *Reading the Numbers, A Survival Guide to the Measurement, Numbers and Sizes Encountered in Everyday Life*. Viking, 1989. *(P; I)*

Brown, Margaret Wise. *Four Fur Feet*. Watermark, 1989. (Fiction) *(P)*

Burningham, John. *The Shopping Basket*. Harcourt, 1980. (Fiction) *(P)*

Burns, Marilyn. *Math for Smarty Pants: Or Who Says Mathematicians Have Little Pig Eyes*. Little, 1983. *(I; A)*

Cushman, Jean. *Do You Wanna Bet? Your Chance to Find Out About Probability*. Clarion, 1991. *(I)*

Duffey, Betsy. *The Math Wiz*. Viking, 1990. (Fiction) *(P)*

Ferrell, Edmund. *Mathopedia*. Omni Books, 1994. *(I; A)*

Flansburg, Scott. *Math Magic*. Morrow, 1993. *(A)*

Gackenbach, Dick. *A Bag Full of Pups*. Houghton, 1981. (Fiction) *(P)*

Gardner, Martin. *Entertaining Mathematical Puzzles*. Dover, 1961. *(P; I)*

Haskins, Jim. *Count Your Way Through Italy*. Carolrhoda, 1990. *(P)*

Hennessey, B. G. *The Dinosaur Who Lived in My Backyard*. Penguin, 1990. (Fiction) *(P)*

Lampton, Christopher. *Science of Chaos*. Watts, 1992. *(I; A)*

Latham, Jean Lee. *Carry On Mr. Bowditch*. Houghton, 1955. *(P; I)*

Mathews, Louise. *Bunches and Bunches of Bunnies*. Scholastic, 1980. (Fiction) *(P)*

Pappas, Theoni. *Fractals, Googols, and Other Mathematical Tales*. Wide World, 1993. *(I; A)*

Pittman, Helena. *A Grain of Rice*. Hastings, 1986. (Fiction) *(P)*

Pomerantz, Charlotte. *The Half-Birthday Party*. Houghton, 1984. (Fiction) *(P)*

Russo, Marisabina. *The Line Up Book*. Greenwillow, 1986. (Fiction) *(P)*

Schwartz, David M. *If You Made a Million*. Lothrop, 1989. *(P; I)*

Sharp, Richard M., and Metzner, Seymour. *The Squeaky Square and 113 Other Math Activities for Kids*. TAB Books, 1990. *(I)*

Tafuri, Nancy. *Have You Seen My Duckling?* Penguin, 1986. (Fiction) *(P)*

Uchida, Yoshiko. *The Dancing Kettle*. Creative Arts, 1977. *(P; I)*

Vancleave, Janice. *Math for Every Kid: Activities That Make Learning Math Fun*. John Wiley, 1991. *(P; I)*

Watson, Clyde. *Tom Fox and the Apple Pie*. HarperCollins, 1972. (Fiction) *(P)*

White, Laurence B., Jr., and Broekel, Ray. *Math-A-Magic: Number Tricks for Magicians*. Albert Whitman, 1990. *(I)*

MATHEMATICS, HISTORY OF

Reimer, Luetta, and Reimer, Wilbert. *Mathematicians Are People, Too*. Dale Seymour, 1990. *(I)*

MATTER. See Physics.

MAURITANIA. See Africa.

MAYFLOWER

DeLage, Ida. *The Pilgrim Children on the Mayflower*. Garrard, 1980. *(P; I)*

See also Thirteen American Colonies.

McCLINTOCK, BARBARA

Kittredge, Mary. *Barbara McClintock: Biologist*. Chelsea House, 1991. *(I; A)*

McKINLEY, WILLIAM

Kent, Zachary. *William McKinley: Twenty-fifth President of the United States*. Childrens, 1988. *(P; I)*

MEAD, MARGARET

Castiglia, Julie. *Margaret Mead*. Silver Burdett, 1989. *(I; A)*

Epstein, Sam, and Epstein, Beryl. *She Never Looked Back: Margaret Mead in Samoa*. Putnam, 1980. *(I)*

Frevert, Patricia. *Margaret Mead Herself*. Creative Education, 1981. *(I; A)*

Ludle, Jacqueline. *Margaret Mead*. Watts, 1983. *(I; A)*

Saunders, Susan. *Margaret Mead: The World Was Her Family*. Viking, 1987. *(P; I)*

MEDICINE

Ardley, Neil. *Health and Medicine*. Watts, 1982. *(P; I)*

Berger, Melvin. *Sports Medicine*. Harper, 1982. *(I; A)*

DeStefano, Susan. *Focus on Medicines*. 21st Century Books, 1991. *(P)*

Drotar, David. L. *Microsurgery: Revolution in the Operating Room*. Beaufort Books NY, 1981. *(I; A)*

Jackson, Gordon. *Medicine: The Body and Healing*. Watts, 1984. *(P; I)*

Oleksy, Walter G. *Paramedics*. Messner, 1983. *(I)*

MENDEL, GREGOR JOHANN

Sootin, Harry. *Gregor Mendel: Father of the Science of Genetics*. Vanguard, 1959. *(I)*

MENSTRUATION

Berger, Gilda. *PMS: Premenstrual Syndrome*. Watts, 1984. *(I; A)*

Marzollo, Jean. *Getting Your Period: A Book About Menstruation*. Dial, 1989. *(I; A)*

Nourse, Alan E., M.D. *Menstruation: Just Plain Talk*. Watts, 1987. *(I; A)*

MENTAL HEALTH

Gilbert, Sara. *What Happens in Therapy*. Lothrop, 1982. *(I; A)*

Myers, Irma, and Myers, Arthur. *Why You Feel Down and What You Can Do About It*. Scribner's, 1982. *(I; A)*

Olshan, Neal H. *Depression*. Watts, 1982. *(I; A)*

MERCURY

Simon, Seymour. *Mercury*. Morrow, 1992. *(P)*

METALS AND METALLURGY

Coombs, Charles. *Gold and Other Precious Metals*. Morrow, 1981. *(P; I)*

Fodor, R. V. *Gold, Copper, Iron: How Metals Are Formed, Found, and Used*. Enslow, 1989. *(A)*

Lambert, Mark. *Spotlight on Copper*. Rourke, 1988. *(P; I)*

Lye, Keith. *Spotlight on Gold*. Rourke, 1988. *(P; I)*

Lyttle, Richard B. *The Golden Path: The Lure of Gold Through History*. Atheneum, 1983. *(I; A)*

Mitgutsch, Ali. *From Ore to Spoon*. Carolrhoda, 1981. *(P)*

Rickard, Graham. *Spotlight on Silver*. Rourke, 1988. *(P; I)*

Whyman, Kathryn. *Metals and Alloys*. Gloucester Press, 1988. *(P; I)*

METRIC SYSTEM. See WEIGHTS AND MEASURES.

MEXICAN WAR

Lawson, Don. *The United States in the Mexican War*. Harper, 1976. *(I; A)*

Murphy, Keith. *The Battle of the Alamo*. Raintree, 1979. *(P; I)*

See also TEXAS.

MEXICO

Casagrande, Louis B., and Johnson, Sylvia A. *Focus on Mexico: Modern Life in an Ancient Land*. Lerner, 1987. *(I)*

Epstein, Sam, and Epstein, Beryl. *Mexico*. Watts, 1983 (rev. ed.). *(I)*

Fincher, E. B. *Mexico and the United States: Their Linked Destinies*. Harper, 1983. *(I; A)*

Jacobsen, Peter O., and Kristensen, Preben S. *A Family in Mexico*. Watts, 1984. *(P; I)*

Jacobson, Karen. *Mexico*. Childrens, 1982. *(P)*

Lye, Keith. *Take a Trip to Mexico*. Watts, 1982. *(P)*

Moran, Tom. *A Family in Mexico*. Lerner, 1987. *(P)*

Smith, Eileen L. *Mexico: Giant of the South*. Dillon, 1983. *(I; A)*

Visual Geography. *Mexico in Pictures*. Lerner, 1987. *(I)*

MICHELANGELO

Ventura, Piero. *Michelangelo's World*. Putnam, 1990. *(P; I)*

MICHIGAN

Hintz, Martin. *Michigan*. Watts, 1987. *(P; I)*

Stein, R. Conrad. *Michigan*. Childrens, 1988. *(P; I)*

Zimmerman, Chanda K. *Detroit*. Dillon, 1989. *(P; I)*

MICROBIOLOGY

Anderson, Lucia. *The Smallest Life Around Us*. Crown, 1978. *(I)*

Giblin, James Cross. *Milk: The Fight for Purity*. Crowell, 1986. *(I)*

Patent, Dorothy Hinshaw. *Bacteria: How They Affect Other Living Things*. Holiday, 1980. *(I)*; *Germs!* Holiday, 1983. *(P; I)*

Taylor, Ron. *Through the Microscope*. Facts on File, 1986. *(I)*

MICROSCOPES

Bleifeld, Maurice. *Experimenting with a Microscope*. Watts, 1988. *(I)*

Johnson, Gaylord, and Bleifeld, Maurice. *Hunting with the Microscope*. Arco, 1980 (rev. ed.). *(I; A)*

Klein, Aaron E. *The Complete Beginner's Guide to Microscopes and Telescopes*. Doubleday, 1980. *(I; A)*

Simon, Seymour. *Hidden Worlds*. Morrow, 1983. *(P; I)*

Stwertka, Eve and Stwertka, Albert. *Microscope: How to Use It and Enjoy It*. Messner, 1989. *(I)*

See also ASTRONOMY; LASERS; LENSES; LIGHT.

MICROWAVES

Asimov, Isaac. *How Did We Find Out About Microwaves?* Walker, 1989. *(P; I)*

MIDDLE AGES

Aliki. *A Medieval Feast*. Harper, 1983. *(P)*

Barber, Richard. *The Reign of Chivalry*. St. Martin's, 1980. *(I)*

Brooks, Polly S. *Queen Eleanor: Independent Spirit of the Medieval World*. Harper, 1983. *(I; A)*

Cosman, Madeleine P. *Medieval Holidays and Festivals: A Calendar of Celebrations*. Scribner's, 1982. *(I; A)*

Crosland, Jessie, tr. *Song of Roland*. Cooper Square, 1970. *(I)*

Fradon, Dana. *Harold the Herald: A Book About Heraldry*. Dutton, 1990. *(P; I)*

Lewis, Brenda R. *Growing Up in the Dark Ages*. David & Charles, 1980. *(I; A)*

Oakes, Catherine. *Exploring the Past: The Middle Ages*. Gulliver Books, 1988. *(I; A)*

Sancha, Sheila. *The Luttrell Village: Country Life in the Middle Ages*. Harper, 1983. *(I; A); Walter Dragun's Town: Crafts and Trades in the Middle Ages*. Crowell, 1989. *(I; A)*

Wood, Audrey. *King Bidgood's in the Bathtub*. Harcourt, 1985. *(P)*

Wright, Sylvia. *The Age of Chivalry: English Society, 1200–1400*. Warwick Press, 1988. *(P; I)*

MIDDLE EAST

Kuwait . . . in Pictures. Lerner, 1989. *(I)*

Beaton, Margaret. *Syria*. Childrens, 1988. *(I)*

Berson, Harold. *Kassim's Shoes*. Crown, 1977. (Fiction) *(P)*

Collinson, Alan. *Mountains*. Dillon, 1992. *(I; A)*

Feinstein, Steve. *Turkey . . . in Pictures*. Lerner, 1988. *(P: I)*

Gell, Anthea, tr. *Stories of the Arabian Nights*. Peter Bedrick, 1982. *(I)*

Heide, Florence Parry, and Gilliland, Judith Heide. *Sami and the Time of the Troubles*. Clarion, 1992. (Fiction) *(I)*

Husain, Akbar. *The Revolution in Iran*. Rourke, 1988. *(A)*

King, John. *The Gulf War*. Dillon: Macmillan, 1991. *(I; A)*

Lawless, Richard, and Bleaney, Heather. *The Middle East Since 1945*. Batsford, 1990. *(A)*

Long, Cathryn J. *The Middle East in Search of Peace*. Millbrook, 1994. *(I)*

McCaughrean, Geraldine. *One Thousand and One Arabian Nights*. Oxford University Press, 1982. *(I)*

Mulloy, Martin. *Kuwait*. Chelsea House, 1989. *(P; I); Syria*. Chelsea House, 1988. *(P)*

Pimlott, John. *Middle East: A Background to the Conflicts*. Gloucester Press, dist. by Watts, 1991. *(I)*

Rice, Edward. *Babylon, Next to Nineveh: Where the World Began*. Scholastic, 1979. *(I; A)*

Spencer, William. *The Islamic States in Conflict*. Watts, 1983. *(I, A); The Land and People of Turkey*. Harper, 1990. *(I; A)*

See also EGYPT; ISRAEL.

MILK. See DAIRYING AND DAIRY PRODUCTS.

MINERALS

Cheney, Glenn Alan. *Mineral Resources*. Watts, 1985. *(I)*

Eckert, Allan W. *Earth Treasures: Where to Collect Minerals, Rocks, and Fossils in the United States*. Harper, 1987. *(I; A)*

Harris, Susan. *Gems and Minerals*. Watts, 1982. *(P)*

Marcus, Elizabeth. *Rocks and Minerals*. Troll, 1983. *(P; I)*

McGowen, Tom. *Album of Rocks and Minerals*. Rand, 1981. *(P; I)*

Podendorf, Illa. *Rocks and Minerals*. Childrens, 1982. *(P)*

Srogi, Lee Ann. *Start Collecting Rocks and Minerals*. Running Press, 1989. *(I; A)*

Symes, R. F. and the staff of the Natural History Museum. *Rocks and Minerals*. Knopf, 1988. *(I)*

Whyman, Kathryn. *Rocks and Minerals*. Gloucester Press, 1989. *(P; I)*

MINES AND MINING

Mitgutsch, Ali. *From Ore to Spoon*. Carolrhoda, 1981. *(P)*

MINNESOTA

Densmore, Frances. *Dakota and Ojibwe People in Minnesota*. Minnesota Historical Society Press, 1977. *(I)*

Finsand, Mary J. *The Town That Moved*. Carolrhoda, 1983. *(P)*

Fradin, Dennis. *Minnesota: In Words and Pictures*. Childrens, 1980. *(P; I)*

Wilder, Laura Ingalls. *On the Banks of Plum Creek*. Harper, 1953. (Fiction) *(I)*

MISSISSIPPI

Carson, Robert. *Mississippi*. Childrens, 1989. *(P; I)*

Fradin, Dennis. *Mississippi: In Words and Pictures*. Childrens, 1980. *(P; I)*

Twain, Mark. *Life on the Mississippi*. Oxford University Press, 1962. *(I; A)*

MISSISSIPPI RIVER

Cooper, Kay. *Journeys on the Mississippi*. Messner, 1981. *(P; I)*

Crisman, Ruth. *The Mississippi*. Watts, 1984. *(I; A)*

St. George, Judith. *The Amazing Voyage of the New Orleans*. Putnam, 1980. *(I; A)*

Zeck, Pam, and Zeck, Gerry. *Mississippi Sternwheelers*. Carolrhoda, 1982. *(P; I)*

MISSOURI

Fradin, Dennis. *Missouri: In Words and Pictures*. Childrens, 1980. *(P; I)*

Wilder, Laura Ingalls, and Lane, Rose Wilder. *On the Way Home: The Diary of a Trip from South Dakota to Mansfield, Missouri, in 1894*. Harper, 1962. *(I)*

MODELING

Cantwell, Lois. *Modeling*. (First Book) Watts, 1986. *(I; A)*

Lasch, Judith. *The Teen Model Book*. Messner, 1986. *(A)*

Moss, Miriam. *Fashion Model*. Crestwood House, 1991. *(I)*

MODERN ART. See ART AND ARTISTS.

MODERN MUSIC. See MUSIC AND MUSICIANS.

MONET, CLAUDE

Venezia, Mike. *Monet*. Childrens, 1990. *(P)*

MONEY

Adler, David A. *All Kinds of Money*. Watts, 1984. *(P)*
Brittain, Bill. *All the Money in the World*. Harper, 1979. *(I)*
Bungum, Jane E. *Money and Financial Institutions*. Lerner, 1991. *(A)*
Byers, Patricia, and Preston, Julia. *The Kids' Money Book*. Liberty Publishing, 1983. *(P; I)*
Cantwell, Lois. *Money and Banking*. Watts, 1984. *(I; A)*
Cribb, Joe. *Money*. Knopf, 1990. *(P; I; A)*
Dolan, Edward F., Jr. *Money Talk*. Messner, 1986. *(I)*
Fodor, R. V. *Nickels, Dimes, and Dollars: How Currency Works*. Morrow, 1980. *(P; I)*
German, Joan. *The Money Book*. Dandelion, 1983. *(P)*
Maestro, Betsy. *The Story of Money*. Clarion, 1993. *(P; I)*
Maestro, Betsy, and Maestro, Guilio. *Dollars and Cents for Harriet*. Crown, 1988. *(P)*
Wyler, Rose, and Elting, Mary. *Math Fun With Money Puzzlers*. Messner, 1992. *(I)*
Young, Robin R. *The Stock Market*. Lerner, 1991. *(A)*

MONKEYS AND THEIR RELATIVES

Anderson, Norman D., and Brown, Walter R. *Lemurs*. Dodd, 1984. *(P)*
Barrett, N. S. *Monkeys and Apes*. Watts, 1988. *(P; I)*
Gelman, Rita Golden. *Monkeys and Apes of the World*. Watts, 1990. *(P)*
Overbeck, Cynthia. *Monkeys*. Lerner, 1981. *(P; I; A)*
Stone, Lynn M. *Baboons*. Rourke, 1990. *(P); Chimpanzees*. Rourke, 1990. *(P); Snow Monkeys*. Rourke, 1990. *(P)*
Whitehead, Patricia. *Monkeys*. Troll, 1982. *(P)*

MONROE, JAMES

Fitzgerald, Christine Maloney. *James Monroe: Fifth President of the United States*. Childrens, 1987. *(I)*
Hanser, James. *The Glorious Hour of Lieutenant Monroe*. Atheneum, 1976. *(P; I)*
Wetzel, Charles. *James Monroe*. Chelsea House, 1989. *(I; A)*
See also PRESIDENCY OF THE UNITED STATES.

MONTANA

Carpenter, Allan. *Montana*. Childrens, 1979. *(I)*
Fradin, Dennis. *Montana: In Words and Pictures*. Childrens, 1981. *(P; I)*

MONTREAL. SEE CANADA.

MOON

Adler, David. *All About the Moon*. Troll, 1983. *(P; I)*
Aiken, Joan. *Moon's Revenge*. Knopf, 1987. (Fiction) *(P; I)*
Apfel, Necia H. *The Moon and Its Exploration*. Watts, 1982. *(I; A)*
Hughes, David. *The Moon*. Facts on File, 1990. *(P; I)*
Jay, Michael, and Henbest, Nigel. *The Moon*. Watts, 1982. *(P)*
Simon, Seymour. *The Moon*. Four Winds, 1984. *(P)*
Vaughan, Jenny. *On the Moon*. Watts, 1983. *(P)*
Zim, Herbert S. *The New Moon*. Morrow, 1980. *(P; I)*

MORMONS

Smith, Gary. *Day of Great Healing in Nauvoo*. Deseret, 1980. *(I; A)*

MOROCCO. See AFRICA.

MORSE, SAMUEL

Kerby, Mona. *Samuel Morse*. Watts, 1991. *(P; I)*

MOSCOW. See UNION OF SOVIET SOCIALIST REPUBLICS.

MOSES. See BIBLE AND BIBLE STORIES.

MOSES, GRANDMA

Kallir, Jane Katherine. *Grandma Moses: The Artist Behind the Myth*. Clarkson Potter, 1982. *(I; A)*
Oneal, Zibby. *Grandma Moses: Painter of Rural America*. Viking Kestrel, 1986. *(I; A)*

MOSQUITOES

Bernard, George, and Cooke, John. *Mosquito*. Putnam, 1982. *(I; A)*
Patent, Dorothy Hinshaw. *Mosquitoes*. Holiday, 1987. *(I)*

MOTION

Ardley, Neil. *Making Things Move*. Watts, 1984. *(P; I); The Science Book of Motion*. Harcourt, 1992. *(P; I)*
Laithwaite, Eric. *Force: The Power Behind Movement*. Watts, 1986. *(I)*
Murphy, Bryan. *Experiment with Movement*. Lerner, 1991. *(P; I)*
Simon, Seymour. *Everything Moves*. Walker, 1976. *(P)*
Taylor, Barbara. *Get it in Gear!* Random, 1991. *(I)*
Taylor, Kim. *Action*. John Wiley, 1992. *(I)*
Watson, Philip. *Super Motion*. Lothrop, 1982. *(I)*
Zubrowski, Bernard. *Raceways: Having Fun with Balls and Tracks*. Morrow, 1985. *(I)*

MOTION PICTURES

Aylesworth, Thomas G. *Monsters from the Movies*. Bantam, 1981. *(P; I)*

Cherrell, Gwen. *How Movies Are Made*. Facts on File, 1989. *(I)*

Cohen, Daniel. *Horror in the Movies*. Houghton, 1982. *(P; I; A)*

Gibbons, Gail. *Lights! Camera! Action! How a Movie Is Made*. Crowell, 1985. *(P)*

Levine, Michael L. *Moviemaking: A Guide for Beginners*. Scribner's, 1980. *(I; A)*

Platt, Richard. *Film*. Knopf, 1992. *(I; A)*

MOTORCYCLES

Baumann, Elwood D. *An Album of Motorcycles and Motorcycle Racing*. Watts, 1982. *(I; A)*

Cave, Joyce, and Cave, Ronald. *What About . . . Motorbikes*. Watts, 1982. *(P)*

Cleary, Beverly. *Lucky Chuck*. Morrow, 1984. (Fiction) *(P)*

Jefferis, David. *Trailbikes*. Watts, 1984. *(P; I)*

Kerrod, Robin. *Motorcycles*. Gloucester Press, 1989. *(I)*

Naden, C. J. *Cycle Chase, the Championship Season*. Troll, 1980. *(P; I; A)*; *High Gear*, 1980. *(P; I; A)*; *I Can Read About Motorcycles*, 1979 (new ed.). *(P; I)*; *Motorcycle Challenge, Trials and Races*, 1980. *(P; I; A)*

Radlauer, Ed, and Radlauer, Ruth. *Minibike Mania; Minibike Winners*. Childrens, 1982. *(P; I)*

MOUNTAINS AND MOUNTAIN CLIMBING

Bain, Ian. *Mountains and Earth Movements*. Bookwright, 1984. *(I)*

Berger, Gilda. *Mountain World*. Coward, 1978. *(P)*

Bramwell, Martin. *Mountains*. Watts, 1987. *(I)*

Catchpole, Clive. *Mountains*. Dial, 1984. *(P)*

Dixon, Dougal. *Mountains*. Watts, 1984. *(P; I; A)* (Atlas format)

Douglas, William O. *Exploring the Himalaya*. Random, 1958. *(I; A)*

Fraser, Mary Ann. *On Top of the World: The Conquest of Mount Everest*. Holt, 1991. *(P; I)*

George, Jean Craighead. *One Day in the Alpine Tundra*. Harper, 1984. *(P; I)*

Hargrove, Jim, and Johnson, S. A. *Mountain Climbing*. Lerner, 1983. *(P; I; A)*

Lye, Keith. *Mountains*. Silver Burdett, 1987. *(P)*

Marcus, Elizabeth. *All About Mountains and Volcanoes*. Troll, 1984. *(P; I)*

Miller, Luree. *The Black Hat Dances: Two Buddhist Boys in the Himalayas*. Dodd, 1987. *(I)*

Radlauer, Ed. *Some Basics About Rock Climbing*. Childrens, 1983. *(P; I; A)*

Rylant, Cynthia. *When I Was Young in the Mountains*. Dutton, 1982. (Fiction) *(P)*

Siebert, Diane. *Sierra*. Harper, 1991. *(P; I)*

Updegraffe, Imelda, and Updegraffe, Robert. *Mountains and Valleys*. Penguin, 1983. *(I; A)*

MOZAMBIQUE

James, R. S. *Mozambique*. Chelsea House, 1987. *(P; I)*

MOZART, WOLFGANG AMADEUS

Downing, Julie. *Mozart Tonight*. Bradbury, 1991. *(P)*

Thompson, Wendy. *Wolfgang Amadeus Mozart*. Viking, 1991. *(I)*

Weil, Lisl. *Wolferl: The First Six Years in the Life of Wolfgang Amadeus Mozart*. Holiday, 1991. *(P)*

See also MUSIC AND MUSICIANS.

MULTICULTURAL*

Adoff, Arnold. *All the Colors of the Race*. Morrow, 1982. (Hispanic) *(I; A)*

Armstrong, Jennifer. *Chin Yu Min and the Ginger Cat*. Crown, 1993. *(P)*

Bemelmans, Ludwig. *Madeline's Rescue*. Viking, 1953. (French) (Fiction) *(P)*

Blumberg, Rhoda. *Commodore Perry in the Land of the Shogun*. Lothrop, 1985. (Japanese) *(I; A)*

Finger, Charles J. *Tales from Silver Lands*. Doubleday, 1924. (Hispanic) *(P; I)*

Friedman, Ina R. *How My Parents Learned to Eat*. Houghton, 1984. (Japanese) (Fiction) *(I)*

Gollub, Matthew. *The Twenty-Five Mixtec Cats*. Tambourine, 1993. *(P)*

Gray, Nigel. *A Country Far Away*. Orchard Books, 1988. (North American/African) *(P)*

Hewett, Joan. *Hector Lives in the United States Now: The Story of a Mexican American Child*. Harper, 1990. (Hispanic) *(P; I)*

Hurwitz, Joanna. *Class President*. Morrow, 1988. (Hispanic) (Fiction) *(P; I)*

Kherdian, David. *The Road from Home*. Greenwillow, 1979. (Armenian) *(I; A)*

Lester, Julius. *How Many Spots Does a Leopard Have?* Scholastic, 1989. *(P; I)*

Lord, Bette. *In the Year of the Boar and Jackie Robinson*. Harper, 1984. (Chinese) (Fiction) *(P; I)*

Louie, Ai-Ling. *Yeh-Shen: A Cinderella Story from China*. Philomel, 1982. (Chinese) (Fiction) *(P; I)*

Lyons, Mary E., ed. *Rawhead, Bloody Bones: African-American Tales of the Supernatural*. Scribner's, 1991. (African) (Fiction) *(I)*

Maruki, Toshi. *Hiroshima No Pika*. Lothrop, 1985. (Japanese) *(I; A)*

Morey, Janet Nomura, and Dunn, Wendy. *Famous Asian Americans*. Dutton, 1992. (Asian) *(I)*

Mosel, Arlene. *The Funny Little Woman*. Dutton, 1972. (Japanese) (Fiction) *(P)*; *Tikki, Tikki, Tembo*. Holt, 1968. (Chinese) (Fiction) *(P)*

Perkins, Mitali. *The Sunita Experiment*. Joy Street/Little, 1993. (Fiction) *(I)*

Polacco, Patricia. *The Keeping Quilt*. Simon & Schuster, 1988. (Russian) (Fiction) *(P)*

---

*This is a popular theme with young readers. However, it is not a separate article in *The New Book of Knowledge*.

Ransome, Arthur. *The Fool of the World and the Flying Ship*. Farrar, 1968. (Russian) (Fiction) *(P; I)*

Steptoe, John. *Mufaro's Beautiful Daughters*. Lothrop, 1987. (African) (Fiction) *(P)*

Taylor, Sydney. *All-of-a-Kind Family*. Follett, 1951. (Jewish) (Fiction) *(P; I)*

Yep, Laurence. *Dragonwings*. Harper, 1975. (Chinese) (Fiction) *(I; A)*

Young, Ed. *Lon Po Po: A Red Riding Hood Story from China*. Philomel, 1989. (Chinese) (Fiction) *(P)*

Young, Richard Alan, and Young, Judy D. *Stories from the Days of Christopher Columbus*. August House, 1992. (Fiction) *(I)*

MUNICIPAL GOVERNMENT

Eichner, James A., and Shields, Linda M. *The First Book of Local Government*. Watts, 1983 (rev. ed.). *(I)*

MUSEUMS

Althea. *Visiting a Museum*. Cambridge University Press, 1983. *(I; A)*

Cutchins, Judy, and Johnston, Ginny. *Are Those Animals Real? How Museums Prepare Wildlife Exhibits*. Morrow, 1984. *(I)*

Papajani, Janet. *Museums*. Childrens, 1983. *(P)*

Sandak, Cass R. *Museums: What They Are and How They Work*. Watts, 1981. *(P; I; A)*

Stan, Susan. *Careers in an Art Museum*. Lerner, 1983. *(P; I)*

Stein, R. Conrad. *The Story of the Smithsonian Institution*. Childrens, 1979. *(P; I)*

MUSHROOMS. See FUNGI.

MUSICAL COMEDY

Powers, Bill. *Behind the Scenes of a Broadway Musical*. Crown, 1982. *(P; I)*

MUSICAL INSTRUMENTS

Anderson, David. *The Piano Makers*. Pantheon, 1982. *(I)*

Blackwood, Alan. *Musical Instruments*. Watts, 1987. *(P)*

Fichter, George S. *American Indian Music and Musical Instruments*. McKay, 1978. *(I; A)*

Kettelkamp, Larry. *Electronic Musical Instruments: What They Do, How They Work*. Morrow, 1984. *(A)*

Walther, Tom. *Make Mine Music*. Little, 1981. *(P; I)*

MUSIC AND MUSICIANS

Ardley, Neil. *Music*. Knopf, 1989. *(P; I; A)*; *Sound and Music*. Watts, 1984. *(P; I)*

Bailey, Eva. *Music and Musicians*. David & Charles, 1983. *(I; A)*

Beirne, Barbara. *A Pianist's Debut: Preparing for the Concert*. Carolrhoda, 1990. *(I)*

Englander, Roger. *Opera! What's All the Screaming About?* Walker, 1983. *(I; A)*

Glazer, Tom. *Music for Ones and Twos: Songs and Games for the Very Young Child*. Doubleday, 1983. *(P)*

Kendall, Catherine W. *Stories of Composers for Young Musicians*. Toadwood, 1982. *(P; I)*

Kogan, Judith. *Nothing but the Best: The Struggle for Perfection at the Juilliard School*. Random, 1987. *(I; A)*

Krementz, Jill. *A Very Young Musician*. Simon & Schuster, 1991. *(P; I)*

Krull, Kathleen. *Lives of the Musicians: Good Times, Bad Times (And What the Neighbors Thought)*. Harcourt, 1993. *(I; A)*

Kuskin, Karla. *The Philharmonic Gets Dressed*. Harper, 1982. *(P; I)*

Meyer, Carolyn. *Music Is for Everyone*. Good Apple, 1980. *(P; I)*

Mitchell, Barbara. *Raggin': A Story About Scott Joplin*. Scholastic, 1986. *(P; I)*

Nichols, Janet. *Women Music Makers: An Introduction to Women Composers*. Walker, 1992. *(I; A)*

Paterson, Katherine. *Come Sing, Jimmy Jo*. Dutton, 1985. (Fiction) *(I; A)*

Price, Leontyne. *Aida*. Harcourt, 1990. (Fiction) *(P; I)*

Schroeder, Alan. *Ragtime Tumpie*. Joy Street, 1989. (Fiction) *(P; I)*

Tanenhaus, Sam. *Louis Armstrong*. Chelsea House, 1989. *(P; I)*

Taylor, Mildred D. *Song of the Trees*. Dial, 1975. (Fiction) *(I; A)*

See also COUNTRY MUSIC; JAZZ; ROCK MUSIC; UNITED STATES (ART, LITERATURE, AND MUSIC).

MUSSOLINI, BENITO

Hartenian, Larry. *Benito Mussolini*. Chelsea House, 1988. *(A)*

Lyttle, Richard B. *Il Duce: The Rise and Fall of Benito Mussolini*. Atheneum, 1987. *(I)*

Mulvihill, Margaret. *Mussolini and Italian Fascism*. Gloucester Press, 1990. *(A)*

MYSTERY*

Duffy, James. *Missing*. Scribner's, 1988. (Fiction) *(I; A)*

Konigsburg, E. L. *From the Mixed-Up Files of Mrs. Basil E. Frankweiler*. Atheneum, 1967. (Fiction) *(P; I)*

Monsell, Mary Elise. *The Mysterious Cases of Mr. Pin*. Atheneum, 1989. (Fiction) *(P; I)*

Pullman, Philip. *The Ruby in the Smoke*. Knopf, 1987. (Fiction) *(I; A)*; *Shadow in the North*. Knopf, 1988. (Fiction) *(I; A)*

Schwartz, Alvin. *Scary Stories to Tell in the Dark*. Lippincott, 1981. (Fiction) *(P; I)*

Shreve, Susan. *Lucy Forever and Miss Rosetree, Shrinks*. Knopf, 1988. (Fiction) *(P; I)*

---

*This is a popular theme with young readers. However, it is not a separate article in *The New Book of Knowledge*.

York, Carol Beach. *Once upon a Dark November*. Holiday, 1989. (Fiction) *(I; A)*

MYTHOLOGY

Benson, Sally. *Stories of the Gods and Heroes*. Dial, 1940. *(P; I)*

Bullfinch, Thomas. *A Book of Myths*. Macmillan, 1942. *(I; A)*

D'Aulaire, Ingri, and D'Aulaire, Edgar P. *D'Aulaire's Book of Greek Myths*. Doubleday, 1962. *(P; I); D'Aulaire's Book of Norse Gods and Giants*. Doubleday, 1962. *(P; I)*

Evslin, Bernard. *Hercules*. Morrow, 1984. *(I)*

Gifford, Douglas. *Warriors, Gods and Spirits*. Eurobook, 1983. *(I)*

Keats, Ezra Jack. *John Henry: An American Legend*. Knopf, 1965. *(P)*

Kellogg, Steven. *Paul Bunyan*. Morrow, 1984. *(P; I)*

Kingsley, Charles. *The Heroes*. W. H. Smith, 1980. *(P; I)*

Lanier, Sidney, ed. *Boy's King Arthur: Sir Thomas Malory's History of King Arthur and His Knights of the Round Table*. Scribner's, 1917. *(I; A)*

Mollel, Tololwa M. *The Orphan Boy*. Clarion, 1991. *(P)*

Richardson, I. M. *Demeter and Persephone: The Seasons of Time; Prometheus and the Story of Fire*. Troll, 1983. *(P; I)*

Ross, Harriet, comp. by. *Myths and Legends of Many Lands*. Lion, 1982. *(I; A)*

Sutcliff, Rosemary. *Sword and the Circle: King Arthur and the Knights of the Round Table*. Dutton, 1981. *(I)*

Switzer, Ellen and Costas. *Greek Myths: Gods, Heroes and Monsters: Their Sources, Their Stories and Their Meanings*. Atheneum, 1988. *(A)*

NAMES AND NICKNAMES

Hazen, Barbara S. *Last, First, Middle, and Nick: All About Names*. Prentice Hall, 1979. *(P)*

Hook, J. N. *The Book of Names*. Watts, 1984. *(A)*

Lee, Mary P. *Your Name: All About It*. Westminster, 1980. *(P; I; A)*

Lee, Mary Price, and Lee, Richard S. *Last Names First . . . And Some First Names, Too*. Westminster, 1985. *(I; A)*

NAMIBIA. See AFRICA.

NAPOLEON I

Marrin, Albert. *Napoleon and the Napoleonic Wars*. Viking, 1991. *(A)*

Masters, Anthony. *Napoleon*. McGraw, 1981. *(I; A)*

NARCOTICS. See DRUGS.

NASSER, GAMAL ABDEL

DeChancie, John. *Gamal Abdel Nasser*. Chelsea House, 1987. *(I: A)*

NATIONAL ANTHEMS AND PATRIOTIC SONGS

Bangs, Edward. *Yankee Doodle*. Scholastic, 1980. *(P)*

Browne, C. A. *The Story of Our National Ballads*. Harper, 1960. *(I)*

Lyons, John Henry. *Stories of Our American Patriotic Songs*. Vanguard, n.d. *(I; A)*

Spier, Peter. *The Star-Spangled Banner*. Doubleday, 1973. *(P; I)*

NATIONAL PARK SYSTEM

Annerino, John. *Hiking the Grand Canyon*. Sierra Club Books, 1986. *(A)*

Lovett, Sarah. *The National Parks of the Southwest: A Young Person's Guide*. John Muir, 1990. *(P; I)*

National Park Service, Department of the Interior, Washington. D.C. 20240—a source of printed materials about the National Park System and the individual units.

Radlauer, Ruth. Books describing individual U.S. national parks: *Acadia; Bryce Canyon; Denali; Glacier; Grand Canyon; Grand Teton; Haleakala, Mammoth Cave; Mesa Verde; Olympic; Shenandoah; Zion*. Childrens, 1977–1982. *(P; I; A)*

NATURAL GAS. See ENERGY.

NATURE, STUDY OF

Burnie, David. *How Nature Works: 100 Ways Parents and Kids Can Share the Secrets of Nature*. Reader's Digest, 1991 *(I)*

Faber, Doris, and Faber, Harold. *Great Lives: Nature and the Environment*. Scribner's, 1991. *(I; A)*

Huber, Carey. *Nature Explorer: A Step-by Step Guide*. Troll, 1990. *(I)*

Keene, Ann T. *Earthkeepers: Observers and Protectors of Nature*. Oxford, 1993. *(I; A)*

Parker, Steve. *The Random House Book of How Nature Works*. Random, 1993. *(I)*

NEBRASKA

Fradin, Dennis. *Nebraska: In Words and Pictures*. Childrens, 1980. *(P; I)*

Hargrove, Jim. *Nebraska*. Childrens, 1989. *(P; I)*

Manley, Robert N. *Nebraska: Our Pioneer Heritage*. Media Productions, 1981. *(I)*

Talbot, Charlene. *An Orphan for Nebraska*. Atheneum, 1979. (Fiction) *(I)*

Thompson, Kathleen. *Nebraska*. Raintree, 1988. *(P; I)*

NEBULAS. See ASTRONOMY.

NEEDLEPOINT. See Sewing and Needlecraft.

NEHRU, JAWAHARLAL. See India.

NEPAL

Nepal . . . in Pictures. Lerner, 1989. *(I; A)*
Knowlton, MaryLee, and Sachner, Mark J. *Nepal.* Gareth Stevens, 1987. *(P)*
Margolies, Barbara A. *Kanu of Kathmandu: A Journey in Nepal.* Four Winds, 1992. *(P; I)*
Watanabe, Hitomi. *Nepal.* Gareth Stevens, 1987. *(P)*

NEPTUNE

Asimov, Isaac. *How Did We Find Out About Neptune?* Walker, 1990. *(I; A)*
Simon, Seymour. *Neptune.* Morrow, 1991. *(P; I)*

NERO. See Rome, Ancient.

NETHERLANDS

Dodge, Mary M. *Hans Brinker.* Putnam, n.d. (Fiction) *(I)*
Fairclough, Chris. *Take a Trip to Holland.* Watts, 1984. *(P; I)*
Fradin, Dennis B. *The Netherlands.* Childrens, 1983. *(I; A)*
Jacobsen, Peter O., and Kristensen, Preben S. *A Family in Holland.* Watts, 1984. *(P; I)*

NEVADA

Carpenter, Allan. *Nevada.* Childrens, 1979. *(I)*
Fradin, Dennis. *Nevada: In Words and Pictures.* Childrens, 1981.

NEW BRUNSWICK. See Canada.

NEWFOUNDLAND. See Canada.

NEW GUINEA. See Southeast Asia.

NEW HAMPSHIRE

Fradin, Dennis. *New Hampshire: In Words and Pictures.* Childrens, 1981; *The New Hampshire Colony,* 1988. *(P; I)*

NEW JERSEY

Homer, Larona. *The Shore Ghosts and Other Stories of New Jersey.* Middle Atlantic Press, 1981. *(P; I)*
Kent, Deborah. *New Jersey.* Childrens, 1988. *(P; I)*
Murray, Thomas C., and Barnes, Valerie. *The Seven Wonders of New Jersey—And Then Some.* Enslow, 1981. *(P; I)*
Rabold, Ted, and Fair, Phillip. *New Jersey: Yesterday and Today.* Penns Valley, 1982. *(P; I)*

NEW MEXICO

Fradin, Dennis. *New Mexico: In Words and Pictures.* Childrens, 1981. *(P; I)*
Stein, R. Conrad. *New Mexico.* Childrens, 1988. *(P)*

NEWSPAPERS

Carey, Helen, and Greenberg, Judith H. *How to Read a Newspaper.* Watts, 1983. *(I; A)*
Crisman, Ruth. *Hot off the Press: Getting the News into Print.* Lerner, 1991. *(I; A)*
English, Betty Lou. *Behind the Headlines at a Big City Paper.* Lothrop, 1985. *(A)*
Leedy, Loreen. *The Furry News: How to Make a Newspaper.* Holiday, 1990. *(P)*
Lipson, Greta, and Greenberg, Bernice. *Extra! Extra! Read All About It.* Good Apple, 1981. *(P; I)*
Miller, Margaret. *Hot off the Press! A Day at the Daily News.* Crown, 1985. *(I)*
Tebbel, John. *Opportunities in Journalism.* VGM Career Horizons, 1982. *(I; A)*
Waters, Sarah. *How Newspapers Are Made.* Facts on File, 1989. *(I)*

NEWTON, ISAAC

Ipsen, D. C. *Isaac Newton: Reluctant Genius.* Enslow, 1986. *(I; A)*
Tiner, John H. *Isaac Newton: The True Story of His Life.* Mott, 1976. *(P; I)*

NEW YEAR CELEBRATIONS AROUND THE WORLD. See Holidays.

NEW YORK

Asch, Sholem. "Summer in New York" from *East River.* Carroll & Graf, 1983. (Fiction) *(I)*
Stein, R. Conrad. *New York.* Childrens, 1989. *(P; I)*
Thompson, Kathleen. *New York.* Raintree, 1988. *(P; I)*

NEW YORK CITY

Adams, Barbara Johnston. *New York City.* Dillon, 1988. *(P)*
Cooney, Barbara. *Hattie and the Wild Waves.* Viking, 1990. (Fiction) *(P; I)*
Konigsburg, E. L. *Amy Elizabeth Explores Bloomingdale's.* Atheneum, 1992. (Fiction) *(P)*
Krustrup, Erik V. *Gateway to America: New York City.* Creative Education, 1982. *(I; A)*
Lovett, Sarah. *Kidding Around New York City: A Young Person's Guide to the City.* John Muir, 1989. *(I; A)*
Munro, Roxie. *The Inside-Outside Book of New York City.* Dodd, 1985. *(P)*

NEW ZEALAND

Anderson, Margaret J. *Light in the Mountain.* Knopf, 1982. *(I)*

Armitage, Ronda. *New Zealand*. Bookwright, 1988. *(P)*

Ball, John. *We Live in New Zealand*. Watts, 1984. *(I; A)*

Keyworth, Valerie. *New Zealand: Land of the Long White Cloud*. Dillon, 1990. *(I)*

Knowlton, MaryLee, and Sachner, Mark J. *New Zealand*. Gareth Stevens, 1987. *(P)*

Yanagi, Akinobu. *New Zealand*. Gareth Stevens, 1987. *(P; I)*

NICARAGUA. See CENTRAL AMERICA.

NIGER. See AFRICA.

NIGERIA

Nigeria . . . in Pictures. Lerner, 1988. *(P; I)*

Barker, Carol. *A Family in Nigeria*. Lerner, 1985. *(P)*

NIGHTINGALE, FLORENCE

Koch, Charlotte. *Florence Nightingale*. Dandelion, 1979. *(P; I)*

NILE RIVER

Percefull, Aaron W. *The Nile*. Watts, 1984. *(I; A)*

NIXON, RICHARD M.

Cook, Fred J. *The Crimes of Watergate*. Watts, 1981. *(A)*

Lillegard, Dee. *Richard Nixon: Thirty-seventh President of the United States*. Childrens, 1988. *(P; I)*

Ripley, C. Peter. *Richard Nixon*. Chelsea House, 1987. *(A)*

See also PRESIDENCY OF THE UNITED STATES.

NOBEL PRIZES

Abrams, Irwin. *The Nobel Peace Prize and the Laureates: An Illustrated Biographical History 1901–1987*. G. K. Hall, 1988. *(A)*

Asseng, Nathan. *The Disease Fighters: The Nobel Prize in Medicine*. Lerner, 1987. *(P; I)*; *The Inventors: Nobel Prizes in Chemistry, Physics, and Medicine*, 1988. *(I)*; *The Peace Seekers: The Nobel Peace Prize*, 1987. *(I)*

McGrayne, Sharon Bertsch. *Nobel Prize Women in Science*. Birch Lane Press, 1993. *(A)*

Meyer, Edith P. *In Search of Peace: The Winners of the Nobel Peace Prize, 1901–1975*. Abingdon, 1978. *(A)*

NOISE

Finney, Shan. *Noise Pollution*. Watts, 1984. *(I; A)*

NORSE MYTHOLOGY

Colum, Padraic. *The Children of Odin*. Haverton Books, 1920. *(I; A)*

Coolidge, Olivia. *Legends of the North*. Houghton, 1951. *(I; A)*

D'Aulaire, Ingri, and D'Aulaire, Edgar P. *Norse Gods and Giants*. Doubleday, 1967. *(P; I)*

Green, Roger L. *Myths of the Norsemen*. Penguin, 1970. *(I; A)*

Hodges, Margaret. *Baldur and the Mistletoe: A Myth of the Vikings*. Little, 1974. *(P)*

NORTH AMERICA

Asimov, Isaac. *The Shaping of North America*. Houghton, 1973. *(I; A)*

See also individual countries, states, and provinces.

NORTH CAROLINA

Carpenter, Allan. *North Carolina*. Childrens, 1979. *(I)*

Fradin, Dennis. *North Carolina: In Words and Pictures*. Childrens, 1980. *(P; I)*

NORTH DAKOTA

Fradin, Dennis. *North Dakota: In Words and Pictures*. Childrens, 1981. *(P; I)*

Herguth, Margaret S. *North Dakota*. Childrens, 1990. *(I)*

Tweton, D. Jerome, and Jelliff, Theodore B. *North Dakota: The Heritage of a People*. North Dakota Institute, 1976. *(I; A)*

NORTHERN IRELAND

Parker, Tony. *May the Lord in His Mercy Be Kind to Belfast*. Holt, 1994. *(A)*

NORTHWEST PASSAGE. See EXPLORATION AND DISCOVERY.

NORTHWEST TERRITORIES

Levert, Suzanne. *Northwest Territories*. Chelsea House, 1992. *(I; A)*

NORWAY

Hintz, Martin. *Norway*. Childrens, 1982. *(I; A)*

St. John, Jetty. *A Family in Norway*. Lerner, 1988. *(P)*

NOVA SCOTIA. See CANADA.

NUCLEAR ENERGY

Beyer, Don E. *The Manhattan Project: America Makes the First Atomic Bomb*. Watts, 1991. *(A)*

Coble, Charles. *Nuclear Energy*. Raintree, 1983. *(I; A)*

Dolan, Edward F., and Scariano, Margaret M. *Nuclear Waste: The 10,000-Year Challenge*. Watts, 1990. *(A)*

Feldbaum, Carl B., and Bee, Ronald J. *Looking the Tiger in the Eye: Confronting the Nuclear Threat*. Harper, 1988. *(A)*

Fradin, Dennis B. *Nuclear Energy*. Childrens, 1987. *(P)*

Halacy, Daniel. *Nuclear Energy*. Watts, 1984 (rev. ed.). *(I; A)*

Hare, Tony. *Nuclear Waste Disposal*. Gloucester Press, dist. by Watts, 1991. *(I)*

Lampton, Christopher. *Nuclear Accident*. Millbrook, 1992. *(I)*

Nardo, Don. *Chernobyl*. Lucent Books, 1990. *(I; A)*

Pringle, Laurence. *Nuclear Energy: Troubled Past, Uncertain Future*. Macmillan, 1989. *(I; A); Radiation: Waves and Particles, Benefits and Risks*. Enslow, 1983. *(I; A)*

Smoke, Richard. *Nuclear Arms Control: Understanding the Arms Race*. Walker, 1988. *(A)*

Williams, Gene B. *Nuclear War, Nuclear Winter*. Watts, 1987. *(I; A)*

NUMBER PATTERNS

Smoothey, Marion. *Let's Investigate Number Patterns*. Marshall Cavendish, 1993. *(I); Let's Investigate Shape Patterns*. Marshall Cavendish, 1993. *(I)*

NUMBER PUZZLES AND GAMES

Buller, Laura, and Taylor, Ron. *Calculation and Chance*. Marshall Cavendish, 1990. *(I)*

Weaver, Charles. *Hidden Logic Puzzles*. Sterling, 1992. *(I; A)*

NUMBERS AND NUMBER SYSTEMS

Challoner, Jack. *The Science Book of Numbers*. Harcourt, 1992. *(P; I)*

Heinst, Marie. *My First Number Book*. Dorling Kindersley, 1992. *(P)*

Sitomer, Harry, and Sitomer, Mindel. *How Did Numbers Begin?* Harper, 1976; *Zero Is Not Nothing*. Crowell, 1978. *(P)*

Smoothey, Marion. *Let's Investigate Numbers*. Marshall Cavendish, 1993. *(I)*

Srivastava, Jane. *Number Families*. Harper, 1979. *(P)*

Tallarico, Tony. *Numbers*. Tuffy Books, 1982. *(P; I)*

Watson, Clyde. *Binary Numbers*. Harper, 1977. *(I)*

NURSERY RHYMES

Blegvad, Lenore, ed. *Hark! Hark! the Dogs Do Bark: And Other Rhymes About Dogs*. Atheneum, 1976. *(P)*

Bodecker, N. M. *It's Raining Said John Twaining: Danish Nursery Rhymes*. Atheneum, 1973. *(P)*

De Angeli, Marguerite. *Book of Nursery and Mother Goose Rhymes*. Doubleday, 1954. *(P; I)*

DePaola, Tomie. *Tomie dePaola's Mother Goose*. Putnam, 1985. *(P)*

Greenaway, Kate, illus. *Mother Goose: Or, the Old Nursery Rhymes*. Warne, 1882. *(P)*

Lewis, Bobby, illus. *Mother Goose: Home Before Midnight*. Lothrop, 1984. *(P)*

Lobel, Arnold. *The Random House Book of Mother Goose*. Random House, 1986. *(P; I)*

Opie, Iona, and Opie, Peter. *A Nursery Companion*. Oxford University Press, 1980; *Oxford Nursery Rhyme Book*, 1955. *(P)*

Potter, Beatrix. *Appley Dapply's Nursery Rhymes*. Warne, 1917; *Cecily Parsley's Nursery Rhymes*, 1922. *(P)*

Provensen, Alice, and Provensen, Martin, illus. *Old Mother Hubbard*. Random, 1982. *(P)*

Rackham, Arthur, illus. *Mother Goose, the Old Nursery Rhymes*. Sanford J. Durst, 1978. *(P)*

Rockwell, Anne. *Gray Goose and Gander and Other Mother Goose Rhymes*. Harper, 1980. *(P)*

Rojankovsky, Feodor. *Tall Book of Mother Goose*. Harper, 1942. *(P)*

Rossetti, Christina G. *Sing Song: A Nursery Rhyme Book*. Dover, 1969. *(P; I)*

Wyndham, Robert. *Chinese Mother Goose Rhymes*. Putnam, 1982. *(P)*

NURSES AND NURSING

Donahue, M. Patricia. *Nursing, the Finest Art: An Illustrated History*. Abrams, 1986. *(A)*

Seide, Diane. *Nurse Power: New Vistas in Nursing*. Lodestar, 1985. *(A)*

Wandro, Mark, and Blank, Joani. *My Daddy Is a Nurse*. Addison-Wesley, 1981. *(P; I)*

Witty, Margot. *A Day in the Life of an Emergency Room Nurse*. Troll, 1981. *(P; I)*

NUTRITION

Arnold, Caroline. *Too Fat? Too Thin? Do You Have a Choice?* Morrow, 1984. *(I)*

Baldwin, Dorothy, and Lister, Claire. *Your Body Fuel*. Watts, 1984. *(I; A)*

Fretz, Sada. *Going Vegetarian: A Guide for Teenagers*. Morrow, 1983. *(I; A)*

Newton, Lesley. *Meatballs and Molecules: The Science Behind Food*. A. & C. Black, 1984. *(P; I)*

Nottridge, Rhoda. *Fats*. Carolrhoda, 1993. *(I)*

Patent, Dorothy Hinshaw. *Nutrition: What's in the Food We Eat*. Holiday, 1992. *(P; I)*

Peavy, Linda, and Smith, Ursula. *Food, Nutrition, and You*. Scribner's, 1982. *(I; A)*

Sanchez, Gail Jones, and Gerbino, Mary. *Overeating: Let's Talk About It*. Dillon, 1986. *(I; A)*

Sexias, Judith S. *Junk Food: What It Is, What It Does*. Greenwillow, 1984. *(P)*

Silverstein, Dr. Alvin. *Carbohydrates*. Millbrook, 1992. *(I); Fats*. Millbrook, 1992. *(I); Proteins*. Millbrook, 1992. *(I); Vitamins and Minerals*. Millbrook, 1992. *(I)*

Smaridge, Norah. *What's on Your Plate?* Abingdon, 1982. *(P)*

Thompson, Paul. *Nutrition*. Watts, 1981. *(I; A)*

NYLON AND OTHER SYNTHETIC FIBERS. See TEXTILES.

OAKLEY, ANNIE

Alderman, Clifford L. *Annie Oakley and the World of Her Time.* Macmillan, 1979. *(I; A)*

Harrison, and others. *Annie Oakley.* Dormac, 1981. *(P; I; A)*

OASES. See DESERTS.

OATS. See GRAIN AND GRAIN PRODUCTS.

OCEANS AND OCEANOGRAPHY

Adler, David. *Our Amazing Oceans.* Troll, 1983. *(P; I)*

Althea. *Signposts of the Sea.* Cambridge U Press, 1983. *(A)*

Asimov, Isaac. *How Did We Find Out About Life in the Deep Sea?* Walker, 1981. *(I)*

Ballard, Robert D. *Exploring the Titanic.* Scholastic, 1988. *(P; I)*

Blair, Carvel Hall. *Exploring the Sea: Oceanography Today.* Random, 1986. *(I)*

Blumberg, Rhoda. *The First Travel Guide to the Bottom of the Sea.* Lothrop, 1983. *(I)*

Bramwell, Martyn. *Oceanography.* Watts, 1989. *(P; I); Oceans.* Watts, 1984. *(P; I)* (Atlas format)

Carson, Rachel L. *The Sea Around Us.* Oxford University Press, 1961. *(A)*

Carter, Katherine J. *Oceans.* Childrens, 1982. *(P)*

Cole, Joanna. *The Magic School Bus on the Ocean Floor.* Scholastic, 1992. *(P)*

Doubilet, Anne. *Under the Sea from A to Z.* Crown, 1991. *(P)*

Elting, Mary. *Mysterious Seas.* Putnam, 1983. *(P; I)*

Fine, John Christopher. *Oceans in Peril.* Atheneum, 1987. *(A)*

Gibbons, Gail. *Sunken Treasure.* Crowell, 1988. *(P)*

Lambert, David. *The Oceans.* Watts, 1984. *(I; A)*

Lampton, Christopher. *Undersea Archaeology.* Watts, 1988. *(I)*

Levinson, Riki. *Our Home Is the Sea.* Dutton, 1988. *(P)*

Mattson, Robert A. *The Living Ocean.* Enslow, 1991. *(I)*

McClung, Robert. *Treasures in the Sea.* National Geographic, 1972. *(P; I)*

Meyerson, A. Lee. *Seawater: A Delicate Balance.* Enslow, 1988. *(I; A)*

Polking, Kirk. *Oceans of the World: Our Essential Resource.* Putnam, 1983. *(I; A)*

Rayner, Ralph. *Undersea Technology.* Bookwright, 1990. *(I)*

Sedge, Michael H. *Commercialization of the Oceans.* Watts, 1987. *(I; A)*

Simon, Anne W. *Neptune's Revenge: The Ocean of Tomorrow.* Watts, 1984. *(A)*

Simon, Seymour. *How to Be an Ocean Scientist in Your Own Home.* Lippincott, 1988. *(I; A); Oceans.* Morrow, 1990. *(P; I)*

Wu, Norbert. *Life in the Oceans.* Little, 1991. *(I)*

OHIO

Cockley, David H. *Over the Falls: A Child's Guide to Chagrin Falls.* Aschley Press, 1981. *(P; I)*

Fox, Mary Virginia. *Ohio.* Watts, 1987. *(P; I)*

Kent, Deborah. *Ohio.* Childrens, 1989. *(P; I)*

O'KEEFFE, GEORGIA

Berry, Michael. *Georgia O'Keeffe.* Chelsea House, 1988. *(A)*

Gherman, Beverly. *Georgia O'Keeffe: The Wideness and Wonder of Her World.* Atheneum, 1986. *(I; A)*

OKLAHOMA

Fradin, Dennis. *Oklahoma: In Words and Pictures.* Childrens, 1981. *(P; I)*

Heinrichs, Ann. *Oklahoma.* Childrens, 1989. *(P; I)*

Newsom, D. Earl. *The Birth of Oklahoma.* Evans Publications, 1983. *(I; A)*

OLD AGE. See AGING.

OLYMPIC GAMES

Aaseng, Nate. *Great Summer Olympic Moments.* Lerner, 1990. *(I; A); Great Winter Olympic Moments.* Lerner, 1990. *(I; A)*

Glubok, Shirley, and Tamarin, Alfred. *Olympic Games in Ancient Greece.* Harper, 1976. *(A)*

Knight, Theodore. *The Olympic Games.* Lucent, 1991. *(P; I)*

Wallechinsky, David. *The Complete Book of the Olympics.* Viking, 1987. *(A)*

ONTARIO. See CANADA.

OPERA. See MUSIC AND MUSICIANS.

OPERETTA. See MUSIC AND MUSICIANS.

OPOSSUMS

Rue, Leonard Lee, and Owen, William. *Meet the Opossum.* Dodd, 1983. *(P; I)*

OPTICAL ILLUSIONS

O'Neill, Catherine. *You Won't Believe Your Eyes!* National Geographic, 1987. *(P; I)*

Simon, Seymour. *The Optical Illusion Book.* Scholastic, 1976. *(I)*

White, Laurence B., and Broekel, Ray. *Optical Illusions.* Watts, 1986. *(P; I)*

OPTICAL INSTRUMENTS. See MICROSCOPES.

ORCHESTRA

Blackwood, Alan. *The Orchestra: An Introduction to the World of Classical Music*. Millbrook, 1993. *(I; A)*

English, Betty Lou. *You Can't Be Timid with a Trumpet: Notes from the Orchestra*. Lothrop, 1980. *(I)*

Hayes, Ann. *Meet the Orchestra*. Gulliver Books, 1991. *(P)*

Kuskin, Karla. *The Philharmonic Gets Dressed*. Harper, 1982. *(P)*

Rubin, Mark. *The Orchestra*. Douglas & McIntyre, 1984. *(P)*

Storms, Laura. *Careers with an Orchestra*. Lerner, 1983. *(P; I)*

OREGON

Bratvold, Gretchen. *Oregon*. Lerner, 1991. *(I)*

Cloutier, James. *This Day in Oregon*. Image West, 1981. *(I; A)*

Fradin, Dennis. *Oregon: In Words and Pictures*. Childrens, 1980. *(P; I)*

Stein, R. Conrad. *Oregon*. Childrens, 1989. *(P; I)*

ORGAN. See MUSICAL INSTRUMENTS.

ORIGAMI

Nakano, Dokuohtei. *Easy Origami*. Viking Kestrel, 1986. *(P)*

Takahama, Toshie. *Origami for Fun: Thirty-one Basic Models*. Tuttle, 1980. *(P; I)*

ORTHODONTICS. See DENTISTRY.

OSMOSIS. See PLANTS.

OSTRICHES AND OTHER FLIGHTLESS BIRDS

Arnold, Carolyn. *Ostriches and Other Flightless Birds*. Carolrhoda, 1990. *(I)*

Lavine, Sigmund A. *Wonders of Flightless Birds*. Dodd, 1981. *(I; A)*

OTTAWA. See CANADA.

OTTERS AND OTHER MUSTELIDS

Aronsky, Jim. *Otters Under Water*. Putnam, 1992. *(P)*

Ashby, Ruth. *Sea Otters*. Atheneum, 1990. *(I)*

Hurd, Edith T. *Song of the Sea Otter*. Pantheon, 1983. *(P; I)*

Lavine, Sigmund A. *Wonders of Badgers*. Dodd, 1985. *(I)*

Scheffer, Victor B. *The Amazing Sea Otter*. Scribner's, 1981. *(I)* (Story)

Smith, Roland. *Sea Otter Rescue: The Aftermath of an Oil Spill*. Cobblehill, 1990. *(I)*

OUTDOOR COOKING AND PICNICS

Haines, Gail K. *Baking in a Box, Cooking on a Can*. Morrow, 1981. *(I)*

OVERLAND TRAILS. See WESTWARD MOVEMENT AND PIONEER LIFE.

OWLS

Burton, Jane. *Buffy the Barn Owl*. Gareth Stevens, 1989. *(P)*

Esbensen, Barbara Juster. *Tiger with Wings: The Great Horned Owl*. Orchard: Watts, 1991. *(P)*

George, Jean Craighead. *The Moon of the Owls*. HarperCollins, 1993. *(I)*

Hunt, Patricia. *Snowy Owls*, Dodd, 1982. *(P; I)*

Sadoway, Margaret W. *Owls: Hunters of the Night*. Lerner, 1981. *(P; I)*

Storms, Laura. *The Owl Book*. Lerner, 1983. *(P; I)*

Zim, Herbert S. *Owls*. Morrow, 1977 (rev. ed.). *(P; I)*

OYSTERS, OCTOPUSES, AND OTHER MOLLUSKS

Bunting, Eve. *The Giant Squid*. Messner, 1981. *(I)*

Carrick, Carol. *Octopus*. Houghton, 1978. *(P)*

Johnson, Sylvia A. *Snails*. Lerner, 1982. *(I)*

Martin, James. *Tentacles: The Amazing World of Octopus, Squid, and Their Relatives*. Crown, 1993. *(I)*

PACIFIC OCEAN AND ISLANDS

Deverell, Gweneth. *Follow the Sun . . . to Tahiti, to Western Samoa, to Fiji, to Melanesia, to Micronesia*. Friends Press, 1982. *(P)*

Gittins, Anne. *Tales from the South Pacific Islands*. Stemmer House, 1977. *(I)*

Kamikamica, Esiteri, comp. by. *Come to My Place: Meet My Island Family*. Friends Press, 1982. *(P; I)*

PADDLE TENNIS. See TENNIS.

PAINTING

Couch, Tony. *Watercolor: You Can Do It!* North Light Books, 1987. *(A)*

Cumming, Robert. *Just Look: A Book About Paintings*. Scribner's, 1980. *(P; I)*

Foste. *A Guide to Painting*. EDC Publishing, 1981. *(P; I)*

Holme, Bryan. *Creatures of Paradise: Pictures to Grow Up With*. Oxford University Press, 1980; *Enchanted World: The Magic of Pictures*, 1979. *(I; A)*

See also ART AND ARTISTS.

PAKISTAN

Hughes, Libby. *From Prison to Prime Minister: A Biography of Benazir Bhutto*. Dillon, 1990. *(I; A)*

Rumalshah, Mano. *Pakistan*. Hamish Hamilton, 1992. *(P; I)*

Weston, Mark. *The Land and People of Pakistan.* HarperCollins, 1992. *(A)*

Yusufali, Jabeen. *Pakistan: An Islamic Treasure.* Dillon, 1990. *(I)*

PALESTINE. See ISRAEL; MIDDLE EAST.

PANAMA. See CENTRAL AMERICA.

PANAMA CANAL AND ZONE. See CANALS.

PANDAS

Bailey, Jill. *Project Panda.* Steck-Vaughn, 1990. *(P; I)*

Barrett, N. S. *Pandas.* Watts, 1988. *(P; I)*

McClung, Robert M. *Lili: A Giant Panda of Sichuan.* Morrow, 1988. *(P: I)*

Wexo, John Bonnett. *Giant Pandas.* Creative Education, 1988. *(P)*

PAPER

Perrins, Lesley. *How Paper is Made.* Facts on File, 1985. *(P; I)*

PAPUA NEW GUINEA. See SOUTHEAST ASIA.

PARAGUAY AND URUGUAY

Naverstock, Nathan A. *Paraguay in Pictures.* Lerner, 1988. *(P: I)*

PARIS. See FRANCE.

PARKS AND PLAYGROUNDS

Anderson, Norman D., and Brown, Walter R. *Ferris Wheels.* Pantheon, 1983. *(I)*

Hahn, Christine. *Amusement Park Machines.* Raintree, 1979. *(P)*

Silverstein, Herma. *Scream Machines: Roller Coasters, Past, Present, and Future.* Walker, 1986. *(I; A)*

Van Steenwyk, Elizabeth. *Behind the Scenes at the Amusement Park.* Albert Whitman, 1983. *(P; I)*

PARLIAMENTARY PROCEDURE

Jones, O. Garfield. *Parliamentary Procedure at a Glance.* Dutton, 1971. *(A)*

PARROTS AND OTHER "TALKING" BIRDS. See BIRDS.

PARTIES

Brinn, Ruth E., and Saypol, Judyth R. *101 Mix and Match Party Ideas for the Jewish Holidays.* Kar-Ben, 1981. *(P)*

Highlights editors. *Party Ideas with Crafts Kids Can Make.* Highlights, 1981. *(P; I)*

Pitcher, Caroline. *Party Time.* Watts, 1984. *(P)*

Wilkes, Angela. *My First Party Book.* Knopf, 1991. *(P; I)*

PASSOVER

Adler, David A. *Passover Fun Book: Puzzles, Riddles, and More.* Hebrew Publishing, 1978. *(P; I); A Picture Book of Passover.* Holiday, 1982. *(P)*

DePaola, Tomie. *My First Passover.* Putnam, 1991. *(P)*

Drucker, Malka. *Passover: A Season of Freedom.* Holiday, 1981. *(I; A)*

Fluek, Toby Knobel. *Passover As I Remember It.* Knopf, 1994. *(P; I; A)*

Kustanowitz, Shulamit, and Foont, Ronnie. *A First Haggadah.* Hebrew Publishing, 1980. *(P; I)*

Rosen, Anne, and others. *Family Passover.* Jewish Publication Society, 1980. *(P; I; A)*

Zalben, Jane B. *Happy Passover, Rosie.* Holt, 1990. *(P)*

PASTEUR, LOUIS

Birch, Beverley. *Louis Pasteur.* Gareth Stevens, 1989. *(I)*

Johnson, Spencer, and Johnson, Ann D. *The Value of Believing in Yourself: The Story of Louis Pasteur.* Western, 1979. *(P; I)*

Sabin, Francene. *Louis Pasteur: Young Scientist.* Troll, 1983. *(P; I)*

PATRICK, SAINT

Corfe, Tom. *St. Patrick and Irish Christianity.* Lerner, 1978. *(I; A)*

PEACE MOVEMENTS

Fitzgerald, Merni Ingrassia. *The Peace Corps Today.* Dodd, 1986. *(P; I)*

Meltzer, Milton. *Ain't Gonna Study War No More: The Story of America's Peace Seekers.* Harper, 1985. *(A)*

PELICANS

Stone, Lynn. *The Pelican.* Dillon, 1990. *(I)*

Wildsmith, Brian. *Pelican.* Pantheon, 1983. *(P)*

PENGUINS

Arnold, Caroline. *Penguin.* Morrow, 1988. *(P; I)*

Bonners, Susan. *A Penguin Year.* Delacorte, 1981. *(P)*

Coldrey, Jennifer. *Penguins.* Andre Deutsch, 1983. *(P)*

Lepthien, Emilie U. *Penguins.* Childrens, 1983. *(P)*

Paladino, Catherine. *Pomona: The Birth of a Penguin.* Watts, 1991. *(P)*

Sømme, Lauritz, and Kalas, Sybille. *The Penguin Family Book.* Picture Book Studio, 1988. *(P)*

Strange, Ian J. *Penguin World.* Dodd, 1981. *(I; A)*

Tenaza, Richard. *Penguins.* Watts, 1982. *(I; A)*

Vernon, Adele. *The Hoiho: New Zealand's Yellow-Eyed Penguin.* Putnam, 1991. *(I)*

PENN, WILLIAM

Foster, Genevieve. *The World of William Penn.* Scribner's, 1973. *(I)*

PENNSYLVANIA

Cornell, William A., and Altland, Millard. *Our Pennsylvania Heritage.* Penns Valley, 1978. *(I; A)*

Costabel, Eva D. *The Pennsylvania Dutch.* Atheneum, 1986. *(P; I)*

De Angeli, Marguerite. *Henner's Lydia.* Doubleday, 1936; *Whistle for the Crossing,* 1977. *(P; I)*

Faber, Doris. *The Amish.* Doubleday, 1991. *(P; I)*

Fritz, Jean. *Brady.* Putnam, 1960; *The Cabin Faced West,* 1958. *(P; I)*

Kent, Deborah. *Pennsylvania.* Childrens, 1988. *(P)*

Knight, James E. *The Farm, Life in Colonial Pennsylvania.* Troll, 1982 *(I; A)*

PERCUSSION INSTRUMENTS. See MUSICAL INSTRUMENTS.

PERRY, COMMODORE

Blumberg, Rhoda. *Commodore Perry in the Land of the Shogun.* Lothrop, 1985. *(I; A)*

PERU

Clark, Ann Nolan. *Secret of the Andes.* Viking, 1952. *(A)*

Dewey, Ariane. *The Thunder God's Son: A Peruvian Folktale.* Greenwillow, 1981. *(P)*

Gemming, Elizabeth. *Lost City in the Clouds: The Discovery of Machu Picchu.* Putnam, 1980. *(P; I)*

Mangurian, David. *Children of the Incas.* Scholastic, 1979. *(P; I)*

Visual Geography. *PERU . . . In Pictures.* Lerner, 1987. *(I; A)*

PETER THE GREAT

Stanley, Diane. *Peter the Great.* Four Winds, 1986. *(P; I)*

PETROLEUM

Alvarez, A. *Offshore: a North Sea Journey.* Houghton, 1986. *(A)*

Asimov, Isaac. *How Did We Find Out About Oil?* Walker, 1980. *(I)*

Mitgutsch, Ali. *From Oil to Gasoline.* Carolrhoda, 1981. *(P)*

Pampe, William R. *Petroleum: How it is Found and Used.* Enslow, 1984. *(A)*

Piper, Allan. *Oil.* Watts, 1980. *(I)*

Rutland, Jonathan. *See Inside an Oil Rig and Tanker.* Watts, 1979. *(I; A)*

Scott, Elaine. *Doodlebugging: The Treasure Hunt for Oil.* Warne, 1982. *(I)*

Stephen, R. J. *Oil Rigs.* Watts, 1987. *(P)*

PETS

Arnold, Caroline. *Pets Without Homes.* Houghton, 1983. *(P)*

Blumberg, Leda. *Pets.* Watts, 1983. *(P; I)*

Fields, Alice. *Pets.* Watts, 1981. *(P)*

Hess, Lilo. *Bird Companions.* Scribner's, 1981. *(I)*

Marrs, Texe, and Marrs, Wanda. *The Perfect Name for Your Pet.* Heian International, 1983. *(P; I; A)*

PHILADELPHIA

Balcer, Bernadette and O'Byrne-Pelham, Fran. *Philadelphia.* Dillon, 1989. *(P; I)*

Clay, Rebecca. *Kidding Around Philadelphia: A Young Person's Guide to the City.* John Muir, 1990. *(P; I)*

Knight, James E. *Seventh and Walnut, Life in Colonial Philadelphia.* Troll, 1982. *(I; A)*

Loeper, John J. *The House on Spruce Street.* Atheneum, 1982. *(I)*

PHILIPPINES. See SOUTHEAST ASIA.

PHILOSOPHY

Allington, Richard L., and Krull, Kathleen. *Thinking.* Raintree, 1980. *(P)*

Plato. *The Republic.* Penguin, 1955. *(I; A)*

Post, Beverly, and Eads, Sandra. *Logic, Anyone? One Hundred Sixty-five Brain-Stretching Problems.* Pitman, 1982. *(I; A)*

PHOTOGRAPHY

Boy Scouts of America. *Photography.* Boy Scouts, 1983. *(I; A)*

Cooper, Miriam. *Snap! Photography.* Messner, 1981. *(I)*

Craven, John, and Wasley, John. *Young Photographer.* Sterling, 1982. *(I)*

Cumming, David. *Photography.* Steck-Vaughn, 1989. *(I)*

Henderson, Kathy. *Market Guide for Young Artists & Photographers.* Betterway, 1990. *(I; A)*

Knudsen-Owens, Vic. *Photography Basics: An Introduction for Young People.* Prentice-Hall, 1983. *(P; I)*

Lasky, Kathryn. *Think Like an Eagle: At Work With A Wildlife Photographer.* Joy Street; Little, 1992. *(I)*

Moss, Miriam. *Fashion Photographer.* Crestwood, 1991. *(I)*

Sandler, Martin W. *The Story of American Photography.* Little, 1979. *(A)*

PHOTOSYNTHESIS. See PLANTS.

PHYSICAL FITNESS. See HEALTH AND PHYSICAL FITNESS.

PHYSICS

Ardley, Neil. *Exploring Magnetism.* Watts, 1984. *(I); Hot and Cold,* 1983. *(P; I; A); Making Things Move.* 1984. *(P; I; A)*

Berger, Melvin. *Our Atomic World.* Watts, 1989. *(P; I); Solids, Liquids, and Gases.* Putnam, 1989. *(I; A)*

Chester, Michael. *Particles: An Introduction to Particle Physics.* Macmillan, 1978. *(I; A)*

Cobb, Vicki. *Why Can't You Unscramble An Egg?: and Other Not Such Dumb Questions About Matter*. Lodestar, 1990. *(P; I)*

Fleisher, Paul. *Secrets of the Universe: Discovering the Universal Laws of Science*. Atheneum, 1987. *(I; A)*

Henbest, Nigel, and Couper, Heather. *Physics*. Watts, 1983. *(I; A)*

McGrath, Susan. *Fun with Physics*. National Geographic, 1986. *(I)*

Sherwood, Martin, and Sutton, Christine. *The Physical World*. Oxford University Press, 1988. *(A)*

Watson, Philip. *Liquid Magic*. Lothrop, 1983. *(P; I)*

Weiss, Malcolm E. *Why Glass Breaks, Rubber Bends, and Glue Sticks*. Harcourt, 1979. *(I)*

PIANO. See MUSICAL INSTRUMENTS.

PICASSO, PABLO

Frevert, Patricia D. *Pablo Picasso: Twentieth Century Genius*. Creative Education, 1981. *(I; A)*

Raboff, Ernest. *Pablo Picasso*. Doubleday, 1982. *(P; I)*

Venezia, Mike. *Picasso*. Childrens, 1988. *(P)*

PIERCE, FRANKLIN

Brown, Fern G. *Franklin Pierce*. Garrett Educational, 1989. *(I)*

Simon, Charnan. *Franklin Pierce*. Childrens, 1988. *(I)*

See also PRESIDENCY OF THE UNITED STATES.

PIGS

Ling, Mary. *Pig*. Dorling Kindersley, 1993. *(P)*

Scott, Jack Denton. *The Book of the Pig*. Putnam, 1981. *(I)*

PIONEER LIFE. See WESTWARD MOVEMENT AND PIONEER LIFE.

PIRATES AND PIRACY

McCall, Edith. *Pirates and Privateers*. Childrens, 1980. *(P; I; A)*

Stein, R. Conrad. *The Story of the Barbary Pirates*. Childrens, 1982. *(P; I)*

PIZARRO, FRANCISCO. See EXPLORATION AND DISCOVERY.

PLANETARIUM. See ASTRONOMY.

PLANETS

Asimov, Isaac. *Colonizing the Planets and Stars*. Gareth Stevens, 1990. *(P; I)*

Branley, Franklyn M. *The Planets in Our Solar System*. Crowell, 1987. *(P)*

Lampton, Christopher. *Stars and Planets*. Doubleday, 1988. *(P)*

Lauber, Patricia. *Journey to the Planets*. Crown, 1993 (rev. ed.). *(I; A)*

Levasseur-Regourd, Anny Chantal. *Our Sun and the Inner Planets*. Facts on File, 1990. *(P; I)*

Nourse, Alan E. *The Giant Planets*. Watts, 1982. *(I; A)*

Petty, Kate. *The Planets*. Watts, 1984. *(P)*

Vogt, Gregory. *Mars and the Inner Planets*. Watts, 1982. *(I; A)*

Yeomans, Don K. *The Distant Planets*. Facts on File, 1990. *(P; I)*

See also names of individual planets.

PLANTS

Burnie, David. *Plant*. Knopf, 1989. *(I)*

Coil, Suzanne M. *Poisonous Plants*. Watts, 1991. *(P; I)*

Cross, Diana H. *Some Plants Have Funny Names*. Crown, 1983. *(P)*

Dowden, Anne O. *From Flower to Fruit*. Harper, 1984. *(I; A)*

Facklam, Howard, and Facklam, Margery. *Plants: Extinction or Survival?* Enslow, 1990. *(I; A)*

Janulewicz, Mike. *Plants*. Watts, 1984. *(I; A)*

Johnson, Sylvia A. *Mosses*. Lerner, 1983. *(I)*

Lambert, Mark. *Plant Life*. Watts, 1983. *(I; A)*

Lauber, Patricia. *Seeds: Pop, Stick, Glide*. Crown, 1981. *(P)*

Lerner, Carol. *Pitcher Plants: The Elegant Insect Traps*. Morrow, 1983. *(P; I)*; *Plant Families*. Morrow, 1989. *(P; I)*; *Dumb Cane and Daffodils: Poisonous Plants in the House and Garden*. Morrow, 1990. *(I; A)*

Marcus, Elizabeth. *Amazing World of Plants*. Troll, 1984. *(P; I)*

Podendorf, Illa. *Weeds and Wildflowers*. Childrens, 1981. *(P)*

Pringle, Laurence P. *Being a Plant*. Crowell, 1983. *(I; A)*

Rahn, Joan E. *Plants Close Up*. Houghton, 1981; *Plants That Changed History*. Atheneum, 1982. *(I)*; *Seven Ways to Collect Plants*. Atheneum, 1978. *(P; I)*

Selsam, Millicent E. *Catnip*. 1983; *Eat the Fruit, Plant the Seed*. 1980; *The Plants We Eat*. Morrow, 1981 (rev. ed.). *(P; I)*

Welch, Martha M. *Close Looks in a Spring Woods*. Dodd, 1982. *(P; I)*

Wexler, Jerome. *Jack-in-the-Pulpit*. Dutton, 1993. *(I)*; *Secrets of the Venus Fly Trap*. Dodd, 1981. *(P; I)*

PLASTICS

Dineen, Jacqueline. *Plastics*. Enslow, 1988. *(I)*

Lambert, Mark. *Spotlight on Plastics*. Rourke, 1988. *(P; I)*

Whyman, Kathryn. *Plastics*. Gloucester Press, 1988. *(P; I)*

PLATYPUS AND SPINY ANTEATERS. See MAMMALS.

PLUMBING

Zim, Herbert S., and Skelly, James R. *Pipes and Plumbing Systems*. Morrow, 1974. *(I)*

PLUTO

Asimov, Isaac. *How Did We Find Out About Pluto?* Walker, 1991. *(I; A); Pluto: A Double Planet?* Gareth Stevens, 1990. *(P; I)*

PLYMOUTH COLONY. See THIRTEEN AMERICAN COLONIES.

POCAHONTAS. See SMITH, JOHN.

POETRY

Adoff, Arnold. *All the Colors of the Race*. Lothrop, 1982. *(P; I)*

Adoff, Arnold, ed. *I Am the Darker Brother: An Anthology of Modern Poems by Black Americans*. Macmillan, 1970; *The Poetry of Black America: Anthology of the Twentieth Century*. Harper, 1973. *(I; A)*

Bierhorst, John, ed. *The Sacred Path: Spells, Prayers, and Power Songs of the American Indians*. Morrow, 1983. *(I)*

Booth, David, sel. *'Til All the Stars Have Fallen: A Collection of Poems for Children*. Viking, 1990. *(P; I)*

Brooks, Gwendolyn. *Bronzeville Boys and Girls*. Harper, 1956. *(P; I)*

Brown, Marcia. *Sing a Song of Popcorn: Every Child's Book of Poems*. Scholastic, 1988. *(P; I)*

Bryan, Ashley, ed. *Beat the Story-Drum, Pum-Pum*. Atheneum, 1987. *(P; I)*

Cole, Joanna, comp. *A New Treasury of Children's Poetry: Old Favorites and New Discoveries*. Doubleday, 1984. *(P; I)*

Cummings, E. E. *Hist Whist and Other Poems for Children*, ed. by George J. Firmage. Liveright, 1983. *(P; I)*

Fleischman, Paul. *Joyful Noise: Poems for Two Voices*. Harper, 1988. *(P; I)*

Froman, Robert. *Seeing Things: A Book of Poems*. Harper, 1974. *(P; I)*

Hopkins, Lee Bennett. *Side by Side: Poems to Read Together*. Simon & Schuster, 1988. *(P; I)*

Hodges, Margaret, ad. *Saint George and the Dragon*, ad. from Edmund Spenser's *Faerie Queene*. Little, 1984. *(P; I)*

Janeczko, Paul. *The Place My Words Are Looking for: What Poets Say About and Through Their Work*. Bradbury, 1990. *(I; A)*

Janeczko, Paul B., ed. *Strings: A Gathering of Family Poems*. Bradbury, 1984. *(I; A)*

Janeczko, Paul, sel. *Preposterous: Poems of Youth*. Orchard Books, 1991. *(I; A)*

Jones, Hettie, ed. *The Trees Stand Shining: The Poetry of the North American Indians*. Dial, 1976. *(P; I; A)*

Katz, Bobbi. *Puddle Wonderful: Poems to Welcome Spring*. Random, 1992. *(P)*

Knudson, R. R., and Swenson, May, selector and ed. *American Sports Poems*. Orchard Books, 1988. *(I; A)*

Larrick, Nancy, ed. *Piping Down the Valleys Wild*. Dell, 1982. *(I; A)*

Lear, Edward. *How Pleasant to Know Mr. Lear*. Holiday, 1982. *(P; I); Of Pelicans and Pussycats: Poems and Limericks*. Dial, 1990. *(P)*

Lindsay, Vachel. *Johnny Appleseed and Other Poems*. Buccaneer, 1981. *(I)*

Livingston, Myra Cohn, ed. *Listen, Children, Listen: An Anthology of Poems for the Very Young*. Harcourt, 1972. *(P); Sky Songs*. Holiday, 1984. *(P; I; A)*

Lobel, Arnold. *The Book of Pigericks*. Harper, 1983. *(P)*

Merriam, Eve. *If Only I Could Tell You*. Knopf, 1983. *(I; A)*

Millay, Edna St. Vincent. *Collected Poems*. Harper, 1981. *(P); Poems Selected for Young People*. Harper, 1979. *(I; A)*

Prelutsky, Jack. *It's Snowing! It's Snowing!* Greenwillow, 1984. *(P); Poems of A. Nonny Mouse*. Knopf, 1991. *(P); The Random House Book of Poetry for Children*. Random, 1983. *(P; I)*

Stevenson, Robert Louis. *A Child's Garden of Verses*. Scribner's, n.d. (Other eds. and pubs.) *(P; I)*

Wildsmith, Brian, illus. *Oxford Book of Poetry for Children*. Merrimack, n.d. *(P; I)*

POLAND

Greene, Carol. *Poland*, Childrens, 1983. *(I; A)*

Heale, Jay. *Poland*. Marshall Cavendish, 1994. *(I; A)*

Kelly, Eric. *The Trumpeter of Krakow*. Macmillan, 1966. (Fiction) *(I)*

Sandak, Cass R. *Poland*. Watts, 1986. *(I)*

Zyskind, Sara. *Stolen Years*. Lerner, 1981. *(I; A)*

POLICE

Arnold, Caroline. *Who Keeps Us Safe?* Watts, 1982. *(P)*

Broekel, Ray. *Police*. Childrens, 1981. *(P)*

Hewett, Joan. *Motorcycle on Patrol: The Story of a Highway Officer*. Clarion, 1986. *(P)*

Johnson, Jean. *Police Officers, A to Z*. Walker, 1986. *(P)*

Mathias, Catherine. *I Can Be a Police Officer*. Childrens, 1984. *(P)*

Scott, Paul. *Police Divers*. Messner, 1982. *(I)*

POLITICAL PARTIES

The New World Order. Greenhaven, 1991. *(A)*

Hoopes, Ray. *Political Campaigning*. Watts, 1979. *(I; A)*

Kronenwetter, Michael. *Are You a Liberal? Are You a Conservative?* Watts, 1984. *(I; A)*

Levenson, Dorothy. *Politics: How to Get Involved*. Watts, 1980. *(I; A)*

Raynor, Thomas. *Politics, Power, and People: Four Governments in Action*. Watts, 1983. *(I; A)*

Weiss, Ann E. *Party Politics, Party Problems*. Harper, 1980. *(I; A)*

POLK, JAMES K.

Lillegard, Dee. *James K. Polk: Eleventh President of the United States*. Childrens, 1988. *(P; I)*
See also PRESIDENCY OF THE UNITED STATES.

POLLUTION

Blashfield, Jean F., and Black, Wallace B. *Oil Spills*. Childrens, 1991. *(I)*
Bright, Michael. *The Dying Sea*. Gloucester Press, 1988. *(I)*
Dolan, Edward F. *Our Poisoned Sky*. Cobblehill, 1991. *(I; A)*
Duden, Jane. *The Ozone Layer*. Crestwood, 1990. *(I)*
Gay, Kathlyn. *Global Garbage: Exploring Trash and Toxic Waste*. Watts, 1992. *(I; A); Ozone*. Watts, 1989. *(I; A); Silent Killers: Radon and Other Hazards*. Watts, 1988. *(I; A)*
Harris, Jack C. *The Greenhouse Effect*. Crestwood, 1990. *(I)*
Hawks, Nigel. *Toxic Waste and Recycling*. Gloucester Press, dist. by Watts, 1991. *(P; I)*
Kronenwetter, Michael. *Managing Toxic Wastes*. Messner, 1989. *(I; A)*
O'Connor, Karen. *Garbage*. Lucent Books, 1989. *(P; I)*
Phillips, Anne W. *The Ocean*. Crestwood, 1990. *(I)*
Snodgrass, Mary Ellen. *Air Pollution*. Bancroft-Sage, 1991. *(P; I); Environmental Awareness: Solid Waste*. Bancroft-Sage, 1991. *(P; I); Water Pollution*. Bancroft-Sage, 1991. *(P; I)*
Stenstrup, Allen. *Hazardous Waste*. Childrens, 1991. *(I)*
Weiss, Malcolm E. *Toxic Waste: Clean up or Cover Up?* Watts, 1984. *(I; A)*
Zipko, Stephen J. *Toxic Threat: How Hazardous Substances Poison Our Lives*. Messner, 1990 (rev. ed.). *(A)*
See also NOISE.

POLO, MARCO. See EXPLORATION AND DISCOVERY.

POMPEII. See ROME, ANCIENT.

PONCE DE LÉON, JUAN. See EXPLORATION AND DISCOVERY.

PONY EXPRESS

McCall, Edith. *Mail Riders*. Childrens, 1980. *(P; I; A)*
Stein, R. Conrad. *The Story of the Pony Express*. Childrens, 1981. *(P; I)*

POPULATION

Becklake, John, and Becklake, Sue. *The Population Explosion*. Gloucester Press, 1990. *(I)*
McGraw, Eric. *Population Growth*. Rourke, 1987. *(I; A)*

Nam, Charles B. *Our Population: The Changing Face of America*. Walker, 1988. *(A)*
Winckler, Suzanne, and Rodgers, Mary M. *Population Growth*. Lerner, 1991. *(I)*

PORTUGAL

Lye, Keith. *Take a Trip to Portugal*. Watts, 1986. *(P)*
Skalon, Ana de, and Stadtler, Christa. *We Live in Portugal*. Bookwright, 1987. *(P)*

POSTAL SERVICE

Gibbons, Gail. *The Post Office Book: Mail and How It Moves*. Harper, 1982. *(P)*
McAfee, Cheryl Weant. *The United States Postal Service*. Chelsea House, 1987. *(I; A)*
Roth, Harold. *First Class! The Postal System in Action*. Pantheon, 1983. *(I)*

POTATOES

Hughes, Meredith Sayles. *The Great Potato Book*. Macmillan, 1986. *(P)*
Johnson, Sylvia A. *Potatoes*. Lerner, 1986. *(I)*
Lobel, Anita. *Potatoes, Potatoes*. Harper, 1984. *(P)*
Meltzer, Milton. *The Amazing Potato: A Story in Which the Incas, Conquistadors, Marie Antoinette, Thomas Jefferson, Wars, Famines, Immigrants, and French Fries All Play a Part*. HarperCollins, 1992. *(I)*

POTTER, HELEN BEATRIX

Collins, David R. *The Country Artist: A Story About Beatrix Potter*. Carolrhoda, 1989. *(I)*

POTTERY. See CERAMICS.

POULTRY

Hopf, Alice L. *Chickens and Their Wild Relatives*. Dodd, 1982. *(I)*

POVERTY

Berek, Judith. *No Place to Be: Voices of Homeless Children*. Houghton, 1992. *(I; A)*
Davis, Bertha. *Poverty in America: What We Do About It*. Watts, 1991. *(A)*
Dudley, William, ed. *Poverty*. Greenhaven Press, 1988. *(A)*
Greenberg, Keith Elliot. *Erik is Homeless*. Lerner, 1992. *(P; I)*
Hubbard, Jim, sel. *Shooting Back: A Photographic View of Life by Homeless Children*. Chronicle, 1991. *(P; I; A)*
Hyde, Margaret O. *The Homeless: Profiling the Problem*. Enslow, 1990. *(P; I)*
Kosof, Anna. *Homeless in America*. Watts, 1988. *(I; A)*
Meltzer, Milton. *Poverty in America*. Morrow, 1986. *(A)*

O'Connor, Karen. *Homeless Children*. Lucent Books, 1989. *(I; A)*

O'Neil, Terry. *The Homeless: Distinguishing Between Fact and Opinion*. Greenhaven, 1990. *(I)*

POWER PLANTS. See Energy; Nuclear Energy

PRAIRIES

George, Jean Craighead. *One Day in the Prairie*. Crowell, 1986. *(I)*

PRAYER

Thanks Be to God: Prayers from Around the World. Macmillan, 1990. *(P; I)*

Bogot, Howard, and Syme, Daniel. *Prayer Is Reaching*. UAHC Press, 1981. *(P)*

Cook, Walter L. *Table Prayers for Children*. Bethany, 1977. *(P)*

Field, Rachel. *Prayer for a Child*. Macmillan, 1973. *(P)*

Hallinan, P. K. *I'm Thankful Each Day*. Childrens, 1981. *(P)*

Nystrom, Carolyn. *What Is Prayer?* Moody, 1980. *(P; I)*

Tudor, Tasha. *First Graces*. McKay, 1955. *(P)*

PREHISTORIC ANIMALS

Cohen, Daniel. *Prehistoric Animals*. Doubleday, 1988. *(P; I)*

Cole, Joanna. *Saber-Toothed Tiger and Other Ice Age Mammals*. Morrow, 1977. *(P; I)*

Dixon, Dougal. *A Closer Look at Prehistoric Reptiles*. Watts, 1984. *(I; A)*

Eldridge, David. *Flying Dragons: Ancient Reptiles That Ruled the Air; Sea Monsters: Ancient Reptiles That Ruled the Sea*. Troll, 1980. *(P; I)*.

Hall, Derek. *Prehistoric Mammals*. Watts, 1984. *(P; I)*

Lampton, Christopher. *Prehistoric Animals*. Watts, 1983. *(I)*

Moody, Richard. *100 Prehistoric Animals*. Grosset, 1988. *(P; I)*

National Geographic editors. *Giants from the Past*. National Geographic, 1983. *(P; I; A)*

Zallinger, Peter. *Prehistoric Animals*. Random, 1981. *(P)*

See also Dinosaurs.

PREHISTORIC PEOPLE. See Anthropology.

PRESIDENCY OF THE UNITED STATES

Beard, Charles A. *The Presidents in American History*. Messner, 1985 (rev. ed.). *(A)*

Beckman, Beatrice. *I Can Be President*. Childrens, 1984. *(P)*

Blassingame, Wyatt. *The Look-It-Up Book of Presidents*. Random, 1990. *(I; A)*

Cooke, Donald E. *Atlas of the Presidents*. Hammond, 1981. *(I; A)*

Frank, Sid, and Melick, Arden. *Presidents: Tidbits and Trivia*. Hammond, 1980. *(P; I; A)*

Gray, Lee Learner. *How We Choose a President*. St. Martin's, 1976. *(I)*

Miers, Earl S. *America and Its Presidents*. Putnam, 1982. *(P; I; A)*

Parker, Nancy Winslow. *The President's Cabinet and How it Grew*. HarperCollins, 1991. *(P; I)*; *The President's Car*. Harper, 1981. *(P; I)*

Reische, Diana. *Electing a U.S. President*. Watts, 1992. *(I; A)*

Seuling, Barbara. *The Last Cow on the White House Lawn, and Other Little-Known Facts About the Presidency*. Doubleday, 1978. *(P; I; A)*

Sullivan, George. *How the White House Really Works*. Dutton, 1989. *(P)*; *Mr. President: A Book of U.S. Presidents*. Scholastic, 1989. *(P; I)*

PRINCE EDWARD ISLAND. See Canada.

PRINTING

Caselli, Giovanni. *A German Printer*. Peter Bedrick, 1986. *(I)*

PRISONS

Hickman, Martha Whitmore. *When Andy's Father Went to Prison*. Albert Whitman, 1990. (Fiction) *(P)*

Owens, Lois Smith, and Gordon, Vivian Verdell. *Think About Prisons and the Criminal Justice System*. Walker, 1991. *(I; A)*

Rickard, Graham. *Prisons and Punishments*. Watts, 1987. *(P)*

Warburton, Lois. *Prisons*. Lucent, 1993. *(I; A)*

Weiss, Anne E. *Prisons: A System in Trouble*. Enslow, 1988. *(A)*

PROBABILITY. See Statistics.

PSYCHOLOGY

Stwertka, Eve. *Psychoanalysis: From Freud to the Age of Therapy*. Watts, 1988 *(I; A)*

Weinstein, Grace W. *People Study People: The Story of Psychology*. Dutton, 1979. *(I; A)*

PUBLIC SPEAKING

Detz, Joan. *You Mean I Have To Stand Up and Say Something?* Atheneum, 1986. *(I; A)*

Gilbert, Sara. *You Can Speak Up in Class*. Morrow, 1991. *(I; A)*

Gilford, Henry. *How to Give a Speech*. Watts, 1980. *(I; A)*

PUBLISHING. See Books.

PUERTO RICO

Griffiths, John. *Take a Trip to Puerto Rico*. Watts, 1989. *(P; I)*

Visual Geography. *Puerto Rico in Pictures*. Lerner, 1987. *(I)*

PULSARS. See ASTRONOMY.

PUMPS

Zubrowski, Bernie. *Messing Around with Water Pumps and Siphons: A Children's Museum Activity Book*. Little, 1981. *(P; I)*

PUNCTUATION

Forte, Imogene. *Punctuation Power*. Incentive Publications, 1981. *(P; I)*

Gregorich, Barbara. *Apostrophe, Colon, Hyphen*. 1980; *Comma*. 1980; *Period, Question Mark, Exclamation Mark*. EDC Publishing, 1980. *(P; I)*

Rigsby, Annelle. *Punctuation*. Enrich, 1980. *(P)*

Tilkin, Sheldon L. *Quotation Marks and Underlining*. EDC, 1980. *(P; I)*

PUNIC WARS. See HANNIBAL; ROME, ANCIENT.

PUPPETS AND MARIONETTES

Griffith, Bonnie. *The Tree House Gang: Puppet Plays for Children*. Standard Publishing, 1983. *(P; I)*

Krisvoy, Juel. *The Good Apple Puppet Book*. Good Apple, 1981. *(P; I)*

Lasky, Kathryn. *Puppeteer*. Macmillan, 1985. *(I)*

Marks, Burton, and Marks, Rita. *Puppets and Puppet-Making*. Plays, 1982. *(P; I)*

Oldfield, Margaret J. *Finger Puppets and Finger Plays*. Creative Storytime Press, 1981; *Tell and Draw Paper Bag Puppet Book*, 1981 (2nd ed.). *(P)*

Supraner, Robyn, and Supraner, Lauren. *Plenty of Puppets to Make*. Troll, 1981. *(P; I)*

Venning, Sue, illus. *Jim Henson's Muppet Show Bill*. Random, 1983. *(P; I)*

Wright, Lyndie. *Puppets*. Watts, 1989. *(P)*

PURIM

Chaikin, Miriam. *Make Noise, Make Merry: The Story and Meaning of Purim*. Houghton, 1983. *(I)*

Cohen, Barbara. *Here Comes the Purim Players*. Lothrop, 1984. *(P)*

Goldin, Barbara Diamond. *Cakes and Miracles: A Purim Tale*. Viking, 1991. (Fiction) *(P)*

Greenfeld, Howard. *Purim*. Holt, 1983. *(P; I)*

QUAKERS. See RELIGIONS OF THE WORLD.

QUASARS. See ASTRONOMY.

QUEBEC. See CANADA.

QUEBEC CITY. See CANADA.

RABBITS AND HARES

Bare, Colleen S. *Rabbits and Hares*. Dodd, 1983. *(P; I)*

Burton, Jane. *Freckles the Rabbit*. Gareth Stevens, 1989. *(P)*

Henrie, Fiona. *Rabbits*. Watts, 1980. *(P; I)*

Hess, Lilo. *Diary of a Rabbit*. Scribner's, 1982. *(I)*

Oxford Scientific Films. *The Wild Rabbit*. Putnam, 1980. *(I; A)*

RACCOONS AND THEIR RELATIVES

Freschet, Berniece. *Raccoon Baby*. Putnam, 1984. *(P)*

MacClintock, Dorcas. *A Natural History of Raccoons*. Scribner's, 1981. *(I); A Raccoon's First Year*. 1982. *(P)*

Patent, Dorothy H. *Raccoons, Coatimundis, and Their Family*. Holiday, 1979. *(I; A)*

RACES, HUMAN. See ANTHROPOLOGY; GENETICS AND GENETIC ENGINEERING.

RACQUETBALL

Hogan, Marty, and Wong, Ken. *High-performance Racquetball*. HP Books, 1985. *(A)*

RADIATION

McGowen, Tom. *Radioactivity: From the Curies to the Atomic Age*. Watts, 1986. *(I)*

Milne, Lorus, and Milne, Margery. *Understanding Radioactivity*. Atheneum, 1989. *(I)*

Pettigrew, Mark. *Radiation*. Gloucester Press, 1986. *(I)*

Pringle, Laurence. *Radiation: Waves and Particles, Benefits and Risks*. Enslow, 1983. *(I)*

See also NUCLEAR ENERGY.

RADIO, AMATEUR

Ferrell, Nancy Warren. *The New World of Amateur Radio*. Watts, 1986. *(I; A)*

Kuslan, Louis I., and Kuslan, Richard D. *Ham Radio*. Prentice-Hall, n.d. *(I: A)*

RADIO

Carter, Alden R. *Radio: From Marconi To the Space Age*. Watts, 1987. *(P; I)*

Edmonds, I. G., and Gebhardt, William H. *Broadcasting for Beginners*. Holt, 1980. *(I; A)*

Gilmore, Susan. *What Goes On at a Radio Station?* Carolrhoda, 1983. *(P; I)*

Hawkins. *Audio and Radio*. EDC Publishing, 1982. *(I; A)*

Lerner, Mark. *Careers with a Radio Station*. Lerner, 1983. *(P; I)*

RAILROADS

Macdonald, Fiona. *A 19th Century Railway Station*. Peter Bedrick, 1990. *(I)*

Marshall, Ray. *The Train: Watch it Work by Operating the Moving Diagrams!* Viking, 1986. *(P)*

Pollard, Michael. *Train Technology*. Bookwright, 1990. *(I)*

Sheffer, H. R. *Trains*. Crestwood, 1982. *(P; I)*

Siebert, Diane. *Train Song*. Harper, 1990. (Fiction) *(P)*

Smith, E. Boyd. *The Railroad Book*. Houghton, 1983. *(I)*

Wilson, Keith. *Railways in Canada: The Iron Link*. Watts, 1982. *(I; A)*

Yepsen, Roger. *Train Talk*. Pantheon, 1983. *(I; A)*

RAIN, SNOW, SLEET, AND HAIL

Aardema, Verna. *Bringing the Rain to Kapiti Plain*. Dial, 1981. (Fiction) *(P)*

Bennett, David. *Rain*. Bantam, 1988. *(P)*

Brandt, Keith. *What Makes It Rain?* Troll, 1981. *(P)*

Branley, Franklyn M. *Rain and Hail*. Harper, 1983. *(P)*

Burton, Virginia. *Katy and the Big Snow*. Houghton, 1974. (Fiction) *(P)*

Coutant, Helen. *First Snow*. Knopf, 1974. (Fiction) *(P)*

Williams, Terry T., and Major, Ted. *The Secret Language of Snow*. Pantheon, 1984. *(I; A)*

RALEIGH, SIR WALTER. See ENGLAND, HISTORY OF.

RANCH LIFE. See COWBOYS.

REAGAN, RONALD WILSON

Fox, Mary Virginia. *Mister President: The Story of Ronald Reagan*. Enslow, 1986 (rev. ed.). *(I; A)*

Sullivan, George. *Ronald Reagan*. Messner, 1985. *(A)*

Tax, Mary V. *Mister President: The Story of Ronald Reagan*. Enslow, 1982. *(I; A)*

See also PRESIDENCY OF THE UNITED STATES.

RECIPES. See COOKING.

RECONSTRUCTION PERIOD

Sterling, Dorothy, ed. *The Trouble They Seen: Black People Tell the Story of Reconstruction*. Doubleday, 1976. *(I; A)*

RED CROSS

Barton, Clara. *The Story of the Red Cross*. Airmont, 1968. *(P; I)*

Gilbo, Patrick. *The American Red Cross*. Chelsea House, 1987. *(I; A)*

See also BARTON, CLARA.

REFERENCE BOOKS

Adams, Simon, et al. *Illustrated Atlas of World History*. Random, 1992. *(I; A)*

Paton, John. *Picture Encyclopedia for Children*. Grosset, 1987. *(P; I)*

Reader's Digest. *The Reader's Digest Children's World Atlas*. Reader's Digest, 1991. *(I)*

REFRIGERATION

Ford, Barbara. *Keeping Things Cool: The Story of Refrigeration and Air Conditioning*. Walker, 1986. *(I; A)*

REFUGEES

Ashabranner, Brent, and Ashabranner, Melissa. *Into A Strange Land*. Dodd, 1987. *(I; A)*

Bentley, Judith. *Refugees: Search for a Haven*. Messner, 1986. *(P; I)*

Graff, Nancy Price. *Where the River Runs: A Portrait of a Refugee Family*. Little, 1993. *(I; A)*

Loescher, Gil, and Loescher, Ann D. *The World's Refugees: A Test of Humanity*. Harcourt, 1982. *(I; A)*

RELATIVITY

Apfel, Necia H. *It's All Relative: Einstein's Theory of Relativity*. Lothrop, 1981. *(I)*

Fisher, David E. *The Ideas of Einstein*. Holt, 1980. *(P; I)*

Swisher, Clarice. *Relativity*. Greenhaven Press, 1990. *(I)*

Tauber, Gerald E. *Relativity: From Einstein to Black Holes*. Watts, 1988. *(I; A)*

RELIGIONS OF THE WORLD

Ahsan, M. M. *Muslim Festivals*. Rourke, 1987. *(P; I)*

Bahree, Patricia. *The Hindu World*. Silver Burdett, 1983. *(I)*

Berger, Gilda. *Religions*. Watts, 1983. *(I; A)*

Edmonds, I. G. *Hinduism*. Watts, 1978. *(I; A)*

Faber, Doris. *The Perfect Life: The Shakers in America*. Farrar, 1974. *(A)*

Kanitkar, V. P. (Hemant). *Hinduism*. Bookwright, 1987. *(I; A)*

Martin, Nancy. *Christianity*. Bookwright, 1987. *(I; A)*

McNeer, May, and Ward, Lynd. *John Wesley*. Abingdon, n.d. *(I)*

Moktefi, Mokhtar. *The Rise of Islam*. Silver Burdett, 1987. *(P; I)*

Moskin, Marietta D. *In the Name of God*. Atheneum, 1980. *(I; A)*

Peare, Catherine O. *John Woolman: Child of Light*. Vanguard, n.d. *(I; A)*

Powell, Anton. *The Rice of Islam*. Warwich, 1980. *(I)*

Rice, Edward. *American Saints and Seers: American-born Religions and the Genius Behind Them*. Scholastic, 1982. *(I; A)*

Snelling, John. *Buddhism*. Bookwright, 1987. *(I; A)*

Stepanek, Sally. *John Calvin*. Chelsea House, 1986. *(I)*

Tames, Richard. *Islam.* (Dictionaries of World Religions Series). David & Charles, 1985. *(A)*

REMBRANDT. See ART AND ARTISTS.

RENAISSANCE

Caselli, Giovanni. *The Renaissance and the New World.* Harper, 1986. *(I; A)*

Howarth, Sarah. *Renaissance People.* Millbrook, 1992. *(I); Renaissance Places.* Millbrook, 1992. *(I)*

REPRODUCTION, HUMAN

Cole, Joanna. *How You Were Born.* Morrow, 1993 (rev. ed.). *(P)*

Girard, Linda W. *You Were Born on Your Very First Birthday.* Albert Whitman, 1983. *(P)*

Jessel, Camilla. *The Joy of Birth.* Hillside Press, 1982. *(P; I)*

Nilsson, Lennart. *How Was I Born? A Photographic Story of Reproduction and Birth for Children.* Delacorte, 1975. *(P; I)*

REPTILES

Ballard, Lois. *Reptiles.* Childrens, 1982. *(P; I)*

Cook, David. *Small World of Reptiles.* Watts, 1981. *(P)*

Daly, Kathleen N. *A Child's Book of Snakes, Lizards, and Other Reptiles.* Doubleday, 1980. *(P)*

DeTreville, Susan, and DeTreville, Stan. *Reptiles and Amphibians.* Troubador, 1981. *(P; I)*

Fichter, George S. *Reptiles and Amphibians of North America.* Random, 1982. *(P; I)*

George, Lindsay Barrett, and George, William T. *Box Turtle at Long Pond.* Greenwillow, 1989. *(P)*

Johnston, Ginny, and Cutchins, Judy. *Scaly Babies: Reptiles Growing Up.* Morrow, 1988. *(I)*

Kuchalla, Susan. *What Is a Reptile?* Troll, 1982. *(P)*

Mattison, Chris. *The Care of Reptiles and Amphibians in Captivity.* Blandford Press, 1987. *(A)*

McCarthy, Colin, and Arnold, Nick. *Reptile.* Knopf, 1991. *(I)*

McNaughton, Lenor. *Turtles, Tadpoles, and Take-Me-Homes.* Good Apple, 1981. *(P; I)*

RETAIL STORES

Gibbons, Gail. *Department Stores.* Harper, 1984. *(P)*

RETARDATION, MENTAL

Byars, Betsy. *The Summer of the Swans.* Viking, 1970. (Fiction) *(I)*

Cleaver, Vera, and Cleaver, Bill. *Me Too.* Harper, 1973. *(I)*

Dunbar, Robert E. *Mental Retardation.* Watts, 1978. *(I)*

Sobol, Harriet Langsam. *My Brother Steven Is Retarded.* Macmillan, 1977. *(I)*

REVERE, PAUL

Brandt, Keith. *Paul Revere: Son of Liberty.* Troll, 1982. *(P; I)*

Forbes, Esther. *America's Paul Revere.* Houghton, 1976. *(P; I)*

Fritz, Jean. *And Then What Happened, Paul Revere?* Coward, 1973. *(I)*

Lee, Martin. *Paul Revere.* Watts, 1987. *(P)*

Longfellow, Henry Wadsworth. ''Paul Revere's Ride'' from *The Works of Henry Wadsworth Longfellow.* AMS Press, 1976. *(I)*

REVOLUTIONARY WAR

Benchley, Nathaniel. *George the Drummer Boy.* Harper, 1977. *(P)*

Bliven, Bruce, Jr. *The American Revolution.* Random, 1981. *(I; A)*

Carter, Alden R. *At the Forge of Liberty; Birth of the Republic; Colonies in Revolt; Darkest Hours.* Watts, 1988. *(P; I)*

Clapp, Patricia. *I'm Deborah Sampson: A Soldier in the War of the Revolution.* Lothrop, 1977. *(I)*

Collier, James Lincoln, and Collier, Christopher. *My Brother Sam Is Dead.* Four Winds, 1974. *(I; A)*

Davis, Burke. *George Washington and the American Revolution.* Random, 1975. *(I; A)*

Egger-Bovet, Howard, and Smith-Baranzini, Marlene. *Book of the American Revolution.* Little, 1994. *(I)*

Fleishman, Sid. *The Whipping Boy.* Greenwillow, 1986. (Fiction) *(P; I)*

Forbes, Esther. *Johnny Tremain.* Houghton, 1943. (Fiction) *(I)*

Fritz, Jean. *And Then What Happened, Paul Revere?* Coward, 1982. *(P; I); Early Thunder.* Coward, 1967 (Fiction) *(I; A); Why Can't You Make Them Behave, King George?* Putnam, 1982. *(P; I)*

Lawson, Robert. *Ben and Me.* Little, 1939. (Fiction) *(P; I)*

Marrin, Albert. *The War for Independence: The Story of the American Revolution.* Atheneum, 1988. *(I)*

McGovern, Ann. *The Secret Soldier: The Story of Deborah Sampson.* Four Winds, 1975. *(I)*

Meltzer, Milton. *The American Revolutionaries.* Crowell, 1987. *(A)*

O'Dell, Scott. *Sarah Bishop.* Houghton, 1980. (Fiction) *(I; A)*

Phelan, Mary K. *The Story of the Boston Massacre.* Harper, 1976. *(I; A)*

Rappaport, Dorene. *The Boston Coffee Party.* Harper, 1988. (Fiction) *(P)*

Roop, Connie, and Roop, Peter. *Buttons for General Washington.* Carolrhoda, 1985. (Fiction) *(P)*

Smith, Carter, eds. *The Revolutionary War.* Millbrook, 1991. *(I)*

Stein, R. Conrad. *The Story of Lexington and Concord.* Childrens, 1983. *(P; I)*

RHINOCEROSES

Bailey, Jill. *Mission Rhino*. Steck-Vaughn, 1990. *(P; I)*
Lavine, Sigmund A. *Wonders of Rhinos*. Dodd, 1982. *(I)*
Yoshida, Toshi. *Rhinoceros Mother*. Philomel, 1991. *(P)*

RHODE ISLAND

Eaton, Jeannette. *Lone Journey: The Life of Roger Williams*. Harcourt, 1966. *(A)*
Fradin, Dennis. *Rhode Island: In Words and Pictures*. Childrens, 1981. *(P; I); The Rhode Island Colony*. Childrens, 1989. *(P; I)*

RICE. See GRAIN AND GRAIN PRODUCTS.

RICHELIEU, CARDINAL. See FRANCE.

RIO DE JANEIRO. See BRAZIL.

RIVERS

Bains, Rae. *Wonders of Rivers*. Troll, 1981. *(P)*
Bellamy, David. *The River*. Clarkson Potter, 1988. *(P)*
Carlisle, Norman, and Carlisle, Madelyn. *Rivers*. Childrens, 1982. *(P)*
Crump, Donald. *Let's Explore a River*. National Geographic, 1988. *(P)*
Dabcovich, Lydia. *Follow the River*. Dutton, 1980. *(P)*
Emil, Jane, and Veno, Joseph. *All About Rivers*. Troll, 1984. *(P; I)*
Hoff, Mary, and Rodgers, Mary M. *Rivers and Lakes*. Lerner, 1991. *(I)*
Mulherin, Jenny. *Rivers and Lakes*. Watts, 1984. *(P; I)* (Atlas format)
Oppenheim, Joanne. *On the Other Side of the River*. Watts, 1972. (Fiction) *(P)*
Rowland-Entwistle, Theodore. *Rivers and Lakes*. Silver Burdett, 1987. *(P; I)*
Updegraffe, Imelda, and Updegraffe, Robert. *Rivers and Lakes*. Penguin, 1983. *(I; A)*

ROADS AND HIGHWAYS

Crockett, Mary. *Roads and Traveling*. Sportshelf, n.d. *(P; I)*
Gibbons, Gail. *New Road!* Harper, 1983. *(P)*
Sauvain, Philip. *Roads*. Garrett Educational, 1990. *(P; I)*
Williams, Owen. *How Roads Are Made*. Facts on File, 1989. *(I)*

ROBINSON, JACK ROOSEVELT (JACKIE)

Farr, Naunerle C. *Babe Ruth—Jackie Robinson*. Pendulum Press, 1979. *(P; I; A)*
Frommer, Harvey. *Jackie Robinson*. Watts, 1984. *(I; A)*
Scott, Richard. *Jackie Robinson*. Chelsea House, 1987. *(I; A)*

ROBOTS

Berger, Fredericka. *Robots: What They Are, What They Do*. Greenwillow, 1992. *(P)*
Billard, Mary. *All About Robots*. Putnam, 1982. *(P; I)*
Chester, Michael. *Robots: Facts Behind Fiction*. Macmillan, 1983. *(P; I)*
Hawkes, Nigel. *Robots and Computers*. Watts, 1984. *(I; A)*
Knight, David C. *Robotics: Past, Present and Future*. Morrow, 1983. *(I; A)*
Liptak, Karen. *Robotics Basics: An Introduction for Young People*. Prentice-Hall, 1984. *(I)*
Litterick, Ian. *Robots and Intelligent Machines*. Watts, 1984. *(I)*
Silverstein, Alvin, and Silverstein, Virginia. *The Robots Are Here*. Prentice-Hall, 1983. *(P; I)*
Skurzynski, Gloria. *Robots: Your High-Tech World*. Bradbury, 1990. *(I)*

ROCKETS. See SATELLITES; SPACE EXPLORATION AND TRAVEL.

ROCK MUSIC

Fornatale, Pete. *The Story of Rock 'n' Roll*. Morrow, 1987. *(A)*
Hanmer, Trudy J. *An Album of Rock and Roll*. Watts, 1988. *(P; I)*
Tobler, John. *Thirty Years of Rock*. Exeter Books, 1985. *(A)*

ROCKS

Baylor, Byrd. *Everybody Needs a Rock*. Scribner's, 1974. (Fiction) *(P)*
Cheney, Glenn Alan. *Mineral Resources*. Watts, 1985. *(I)*
Eckert, Allan W. *Earth Treasures: Where to Collect Minerals, Rocks, and Fossils in the United States*. Harper, 1987. *(I; A)*
Harris, Susan. *Gems and Minerals*. Watts, 1982. *(P)*
Hiscock, Bruce. *The Big Rock*. Atheneum, 1988. *(P; I)*
Horenstein, Sidney. *Rocks Tell Stories*. Millbrook, 1993. *(I)*
Kehoe, Michael. *The Rock Quarry Book*. Carolrhoda, 1981. *(P)*
Marcus, Elizabeth. *Rocks and Minerals*. Troll, 1983. *(P; I)*
McGowen, Tom. *Album of Rocks and Minerals*. Rand, 1981. *(P; I)*
O'Neil, Paul. *Gemstones*. Time-Life, 1983. *(I)*
Podendorf, Illa. *Rocks and Minerals*. Childrens, 1982. *(P)*
Srogi, Lee Ann. *Start Collecting Rocks and Minerals*. Running Press, 1989. *(I; A)*
Symes, R. F., and Harding, Roger. *Crystal & Gem*. Knopf, 1991. *(I)*
Symes, R. F. and the staff of the Natural History Museum. *Rocks and Minerals*. Knopf, 1988. *(I)*

Whyman, Kathryn. *Rocks and Minerals.* Gloucester Press, 1989. *(P; I)*

RODENTS

Bare, Colleen S. *Tree Squirrels.* Dodd, 1983. *(P; I)*

Lane, Margaret. *The Squirrel.* Dial, 1981. *(P)*

Lavine, Sigmund. *Wonders of Mice.* Dodd, 1980; *Wonders of Woodchucks,* 1984. *(I)*

McConoughey, Jana. *The Squirrels.* Crestwood, 1983. *(P; I)*

Newton, James R. *The March of the Lemmings.* Harper, 1976. *(P)*

See also GUINEA PIGS, HAMSTERS, AND GERBILS.

RODEOS

Fain, James W. *Rodeos.* Childrens, 1983. *(P)*

Munn, Vella. *Rodeo Riders.* Harvey, 1981. *(P; I; A)*

Tinkelman, Murray. *Rodeo: The Great American Sport.* Greenwillow, 1982. *(I; A)*

ROLLER SKATING

Herda, D. J. *Roller Skating.* Watts, 1979. *(I; A)*

Olney, Ross R., and Bush, Chan. *Roller Skating!* Lothrop, 1979. *(I)*

ROMANIA

Carran, Betty B. *Romania.* Childrens, 1988. *(P; I)*

Diamond, Arthur. *The Romanian Americans.* Chelsea House, 1988. *(I; A)*

Sheehan, Sean. *Romania.* Marshall Cavendish, 1994. *(I; A)*

ROMAN NUMERALS. See NUMBERS AND NUMBER SYSTEMS.

ROME, ANCIENT

Chisholm, Jan. *Roman Times.* EDC Publishing, 1982. *(I; A)*

Corbishley, Mike. *The Romans.* Watts, 1984. *(I; A)*

Goodenough, Simon. *Citizens of Rome.* Crown, 1979. *(I)*

James, Simon. *Rome: 750 B.C.–500 A.D.* Watts, 1987. *(I)*

Lapper, Ivan. *Small World of Romans.* Watts, 1982. *(P)*

Lewis, Brenda R. *Growing Up in Ancient Rome.* David & Charles, 1980. *(I; A)*

Miguel, Pierre. *Life in Ancient Rome.* Silver Burdett, 1981. *(I)*

Mulvihill, Margaret. *Roman Forts.* Watts, 1990. *(I)*

Purdy, Susan, and Sandak, Cass R. *Ancient Rome.* (Civilization Project Book) Watts, 1982. *(I)*

Robinson, Charles A., Jr. *Ancient Rome,* rev. by Lorna Greenberg. Watts, 1984. *(I; A)*

Rutland, Jonathan. *See Inside a Roman Town.* Warwick Press, 1986. *(I)*

ROME, ART AND ARCHITECTURE OF. See ROME, ANCIENT.

ROOSEVELT, ELEANOR

Freedman, Russell. *Eleanor Roosevelt: A Life of Discovery.* Clarion, 1993. *(I; A)*

Jacobs, William J. *Eleanor Roosevelt: A Life of Happiness and Tears.* Putnam, 1983. *(I)*

Roosevelt, Eleanor. *The Autobiography of Eleanor Roosevelt.* Harper, 1961. *(A)*

Roosevelt, Elliott. *Eleanor Roosevelt, With Love: A Centenary Remembrance.* Lodestar, 1984. *(A)*

Toor, Rachel. *Eleanor Roosevelt.* Chelsea House, 1989. *(I; A)*

ROOSEVELT, FRANKLIN D.

Devaney, John. *Franklin Delano Roosevelt, President.* Walker, 1987. *(I; A)*

Freedman, Russell. *Franklin Delano Roosevelt.* Clarion, 1990. *(I)*

Greenblatt, Miriam. *Franklin D. Roosevelt: 32nd President of the United States.* Garrett Educational, 1989. *(I)*

Hacker, Jeffrey H. *Franklin D. Roosevelt.* Watts, 1983. *(I; A)*

Lawson, Don. *FDR's New Deal.* Harper, 1979. *(A)*

Osinski, Alice. *Franklin D. Roosevelt.* Childrens, 1988. *(P; I)*

See also PRESIDENCY OF THE UNITED STATES.

ROOSEVELT, THEODORE

Fritz, Jean. *Bully for You, Teddy Roosevelt!* Putnam, 1991. *(I)*

Kent, Zachary. *Theodore Roosevelt: Twenty-sixth President of the United States.* Childrens, 1988. *(P; I)*

Sabin, Louis. *Teddy Roosevelt: Rough Rider.* (Easy Biography Series) Troll, 1986. *(P; I)*

Stefoff, Rebecca. *Theodore Roosevelt: 26th President of the United States.* Garrett Educational, 1988. *(A)*

See also PRESIDENCY OF THE UNITED STATES.

RUBBER

Cosner, Sharon. *Rubber.* Walker, 1986. *(I)*

RUSSIA

Adelman, Deborah. *The "Children of Perestroika" Come of Age: Young People of Moscow Talk About Life in the New Russia.* Sharpe, 1994. *(A)*

RWANDA. See AFRICA.

SAFETY

Brown, Marc, and Krensky, Stephen. *Dinosaurs, Beware! A Safety Guide.* Little, 1982. *(P)*

Chlad, Dorothy. *Matches and Fireworks Are Not Toys; Strangers; When I Cross the Street—By Myself.* Childrens, 1982. *(P)*

Girard, Linda Walvoord. *Who Is a Stranger and What Should I Do?* Albert Whitman, 1985. *(P)*

Keller, Irene. *Thingumajig Book of Health and Safety.* Childrens, 1982. *(P)*

Vogel, Carol G., and Goldner, Kathryn A. *The Danger of Strangers.* Dillon, 1983. *(I)*

SAILING

Adkins, Jan. *The Craft of Sail: A Primer of Sailing.* Walker, 1983. *(I)*

Burchard, Peter. *Venturing: An Introduction to Sailing.* Little, 1986. *(I; A)*

Paulsen, Gary. *Sailing: From Jibs to Jibbing.* Messner, 1981. *(I; A)*

Slocombe, Lorna. *Sailing Basics.* Prentice-Hall, 1982. *(P; I)*

Vandervoort, Tom. *Sailing Is for Me.* Lerner, 1981. *(P; I)*

SAINT KITTS AND NEVIS. See CARIBBEAN SEA AND ISLANDS.

SAINT LAWRENCE RIVER AND SEAWAY

Hanmer, Trudy J. *The St. Lawrence.* Watts, 1984. *(I; A)*

SAINT LUCIA. See CARIBBEAN SEA AND ISLANDS.

SAINT VINCENT AND THE GRENADINES. See CARIBBEAN SEA AND ISLANDS.

SALES AND MARKETING

Boy Scouts of America. *Salesmanship.* Boy Scouts, 1971. *(I; A)*

SAMOA. See PACIFIC OCEAN AND ISLANDS.

SANDBURG, CARL

Hacker, Jeffrey H. *Carl Sandburg.* Watts, 1984. *(I; A)*

Melin, Grace. *Carl Sandburg: Young Singing Poet.* Bobbs, n.d. *(P; I)*

Sandburg, Carl. *Prairie-Town Boy.* Harcourt, 1977. *(A); Rootabaga Stories,* n.d. *(P; I)*

SAN FRANCISCO. See CALIFORNIA.

SAO TOME AND PRINCIPE. See AFRICA.

SASKATCHEWAN. See CANADA.

SATELLITES

Barrett, Norman. *The Picture World of Rockets and Satellites.* Watts, 1990. *(P); The Picture World of Space Shuttles.* Watts, 1990. *(P)*

Berger, Melvin. *Space Shots, Shuttles, and Satellites.* Putnam, 1983. *(I; A)*

Furniss, Tim. *Space Rocket.* Gloucester Press, 1988. *(P; I)*

Irvine, Mat. *Satellites and Computers.* Watts, 1984. *(I; A)*

Petty, Kate. *Satellites.* Watts, 1984. *(P)*

White, Jack R. *Satellites of Today and Tomorrow.* Dodd, 1985. *(I; A)*

SATURN

Asimov, Isaac. *Saturn: The Ringed Beauty.* Gareth Stevens. 1989. *(P; I)*

Halliday, Ian. *Saturn.* Facts on File, 1990. *(P; I)*

Landau, Elaine. *Saturn.* Watts, 1991. *(P; I)*

Simon, Seymour. *Saturn.* Morrow, 1985. *(P)*

SAUDI ARABIA

Saudi Arabia . . . in Pictures. Lerner, 1989. *(I)*

Lye, Keith. *Take a Trip to Saudi Arabia.* Watts, 1984. *(P; I)*

SCANDINAVIA

Booss, Claire, ed. *Scandinavian Folk & Fairy Tales.* Crown, 1985. *(A)*

Franck, Irene M. *The Scandinavian-American Heritage.* Facts on File, 1988. *(I; A)*

See also DENMARK; FINLAND; LAPLAND; NORSE MYTHOLOGY; NORWAY; SWEDEN.

SCHLIEMANN, HEINRICH. See ARCHAEOLOGY.

SCHOOLS. See EDUCATION.

SCHWEITZER, ALBERT

Daniel, Anita. *The Story of Albert Schweitzer,* Random, 1957. *(I)*

SCIENCE, HISTORY OF

Asimov, Isaac. *Great Ideas of Science.* Houghton, 1969. *(A)*

Folsom, Franklin. *Science and the Secret of Man's Past.* Harvey House, 1966. *(I)*

Ross, Frank, Jr. *Oracle Bones, Stars, and Wheelbarrows: Ancient Chinese Science and Technology.* Houghton, 1982. *(I; A)*

Tannenbaum, Beulah and Tannenbaum, Harold E. *Science of the Early American Indians.* Watts, 1988. *(I)*

Temple, Robert. *The Genius of China: 3000 Years of Science, Discovery and Invention.* Simon & Schuster, 1986. *(I; A)*

SCIENCE FICTION

Science Fiction Hall of Fame, 2 vols. Avon, 1983. *(I; A)*

Christopher, John. *The White Mountains.* Macmillan, 1967. (Fiction) *(I; A)*

Cohen, Daniel. *The Monsters of Star Trek*. Archway, 1980. *(P; I)*

Cooper, Susan. *The Dark Is Rising*. Windrush, 1988 (1973). (Fiction) *(P; I)*

Engdahl, Sylvia. *Universe Ahead: Stories of the Future*. Atheneum, 1975. (Fiction) *(I)*

Greer, Gery, and Ruddick, Bob. *Max and Me and the Time Machine*. Harcourt, 1983. (Fiction) *(P; I)*

Heinlein, Robert A., ed. *Tomorrow, the Stars*. Berkley, 1983. *(I; A)*

Key, Alexander. *Escape to Witch Mountain*. Westminster, 1968. (Fiction) *(P; I)*

LeGuin, Ursula. *The Last Book of Earthsea*. Atheneum, 1990. *(I)*

L'Engle, Madeleine. *A Wrinkle in Time*. Farrar, 1962. (Fiction) *(I; A)*

Liebman, Arthur, ed. *Science Fiction: Creators and Pioneers*. Rosen, 1979. *(I; A)*

McCaffrey, Anne. *Dragonsinger*. Atheneum, 1977. (Fiction) *(I; A); Dragonsong*. Atheneum, 1976. (Fiction) *(I; A)*

Wells, H. G. *The Time Machine*. Airmont, 1964. (Fiction) *(I; A)*

Yolen, Jane, ed. *2041*. Delacorte, 1991. *(I)*

SCIENCE PROJECTS. See EXPERIMENTS AND OTHER SCIENCE ACTIVITIES.

SCOTLAND

Lye, Kenneth. *Take a Trip to Scotland*. Watts, 1984. *(P; I)*

Meek, James. *The Land and People of Scotland*. Lippincott, 1990. *(I; A)*

Mitcheson, Rosalind. *Life in Scotland*. David & Charles, 1978. *(I; A)*

Sutcliff, Rosemary. *Bonnie Dundee*. Dutton, 1984. *(I; A)*

SCULPTURE

Fine, Joan. *I Carve Stone*. Harper, 1979. *(I)*

Haldane, Suzanne. *Faces on Places: About Gargoyles and Other Stone Creatures*. Viking, 1980. *(P; I)*

SEA LIONS

Patent, Dorothy Hinshaw. *Seals, Sea Lions and Walruses*. Holiday, 1990. *(P; I)*

Sherrow, Victoria. *Seals, Sea Lions & Walruses*. Watts, 1991. *(P)*

SEALS

Fields, Alice. *Seals*. Watts, 1980. *(P)*

Grace, Eric S. *Seals*. Sierra Club Books/Little, 1991. *(I; A)*

Myers, Susan. *Pearson: A Harbor Seal Pup*. Dutton, 1981. *(P; I)*

Patent, Dorothy Hinshaw. *Seals, Sea Lions and Walruses*. Holiday, 1990. *(P; I)*

Sherrow, Victoria. *Seals, Sea Lions & Walruses*. Watts, 1991. *(P)*

SEASONS

Bennett, David. *Seasons*. Bantam, 1988. *(P)*

Briggs, Raymond. *The Snowman*. Random, 1978. (Fiction) *(P)*

Burton, Virginia Lee. *The Little House*. Houghton, 1942. (Fiction) *(P)*

Clifton, Lucille. *The Boy Who Didn't Believe in Spring*. Dutton, 1978. (Fiction) *(P)*

Hall, Donald. *Ox-Cart Man*. Viking, 1978. (Fiction) *(P; I)*

Hartley, Deborah. *Up North in Winter*. Dutton, 1986. (Fiction) *(P)*

Hirschi, Ron. *Spring*. Cobblehill, 1990. *(P); Winter*. Cobblehill, 1990. *(P)*

Keats, Ezra Jack. *The Snowy Day*. Viking, 1962. (Fiction) *(P)*

Kurelek, William. *A Prairie Boy's Winter*. Houghton, 1973. (Fiction) *(P)*

Lambert David. *The Seasons*. Watts, 1983. *(P)*

Locker, Thomas. *Mare on the Hill*. Dial, 1985. (Fiction) *(P; I)*

Markle, Sandra. *Exploring Autumn: A Season of Science Activities, Puzzlers, and Games*. Atheneum, 1991. *(I); Exploring Winter*. Atheneum, 1984. *(I)*

McNaughton, Colin. *Autumn*. Dial, 1983; *Spring*, 1983; *Summer*, 1983; *Winter*, 1983. *(P)*

Penn, Linda. *Young Scientists Explore the Seasons*. Good Apple, 1983. *(P)*

Provensen, Alice, and Provensen, Martin. *A Book of Seasons*. Random, 1978. *(P)*

Purdy, Carol. *Iva Dunnit and the Big Wind*. Dial, 1985. (Fiction) *(P)*

Sendak, Maurice. *Chicken Soup with Rice*. Harper, 1962. (Fiction) *(P)*

Vaughan, Jenny. *The Four Seasons*. Watts, 1983. *(P)*

Zolotow, Charlotte. *Summer Is. . . .* Harper, 1983. *(P)*

SEGREGATION

Bentley, Judith. *Busing: The Continuing Controversy*. Watts, 1982. *(I; A)*

Bullard, Pamela, and Stoia, Judith. *The Hardest Lesson: Personal Stories of a School Desegregation Crisis*. Little, 1980. *(I; A)*

SELF-DISCOVERY/GROWING UP *

Bridges, Sue Ellen. *Home Before Dark*. Knopf, 1976. (Fiction) *(I; A)*

Burnett, Frances Hodgson. *The Secret Garden*. Holt, 1987 (1909). (Fiction) *(P; I)*

Cleary, Beverly. *Dear Mr. Henshaw*. Morrow, 1983. (Fiction) *(P; I)*

Duncan, Lois. *Killing Mr. Griffin*. Little, 1978. (Fiction) *(I; A)*

---

*This is a popular theme with young readers. However, it is not a separate article in *The New Book of Knowledge*.

Fitzhugh, Louise. *Harriet the Spy*. Harper, 1964. (Fiction) *(P; I)*
Hinton, S. E. *The Outsiders*. Viking, 1967. (Fiction) *(I; A)*
Kraus, Robert. *Leo the Late Bloomer*. Prentice Hall, 1971. (Fiction) *(P)*
Peck, Robert Newton. *Soup*. Knopf, 1974. *(P; I)*
Rawls, Wilson. *Where the Red Fern Grows*. Doubleday, 1961. (Fiction) *(I; A)*
Sharpe, Susan. *Waterman's Boy*. Bradbury, 1990. (Fiction) *(I; A)*
Zindel, Paul. *The Pigman*. Harper, 1968. (Fiction) *(I; A)*

SENEGAL

Lutz, William. *Senegal*. Chelsea House, 1987. *(P; I)*
Senegal . . . in Pictures. Lerner, 1988. *(I; A)*

SETS. See NUMBERS AND NUMBER SYSTEMS.

SEWING AND NEEDLECRAFT

Cone, Ferne G. *Classy Knitting: A Guide to Creative Sweatering for Beginners*. Atheneum, 1984; *Crazy Crocheting*. Atheneum, 1981. *(I; A)*
Eaton, Jan. *The Encyclopedia of Sewing Techniques*. Barron, 1987. *(A)*
Harayda, Marel. *Needlework Magic with Two Basic Stitches*. McKay, 1978. *(A)*
Hodgson, Mary Anne, and Paine, Josephine Ruth. *Fast and Easy Needlepoint*. Doubleday, 1978. *(I)*
Mahler, Celine. *Once Upon a Quilt: Patchwork Design and Technique*. Van Nostrand, 1973. *(I; A)*
Rubenstone, Jessie. *Knitting for Beginners*. Harper, 1973. *(P; I)*
Sommer, Elyse, and Sommer, Joeellen. *A Patchwork, Applique, and Quilting Primer*. Lothrop, 1975. *(P; I)*
Wilson, Erica. *Erica Wilson's Children's World: Needlework Ideas from Childhood Classics*. 1983; *Erica Wilson's Christmas World*. 1982; *Erica Wilson's Embroidery Book*. 1979; *Fun with Crewel Embroidery*. 1965; *More Needleplay*. 1979; *Needleplay*. Scribner's, 1975; *Erica Wilson's Quilts of America*, Oxmoor House, 1979. *(I; A)*

SHAKESPEARE, WILLIAM

Brown, John Russell. *Shakespeare and His Theatre*. Lothrop, 1982. *(I)*
Chute, Marchette. *An Introduction to Shakespeare*. Dutton, 1957; *Stories from Shakespeare*. New American Library, 1971. *(I; A)*
Garfield, Leon. *Shakespeare Stories*. Houghton, 1991. (Fiction) *(I; A)*
Hodges, C. Walter. *Shakespeare's Theatre*. Putnam, 1980. *(I)*
Lamb, Charles, and Lamb, Mary. *Tales from Shakespeare*. Puffin, 1988. *(I)*
Miles, Bernard. *Favorite Tales from Shakespeare*. Rand, 1977. *(I)*

SHARKS, SKATES, AND RAYS

Sharks. Facts on File, 1990. *(I)*
Albert, Burton. *Sharks and Whales*. Grosset, 1989. *(P)*
Blassingame, Wyatt. *Wonders of Sharks*. Dodd, 1984. *(P; I)*
Bunting, Eve. *The Great White Shark*. Messner, 1982. *(I)*
Dingerkus, Guido. *The Shark Watcher's Guide*. Messner, 1985. *(I)*
Gay, Tanner Ottley. *Sharks in Action*. Aladdin, 1990. *(P)*
Gibbons, Gail. *Sharks*. Holiday, 1992. *(P)*
Langley, Andrew. *The World of Sharks*. Bookwright, 1988. *(P)*
Selsam, Millicent, and others. *A First Look at Sharks*. Walker, 1979. *(P)*

SHEEP AND GOATS

Chiefari, Janet. *Kids Are Baby Goats*. Dodd, 1984. *(P; I)*
Levine, Sigmund A., and Scuro, Vincent. *Wonders of Goats*. Dodd, 1980; *Wonders of Sheep*, 1983. *(P; I)*
McDearmon, Kay. *Rocky Mountain Bighorns*. Dodd, 1983. *(P; I)*
Moon, Cliff. *Sheep on the Farm*. Watts, 1983. *(P; I)*
Paladino, Catherine. *Springfleece: A Day of Sheepshearing*. Little, 1990. *(P; I)*

SHELLS

Arthur, Alex. *Shell*. Knopf, 1989. *(I)*
Goudey, Alice E. *Houses from the Sea*. Scribner's, 1959. *(P)*
Morris, Dean. *Animals That Live in Shells*. Raintree, 1977. *(P)*
Selsam, Millicent E., and Hunt, Joyce A. *A First Look at Seashells*. Walker, 1983. *(P)*

SHIPS AND SHIPPING

Bushey, Jerry. *The Barge Book*. Carolrhoda, 1984. *(P; I)*
Carter, Katherine. *Ships and Seaports*. Childrens, 1982. *(P)*
Gibbons, Gail. *Boat Book*. Holiday, 1983. *(P)*
Graham, Ian. *Boats, Ships, Submarines, and Other Floating Machines*. Kingfisher, 1993. *(I)*
Lambert, Mark. *Ship Technology*. Bookwright, 1990. *(I)*
Lewis, Thomas. *Clipper Ship*. Harper, 1978. *(P)*
Maestro, Betsy, and DelVecchio, Ellen. *Big City Port*. Four Winds, 1983. *(P)*
Melville, Herman. *Moby Dick*. Bantam, 1981. (Fiction) *(I; A)*
Rutland, Jonathan. *Ships*. Watts, 1982 (updated ed.). *(I; A)*
Stephen, R. J. *The Picture World of Warships*. Watts, 1990. *(P)*
Thomas, David A. *How Ships Are Made*. Facts on File, 1989. *(I)*
Tunis, Edwin. *Oars, Sails, and Steam: A Picture Book of Ships*. Harper, 1977. *(I)*

Williams, Brian. *Ships and Other Seacraft*. Watts, 1984. *(P; I; A)*

SIERRA LEONE. See AFRICA.

SILK

Johnson, Sylvia A. *Silkworms*. Lerner, 1982. *(P; I)*

SILVER. See METALS AND METALLURGY.

SINGAPORE. See SOUTHEAST ASIA.

SKATEBOARDING

Cassorla, Albert. *The Ultimate Skateboard Book*. Running Press, 1989. *(I; A)*
Thatcher, Kevin J., and Brannon, Brian. *Thrasher: The Radical Skateboard Book*. Random, 1992. *(I; A)*

SKELETAL SYSTEM

Broekel, Ray. *Your Skeleton and Skin*. Childrens, 1984. *(P)*
Ward, Brian T. *The Skeleton and Movement*. Watts, 1981. *(I)*

SKIING

Berry, I. William. *The Great North American Ski Book*. Scribner's, 1982 (rev. ed.). *(I)*
Campbell, Stu, and others. *The Way to Ski!* HP Books, 1987. *(A)*
Krementz, Jill. *A Very Young Skier*. Dial, 1990. *(P; I)*
Marozzi, Alfred. *Skiing Basics*. Prentice Hall, 1984. *(P; I)*
Sullivan, George. *Cross-country Skiing; A Complete Beginner's Book*. Messner, 1980. *(P; I)*
Washington, Rosemary G. *Cross-Country Skiing Is for Me*. Lerner, 1982. *(I)*

SKIN DIVING. See SWIMMING AND DIVING.

SKYDIVING

Benson, Rolf. *Skydiving*. Lerner, 1979. *(P; I; A)*
Nentl, Jerolyn. *Skydiving*. Crestwood, 1978. *(P)*

SLAVERY

Buckmaster, Henrietta. *Flight to Freedom: The Story of the Underground Railroad*. Harper, 1958. *(A)*
Cosner, Shaaron. *The Underground Railroad*. Watts, 1991. *(I; A)*
Everett, Gwen. *John Brown: One Man Against Slavery*. Rizzoli, 1994. *(I; A)*
Fox, Paula. *The Slave Dancer*. Bradbury, 1973. (Fiction) *(I)*
Haskins, Jim. *Get on Board: The Story of the Underground Railroad*. Scholastic, 1993. *(I; A)*
Katz, William Loren. *Breaking the Chains: African-American Slave Resistance*. Atheneum, 1990. *(A)*

Lawrence, Jacob. *Harriet and the Promised Land*. Simon and Schuster, 1994. *(P; I)*
Lester, Julius. *To Be a Slave*. Dial, 1968. *(I; A)*
Meltzer, Milton. *All Times, All Peoples: A World History of Slavery*. Harper, 1980. *(A)*
Monjo, F. N. *The Drinking Gourd*. Harper, 1969; 1983 (paper). (Fiction) *(P)*
Ofosu-Appiah, L. H. *People in Bondage: African Slavery Since the 15th Century*. Runestone Press, 1993. *(I; A)*
Rinaldi, Ann. *Wolf by the Ears*. Scholastic, 1991. (Fiction) *(I; A)*
Smucker, Barbara. *Runaway to Freedom*. Harper, 1979. (Fiction) *(P; I)*
Stowe, Harriet Beecher. *Uncle Tom's Cabin*. Macmillan, 1985 reprint. (Fiction) *(I; A)*
Winter, Jeanette. *Follow the Drinking Gourd*. Knopf, 1992. *(P)*
See also CIVIL WAR, UNITED STATES; DOUGLASS, FREDERICK; TUBMAN, HARRIET.

SLEEP

Eldred, Patricia M. *What Do We Do When We're Asleep?* Creative Education, 1981. *(P)*
Selsam, Millicent. *How Animals Sleep*. Scholastic, 1969. *(P)*
Silverstein, Alvin, and Silverstein, Virginia. *The Mystery of Sleep*. Little, 1987. *(P; I)*

SMITH, JOHN

Fritz, Jean. *The Double Life of Pocahontas*. Putnam, 1983. *(P; I)*

SMOKING

Berger, Gilda. *Smoking Not Allowed: The Debate*. Watts, 1987. *(A)*
Gano, Lila. *Smoking*. Lucent Books, 1989. *(I; A)*
Sonnett, Sherry. *Smoking*. Watts, 1988. *(I: A)*
Ward, Brian R. *Smoking and Health*. Watts, 1986. *(I; A)*

SNAKES

Anderson, Robert. *A Step-By-Step Book About Snakes*. TFH Publications, 1988. *(I; A)*
Arnold, Caroline. *Snake*. Morrow, 1991. *(P; I)*
Broekel, Ray. *Snakes*. Childrens, 1982. *(P)*
Chace, G. Earl. *Rattlesnakes*. Dodd, 1984. *(I)*
Cole, Joanna. *A Snake's Body*. Morrow, 1981. *(P)*
Fichter, George S. *Poisonous Snakes*. Watts, 1982. *(P; I)*; *Snakes Around the World*, 1980. *(P)*
Freedman, Russell. *Rattlesnakes*. Holiday, 1984. *(P)*
Gove, Dors. *A Water Snake's Year*. Atheneum, 1991. *(P; I)*
Lauber, Patricia. *Snakes Are Hunters*. Crowell, 1988. *(P)*
Lavies, Bianca. *The Secretive Timber Rattlesnake*. Dutton, 1990. *(P)*
Maestro, Betsy. *Take a Look at Snakes*. Scholastic, 1992. *(P)*

McClung, Robert M. *Snakes: Their Place in the Sun*. Garrard, 1991 (rev. ed.). *(P; I)*

SOAP BOX DERBY

Radlauer, Ed, and Radlauer, Ruth. *Soap Box Winners*. Childrens, 1983. *(P; I)*

SOCCER

Arnold, Caroline. *Soccer: From Neighborhood Play to the World Cup*. Watts, 1991. *(P; I)*

Butterfield, S. M. *The Wonderful World of Soccer*. Putnam, 1982. *(P; I; A)*

Cohen, Mervyn D. *Soccer for Children and Their Parents*. Brunswick, 1983. *(P; I)*

Delson, Paul. *Soccer Sense: Terms, Tips, and Techniques*. Bradson, 1983. *(I; A)*

Gutman, Bill. *Modern Soccer Superstars*. Dodd, 1980. *(P; I; A)*

Rosenthal, Bert. *Soccer*. Childrens, 1983. *(P)*

Yannis, Alex. *Soccer Basics*. Prentice-Hall, 1982. *(P; I)*

SOFTBALL

Madison, Arnold. *How to Play Girls' Softball*. Messner, 1981. *(P; I)*

Sandak, Cass R. *Baseball and Softball*. Watts, 1982. *(P)*

Washington, Rosemary G. *Softball Is for Me*. Lerner, 1982. *(P; I)*

SOILS

Leutscher, Alfred. *Earth*. Dial, 1983. *(P; I)* (A book about soils)

SOLAR ENERGY

Asimov, Isaac. *How Did We Find Out About Solar Power?* Walker, 1981. *(P; I)*

Kaplan, Sheila. *Solar Energy*. Raintree, 1983. *(P; I)*

Spetgang, Tilly, and Wells, Malcolm. *The Children's Solar Energy Book*. Sterling, 1982. *(P; I)*

SOLAR SYSTEM

Adams, Richard. *Our Wonderful Solar System*. Troll, 1983. *(P; I)*

Cole, Joanna. *The Magic Schoolbus: Lost in the Solar System*. Scholastic, 1990. *(I)*

Lambert, David. *The Solar System*. Watts, 1984. *(I; A)*

Roop, Peter, and Roop, Connie. *The Solar System*. Greenhaven Press, 1988. *(A)*

Smoluchowski, Roman. *The Solar System*. Freeman, 1983. *(I)*

See also PLANETS; SUN.

SOLIDS. See MATTER.

SOLOMON ISLANDS. See PACIFIC OCEAN AND ISLANDS.

SOMALIA. See AFRICA.

SOUND AND ULTRASONICS

Broekel, Ray. *Sound Experiments*. Childrens, 1983. *(P)*

Kettelkamp, Larry. *The Magic of Sound*. Morrow, 1982. *(I)*

Knight, David. *All About Sound*. Troll, 1983. *(P; I)*

Lampton, Christopher. *Sound: More Than What You Hear*. Enslow, 1992. *(I; A)*

Taylor, Barbara. *Hear! Hear! The Science of Sound*. Random, 1991. *(P; I)*

Wicks, Keith. *Sound and Recording*. Watts, 1982. *(I; A)*

SOUTH AFRICA

Denenberg, Barry. *Nelson Mandela: No Easy Walk to Freedom*. Scholastic, 1991. *(I)*

Harris, Sarah. *Timeline: South Africa*. Dryad Press, 1988. *(I; A)*

Isadora, Rachel. *At the Crossroads*. Greenwillow, 1991. (Fiction) *(P)*

Jacobsen, Karen. *South Africa*. Childrens, 1989. *(P)*

Maartens, Maretha. *Paper Bird: A Novel of South Africa.*Clarion, 1991. (Fiction) *(I; A)*

Meyer, Carolyn. *Voices of South Africa: Growing up in a Troubled Land*. Gulliver Books, 1986. *(I; A)*

Naidoo, Beverley. *Chain of Fire*. Harper, 1990. (Fiction) *(I; A); Journey to Jo'burg: A South African Story*. Lippincott, 1986. *(I; A)*

Pascoe, Elaine. *South Africa: Troubled Land*. Watts, 1992. (rev. ed.) *(A)*

Paton, Jonathan. *The Land and People of South Africa*. Lippincott, 1990. *(A)*

Stein, R. Conrad. *South Africa*. Childrens, 1986. *(P)*

Watson, R. L. *South Africa . . . in Pictures*. Lerner, 1988. *(P; I)*

SOUTH AMERICA

Beatty, Noelle B. *Suriname*. Chelsea House, 1987. *(P; I)*

Carter, William E. *South America*. Watts, 1983 (rev. ed.). *(I; A)*

See also individual countries.

SOUTH CAROLINA

Burney, Eugenia. *Fort Sumter*. Childrens, 1975. *(P; I)*

Carpenter, Allan. *South Carolina*. Childrens, 1979. *(I)*

Fradin, Dennis. *South Carolina: In Words and Pictures*. Childrens, 1980. *(P; I)*

Osborne, Anne R. *A History of South Carolina*. Sandlapper Publishing, 1983. *(P; I)*

SOUTH DAKOTA

Carpenter, Allan. *South Dakota*. Childrens, 1978. *(P; I)*

Fradin, Dennis. *South Dakota: In Words and Pictures*. Childrens, 1981. *(P; I)*

Wilder, Laura Ingalls. *Little Town on the Prairie*. Harper, 1953. *(I); The Long Winter*, 1953. *(I)*

SOUTHEAST ASIA

Malaysia . . . in Pictures. Lerner, 1989. *(I)*

Thailand . . . in Pictures. Lerner, 1989. *(I)*

Bjener, Tamiko. *Philippines*. Gareth Stevens, 1987. *(P)*

Chandler, David P. *The Land and People of Cambodia*. Harper, 1991. *(I; A)*

Cordero Fernando, Gilda. *We Live in the Philippines*. Bookwright, 1986. *(P; I)*

Elder, Bruce. *Malaysia. Singapore*. Watts, 1985. *(P)*

Fairclough, Chris. *We Live in Indonesia*. Bookwright, 1986. *(P; I)*

Fox, Mary Virginia. *Papua New Guinea*. Childrens, 1994. *(I; A)*

Goldfarb, Mace. *Fighters, Refugees, Immigrants: A Story of the Hmong*. Carolrhoda, 1982. *(P; I)*

Huynh Quang Nhuong. *The Land I Lost: Adventures of a Boy in Vietnam*. Harper, 1982. *(I)*

Knowlton, MaryLee, and Sachner, Mark J. *Burma*. Gareth Stevens, 1987. *(P); Indonesia*, 1987. *(P); Malaysia*, 1987. *(P)*

Layton, Lesley. *Singapore*. Marshall Cavendish, 1990. *(I)*

Lee, Jeanne. *Toad Is the Uncle of Heaven: A Vietnamese Folk Tale*. Holt, 1985. *(P)*

Lye, Keith. *Indonesia*. Watts, 1985. *(P)*

Nickelson, Harry. *Vietnam*. Lucent Books, 1989. *(I; A)*

Smith, Datus C., Jr. *The Land and People of Indonesia*. Harper, 1983 (rev. ed.). *(I)*

Stein, R. Conrad. *The Fall of Singapore*. Childrens, 1982. *(P; I)*

Thomson, Ruth and Neil. *A Family in Thailand*. Lerner, 1988. *(P)*

Withington, William A. *Southeast Asia*. Gateway Press, 1988. *(I; A)*

Wright, David K. *Burma*. Childrens, 1991. *(I); Malaysia*. Childrens, 1988. *(P; I)*

Zickgraf, Ralph. *Laos*. Chelsea House, 1990. *(I)*

SOUTH POLE. See ANTARCTICA.

SPACE EXPLORATION AND TRAVEL

Apfel, Necia H. *Voyager to the Planets*. Clarion, 1991. *(P; I)*

Asimov, Isaac. *Piloted Space Flights*. Gareth Stevens, 1990. *(P; I)*

Baird, Anne. *Space Camp: The Great Adventure for NASA Hopefuls*. Morrow, 1992. *(I)*

Becklake, Sue. *Space: Stars, Planets, and Spacecraft*. Dorling Kindersley, 1991. *(I; A)*

Berger, Melvin. *Space Shots, Shuttles, and Satellites*. Putnam, 1983. *(I; A)*

Bernards, Neal. *Living in Space*. Greenhaven Press, 1990. *(I; A)*

Branley, Franklyn M. *From Sputnik to Space Shuttles: Into the New Space Age*. Crowell, 1986. *(P; I)*

Burrows, William E. *Mission to Deep Space: Voyagers' Journey of Discovery*. Freeman, 1993. *(I; A)*

Darling, David. *Could You Ever Fly to the Stars?* Dillon, 1990. *(P; I)*

Dwiggins, Don. *Flying the Space Shuttles*. Dodd, 1985. *(I); Hello? Who's Out There?: The Search for Extraterrestrial Life*, 1987. *(P; I)*

Embury, Barbara. *The Dream Is Alive*. Harper, 1990. *(I)*

Ferguson, Kitty. *Black Holes in Spacetime*. Watts, 1991. *(I; A)*

Fox, Mary Virginia. *Women Astronauts Aboard the Shuttle*. Messner, 1984. *(P; I)*

Harris, Alan, and Weissman, Paul. *The Great Voyager Adventure: A Guided Tour Through the Solar System*. Messner, 1990. *(I)*

Kelch, Joseph W. *Small Worlds: Exploring the 60 Moons of Our Solar System*. Messner, 1989. *(I; A)*

Lampton, Christopher. *Rocketry: From Goddard to Space Travel*. Watts, 1988. *(P; I)*

Long, Kim. *The Astronaut Training Book for Kids*. Lodestar, 1990. *(I)*

Maurer, Richard. *Junk in Space*. Simon & Schuster, 1989. *(P; I); The Nova Space Explorer's Guide: Where to Go and What to See*. Crown, 1985. *(I; A)*

Moulton, Robert R. *First to Fly*. Lerner, 1983. *(P; I)*

O'Conner, Karen. *Sally Ride and the New Astronauts: Scientists in Space*. Watts, 1983. *(I; A)*

Sandak, Cass R. *The World of Space*. Watts, 1989. *(P; I)*

Schefter, James L. *Aerospace Careers*. Watts, 1987. *(A)*

Schick, Ron, and Van Haaften, Julia. *The View from Space*. Clarkson N. Potter, 1988. *(A)*

Solomon, Maury. *An Album of Voyager*. Watts, 1990. *(I)*

Spangenburg, Ray, and Moser, Diane. *Opening the Space Frontier*. Facts on File, 1989. *(I; A)*

Vogt, Gregory. *Space Laboratories*. Watts, 1990. *(P; I); Spaceships*. Watts, 1990. *(P; I)*

SPACE PROBES

Ride, Sally, and O'Shaughnessy, Tam. *Voyager: An Adventure to the Edge of the Solar System*. Crown, 1992. *(P; I)*

SPAIN

De Cervantes, Miguel. *Don Quixote*. Farrar, 1986. (Fiction) *(I; A)*

Hodges, Margaret. *Don Quixote and Sancho Panza*. Scribner's, 1992. *(I; A)*

Lye, Keith. *Passport to Spain*. Watts, 1987. *(P)*

Miller, Arthur. *Spain*. Chelsea House, 1989. *(P; I)*

Selby, Anna. *Spain*. Steck-Vaughn, 1994. *(I)*

Woods, Geraldine. *Spain: A Shining New Democracy.* Dillon, 1987. *(P; I)*

Yokoyama, Masami. *Spain.* Gareth Stevens, 1987. *(P; I)*

SPANISH-AMERICAN WAR

Marrin, Albert. *The Spanish-American War.* Atheneum, 1991. *(I; A)*

SPEECH AND SPEECH DISORDERS

Adams, Edith. *The Noisy Book Starring Yakety Yak.* Random, 1983. *(P)*

Berger, Gilda. *Speech and Language Disorders.* Watts, 1981. *(I; A)*

Carlisle, Jock A. *Tangled Tongue.* University of Toronto Press, 1985. *(A)*

Minn, Loretta. *Teach Speech.* Good Apple, 1982. *(P; I)*

Showers, Paul. *How You Talk.* Harper, 1967; 1975; 1992 (paper). *(P)*

Silverstein, Alvin and Virginia. *Wonders of Speech.* Morrow, 1988. *(A)*

See also PUBLIC SPEAKING.

SPELLING

Gordon, Sharon. *The Spelling Bee.* Troll, 1981. *(P)*

Wittels, Harriet, and Greisman, Joan. *How to Spell It: A Dictionary of Commonly Misspelled Words.* Putnam, 1982. *(P; I; A)*

SPELUNKING. See CAVES AND CAVERNS.

SPIDERS

Dallinger, Jane. *Spiders.* Lerner, 1981. *(P; I; A)*

Lane, Margaret. *The Spider.* Dial, 1982. *(P)*

Schnieper, Claudia. *Amazing Spiders.* Carolrhoda, 1989. *(P; I)*

Selsam, Millicent E., and Hunt, Joyce A. *A First Look at Spiders.* Walker, 1983. *(P)*

Webster, David. *Spider Watching.* Messner, 1984. *(I)*

SPIRITUALS. See HYMNS AND SPIRITUALS.

SQUIRRELS

Gurnell, John. *The Natural History of Squirrels.* Facts on File, 1987. *(A)*

Schlein, Miriam. *Squirrel Watching.* Harper, 1992. *(P; I)*

SRI LANKA

Sri Lanka . . . in Pictures. Lerner, 1989. *(I; A)*

Wilber, Donald N. *The Land and People of Ceylon.* Harper, 1972. *(I; A)*

STAINED-GLASS WINDOWS. See CATHEDRALS.

STALIN, JOSEPH

Caulkins, Janet. *Joseph Stalin.* Watts, 1990. *(I; A)*

Marrin, Albert. *Stalin: Russia's Man of Steel.* Viking, 1988. *(A)*

STAMPS AND STAMP COLLECTING

Allen, Judy. *Guide to Stamps and Stamp Collecting.* EDC Publishing, 1981. *(P; I)*

Boy Scouts of America. *Stamp Collecting.* Boy Scouts, 1974. *(I; A)*

Hobson, Burton. *Getting Started in Stamp Collecting.* Sterling. 1982 (rev. ed.) *(I; A)*

Lewis, Brenda Ralph. *Stamps!* Lodestar, 1991. *(I; A)*

STARFISHES AND THEIR RELATIVES

Zim, Herbert S., and Krantz, Lucretia. *Sea Stars and Their Kin.* Morrow, 1976. *(P; I)*

STARS

Adler, Irving. *The Stars: Decoding Their Messages.* Crowell, 1980. *(I)*

Apfel, Necia H. *Nebulae: The Birth and Death of Stars.* Lothrop, 1988. *(P); Stars and Galaxies.* Watts, 1982. *(I; A)*

Berger, Melvin. *Bright Stars, Red Giants, and White Dwarfs.* Putnam, 1983. *(I; A); Star Gazing, Comet Tracking, and Sky Mapping.* Putnam, 1986. *(I)*

Berry, Richard. *Discover the Stars.* Harmony, 1987. *(P; I)*

Branley, Franklyn M. *Journey into a Black Hole.* Crowell, 1986. *(P); The Sky Is Full of Stars.* Crowell, 1981. *(P); Star Guide.* Crowell, 1987. *(P; I)*

Couper, Heather, and Henbest, Nigel. *Galaxies and Quasars.* Watts, 1986. *(I)*

Gallant, Roy A. *The Constellations: How They Came to Be.* Scholastic, 1979. *(I; A)*

Gibbons, Gail. *Stargazers.* Holiday, 1992. *(P)*

Gustafson, John. *The Young Stargazer's Guide to the Galaxy.* Messner, 1993. *(I; A)*

Levinson, Riki. *Watch the Stars Come Out.* Dutton, 1985. (Fiction) *(P)*

Lurie, Alison. *The Heavenly Zoo: Legends and Tales of the Stars.* Farrar, 1979. *(I)*

Monroe, Jean. *They Dance in the Sky: Native American Star Myths.* Houghton, 1987. *(I)*

STATE GOVERNMENTS

Bentley, Judith. *State Government.* Watts, 1978. *(I; A)*

Goode, Stephen. *The New Federalism: States' Rights in American History.* Watts, 1983. *(I; A)*

STATISTICS

Arthur, Lee, and others. *Sportsmath: How It Works.* Lothrop, 1975. *(I; A)*

Riedel, Manfred G. *Winning with Numbers: A Kid's Guide to Statistics*. Prentice-Hall, 1978. *(I; A)*

STEAM ENGINES. See TECHNOLOGY.

STORYTELLING

Trelease, Jim, ed. *Hey! Listen to This: Stories to Read Aloud*. Viking Penguin, 1992. *(A)*
Trelease, Jim. *The New Read-Aloud Handbook*. Viking Penguin, 1989. *(A)*

STOWE, HARRIET BEECHER

Jakoubek, Robert E. *Harriet Beecher Stowe: Author and Abolitionist*. Chelsea House, 1989. *(I; A)*
Scott, John A. *Woman Against Slavery: The Story of Harriet Beecher Stowe*. Harper, 1978. *(I; A)*
Stowe, Harriet Beecher. *Uncle Tom's Cabin*. Macmillan, 1985 reprint. (Fiction) *(I; A)*

STRINGED INSTRUMENTS. See MUSICAL INSTRUMENTS.

STUDY, HOW TO

Farnette, Cherrie. *The Study Skills Shop*. Incentive Publications, 1980. *(P; I)*
James, Elizabeth, and Barkin, Carol. *How to Be School Smart: Secrets of Successful Schoolwork*. Lothrop, 1988. *(I; A)*
Kesselman-Turkel, Judi, and Peterson, Franklynn. *Study Smarts: How to Learn More in Less Time*. Contemporary Books, 1981. *(I; A)*

SUBMARINES

Graham, Ian. *Submarines*. Gloucester Press, 1989. *(I)*
Rossiter, Mike. *Nuclear Submarine*. Watts, 1983. *(I; A)*
Stephen, R. J. *The Picture World of Submarines*. Watts, 1990. *(P)*
Sullivan, George. *Inside Nuclear Submarines*. Dodd, 1982. *(I; A)*
Weiss, Harvey. *Submarines and Other Underwater Craft*. Crowell, 1990. *(P; I)*
White, David. *Submarines*. Rourke, 1988. *(P)*

SUDAN

Sudan . . . in Pictures. Lerner, 1988. *(I)*
Stewart, Judy. *A Family in Sudan*. Lerner, 1988. *(P)*

SUEZ CANAL. See CANALS.

SUGAR

Cobb, Vicki. *Gobs of Goo*. Harper, 1983. *(P)*
Mitgutsch, Ali. *From Beet to Sugar*. Carolrhoda, 1981. *(P)*

SUN

Adams, Richard. *Our Amazing Sun*. Troll, 1983. *(P; I)*
Ardley, Neil. *Sun and Light*. Watts, 1983. *(P; I)*
Asimov, Isaac. *How Did We Find Out About Sunshine?* Walker, 1987. *(P; I)*
Darling, David. *The Sun: Our Neighborhood Star*. Dillon, 1984. *(I)*
Fields, Alice. *The Sun*. Watts, 1980. *(P)*
Gibbons, Gail. *Sun Up, Sun Down*. Harcourt, 1983. *(P; I)*
Jaber, William. *Exploring the Sun*. Messner, 1980. *(P; I)*
Lampton, Christopher. *The Sun*. Watts, 1982. *(I; A)*
Palazzo, Janet. *Our Friend the Sun*. Troll, 1982. *(P)*

SUPERMARKETS. See RETAIL STORES.

SUPERSTITIONS

Nevins, Ann. *Super Stitches: A Book of Superstitions*. Holiday, 1983. *(P)*
Perl, Lila. *Don't Sing Before Breakfast, Don't Sleep in the Moonlight: Everyday Superstitions and How They Began*. Clarion, 1988. *(I)*

SUPREME COURT OF THE UNITED STATES

Coy, Harold. *The Supreme Court*, rev. by Lorna Greenberg. Watts, 1981. *(I; A)*
Fox, Mary V. *Justice Sandra Day O'Connor*. Enslow, 1983. *(I; A)*
Goode, Stephen. *The Controversial Court: Supreme Court Influences on American Life*. Messner, 1982. *(I; A)*
Greene, Carol. *Sandra Day O'Connor: First Woman of the Supreme Court*. Childrens, 1982. *(P)*; *The Supreme Court*. Childrens, 1985. *(P)*
Peterson, Helen Stone. *The Supreme Court in America's Story*. Garrard, 1976. *(I)*
Rierden, Anne B. *Reshaping the Supreme Court: New Justices, New Directions*. Watts, 1988. *(A)*
Stein, R. Conrad. *The Story of the Powers of the Supreme Court*. Childrens, 1989. *(I)*

SURFING

Coombs, Charles. *Be a Winner in Windsurfing*. Morrow, 1982. *(P; I)*
Evans, Jeremy. *The Complete Guide To Short Board Sailing*. International Marine Publishing, 1987. *(A)*
Freeman, Tony. *Beginning Surfing*. Childrens, 1980. *(P; I)*
Wardlaw, Lee. *Cowabunga! The Complete Book of Surfing*. Avon, 1991. *(I; A)*

SURINAME. See SOUTH AMERICA.

SURVIVAL *

Cleaver, Vera, and Cleaver, Bill. *Where the Lilies Bloom*. Lippincott, 1969. (Fiction) *(I; A)*

*This is a popular theme with young readers. However, it is not a separate article in *The New Book of Knowledge*.

George, Jean C. *Julie of the Wolves*. Harper, 1972. (Fiction) *(I; A)*

Lane, Rose Wilder. *Let the Hurricanes Roar*. Harper, 1961. (Fiction) *(I; A)*

Paulsen, Gary. *Hatchet*. Bradbury, 1987. (Fiction) *(I; A)*

Strieber, Whitley. *Wolf of Shadows*. Knopf, 1985. (Fiction) *(I; A)*

Warner, Gertrude Chandler. *The Boxcar Children*. Albert Whitman, 1977. *(P)*

SWAZILAND. See AFRICA.

SWEDEN

Bjener, Tamiko. *Sweden*. Gareth Stevens, 1987. *(P; I)*

Knowlton, MaryLee, and Sachner, Mark J. *Sweden*. Gareth Stevens, 1987. *(P)*

Lye, Keith. *Take a Trip to Sweden*. Watts, 1983. *(P)*

McGill, Allyson. *The Swedish Americans*. Chelsea House, 1988. *(I; A)*

Olsson, Kari. *Sweden: A Good Life for All*. Dillon, 1983. *(I; A)*

SWIMMING AND DIVING

Boy Scouts of America. *Swimming*. Boy Scouts, 1980. *(I; A)*

Briggs, Carole S. *Diving Is for Me*. Lerner, 1983. *(P; I)*

Chiefari, Jane, and Wightman, Nancy. *Better Synchronized Swimming for Girls*. Dodd, 1981. *(I)*

Gleasner, Diana C. *Illustrated Swimming, Diving, and Surfing Dictionary for Young People*. Harvey, 1980. *(P; I; A)*

Libby, Bill. *The Young Swimmer*. Lothrop, 1983. *(P; I)*

Orr, C. Rob, and Tyler, Jane B. *Swimming Basics*. Prentice-Hall, 1980. *(P; I; A)*

Sullivan, George. *Better Swimming for Boys and Girls*. Dodd, 1982. *(A)*

SWITZERLAND

Cameron, Fiona, and Kristensen, Preben. *We Live in Switzerland*. Bookwright, 1987. *(P)*

Hintz, Martin. *Switzerland*. Childrens, 1986. *(P)*

Lye, Keith. *Take a Trip to Switzerland*. Watts, 1984. *(P; I)*

Schrepfer, Margaret. *Switzerland: The Summit of Europe*. Dillon, 1989. *(P; I)*

Spyri, Johanna. *Heidi*. Knopf, 1980. (Fiction) *(P; I)*

SYRIA. See MIDDLE EAST.

TABLE TENNIS

Sullivan, George. *Better Table Tennis for Boys and Girls*. Putnam, 1972. *(I)*

TAFT, WILLIAM HOWARD

Casey, Jane Clark. *William Howard Taft*. Childrens, 1989. *(P; I)*

TAIWAN

Cooke, David C. *Taiwan, Island China*. Dodd, 1975. *(I)*

Yu, Ling. *A Family in Taiwan*. Lerner, 1990. *(P); Taiwan . . . in Pictures*. Lerner, 1989. *(I)*

TAJ MAHAL. See INDIA.

TANZANIA. See AFRICA.

TAXATION

Taylor, Jack. *The Internal Revenue Service*. Chelsea House, 1987. *(A)*

TAXIDERMY

Cutchins, Judy, and Johnston, Ginny. *Are Those Animals Real? How Museums Prepare Wildlife Exhibits*. Morrow, 1984. *(P; I)*

TAXONOMY

Gutnik, Martin J. *The Science of Classification: Finding Order Among Living and Non-Living Objects*. Watts, 1980. *(I; A)*

TAYLOR, ZACHARY

Collins, David R. *Zachary Taylor: 12th President of the United States*. Garrett Educational, 1989. *(I)*

Kent, Zachary. *Zachary Taylor: Twelfth President of the United States*. Childrens, 1988. *(P; I)*

See also PRESIDENCY OF THE UNITED STATES.

TCHAIKOVSKY, PETER ILYICH. See MUSIC AND MUSICIANS.

TEACHERS AND TEACHING

Shockley, Robert J., and Cutlip, Glen W. *Careers in Teaching*. Rosen, 1988. *(A)*

TECHNOLOGY

Adkins, Jan. *Moving Heavy Things*. Houghton, 1980. *(I; A)*

Ardley, Neil. *Fact or Fantasy*. Watts, 1982. *(I; A); Force and Strength*. Watts, 1985. *(P; I); Muscles to Machines*. Gloucester Press, 1990. *(I)*

Brown, David J. *The Random House Book of How Things Were Built*. Random, 1992. *(I; A)*

Burnie, David. *Machines and How They Work*. Dorling Kindersley, 1991. *(I; A)*

Diagram Group. *Weapons: An International Encyclopedia from 5000 B.C. to 2000 A.D.* St. Martin's, *(I; A)*

Dunn, Andrew. *Wheels at Work*. Thomson Learning, 1993. *(I)*; *The Power of Pressure*. Thomson Learning, 1993. *(I)*

Gaff, Jackie. *Buildings, Bridges & Tunnels*. Random, 1992. *(P; I)*

Gardner, Robert. *This Is the Way It Works: A Collection of Machines*. Doubleday, 1980. *(I; A)*

Gies, Frances, and Gies, Joseph. *Cathedral, Forge, and Waterwheel: Technology and Invention in the Middle Ages*. HarperCollins, 1994. *(A)*

Gross, Cynthia S. *The New Biotechnology; Putting Microbes to Work*. Lerner, 1988. *(I; A)*

Hodges, Henry. *Technology in the Ancient World*. Knopf, 1970. *(I)*

Horvatic, Anne. *Simple Machines*. Dutton, 1989. *(P)*

Lambert, David, and Insley, Jane. *Great Discoveries and Inventions*. Facts on File, 1985. *(I; A)*

Macaulay, David. *The Way Things Work*. Houghton, 1988. *(I; A)*

Math, Irwin. *Tomorrow's Technology: Experimenting With the Science of the Future*. Scribner's, 1992. *(I; A)*

McKie, Robin. *Technology: Science at Work*. Watts, 1984. *(I; A)*

Morgan, Kate. *The Story of Things*. Walker, 1991. *(P; I)*

National Geographic editors. *How Things Work*. National Geographic, 1983 *(P; I; A)*

Parker, Steve. *Everyday Things & How They Work*. Random, 1991. *(P; I)*; *The Random House Book of How Things Work*. Random, 1991. *(I)*

Pollard, Michael. *How Things Work*. Larousse, 1979. *(I)*

Rockwell, Anne, and Rockwell, Harlow. *Machines*. Macmillan, 1985. *(P)*

Skurzynski, Gloria. *Almost the Real Thing: Simulation in Your High-Tech World*. Bradbury, 1991. *(I)*

Smith, Norman F., and Douglas W. *Simulators*. Watts, 1989. *(I; A)*

Stacy, Tom. *Wings, Wheel & Sails*. Random, 1991. *(P; I)*

Weiss, Harvey. *Machines and How They Work*. Crowell, 1983. *(I)*

Zubrowski, Bernie. *Wheels at Work: Building and Experimenting with Models of Machines*. Morrow, 1986. *(I)*

TEETH

Brown, Marc. *Arthur's Tooth*. Little, 1985. (Fiction) *(P)*

Pluckrose, Henry. *Teeth*. Watts, 1988. *(P)*

See also DENTISTRY.

TELEPHONE AND TELEGRAPH

Ault, Phil. *Wires West*. Dodd, 1974. *(I)*

Cavanagh, Mary. *Telephone Power*. Enrich, 1980. *(P; I)*

Math, Irwin. *Morse, Marconi, and You: Understanding and Building Telegraph, Telephone, and Radio Sets*. Scribner's, 1979. *(I; A)*

Webb, Marcus. *Telephones: Words Over Wires*. Lucent Books, 1992. *(I)*

See also BELL, ALEXANDER GRAHAM.

TELESCOPES. See ASTRONOMY.

TELEVISION

Beale, Griffin. *TV and Video*. EDC Publishing, 1983. *(P; I)*

Calabro, Marian. *ZAP! A Brief History of Television*. Four Winds, 1992. *(I)*

Drucker, Malka, and James, Elizabeth. *Series TV: How a Television Show Is Made*. Houghton, 1983. *(I; A)*

Fields, Alice. *Television*. Watts, 1981. *(P)*

Jaspersohn, William. *A Day in the Life of a Television News Reporter*. Little, 1981. *(I)*

Scott, Elaine. *Ramona: Behind the Scenes of a Television Show*. Morrow, 1988. *(P; I)*

Smith, Betsy. *Breakthrough: Women in Television*. Walker, 1981. *(A)*

TENNESSEE

Carpenter, Allan. *Tennessee*. Childrens, 1979. *(I)*

Fradin, Dennis. *Tennessee: In Words and Pictures*. Childrens, 1980. *(P; I)*

Steele, William O. *The Perilous Road*. Harcourt, 1965. *(P; I)*

TENNIS

Ashe, Arthur, and Robinson, Louie. *Getting Started in Tennis*. Atheneum, 1977. *(I; A)*

Braden, Vic, and Bruns, Bill. *Vic Braden's Quick Fixes*. Little, 1988. *(I; A)*

Knudson, R. R. *Martina Navratilova: Tennis Power*. Viking Kestrel, 1986. *(P; I)*

LaMarche, Bob. *Tennis Basics*. Prentice-Hall, 1983. *(P; I)*

Sullivan, George. *Better Tennis for Boys and Girls*. Dodd, 1987. *(I)*

TERRARIUMS

Broekel, Ray. *Aquariums and Terrariums*. Childrens, 1982. *(P)*

Mattison, Christopher. *The Care of Reptiles and Amphibians in Captivity*. Blandford Press, 1987. *(I; A)*

Steinberg, Phil. *You and Your Pet: Terrarium Pets*. Lerner, 1978. *(P; I)*

TERRORISM

Arnold, Terrell E., and Kennedy, Moorhead. *Think About Terrorism: The New Warfare*. Walker, 1988. *(A)*

Coker, Chris. *Terrorism and Civil Strife*. Watts, 1987. *(I)*

Edwards, Richard. *International Terrorism*. Rourke, 1988. *(I)*

TESTS AND TEST TAKING

How to Get Better Test Scores: Grades 3–4; How to Get Better Test Scores: Grades 5–6; How to Get Better Test Scores: Grades 7–8. Random, 1991. *(P; I)*

TEXAS

Adams, Carolyn. *Stars over Texas*. Eakin Press, 1983. *(P; I)*

DePaola, Tomie. *The Legend of the Bluebonnet: An Old Tale of Texas*. Putnam, 1983. *(P)*

Fisher, Leonard. *The Alamo*. Holiday, 1987. *(I)*

Meadowcroft, Enid. *Texas Star*. Crowell, 1950. *(I)*

Peacock, Howard. *The Big Thicket of Texas: America's Ecological Wonder*. Little, 1984. *(I; A)*

Phillips, Betty Lou and Bryce. *Texas*. Watts, 1987. *(P; I)*

Roderus, Frank. *Duster: The Story of a Texas Cattle Drive*. Texas Christian University Press, 1987. *(I)*

Stein, R. Conrad. *Texas*. Childrens, 1989. *(P; I)*

Warren, Betsy. *Let's Remember When Texas Belonged to Spain*. Hendrick-Long, 1982; *Let's Remember When Texas Was a Republic,* 1983; *Texas in Historic Sites and Symbols,* 1982. *(I; A)*

Younger, Jassamine. *If These Walls Could Speak: A Story of Early Settlement in Texas*. Hendrick-Long, 1981. *(I)*

See also MEXICAN WAR.

TEXTILES

Cobb, Vicki. *Fuzz Does It!* Harper, 1982. *(P)*

Macaulay, David. *Mill*. Houghton, 1983. *(I; A)*

Whyman, Kathryn. *Textiles*. Gloucester Press, 1988. *(P; I)*

See also CLOTHING; COTTON; SILK; WEAVING; WOOL.

THAILAND. See SOUTHEAST ASIA.

THANKSGIVING DAY

Anderson, Joan. *The First Thanksgiving Feast*. Clarion, 1984. *(I)*

Baldwin, Margaret. *Thanksgiving*. Watts, 1983. *(I; A)*

Barkin, Carol, and James, Elizabeth. *Happy Thanksgiving!* Lothrop, 1987. *(P; I)*

Barth, Edna. *Turkey, Pilgrims, and Indian Corn: The Story of the Thanksgiving Symbols*. Houghton, 1981. *(P; I)*

Gibbons, Gale. *Thanksgiving Day*. Holiday, 1983. (I)

Kessel, Joyce K. *Squanto and the First Thanksgiving*. Carolrhoda, 1983. *(P)*

Penner, Ruth. *The Thanksgiving Book*. Hastings, 1983. *(I; A)*

THATCHER, MARGARET

Faber, Doris. *Margaret Thatcher: Britain's "Iron Lady."* Viking Kestrel, 1985. *(I)*

Levin, Angela. *Margaret Thatcher*. David & Charles, 1981. *(P; I)*

Moskin, Marietta D. *Margaret Thatcher of Great Britain*. Silver Burdett, 1990. *(I; A)*

THEATER

Cummings, Richard. *Simple Makeup for Young Actors*. Plays, 1990. *(A)*

Gallo, Donald R. *Center Stage: One-Act Plays for Teenage Readers and Actors*. Harper, 1991. *(I; A)*

Gillette, J. Michael. *Theatrical Design and Production*. Mayfield, 1987. *(A)*

Greenberg, Jan. *Theater Careers*. Holt, 1983. *(I; A)*

Haskins, James S. *Black Theater in America*. Harper, 1982. *(I; A)*

Hewett, Joan. *On Camera: The Story of a Child Actor*. Clarion, 1987. *(P)*

Huberman, Caryn, and Wetzel, JoAnne. *Onstage/Backstage*. Carolrhoda, 1987. *(P)*

Judy, Susan, and Judy, Stephen. *Putting On a Play*. Scribner's, 1982. *(I)*

Krementz, Jill. *A Very Young Actress*. Knopf, 1991. *(P; I)*

Lowndes, Rosemary. *Make Your Own World of the Theater*. Little, 1982. *(I; A)*

Loxton, Howard, *Theater*. Steck-Vaughn, 1989. *(I)*

Williamson, Walter. *Behind the Scenes: The Unseen People Who Make Theater Work*. Walker, 1987. *(I; A)*

THIRTEEN AMERICAN COLONIES

Anderson, Joan. *A Williamsburg Household*. Clarion, 1988. *(I)*

Blackburn, Joyce. *James Edward Oglethorpe*. Dodd, 1983. *(I; A)*

Blos, Joan. *A Gathering of Days: A New England Girl's Journal*. Scribner's, 1979. (Fiction) *(I)*

Cohen, Barbara. *Molly's Pilgrim*. Lothrop, 1983. (Fiction) *(P)*

Edwards, Cecile. *John Alden Steadfast Pilgrim*. Houghton, 1965. *(P)*

Fradin, Dennis B. *The Virginia Colony*. Childrens, 1987. *(I)*

Fritz, Jean. *The Double Life of Pocahontas*. Putnam, 1983; *Who's That Stepping on Plymouth Rock?* 1975. *(P; I)*

Knight, James. *The Farm: Life in Colonial Pennsylvania; Sailing to America: Colonists at Sea; Salem Days: Life in a Colonial Seaport; The Village: Life in Colonial Times*. Troll, 1982. *(I; A)*

Lacy, Dan. *The Colony of Virginia*. Watts, 1973. *(I)*

Lobel, Arnold. *On the Day Peter Stuyvesant Sailed into Town*. Harper, 1971. (Fiction) *(P)*

O'Dell, Scott. *The Serpent Never Sleeps: A Novel of Jamestown and Pocahontas*. Houghton, 1987. (Fiction) *(I)*

Reische, Diana. *Founding the American Colonies*. Watts, 1989. *(P; I)*

Scott, John Anthony. *Settlers on the Eastern Shore*. Facts on File, 1991. *(A)*

Sewall, Marcia. *The Pilgrims of Plimoth*. Atheneum, 1986. *(P)*

Speare, Elizabeth George. *The Witch of Blackbird Pond.* Houghton, 1958. (Fiction) *(I; A)*
Tunis, Edwin. *Colonial Living.* Harper, 1976. *(I)*
Waters, Kate. *Sarah Morton's Day: A Day in the Life of a Pilgrim Girl.* Scholastic, 1990. *(P)*

THOREAU, HENRY DAVID

Burleigh, Robert. *A Man Named Thoreau.* Atheneum, 1985. *(P)*
Reef, Catherine. *Henry David Thoreau: A Neighbor to Nature.* 21st Century Books, 1991. *(P; I)*

THUNDER AND LIGHTNING

Branley, Franklyn M. *Flash, Crash, Rumble, and Roll.* Harper, 1964. *(P)*
Cutts, David. *I Can Read About Thunder and Lightning.* Troll, 1979 (new ed.). *(P; I)*

TIDES

Bowden, Joan. *Why the Tides Ebb and Flow.* Houghton, 1979. *(P)*
Stephens, William. *Life in the Tidepool.* McGraw, 1975. *(P; I)*

TIGERS. See LIONS AND TIGERS.

TIME

Baumann, Hans. *What Time Is It Around the World?* Scroll, 1979. *(P; I)*
Branley, Franklyn. *Keeping Time.* Houghton, 1993. *(I)*
Burns, Marilyn. *This Book Is About Time.* Little, 1978. *(I; A)*
Grey, Judith. *What Time Is It?* Troll, 1981. *(P)*
Humphrey, Henry, and Humphrey, Deirdre. *When Is Now: Experiments with Time and Timekeeping Devices.* Doubleday, 1981. *(I)*
Livoni, Cathy. *Elements of Time.* Harcourt, 1983. *(I; A)*
Llewellyn, Claire. *My First Book of Time.* Dorling Kindersley, 1992. *(P)*
Simon, Seymour. *The Secret Clocks: Time Senses of Living Things.* Penguin, 1981. *(I; A)*
Ziner, Feenie, and Thompson, Elizabeth. *Time.* Childrens, 1982. *(P)*

TOGO

Winslow, Zachery. *Togo.* Chelsea House, 1987. *(P; I)*

TOLKIEN, J. R. R.

Collins, David R. *J.R.R. Tolkien: Master of Fantasy.* Lerner, 1991. *(I; A)*
Helms, Randel. *Tolkien's World.* Houghton, 1975. *(I; A)*

TONGA. See PACIFIC OCEAN AND ISLANDS.

TOOLS

Gibbons, Gail. *The Tool Book.* Holiday, 1982. *(P)*
Robbins, Ken. *Tools.* Scholastic, 1983. *(P)*
Rockwell, Anne. *The Toolbox.* Macmillan, 1971. *(P)*

TOPOLOGY

Froman, Robert. *Rubber Bands, Baseballs, and Doughnuts: A Book About Topology.* Harper, 1972. *(P)*

TORNADOES

Alth, Max, and Alth, Charlotte. *Disastrous Hurricanes and Tornadoes.* Watts, 1981. *(P; I)*
Fradin, Dennis Brindel. *Disaster! Tornadoes.* Childrens, 1982. *(I)*
Ruckman, Ivy. *Night of the Twisters.* Crowell, 1984. *(P)*

TORONTO. See CANADA.

TOYS

Churchill, E. Richard. *Fast & Funny Paper Toys You Can Make.* Sterling, 1990. *(P; I; A)*
Gogniat, Maurice. *Indian and Wild West Toys You Can Make.* Sterling, 1980. *(P; I; A)*
Lerner, Mark. *Careers in Toy Making.* Lerner, 1980. *(P; I)*
Loeper, John J. *The Shop on High Street: Toys and Games of Early America.* Atheneum, 1978. *(P; I)*
Olney, Ross. *The Amazing Yo-Yo.* Lothrop, 1980; *Tricky Discs: Frisbee Saucer Flying,* 1979. *(P; I; A)*
Sibbett, Ed, Jr. *Easy-to-Make Articulated Wooden Toys: Patterns and Instructions for 18 Playthings That Move.* Dover, 1983. *(P; I; A)*

TRACK AND FIELD

Aaseng, Nathan. *Track's Magnificent Milers.* Lerner, 1981. *(P; I; A)*
Lyttle, Richard B. *Jogging and Running.* Watts, 1979. *(I; A)*
McMane, Fred. *Track and Field Basics.* Prentice-Hall, 1983. *(P; I)*
Owens, Jesse, and O'Connor, Dick. *Track and Field.* Atheneum, 1976. *(I; A)*
Ryan, Frank. *Jumping for Joy: The High Jump, the Pole Vault, the Long Jump, and the Triple Jump.* Scribner's, 1980. *(P; I)*
Sullivan, George. *Better Cross-country Running for Boys and Girls,* 1983; *Better Field Events for Girls,* 1982; *Better Track for Boys,* 1985; *Better Track for Girls,* 1981; *Marathon: The Longest Race,* 1980; *Run, Run Fast,* 1980; *Track and Field: Secrets of the Champions,* 1980. Dodd. *(I; A)*

TRADEMARKS

Arnold, Oren. *What's In a Name: Famous Brand Names.* Messner, 1979. *(I; A)*

TRANSPORTATION

Arnold, Caroline. *How Do We Travel?* Watts, 1983. *(P)*
Graham, Ian. *Transportation.* Watts, 1989. *(P; I)*
Hamer, Mick. *Transport.* Watts, 1982. *(I)*
Kalman, Bobbie. *Early Travel.* Crabtree, 1981. *(I)*
Scarry, Huck. *On Wheels.* Philomel, 1980. *(P)*
Taylor, Ron. *50 Facts About Speed and Power.* Watts, 1983. *(I)*
See also AUTOMOBILES; AVIATION; RAILROADS; ROADS AND HIGHWAYS; SHIPS AND SHIPPING; TRUCKS AND TRUCKING.

TREES

Arnold, Caroline. *The Biggest Living Thing.* Carolrhoda, 1983. *(P; I)*
Arnosky, Jim. *Crinkleroot's Guide to Knowing the Trees.* Bradbury, 1992. *(P)*
Boulton, Carolyn. *Trees.* Watts, 1984. *(P; I)*
Brandt, Keith. *Discovering Trees.* Troll, 1981. *(P)*
Burnie, David. *Tree.* Knopf, 1988. *(P; I)*
Dickinson, Jane. *All About Trees.* Troll, 1983. *(P; I)*
Mabley, Richard. *Oak and Company.* Greenwillow, 1983. *(P)*
Podendorf, Illa. *Trees.* Childrens, 1982. *(P)*
Selsam, Millicent E. *Tree Flowers.* Morrow, 1984. *(P; I)*
Udry, Janice May. *A Tree Is Nice.* Harper, 1956. *(P)*
Wiggers, Ray. *Picture Guide to Tree Leaves.* Watts, 1991. *(I)*
See also FORESTS AND FORESTRY.

TRICKS AND PUZZLES

Anderson, Doug. *Picture Puzzles for Armchair Detectives.* Sterling, 1983. *(I; A)*
Barry, Sheila Anne. *Super-Colossal Book of Puzzles, Tricks, and Games.* Sterling, 1978. *(I)*
Churchill, Richard. *I Bet I Can—I Bet You Can't.* Sterling, 1982. *(P; I)*

TRINIDAD AND TOBAGO. See CARIBBEAN SEA AND ISLANDS.

TROPICS. See JUNGLES.

TRUCKS AND TRUCKING

Abrams, Kathleen S., and Abrams, Lawrence F. *The Big Rigs: Trucks, Truckers, and Trucking.* Messner, 1981. *(P; I)*
Bushey, Jerry. *Monster Trucks and Other Giant Machines on Wheels.* Carolrhoda, 1985. *(P)*
Gibbons, Gail. *Trucks.* Harper, 1981. *(P)*
Haddad, Helen R. *Truck and Loader.* Greenwillow, 1982. *(P)*
Herman, Gail. *Make Way for Trucks: Big Machines on Wheels.* Random, 1990. *(P)*
Horenstein, Henry. *Sam Goes Trucking.* Houghton, 1989. (Fiction) *(P)*

Lerner, Mark. *Careers in Trucking.* Lerner, 1979. *(P; I)*
Lines, Cliff. *Looking at Trucks.* Watts, 1984. *(P; I)*
Radlauer, Ed. *Some Basics About Minitrucks.* Childrens, 1982; *Some Basics About Vans,* 1978; *Trucks,* 1980. *(P; I)*
Rockwell, Anne F. *Trucks.* Dutton, 1984. *(P)*
Siebert, Diane. *Truck Song.* Crowell, 1984. *(P)*
Wolverton, Ruth, and Wolverton, Mike. *Trucks and Trucking.* Watts, 1983. *(I; A)*

TRUMAN, HARRY S.

Greenberg, Morrie. *The Buck Stops Here: A Biography of Harry Truman.* Dillon, 1989. *(I)*
Hargrove, Jim. *Harry S. Truman: Thirty-third President of the United States.* Childrens, 1987. *(P; I)*
Leavell, J. Perry, Jr. *Harry S. Truman.* Chelsea House, 1987. *(A)*
Melton, David. *Harry S Truman: The Man Who Walked with Giants.* Independence Press, MO, 1980. *(I; A)*
See also PRESIDENCY OF THE UNITED STATES.

TRUST FUND. See ECONOMICS.

TUBMAN, HARRIET

Bentley, Judith. *Harriet Tubman.* Watts, 1990. *(A)*
Epstein, Sam, and Epstein, Beryl. *Harriet Tubman: Guide to Freedom.* Garrard, 1968. *(P; I)*
Humphreville, Frances. *Harriet Tubman: Flame of Freedom.* Houghton, 1967. *(I)*
McClard, Megan. *Harriet Tubman: Slavery and the Underground Railroad.* Silver Burdett, 1991. *(I; A)*
Petry, Ann. *Harriet Tubman: Conductor on the Underground Railroad.* Archway, 1971. *(I; A)*
Taylor, M. W. *Harriet Tubman.* Chelsea House, 1990. *(I)*

TUNISIA. See AFRICA.

TUNNELS

Dunn, Andrew. *Tunnels.* Thomson Learning, 1993. *(I)*
Epstein, Sam, and Epstein, Beryl. *Tunnels.* Little, 1985. *(I)*
Gibbons, Gail. *Tunnels.* Holiday, 1984. *(P)*
Rickard, Graham. *Tunnels.* Bookwright, 1988. *(P)*
Sauvain, Philip. *Tunnels.* Garrett Educational, 1990. *(P; I)*

TURKEY. See MIDDLE EAST.

TURKEYS

Lavine, Sigmund A., and Scuro, Vincent. *Wonders of Turkeys.* Dodd, 1984. *(I)*
Patent, Dorothy Hinshaw. *Wild Turkey, Tame Turkey.* Clarion, 1989. *(I)*

TURKS AND CAICOS ISLANDS. See CARIBBEAN SEA AND ISLANDS.

TURTLES AND TORTOISES

Jahn, Johannes. *A Step-by-Step Book About Turtles.* TFH Publications, 1988. *(I; A)*

Riedman, Sarah R., and Witham, Ross. *Turtles: Extinction or Survival?* Harper, 1974. *(I; A)*

TUVALU. See PACIFIC OCEAN AND ISLANDS.

TWAIN, MARK

Frevert, Patricia D. *Mark Twain, an American Voice.* Creative Education, 1981. *(I; A)*

Meltzer, Milton. *Mark Twain: A Writer's Life.* Watts, 1985. *(I; A)*

Quackenbush, Robert. *Mark Twain? What Kind of Name Is That?* Prentice-Hall, 1984. *(P; I)*

Twain, Mark. *Life on the Mississippi.* Oxford University Press, 1962. *(I; A); Mark Twain's Best.* Scholastic, 1969. *(I; A)*

TYLER, JOHN

Lillegard, Dee. *John Tyler.* Childrens, 1988. *(P; I)*

See also PRESIDENCY OF THE UNITED STATES.

TYPE. See BOOKS.

UGANDA

Creed, Alexander. *Uganda.* Chelsea House, 1987. *(P; I)*

UKRAINE. See UNION OF SOVIET SOCIALIST REPUBLICS.

UNDERWATER EXPLORATION. See OCEANS AND OCEANOGRAPHY.

UNIDENTIFIED FLYING OBJECTS

Asimov, Isaac. *Unidentified Flying Objects.* Gareth Stevens, 1989. *(P; I)*

Berger, Melvin. *UFOs, ETs and Visitors From Space.* Putnam, 1988. *(I)*

Darling, David. *Could You Ever Meet an Alien?* Dillon, 1990. *(I)*

Rasmussen, Richard Michael. *The UFO Challenge.* Lucent Books, 1990. *(I; A)*

UNION OF SOVIET SOCIALIST REPUBLICS

Andrews, William G. *The Land and People of the Soviet Union.* Harper, 1991. *(I; A)*

Bernards, Neal, ed. *The Soviet Union.* Greenhaven Press, 1987. *(A)*

Campling, Elizabeth. *The Russian Revolution.* David & Charles, 1985. *(I; A); How and Why: The Russian Revolution.* Batsford, 1987. *(A); The USSR Since 1945.* Batsford, 1990. *(I; A)*

Dolphin, Laurie. *Georgia to Georgia: Making Friends in the U.S.S.R.* Tambourine, 1991. *(P; I)*

Fannon, Cecilia. *Soviet Union.* Rourke, 1990. *(I)*

Hogrotgian, Nonny. *The Contest: An Armenian Folktale.* Greenwillow, 1976. *(P)*

Jackson, W. A. Douglas. *Soviet Union.* Gateway Press, 1988. *(I; A)*

Keeler, Stephen. *Soviet Union.* (Passport to) Watts, 1988. *(P; I)*

Oparenko, Christina. *The Ukraine.* Chelsea House, 1988. *(P; I)*

Resnick, Abraham. *Russia: A History to 1917.* Childrens, 1983. *(I)*

Riordan, James. *Soviet Union: The Land and Its People.* Silver Burdett, 1987. *(P; I)*

Ross, Stewart. *The Russian Revolution.* Bookwright, 1989. *(I; A)*

Smith, Samantha. *Journey to the Soviet Union.* Little, 1985. *(I)*

UNITED KINGDOM

Lye, Keith. *Take a Trip to Wales.* Watts, 1986. *(P)*

Mitsumasa, Anno. *Anno's Britain.* Philomel, 1986. *(I)*

Sutherland, Dorothy B. *Wales.* (Enchantment of the World) Children's, 1987. *(P; I)*

Warner, Marina. *The Crack in the Teacup: Britain in the Twentieth Century.* Houghton, 1979. *(I; A)*

See also ENGLAND; ENGLAND, HISTORY OF; IRELAND; SCOTLAND.

UNITED NATIONS

Carroll, Raymond. *The Future of the United Nations.* Watts, 1985. *(I; A)*

Parker, Nancy Winslow. *The United Nations from A to Z.* Dodd, 1985. *(I)*

Ross, Stewart. *The United Nations.* Watts, 1990. *(I; A)*

Stein, Conrad. *The Story of the United Nations.* Childrens, 1986. *(I)*

Woods, Harold, and Woods, Geraldine. *The United Nations.* Watts, 1985. *(I)*

UNITED STATES

Berger, Gilda. *The Southeast States.* Watts, 1984. *(I)*

Brandt, Sue R. *Facts About the Fifty States.* Watts, 1979 (rev. ed.). *(I)*

Costabel, Eva. *A New England Village.* Atheneum, 1983. *(I); The Pennsylvania Dutch.* Atheneum, 1986. *(I)*

Gilfond, Henry. *The Northeast States.* Watts, 1984. *(I)*

Jacobson, Daniel. *The North Central States.* Watts, 1984. *(I)*

Lawson, Don. *The Pacific States.* Watts, 1984. *(I)*

Mitsumasa, Anno. *Anno's U.S.A.* Philomel, 1983. *(I)*

Pizer, Vernon. *Ink, Art, and All That: How American Places Got Their Names.* Putnam, 1976. *(I)*

Ronan, Margaret. *All About Our Fifty States.* Random, 1978 (rev. ed.). *(I; A)*

St. George, Judith. *The Mount Rushmore Story.* Putnam, 1985. *(I)*

Taylor, L. B., and Taylor, C. *The Rocky Mountain States.* Watts, 1984. *(I)*

Woods, Harold, and Woods, Geraldine. *The South Central States*. Watts, 1984. *(I)*

See also Mississippi River; National Park System; North America; and names of individual states.

UNITED STATES (Art, Literature, and Music)

Famous American Artists. Denison, n.d. *(I; A)*

Famous American Fiction Writers. Denison, n. d. *(I; A)*

Famous American Musicians. Denison, n.d. *(I; A)*

Foley, Mary M. *The American House*. Harper, 1981. *(I; A)*

Glubock, Shirley. *The Art of America in the Early Twentieth Century*. Macmillan, 1974; *The Art of Colonial America*, 1970; *The Art of the New American Nation*, 1972. *(P; I; A)*

Guthrie, Woody. "Riding in My Car." Folkways Music Publisher, 1969. *(P)*; "This Land Is Your Land." Ludlow Music, 1956. *(I)*

Hancock, Carla. *Seven Founders of American Literature*. John F. Blair, 1976. *(I; A)*

Henderson, Nancy. *Celebrate America: A Baker's Dozen of Plays*. Messner, 1978. *(I)*

Kraske, Robert. *America the Beautiful: Stories of Patriotic Songs*. Garrard, 1972. *(P; I)*

Plotz, Helen, ed. *The Gift Outright: America to Her Poets*. Greenwillow, 1977. *(I; A)*

Thum, Marcella. *Exploring Literary America*. Atheneum, 1979. *(I; A)*

UNITED STATES (History and Government)

Bartz, Carl F. *The Department of State*. Chelsea House, 1988. *(A)*

Bender, David L. *The Arms Race: Opposing Viewpoints*. Greenhaven Press, 1982. *(I; A)*

Bender, David L., ed. *American Government*. Greenhaven Press, 1987. *(A)*

Commager, Henry S. *The Great Constitution*. Bobbs, 1961. *(I; A)*

Coy, Harold. *Congress*, rev. by Barbara L. Dammann. Watts, 1981. *(I; A)*

Ellis, Rafaela. *The Central Intelligence Agency*. Chelsea House, 1987. *(A)*

Faber, Doris, and Faber, Harold. *The Birth of a Nation: The Early Years of the United States*. Scribner's, 1989. *(I; A)*

Fisher, Leonard Everett. *The White House*. Holiday, 1990. *(P; I)*

Fritz, Jean. *Shh! We're Writing the Constitution*. Putnam, 1987. *(I)*

Goode, Stephen. *The New Federalism: States' Rights in American History*. Watts, 1983. *(A)*

Hoopes, Roy. *What a United States Senator Does*. Harper, 1975. *(P; I; A)*

Levy, Elizabeth. *If You Were There When They Signed the Constitution*. Scholastic, 1987. *(I)*

Lindrop, Edmund. *Birth of the Constitution*. Enslow, 1986. *(I)*

Lomask, Milton. *The Spirit of 1787: The Making of Our Constitution*. Farrar, 1980. *(P; I; A)*

Maestro, Betsy. *A More Perfect Union: The Story of Our Constitution*. Lothrop, 1987. *(P; I)*

McGrath, Edward, and Krauss, Bob, eds. *A Child's History of America*. Little, 1976. *(P; I)*

Paine, Thomas. *Common Sense*. Penguin, 1982. *(I; A)*

Parker, Nancy Winslow. *The President's Cabinet and How It Grew*. Harper, 1991. *(P; I)*

Ragsdale, Bruce A. *The House of Representatives*. Chelsea House, 1988. *(A)*

Ritchie, Donald A. *The U.S. Constitution*. Chelsea House, 1988. *(A)*

Sgroi, Peter. *This Constitution*. Watts, 1986. *(I)*

Short, Max H., and Felton, Elizabeth N. *The United States Book: Facts and Legends About the Fifty States*. Lerner, 1975. *(P; I; A)*

Spier, Peter. *We The People: The Constitution of the United States of America*. Doubleday, 1987. *(P)*

Tunis, Edwin. *The Young United States, 1785 to 1830*. Crowell, 1976. *(I)*

See also Civil War, United States; Revolutionary War; Thirteen American Colonies; Westward Movement and Pioneer Life; World War I; World War II.

UNITED STATES, ARMED FORCES OF THE

Bradley, Jeff. *A Young Person's Guide to Military Service*. Kampmann, 1987. *(A)*

Cohen, Andrew and Heinsohn, Beth. *The Department of Defense*. Chelsea House, 1990. *(I; A)*

Colby, C. B. *Two Centuries of Sea Power*. Putnam, 1976. *(P; I)*

Ferrell, Nancy Warren. *The U.S. Air Force*. Lerner, 1990. *(I)*; *The U.S. Coast Guard*. Lerner, 1989. *(I; A)*

Fisch, Arnold G., Jr. *The Department of the Army*. Chelsea House, 1987. *(A)*

Halliburton, Warren. *The Fighting Redtails: America's First Black Airmen*. Silver Burdett, 1978. *(I; A)*

Martin, Nancy. *Search and Rescue: The Story of the Coast Guard Service*. David & Charles, 1975. *(P; I)*

Moran, Tom. *The U.S. Army*. Lerner, 1990. *(I)*

Pelta, Kathy. *The U.S. Navy*. Lerner, 1990. *(I)*

Petersen, Gwenn B. *Careers in the United States Merchant Marine*. Lodestar, 1983. *(I; A)*

Rummel, Jack. *The U.S. Marine Corps*. Chelsea House, 1990. *(I; A)*

Stefoff, Rebecca. *The U.S. Coast Guard*. Chelsea House, 1989. *(I; A)*

Warner, J. F. *The U.S. Marine Corps*. Lerner, 1991. *(I)*

UNIVERSE

Asimov, Isaac. *How Did We Find Out About the Universe?* Walker, 1982. *(I)*

Gallant, Roy. *101 Questions and Answers About the Universe*. Macmillan, 1984. *(I)*; *Our Universe*. National Geographic, 1986. *(I; A)*

Hirst, Robin, and Hirst, Sally. *My Place in Space*. Orchard Books, 1988. *(P)*

Lampton, Christopher. *New Theories on the Birth of the Universe*. Watts, 1989. *(I)*

See also ASTRONOMY.

UNIVERSITIES AND COLLEGES

The *Yale Daily News* Staff, eds. *The Insider's Guide to the Colleges, 1992*. St. Martin's, 18th ed., 1986. *(A)*

Buckalew, M. W., and Hall, L. M. *Coping with Choosing a College*. Rosen, 1990. *(A)*

UPPER VOLTA. See AFRICA.

URANUS

Asimov, Isaac. *Uranus: The Sideways Planet*. Gareth Stevens, 1988. *(P; I)*

Branley, Franklyn M. *Uranus: The Seventh Planet*. Crowell, 1988. *(I; A)*

Simon, Seymour. *Uranus*. Morrow, 1987. *(P)*

URBAN PLANNING. See CITIES.

URUGUAY

Uruguay in Pictures. Lerner, 1987. *(I; A)*

UTAH

Carpenter, Allan. *Utah*. Childrens, 1979. *(I)*

Fradin, Dennis. *Utah: In Words and Pictures*. Childrens, 1980. *(P; I)*

VACCINATION AND IMMUNIZATION. See DISEASES.

VALENTINES

Barth, Edna. *Hearts, Cupids, and Red Roses: The Story of the Valentine Symbols*. Houghton, 1982. *(P; I)*

Brown, Fern G. *Valentine's Day*. Watts, 1983. *(I; A)*

Cohen, Miriam. *Be My Valentine*. Greenwillow, 1978. (Fiction) *(P)*

Fradin, Dennis Brindell. *Valentine's Day*. Enslow, 1990. *(P)*

Graham-Barber, Lynda. *Mushy!: The Complete Book of Valentine Words*. Bradbury, 1990. *(I)*

Prelutsky, Jack. *It's Valentine's Day*. Greenwillow, 1983. *(P)*

Sandak, Cass R. *Valentine's Day*. Watts, 1980. *(P)*

Supraner, Robyn. *Valentine's Day: Things to Make and Do*. Troll, 1981. *(P; I)*

VAN BUREN, MARTIN

Ellis, Rafaela. *Martin Van Buren*. Garrett Educational, 1989. *(I)*

Hargrove, Jim. *Martin Van Buren*. Childrens, 1988. *(P; I)*

See also PRESIDENCY OF THE UNITED STATES.

VANCOUVER. See CANADA.

VAN GOGH, VINCENT

Lucas, Eileen. *Vincent Van Gogh*. Watts, 1991. *(I)*

Venezia, Mike. *Van Gogh*. Childrens, 1988. *(P; I)*

VANUATU. See PACIFIC OCEAN AND ISLANDS.

VEGETABLES

Back, Christine. *Bean and Plant*. Silver Burdett, 1986. *(P)*

Blanchet, Francoise, and Doornekamp, Rinke. *What to Do with . . . Vegetables*. Barron, 1981. *(P; I)*

Brown, Elizabeth B. *Vegetables: An Illustrated History with Recipes*. Prentice Hall, 1981. *(I; A)*

Johnson, Sylvia. *Potatoes*. Lerner, 1984. *(I)*

Sobol, Harriet L. *A Book of Vegetables*. Dodd, 1984. *(P)*

VENEZUELA

Venezuela in Pictures. Lerner, 1987. *(I; A)*

Morrison, Marion. *Venezuela*. Childrens, 1989. *(I)*

VENICE. See ITALY.

VENTRILOQUISM

Bergen, Edgar. *How to Become a Ventriloquist*. Presto Books, 1983. *(P; I; A)*

Hutton, Darryl. *Ventriloquism: How to Put on an Act, Use the Power of Suggestion, Write a Clever Accompanying Patter, and Make Your Own Dummy*. Sterling, 1982. *(I; A)*

Ritchard, Dan, and Moloney, Kathleen. *Ventriloquism for the Total Dummy*. Villard, 1988. *(A)*

VENUS

Schloss, Muriel. *Venus*. Watts, 1991. *(P; I)*

Simon, Seymour. *Venus*. Morrow, 1992. *(P; I)*

VERMONT

Carpenter, Allan. *Vermont*. Childrens, 1979. *(I)*

Cheney, Cora. *Vermont: The State with the Storybook Past*. New England Press, 1981. *(P; I)*

Fradin, Dennis. *Vermont: In Words and Pictures*. Childrens, 1980. *(P; I)*

VERNE, JULES. See SCIENCE FICTION.

VETERINARIANS

Bellville, Rod, and Bellville, Cheryl W. *Large Animal Veterinarians*. Carolrhoda, 1983. *(P)*

Carris, Joan Davenport. *Pets, Vets, and Marty Howard*. Lippincott, 1984. *(I)*

Gibbons, Gail. *Say Woof! The Day of a Country Veterinarian*. Macmillan, 1992. *(P)*

Riser, Wayne H. *Your Future in Veterinary Medicine.* Rosen, 1982. *(I; A)*

Sobol, Harriet Langsam. *Pet Doctor.* Putnam, 1988. *(I)*

VICE PRESIDENCY OF THE UNITED STATES

Alotta, Robert I. *Number Two: A Look at the Vice Presidency.* Messner, 1981. *(I; A)*

Feerick, John D., and Feerick, Amalie P. *Vice-Presidents.* Watts, 1981 (updated ed.). *(I)*

Hoopes, Roy. *The Changing Vice-Presidency.* Harper, 1981. *(I; A)*

VICTORIA, QUEEN. See ENGLAND, HISTORY OF.

VIDEO RECORDING

Andersen, Yvonne. *Make Your Own Animated Movies and Videotapes.* Little, 1991. *(I; A)*

Cooper, Carolyn E. *VCRs.* Watts, 1987. *(P)*

Irvine, Mat. *TV & Video.* Watts, 1984. *(I)*

Meigs, James B., and Stern, Jennifer. *Make Your Own Music Video.* Watts, 1986. *(I; A)*

Schwartz, Perry. *How to Make Your Own Video.* Lerner, 1991. *(I; A)*

Shachtman, Tom and Harriet. *Video Power: A Complete Guide to Writing, Planning, and Shooting Videos.* Holt, 1988. *(I; A)*

Yurko, John. *Video Basics.* Prentice Hall, 1983. *(P; I)*

VIENNA. See AUSTRIA.

VIETNAM. See SOUTHEAST ASIA.

VIETNAM WAR

Bender, David L., ed. *The Vietnam War.* Greenhaven Press, 1984. *(A)*

Bunting, Eve. *The Wall.* Clarion, 1990. *(I; A)*

Dolan, Edward F. *America After Vietnam: Legacies of a Hated War.* Watts, 1989. *(I; A)*

Fincher, E. B. *The Vietnam War.* Watts, 1980. *(I; A)*

Hauptly, Denis J. *In Vietnam.* Atheneum, 1985. *(A)*

Hoobler, Dorothy, and Hoobler, Thomas. *Vietnam: Why We Fought.* Knopf, 1990. *(I; A)*

Kidd, Diana. *Onion Tears.* Orchard Books, 1991. *(Fiction) (P; I)*

Lawson, Don. *The War in Vietnam.* Watts, 1981. *(I); An Album of the Vietnam War,* 1986. *(A)*

Myers, Walter Dean. *Fallen Angels.* Scholastic, 1990. *(Fiction) (I; A)*

Nelson, Theresa. *And One for All.* Dell, 1989. *(Fiction) (I; A)*

Palmer, Laura. *Shrapnel in the Heart—Letters and Remembrances from the Vietnam Memorial.* Random, 1987. *(I; A)*

Paterson, Katherine. *Park's Quest.* Lodestar, 1988. *(Fiction) (I; A)*

Warren, James A. *Portrait of a Tragedy: America and the Vietnam War.* Lothrop, 1990. *(A)*

VIKINGS

Atkinson, Ian. *The Viking Ships.* Lerner, 1980. *(I; A)*

Benchley, Nathaniel. *Snorri and the Strangers.* Harper, 1976. *(P)*

Clare, John D., ed. *The Vikings.* Gulliver, 1992. *(I; A)*

Ferguson, Sheila. *Growing Up in Viking Times.* David & Charles, 1981. *(I)*

Glubok, Shirley. *The Art of the Vikings.* Macmillan, 1978. *(P; I; A)*

Hughes, Jill. *Vikings.* Watts, 1984 (rev. ed.). *(P; I; A)*

Janeway, Elizabeth. *The Vikings.* Random, 1981. *(I; A)*

Jones, Terry. *The Saga of Erik the Viking.* Schocken, 1983. *(P; I)*

Martell, Hazel. *The Vikings.* Warwick Press, 1986. *(I)*

Pluckrose, Henry, ed. *Small World of Vikings.* Watts, 1982. *(P)*

VIOLIN. See MUSICAL INSTRUMENTS.

VIRGINIA

Campbell, Elizabeth A. *The Carving on the Tree.* Little, 1968. *(P)*

McNair, Sylvia. *Virginia.* Childrens, 1989. *(P; I)*

Sirvaitis, Karen. *Virginia.* Lerner, 1991. *(I)*

VIRUSES

Knight, David C. *Viruses: Life's Smallest Enemies.* Morrow, 1981. *(I)*

Nourse, Alan E. *Viruses.* Watts, 1983 (rev. ed.). *(I; A)*

VOCATIONS

Berman, Steve, and Weiss, Vivian. *What to Be.* Prentice-Hall, 1981. *(I)*

Blumenthal, Howard J. *Careers in Television.* Little, 1992. *(I; A)*

Claypool, Jane. *How to Get a Good Job.* Watts, 1982. *(I; A)*

Clayton, Lawrence. *Careers in Psychology.* Rosen, 1992. *(I; A)*

Collins, Robert F. *America at Its Best: Opportunities in the National Guard.* Rosen, 1989. *(A)*

DeGalan, Julie, and Lambert, Stephen. *Great Jobs for Foreign Language Majors.* VGM Career Horizons, 1994. *(A)*

Epstein, Lawrence. *Careers in Computer Sales.* Rosen, 1990. *(A)*

Epstein, Rachel. *Careers in Health Care.* Chelsea House, 1989. *(A)*

Girl Scouts of the U.S.A. *Careers to Explore for Brownie and Junior Girl Scouts.* Girl Scouts, 1979. *(I; A)*

Haddock, Patricia. *Careers in Banking and Finance.* Rosen, 1989. *(A)*

Hirsh, Marilyn. *Ben Goes into Business*. Holiday, 1973. (Fiction) *(P)*

Johnson, Neil. *All in a Day's Work: Twelve Americans Talk About Their Jobs*. Little, 1989. *(I)*

Johnston, Tony. *Odd Jobs*. Putnam, 1982. *(P)*

Lobb, Charlotte. *Exploring Apprenticeship Careers*. Rosen, 1982; *Exploring Vocational School Careers*, 1982 (2nd rev. ed.). *(I; A)*

Marshall, James. *Fox on the Job*. Dial, 1988. (Fiction) *(P)*

Pitz, Mary Elizabeth. *Careers in Government*. VGM Career Horizons, 1994. *(A)*

Schulz, Marjorie Rittenberg. *Hospitality and Recreation*. Watts, 1990. *(I; A); Transportation*. Watts, 1990. *(I; A); Travel and Tourism*. Watts, 1990. *(I; A)*

Sipiera, Paul. *I Can Be an Oceanographer*. Childrens, 1989. *(P)*

Vitkus-Weeks, Jessica. *Television*. Crestwood, 1994. *(I)*
See also names of specific fields.

VOLCANOES

Asimov, Isaac. *How Did We Find Out About Volcanoes?* Walker, 1981. *(P; I)*

Aylesworth, Thomas G., and Aylesworth, Virginia L. *The Mount St. Helens Disaster: What We've Learned*. Watts, 1983. *(I; A)*

Branley, Franklyn M. *Volcanoes*. Crowell, 1985. *(P)*

Carson, James. *Volcanoes*. Watts, 1984. *(I)*

Fradin, Dennis. *Disaster! Volcanoes*. Childrens, 1982. *(I)*

Lauber, Patricia. *Volcano: The Eruption and Healing of Mount St. Helens*. Bradbury, 1986. *(I)*

Marcus, Elizabeth. *All About Mountains and Volcanoes*. Troll, 1984. *(P; I)*

Simon, Seymour. *Volcanoes*. Morrow, 1988. *(P; I)*

Taylor, G. Jeffrey. *Volcanoes in Our Solar System*. Dodd, 1983. *(I; A)*

Tilling, Robert I. *Born of Fire: Volcanoes and Igneous Rocks*. Enslow, 1991. *(I; A)*

VOLLEYBALL

Sullivan, George. *Better Volleyball for Girls*. Lerner, 1980. *(P; I)*

Thomas, Art. *Volleyball Is for Me*. Lerner, 1980. *(P; I)*

WALES. See UNITED KINGDOM.

WALESA, LECH

Craig, Mary. *Lech Walesa*. Gareth Stevens, 1990. *(I; A)*

WALRUSES

Brady, Irene. *Elephants on the Beach*. Scribner's, 1979. *(P; I)*

Darling, Kathy. *Walrus*. Lothrop, 1991. *(P; I)*

Patent, Dorothy Hinshaw. *Seals, Sea Lions and Walruses*. Holiday, 1990. *(P; I)*

Scott, Jack Denton. *The Fur Seals of Pribilof*. Putnam, 1983. *(I; A)*

Sherrow, Victoria. *Seals, Sea Lions & Walruses*. Watts, 1991. *(P)*

WAR OF 1812

Richards, Norman. *The Story of Old Ironsides*. Childrens, 1967. *(P; I)*

WASHINGTON

Carpenter, Allan. *Washington*. Childrens, 1979. *(I)*

Field, Nancy, and Machlis, Sally. *Discovering Mount Rainier*. Dog-Eared Publications, 1980. *(P; I)*

Fradin, Dennis. *Washington: In Words and Pictures*. Childrens, 1980. *(P; I)*

Olson, Joan, and Olson, Gene. *Washington Times and Trails*. Windyridge Press, 1983. *(I; A)*

WASHINGTON, BOOKER T.

Poole, Susan. *Booker T. Washington*. Dandelion, n.d. *(P)*

Washington, Booker T. *Up from Slavery*. Airmont, n.d. *(I; A)*

WASHINGTON, D.C.

Aikman, Lonnelle. *We, the People: The Story of the United States Capital, Its Past and Its Promise*. U.S. Capital Historical Society, 1978. *(I)*

Kent, Deborah. *Washington, D.C.* Childrens, 1990. *(I)*

Krementz, Jill. *A Visit to Washington, D.C.* Scholastic, 1987. *(P)*

Munro, Roxie. *The Inside-Outside Book of Washington, D.C.* Dutton, 1987. *(P)*

Sandak, Cass R. *The White House*. Watts, 1981. *(I)*

WASHINGTON, GEORGE

Adler, David A. *A Picture Book of George Washington*. Holiday, 1989. *(P); George Washington, Father of Our Country: A First Biography*. Holiday, 1988. *(P)*

D'Aulaire, Ingri, and D'Aulaire, Edgar P. *George Washington*. Doubleday, n.d. *(P)*

Falkof, Lucille. *George Washington: 1st President of the United States*. Garrett Educational, 1989. *(I)*

Foster, Genevieve. *George Washington's World*. Scribner's, 1977. *(A)*

Fritz, Jean. *George Washington's Breakfast*. Putnam, 1969. *(I)* (Fiction)

Giblin, James Cross. *George Washington: A Picture Book Biography*. Scholastic, 1992. *(P)*

Kent, Zachary. *George Washington: First President of the United States*. (Encyclopedia of Presidents) Childrens, 1986. *(P; I)*

Meltzer, Milton. *George Washington and the Birth of Our Nation*. Watts, 1986. *(I; A)*

Santrey, Laurence. *George Washington: Young Leader*. Troll, 1982. *(P; I)*

Seigal, Beatrice. *George and Martha Washington Home in New York*. Four Winds, 1989. *(I)*
See also PRESIDENCY OF THE UNITED STATES.

WATCHES AND CLOCKS

Breiter, Herta S. *Time and Clocks*. Raintree, 1978. *(P)*
Jespersen, James, and Fitz-Randolph, Jane. *Time and Clocks for the Space Age*. Atheneum, 1979. *(I; A)*
Perry, Susan. *How Did We Get Clocks and Calendars?* Creative Education, 1981. *(P)*
Trivett, Daphne, and Trivett, John. *Time for Clocks*. Harper, 1979. *(P; I)*

WATER

Ardley, Neil. *The Science Book of Water*. Gulliver Books, 1991. *(P; I)*; *Working with Water*. Watts, 1983. *(P)*
Bain, Iain. *Water on the Land*. Watts, 1984. *(I)*
Branley, Franklyn M. *Water for the World*. Harper, 1982. *(I)*
Dickinson, Jane. *Wonders of Water*. Troll, 1983. *(P; I)*
Dorros, Arthus. *Follow the Water From Brook to Ocean*. HarperCollins, 1991. *(P)*
Gardner, Robert. *Water, the Life Sustaining Resource*. Messner, 1982. *(A)*
Ginsburg, Mirra. *Across the Stream*. Morrow, 1982. *(P)*
Goldin, Augusta. *The Shape of Water*. Doubleday, 1979. *(P)*; *Water—Too Much, Too Little, Too Polluted?* Harcourt, 1983. *(I; A)*
Hoff, Mary, and Rodgers, Mary M. *Groundwater*. Lerner, 1991. *(I)*
Leutscher, Alfred. *Water*. Dutton, 1983. *(P)*
Pringle, Laurence. *Water: The Next Great Resource Battle*. Macmillan, 1982. *(I; A)*
Roy, Ronald. *A Thousand Pails of Water*. Knopf, 1978. (Fiction) *(P)*
Sexias, Judith. *Water—What It Is, What It Does*. Greenwillow, 1987. *(P)*
Smeltzer, Patricia, and Smeltzer, Victor. *Thank You for a Drink of Water*. Winston, 1983. *(P; I)*
Taylor, Barbara. *Sink or Swim? The Science of Water*. Random, 1991. *(I)*
Walker, Sally M. *Water Up, Water Down: The Hydrologic Cycle*. Carolrhoda, 1992. *(I)*

WATER POLLUTION. See POLLUTION.

WATERSKIING

Radlauer, Ed. *Some Basics About Water Skiing*. Childrens, 1980. *(I)*

WEATHER

Adler, David. *The World of Weather*. Troll, 1983. *(P; I)*
Baker, Thomas Richard. *Weather in the Lab*. TAB Books, 1993. *(I)*
Bramwell, Martyn. *Weather*. Watts, 1988. *(I)*
Cosgrove, Brian. *Weather*. Knopf, 1991. *(I)*

DeBruin, Jerry. *Young Scientists Explore the Weather*. Good Apple, 1983. *(P; I)*
Dickinson, Terence. *Exploring the Sky by Day: The Equinox Guide to Weather and the Atmosphere*. Camden House, 1988. *(P; I)*
Gibbons, Gail. *Weather Forecasting*. Four Winds, 1987. *(P)*; *Weather Words and What They Mean*. Holiday, 1990. *(P)*
Kahl, Jonathan D. *Weatherwise: Learning About the Weather*. Lerner, 1992. *(I)*; *Wet Weather: Rain Showers and Snowfall*. Lerner, 1992. *(I)*
Lambert, David. *Weather*. Watts, 1983. *(P)*
Lye, Keith. *Weather and Climate*. Silver Burdett, 1984. *(P)*
Mandell, Muriel. *Simple Weather Experiments with Everyday Materials*. Sterling, 1990. *(I)*
Mason, John. *Weather and Climate*. Silver Burdett, 1991. *(I)*
McMillan, Bruce. *The Weather Sky*. Farrar, 1991. *(I)*
Peters, Lisa. *The Sun, the Wind, and the Rain*. Holt, 1988. *(P)*
Purvis, George, and Purvis, Anne. *Weather and Climate*. Watts, 1984. *(I; A)*
Simon, Seymour. *Weather*. Morrow, 1993. *(I)*
Tannenbaum, Beulah, and Tannenbaum, Harold. *Making and Using Your Own Weather Station*. Watts, 1989. *(I)*
Yvart, Jacques, and Forgeot, Claire. *The Rising of the Wind: Adventures Along the Beaufort Scale*. Green Tiger, 1986. *(I)*
See also CLIMATE.

WEAVING

Alexander, Marthann. *Simple Weaving*. Taplinger, n.d. *(P; I)*
Hobden, Eileen. *Fun with Weaving*. Sportshelf, n.d. *(I)*
Rubenstone, Jessie. *Weaving for Beginners*. Lippincott, 1975. *(I)*

WEEDS

Collins, Pat L. *Tumble, Tumble, Tumbleweed*. Albert Whitman, 1981. *(P)*
Kirkpatrick, Rena K. *Look at Seeds and Weeds*. Raintree, 1978. *(P)*
Podendorf, Illa. *Weeds and Wild Flowers*. Childrens, 1981. *(P)*
Selsam, Millicent E., and Wexler, Jerome. *The Amazing Dandelion*. Morrow, 1977. *(P; I)*

WEIGHT LIFTING

Smith, Tim. *Junior Weight Training and Strength Training*. Sterling, 1985. *(I; A)*

WEIGHTS AND MEASURES

Ardley, Neil. *Making Metric Measurements*. Watts, 1984. *(I)*

Arnold, Caroline. *Measurements: Fun, Facts, and Figures*. Watts, 1984. *(P)*

Bendick, Jeanne. *How Much & How Many? The Story of Weights and Measures*. Watts, 1989. *(P; I)*

WESLEY, JOHN. See RELIGIONS OF THE WORLD.

WEST INDIES. See CARIBBEAN SEA AND ISLANDS.

WEST VIRGINIA

Carpenter, Allan. *West Virginia*. Childrens, 1979. *(I)*

Fradin, Dennis. *West Virginia: In Words and Pictures*. Childrens, 1980. *(P; I)*

WESTWARD MOVEMENT AND PIONEER LIFE

Aliki. *The Story of Johnny Appleseed*. Prentice Hall, 1963. *(P)*

Anderson, Joan. *Pioneer Children of Appalachia*. Clarion, 1986. *(I)*

Bercuson, David, and Palmer, Howard. *Pioneer Life in the West*. Watts, 1984. *(I; A)* (Canadian West)

Brenner, Barbara. *Wagon Wheels*. Harper, 1978. (Fiction) *(P; I)*

Brink, Carol Ryrie. *Caddie Woodlawn*. Macmillan, 1973 (1935). (Fiction) *(P; I)*

Cather, Willa. *O, Pioneers!* Houghton, 1941. (Fiction) *(A)*

Collins, James L. *Exploring the American West*. Watts, 1989. *(P; I)*

Dalgliesh, Alice. *The Courage of Sarah Noble*. Scribner's, 1954. *(P; I)*

Flatley, Dennis R. *The Railroads: Opening the West*. Watts, 1989. *(P; I)*

Fradin, Dennis B. *Pioneers*. Childrens, 1984. *(P)*

Freedman, Russell. *Children of the Wild West*. Houghton, 1983. *(I)*

Fritz, Jean. *Make Way for Sam Houston*. Putnam, 1986. *(P; I)*

Gipson, Fred. *Old Yeller*. Harper, 1956. (Fiction) *(I; A)*

Guthrie, Alfred B., Jr. *The Big Sky: The Way West*. Bantam, 1972. *(I; A)*

Harvey, Brett. *Cassie's Journey: Going West in the 1860's*. Holiday, 1987. (Fiction) *(P); My Prairie Year*. Holiday, 1986. (Fiction) *(P)*

Hilton, Suzanne. *Getting There: Frontier Travel Without Power*. Westminster, 1980. *(I; A)*

Holbrook, Stewart. *Wyatt Earp: U.S. Marshall*. Random, 1956. *(P; I)*

Holling, Holling C. *Tree in the Trail*. Houghton, 1978 (1942). *(P; I)*

Jassem, Kate. *Sacajawea, Wilderness Guide*. Troll, 1979. *(P; I)*

Johnston, Tony. *The Quilt Story*. Putnam, 1985. *(P)*

Lasky, Kathryn. *Beyond the Divide*. Macmillan, 1983. (Fiction) *(I; A)*

Laycock, George. *How the Settlers Lived*. McKay, 1980. *(I; A)*

Lenski, Lois. *Prairie School*. Lippincott, 1951. (Fiction) *(I)*

Lyons, Grant. *Mustangs, Six-Shooters, and Barbed Wire: How the West Was Really Won*. Messner, 1981. *(P; I)*

MacLachlan, Patricia. *Sarah, Plain and Tall*. Harper, 1985. (Fiction) *(I)*

McCall, Edith. *Cumberland Gap and Trails West; Hunters Blaze the Trails; Pioneering on the Plains; Wagons over the Mountains*. Childrens, 1980. *(P; I; A)*

Morrow, Honore. *On to Oregon!* Morrow, 1946. (Fiction) *(I)*

Parkman, Francis. *The Oregon Trail*. New American Library, 1950. *(I)*

Poole, Frederick King. *Early Exploration of North America*. Watts, 1989. *(P; I)*

Sanders, Scott Russell. *Aurora Means Dawn*. Bradbury, 1989. (Fiction) *(P)*

Sandin, Joan. *The Long Way Westward*. Harper, 1988. (Fiction) *(P)*

Schlissel, Lillian, et al. *Far from Home: Families of the Westward Journey*. Schocken, 1989. *(I)*

Scott, Lynn H. *The Covered Wagon and Other Adventures*. University of Nebraska Press, 1987. *(I; A)*

Stein, R. Conrad. *The Story of the Homestead Act*. Childrens, 1978. *(P; I)*

Wilder, Laura Ingalls. *Farmer Boy*. Harper, 1953. (Fiction) *(I); Little House in the Big Woods*. Harper, 1953. (Fiction) *(P; I); Little House on the Prairie*. Harper, 1975. (Fiction) *(P; I)*

WETLANDS

Amsel, Sheri. *A Wetland Walk*. Millbrook, 1993. *(P; I)*

Matthews, Downs. *Wetlands*. Simon & Schuster, 1994. *(P)*

Rood, Ronald. *Wetlands*. HarperCollins, 1994. *(P)*

WHALES AND WHALING

Whales. Facts on File, 1990. *(I)*

Carrick, Carol. *Whaling Days*. Clarion, 1993. *(P; I)*

Gardner, Robert. *The Whale Watchers' Guide*. Messner, 1984. *(P; I)*

Gibbons, Gail. *Whales*. Holiday, 1991. *(P)*

Kraus, Scott, and Mallory, Kenneth. *The Search for the Right Whale: How Scientists Rediscovered the Most Endangered Whale in the Sea*. Crown, 1993. *(I)*

Lauber, Patricia. *Great Whales: The Gentle Giants*. Holt, 1991. *(P; I)*

Mallory, Kenneth, and Conley, Andrea. *Rescue of the Stranded Whales*. Simon & Schuster, 1989. *(I)*

Patent, Dorothy Hinshaw. *Killer Whales*. Holiday, 1993. *(P); Whales: Giants of the Deep*. Holiday, 1984. *(P; I)*

Sattler, Roney Helen. *Whales, the Nomads of the Sea*. Lothrop, 1987. *(P; I)*

Selsam, Millicent E., and Hunt, Joyce. *A First Look at Whales*. Walker, 1980. *(P)*

Siegel, Robert. *Whalesong.* Harper, 1991. (Fiction) *(I; A)*; *White Whale.* Harper, 1991. (Fiction) *(I; A)*

Simon, Seymour. *Whales.* Crowell, 1989. *(P; I)*

Stein, R. C. *The Story of the New England Whalers.* Childrens, 1982. *(P; I)*

Torgersen, Don. *Killer Whales and Dolphin Play.* Childrens, 1982. *(P; I)*

Weller, Frances Ward. *I Wonder If I'll See a Whale.* Philomel, 1991. (Fiction) *(P)*

WHEAT. See Grain and Grain Products.

WHEELS

Barton, Byron. *Wheels.* Harper, 1979. *(P)*

Scarry, Huck. *On Wheels.* Putnam, 1980. *(P)*

Tunis, Edwin. *Wheels: A Pictorial History.* Harper, 1977. *(I)*

WILLIAMS, ROGER

Eaton, Jeanette. *Lone Journey: The Life of Roger Williams.* Harcourt, 1966. *(A)*

WILLIAM THE CONQUEROR. See England, History of.

WILSON, WOODROW

Collins, David R. *Woodrow Wilson: 28th President of the United States.* Garrett Educational, 1989. *(I)*

Jacobs, David. *An American Conscience: Woodrow Wilson's Search for World Peace.* Harper, n.d. *(I; A)*

Osinski, Alice. *Woodrow Wilson.* Childrens, 1989. *(P; I)*

See also Presidency of the United States.

WIND INSTRUMENTS. See Musical Instruments.

WINNIPEG. See Canada.

WISCONSIN

Stein, R. Conrad. *Wisconsin.* Childrens, 1988. *(P; I)*

Wilder, Laura Ingalls. *Little House in the Big Woods.* Harper, 1953. (Fiction) *(I)*

WITCHCRAFT

Jack, Adrienne. *Witches and Witchcraft.* Watts, 1981. *(P; I)*

Jackson, Shirley. *The Witchcraft of Salem Village.* Random, 1956. *(I)*

Petry, Ann. *Tituba of Salem Village.* Harper, 1964. *(I)*

Rinaldi, Ann. *A Break with Charity.* HarBraceJ, 1992. (Fiction) *(I; A)*

Zeinert, Karen. *The Salem Witchcraft Trials.* Watts, 1989. *(I; A)*

WOLVES

George, Jean Craighead. *The Moon of the Gray Wolves.* Harper, 1991. *(I)*

Gibbons, Gail. *Wolves.* Holiday, 1994. *(P)*

Hansen, Rosanna. *Wolves and Coyotes.* Putnam, 1981. *(P; I)*

Johnson, Sylvia A., and Aamodt, Alice. *Wolf Pack: Tracking Wolves in the Wild.* Lerner, 1985. *(I)*

Lawrence, R. D. *Wolves.* Sierra Club Books, 1989. *(P; I)*

Milton, Joyce. *Wild, Wild Wolves.* Random, 1992. *(P)*

Murphy, Jim. *The Call of the Wolves.* Scholastic, 1989. *(P; I)*

Patent, Dorothy H. *Gray Wolf, Red Wolf.* Clarion, 1990. *(I)*

Pringle, Laurence. *Wolfman: Exploring the World of Wolves.* Scribner's, 1983. *(I; A)*

WOMEN'S RIGHTS MOVEMENT

Archer, Jules. *Breaking Barriers: The Feminist Movement from Susan B. Anthony to Margaret Sanger to Betty Friedan.* Viking, 1991. *(A)*

Berger, Gilda. *Women, Work and Wages.* Watts, 1986. *(A)*

Blumberg, Rhoda. *Bloomers!* Bradbury, 1993. (Fiction) *(P; I)*

Briggs, Carole S. *At the Controls: Women in Aviation.* Lerner, 1991. *(I)*

Conta, Marcia Maher. *Women for Human Rights.* Raintree, 1979. *(I)*

Felton, Harold. *Deborah Sampson, Soldier of the Revolution.* Dodd, 1976. *(I)*

Fisher, Maxine P. *Women in the Third World.* Watts, 1989. *(I; A)*

Gutman, Bill. *Women Who Work with Animals.* Dodd, 1982. *(I)*

Haber, Louis. *Women Pioneers of Science.* Harcourt, 1979 (rev. ed.). *(I; A)*

Hodgman, Ann, and Djabbaroff, Ruby. *Skystars: The History of Women in Aviation.* Atheneum, 1981. *(I)*

Ingraham, Gloria D. and Leonard W. *An Album of American Women: Their Changing Role.* Watts, 1987. *(P; I)*

Kibbe, Pat. *My Mother the Mayor, Maybe.* Random, 1981. (Fiction) *(P)*

Levinson, Nancy S. *The First Women Who Spoke Out.* Dillon, 1983. *(I; A)*

McGovern, Ann. *The Secret Soldier: The Story of Deborah Sampson.* Four Winds, 1975. *(I)*

McPherson, Stephanie Sammartino. *I Speak for the Women: A Story About Lucy Stone.* Carolrhoda, 1992. *(I)*

Peavy, Linda, and Smith, Ursula. *Women Who Changed Things.* Scribner's, 1983. *(I; A)*

Rappaport, Doreen, ed. *American Women: Their Lives in Their Words.* Crowell, 1990. *(I; A)*

Saxby, Maurice, and Ingpen, Robert. *The Great Deeds of Heroic Women.* Peter Bedrick, 1990. *(I)*

Scheader, Catherine. *Contributions of Women: Music.* Dillon, 1985. *(I; A)*

Stein, R. Conrad. *The Story of the Nineteenth Amendment*. Childrens, 1982. *(P; I)*

Wekesser, Carol, and Polesetsky, Matthew, eds. *Women in the Military*. Greenhaven, 1991. *(I; A)*

Whitney, Sharon. *The Equal Rights Amendment: The History of the Movement*. Watts, 1984. *(I; A); Women in Politics*, 1986. *(A)*

WOOD, GRANT

Goldstein, Ernest. *Grant Wood: American Gothic*. New American Library, 1984. *(I; A)*

WOOD AND WOOD PRODUCTS. See LUMBER AND LUMBERING.

WOOD CRAFTS

Boy Scouts of America. *Wood Carving*. Boy Scouts, 1966; 1970. *(I; A)*

Brown, William F. *Wood Works: Experiments with Common Wood and Tools*. Atheneum, 1984. *(I)*

WOOL

Mitgutsch, Ali. *From Sheep to Scarf*. Carolrhoda, 1981. *(P)*

WORLD WAR I

Farmer, Penelope. *Charlotte Sometimes*. Dell, 1987 (1969). (Fiction). *(P; I)*

Hoobler, Dorothy, and Hoobler, Thomas. *An Album of World War I*. Watts, 1976. *(I; A)*

Peyton, K. M. *Flambards*. Puffin, 1989. (Fiction) *(I; A)*

Pimlott, John. *The First World War*. Watts, 1986. *(I)*

Ross, Stewart. *The Origins of World War I*. Bookwright, 1989. *(I; A)*

Rostkowski, Margaret I. *After the Dancing Days*. Harper, 1986. (Fiction) *(I; A)*

Stewart, Gail B. *World War I*. Lucent, 1991 *(I; A)*

Wright, Nicolas. *The Red Baron*. McGraw, 1977. *(I)*

WORLD WAR II

Bliven, Bruce. *From Casablanca to Berlin: The War in North Africa and Europe, 1942–1945*. 1965; *From Pearl Harbor to Okinawa: The War in the Pacific, 1941–45*. 1960; *The Story of D-Day*. Random, 1956. *(I; A)*

Bunting, Eve. *Terrible Things: An Allegory of the Holocaust*. Jewish Publication Society, 1990. *(P; I)*

Carter, Hodding. *The Commandos of World War II*. Random, 1981. *(I; A)*

Coerr, Eleanor B. *Sadako and the Thousand Paper Cranes*. Putnam, 1977. (Fiction) *(P; I)*

Dank, Milton. *D-Day*. Watts, 1984. *(I; A)*

Davis, Daniel S. *Behind Barbed Wire: The Imprisonment of Japanese Americans During World War II*. Dutton, 1982. *(I; A)*

Dunnahoo, Terry. *Pearl Harbor: America Enters the War*. Watts, 1991. *(I; A)*

Fink, Ida. *A Scrap of Time and Other Stories*. Schocken, 1987. (Fiction) *(I; A)*

Foreman, Michael. *War Boy: A Country Childhood*. Arcade, 1990. *(I)*

Frank, Anne. *Anne Frank: The Diary of a Young Girl*. Doubleday, 1967 (rev. ed.). *(I); The Diary of Anne Frank*. Random, 1956. *(I)*

Gordon, Sheila. *3rd September 1939*. Batsford, 1988. *(I; A)*

Greene, Bette. *The Summer of My German Soldier*. Dial, 1973. (Fiction) *(I; A)*

Hautzig, Esther. *The Endless Steppe*. Harper, 1968. *(I; A)*

Hest, Amy. *The Ring and the Window Seat*. Scholastic, 1990. (Fiction) *(P)*

Jones, Madeline. *Find Out About Life in the Second World War*. David & Charles, 1983. *(I; A)*

Lawson, Ted. *Thirty Seconds over Tokyo*. Random, 1981. *(I)*

Lowry, Lois. *Number the Stars*. Houghton, 1989. (Fiction) *(P; I)*

Markl, Julia. *The Battle of Britain*. Watts, 1984. *(I; A)*

Marrin, Albert. *The Airman's War: World War II in the Sky*. Atheneum, 1982; *Victory in the Pacific*, 1983. *(I; A)*

Maruki, Toshi. *Hiroshima No Pika*. Lothrop, 1982. *(I; A)*

McGowen, Tom. *Midway and Guadalcanal*. Watts, 1984. *(I; A)*

Messenger, Charles. *The Second World War*. (Conflict in the Twentieth Century) Watts, 1987. *(A)*

Miner, Jane C. *Hiroshima and Nagasaki*. Watts, 1984. *(I; A)*

Morimoto, Junko. *My Hiroshima*. Viking, 1990. *(I)*

Ray, Deborah Kogan. *My Daddy Was a Soldier: A World War II Story*. Holiday, 1990. (Fiction) *(I)*

Reiss, Johanna. *The Upstairs Room*. Crowell, 1972. *(I; A)*

Richardson, Nigel. *How and Why: The Third Reich*. Batsford, 1988. *(I; A)*

Saunders, Alan. *The Invasion of Poland*. Watts, 1984. *(I; A)*

Siegal, Aranka. *Upon the Head of a Goat*. New American Library, 1981. *(I; A)*

Snyder, Louis L. *World War II*. Watts, 1981 (rev. ed.). *(I; A)*

Sullivan, George. *The Day Pearl Harbor Was Bombed: A Photo History of World War II*. Scholastic, 1991. *(P; I); Strange But True Stories of World War II*. Walker, 1983. *(I; A)*

Sweeney, James. *Army Leaders of World War II*. Watts, 1984. *(I)*

Uchida, Yoshiko. *Journey to Topaz*. Scribner's, 1971. (Fiction) *(P; I)*

Westall, Robert. *Blitzcat*. Scholastic, 1989. (Fiction) *(I; A)*

Ziefert, Harriet. *A New Coat for Anna*. Knopf, 1986. (Fiction) *(P)*

WORMS

Hess, Lilo. *The Amazing Earthworm*. Scribner's, 1979. *(I)*

O'Hagan, Caroline, ed. *It's Easy to Have a Worm Visit You*. Lothrop, 1980. *(P)*

WRESTLING

Hellickson, Russ, and Baggott, Andrew. *An Instructional Guide to Amateur Wrestling*. Perigee Books, 1987. *(A)*

Lewin, Ted. *I Was a Teenage Professional Wrestler*. Orchard, 1993. *(I; A)*

Thomas, Art. *Wrestling Is for Me*. Lerner, 1979. *(P; I)*

WRIGHT, WILBUR AND ORVILLE

Freedman, Russell. *The Wright Brothers: How They Invented the Airplane*. Holiday, 1991. *(I)*

Reynolds, Quentin. *The Wright Brothers: Pioneers of American Aviation*. Random, 1981. *(I; A)*

Sabin, Louis. *Wilbur and Orville Wright: The Flight to Adventure*. Troll, 1983. *(I)*

Stein, R. Conrad. *The Story of the Flight at Kitty Hawk*. Childrens, 1981. *(I)*

WRITING (AUTHORSHIP)

Aldis, Dorothy. *Nothing Is Impossible: The Story of Beatrix Potter*. Atheneum, 1969. *(P; I)*

Camerobn, Eleanor. *A Room Made of Windows*. Little, 1971. *(I; A)*

Carpenter, Angelica S., and Shirley, Jean. *Frances Hodgson Burnett: Beyond the Secret Garden*. Lerner, 1990. *(I; A)*

Cleary, Beverly. *A Girl from Yamhill: A Memoir*. Morrow, 1988. *(I; A)*

Conford, Ellen. *Jenny Archer, Author*. Little, 1989. *(P; I)*

Dubrovin, Vivian. *Write Your Own Story*. Watts, 1984. *(I; A)*

Duncan, Lois. *Chapters: My Growth as a Writer*. Little, 1982. *(I)*

Fritz, Jean. *China Homecoming*. Putnam, 1985. *(P; I)*; *Homesick: My Own Story*. Putnam, 1982. *(P; I)*

Henderson, Kathy. *Market Guide for Young Writers*. Shoe Tree Press, 1988. *(I; A)*

James, Elizabeth, and Barkin, Carol. *How to Write Your Best Book Report; How to Write A Great School Report; How to Write a Term Paper*. Lothrop, 1988. *(I; A)*

Livingston, Myra Cohn. *Poem-Making: Ways to Begin Writing Poetry*. Harper, 1991. *(I)*

Peet, Bill. *Bill Peet: An Autobiography*. Houghton, 1989. *(P; I)*

Sears, Peter. *Gonna Bake Me a Rainbow Poem: A Student Guide to Writing Poetry*. Scholastic, 1990. *(I; A)*

Tchudi, Susan. *The Young Writer's Handbook*. Scribner's, 1984. *(I; A)*

Zemach, Margot. *Self-Portrait*. Addison-Wesley, 1978. *(P; I)*

Zindel, Paul. *The Pigman and Me*. Harper, 1992. *(A)*

WYOMING

Carpenter, Allan. *Wyoming*. Childrens, 1979. *(I)*

Fradin, Dennis. *Wyoming: In Words and Pictures*. Childrens, 1980. *(P; I)*

O'Hara, Mary. *Green Grass of Wyoming*. Harper, 1946; *My Friend Flicka*, 1973 (new ed.) *(I; A)*

Willems, Arnold, and Hendrickson, Gordon. *Living Wyoming's Past*. Pruett, 1983. *(P; I)*

YANGTZE RIVER. See CHINA.

YEMEN. See MIDDLE EAST.

YUGOSLAVIA

Kronenwetter, Michael. *The New Eastern Europe*. Watts, 1991. *(I; A)*

Popescu, Julian. *Yugoslavia*. Chelsea House, 1988. *(I; A)*

YUKON TERRITORY

Levert, Suzanne. *Yukon*. Chelsea House, 1992. *(I; A)*

ZÄIRE

Stefoff, Rebecca. *Republic of Zaire*. Chelsea House, 1987. *(A)*

ZAMBIA. See AFRICA.

ZEBRAS

Arnold, Caroline. *Zebra*. Morrow, 1987. *(P; I)*

ZIMBABWE

Barnes-Svarney, Patricia. *Zimbabwe*. Chelsea House, 1989. *(I)*

Cheney, Patricia. *The Land and People of Zimbabwe*. Lippincott, 1990. *(I; A)*

Lauré, Jason. *Zimbabwe*. Childrens, 1988. *(P; I)*

Stark, Al. *Zimbabwe: A Treasure of Africa*. Dillon, 1986. *(I)*

Zimbabwe . . . in Pictures. Lerner, 1988. *(A)*

ZOOS

Altman, Joyce, and Goldberg, Sue. *Dear Bronx Zoo*. Macmillan, 1990. *(I)*

Anderson, Madelyn Klein. *New Zoos*. Watts, 1987. *(P; I)*

Barton, Miles. *Zoos and Game Reserves*. Gloucester Press, 1988. *(P; I)*

Curtis, Patricia. *Animals and the New Zoos*. Lodestar, 1991. *(I)*

Jacobson, Karen. *Zoos*. Childrens, 1982. *(P)*

Moss, Miriam. *Zoos*. Watts, 1987. *(P)*

Rinard, Judith E. *Zoos Without Cages*. National Geographic, 1981. *(P; I)*

Thomson, Peggy. *Keepers and Creatures at the National Zoo*. Crowell, 1988. *(P; I)*

PART II
THE STUDY GUIDE

INTRODUCTION

THE NEW BOOK OF KNOWLEDGE is a valuable source of information. Whether you are searching for the answer to a question that made a conversation with a child memorable or investigating a topic for a young student's school assignment, this encyclopedia will help you find the information you need.

THE NEW BOOK OF KNOWLEDGE can be used in a variety of settings—home, school, and library. It is written in a clear, direct style and organized so that information can be located quickly and easily. Precise and colorful photographs, illustrations, maps, charts, and diagrams assist understanding and encourage further reading and browsing. Articles are written by experts in their fields and cover topics of general interest as well as every important area of the school curriculum. Among the many categories covered are literature, language arts, history, government, geography, mathematics, social, natural, and physical sciences, technology, health and safety, art, music, and sports and physical education.

The HOME AND SCHOOL STUDY GUIDE was prepared to help teachers, librarians, and especially parents make optimal use of THE NEW BOOK OF KNOWLEDGE. The first part of the STUDY GUIDE offers suggestions about how the home-school partnership can assist the education of children. This is followed by an overview of school curriculum areas. The STUDY GUIDE then discusses the school years in three separate sections: Kindergarten through Grade 3; Grades 4 through 6; and Grades 7 through 9. Each section briefly describes what children will be learning in the classroom at those grade levels and then lists some of the articles in the set that are important to each curriculum area at those grade levels. These lists of curriculum-related articles can be used in several ways with young people. For example:

- To identify and skim through articles about a topic before it is actually covered in the classroom. This can provide important background knowledge for youngsters that will help them understand and remember information about the topic presented in class. This activity can also make the topic more interesting.
- The lists can be used to locate articles in which answers to specific questions raised in the classroom or information needed for homework assignments, research projects, or writing reports can be found. As they seek out the information they need, students will also find in the set cross-references to additional articles that will help them complete their assignments.
- Some students want to know more about subjects of particular interest to them, and they will find their interests satisfied and their learning enhanced by reading the variety of articles listed about that subject.

Learning the habit of turning to reference books for information is invaluable, as is the close association of parents and children searching for knowledge together. One of the goals of THE NEW BOOK OF KNOWLEDGE is to help parents share in their children's learning and growing experiences.

Parents of elementary-school children will be particularly interested in the Home Activities in the STUDY GUIDE for the subject areas of Reading, Language, and Literature; Mathematics; Social Studies; and Science and Technology. These simple activities require no special materials or preparation and can be incorporated easily into a busy schedule. An estimation activity in mathematics, for example, asks the child to estimate how many puffs or flakes are in a bowl of cereal. These activities can be used to stimulate and encourage a child's interest and creativity or to help a child achieve a better understanding and increased skill in a difficult subject. There are activities for the four core subject areas in the Kindergarten and Grades 1 through 3 section and in the Grades 4 through 6 section. Each set of activities for a subject area immediately follows the curriculum discussion for it.

Other unique features to be found in THE NEW BOOK OF KNOWLEDGE include the Wonder Questions that cover a broad range of unusual topics young people always find interesting. There are also the many activities, projects, and experiments they can do on their own, along with a complete listing of the variety of literary selections found in the set. Lists of the articles in which all of these can be found are provided in the Appendix at the end of the STUDY GUIDE. The lists of literary selections in the set are also shown organized by grade level. These groupings are included in the lists of curriculum-related articles printed in the appropriate section of the STUDY GUIDE: K through 3; 4 through 6; 7 through 9.

Preschool children will also have enjoyable learning experiences with THE NEW BOOK OF KNOWLEDGE. They can wander through the set with its many illustrations and photographs of the people, places, and objects, past and present, that represent the wide range of knowledge they will acquire as they grow older. They will be delighted to listen to someone read them the nursery rhymes, poems, and stories in the set. When they ask those questions that defy immediate answers, they will observe how answers and explanations are found in its pages, and thereby learn a valuable lesson and skill.

Much of the appeal of THE NEW BOOK OF KNOWLEDGE springs from the articles about subjects that may not be covered in the typical school curriculum but which will broaden a young person's overall education. Just a few of the topics that are covered include those in the cultural arts, popular entertainment, food and cooking, games, clothing and fashions, and hobbies and crafts. The STUDY GUIDE lists some of these articles in the Hobbies and Leisure section of the Appendix.

Today's educators realize that, because the world's body of knowledge is constantly and quickly changing and expanding, one of their most important missions is to teach children how to become independent discoverers, researchers, and learners. The innate curiosity of children turns them into eager questioners. In the classroom, discussions often produce dozens of questions about events, people, and places. Knowing how to find the answers to their questions is not always easy for young people. Out of the mass of resources readily available—books and textbooks, newspapers and magazines, picture files, recordings, videos, films, and electronic data bases—we often direct students to begin their search for a first answer or basic understanding in an encyclopedia.

THE NEW BOOK OF KNOWLEDGE was planned to be an early, authoritative, and efficient resource for school-age children. Many of its editors and advisers have been educators or librarians or have worked in other important ways with young people. Its contributors are experts in their fields and are able to write for young audiences. You can direct students to THE NEW BOOK OF KNOWLEDGE confident that its articles are accurate, up-to-date, and set within the contexts needed to help readers understand and use the information in them. Sometimes an article will tell students as much as they want or need to know about a particular subject. Often the encyclopedia will be only a first resource, providing an overview of basic information and stimulating the student to seek out additional resources.

Educators today are often required to fit new topics such as global studies, environmental education, multicultural studies, and substance-abuse education into their regular programs. These and similar topics have been integrated into the STUDY GUIDE's lists of articles for traditional curriculum areas. Many educators are also concerned about helping children make connections across the curriculum. An encyclopedia is an invaluable tool for implementing such activities, and the lists of curriculum articles will be helpful in making such connections in the classroom or library, as well as in planning and helping students achieve classroom and homework assignments. As the HOME AND SCHOOL STUDY GUIDE is used with THE NEW BOOK OF KNOWLEDGE, you will discover numerous other ways in which the encyclopedia can be used to help young people become better learners.

ARTICLES OF PARTICULAR INTEREST TO PARENTS

▶ SCHOOLS, EDUCATION, AND THE FAMILY

As your children progress from infancy through childhood and adolescence into young adulthood, you will have many questions about their growth, development, and education. Questions like these:

- Is each of us born with a certain level of intelligence that will never change throughout our lives? What does an intelligence test score really mean?
- What important questions should I ask in choosing a good day-care facility?
- What can I do to help my children improve their learning abilities?
- Am I free to provide schooling for my children at home? Are there specific federal or state laws that regulate home schooling?
- Does my adolescent youngster really want me to say "No" to certain requests or demands?

THE NEW BOOK OF KNOWLEDGE contains dozens of informative articles about child development, the family, schools, curriculum subjects, and various other aspects of education that will help you find answers to these questions. You will find helpful information about these topics, for example, in the articles INTELLIGENCE, DAY CARE, LEARNING, EDUCATION, and ADOLESCENCE. If you are the parent of a preschool or school-age child, you will find the following list of a few of the key articles in the set that will be of special interest to you.

FAMILY AND CHILD DEVELOPMENT

Volume	Articles
A	Adolescence
	Adoption
B	Baby
C	Child Abuse
	Child Development
D	Divorce
E	Ethnic Groups
	Etiquette
F	Family
	Foster Care
G	Genealogy
I	Intelligence
J-K	Juvenile Crime
L	Learning
P	Psychology
Q-R	Reproduction
S	Speech Disorders

EDUCATION AND SCHOOLS

Volume	Articles
C	Children's Literature
D	Day Care
E	Education
G	Guidance Counseling
J-K	Kindergarten and Nursery Schools
L	Libraries
P	Parent-Teacher Associations
	Preparatory Schools
Q-R	Reference Books
	Research
S	Schools
	Storytelling
	Study, How to
T	Teachers and Teaching
	Tests and Test Taking
	Textbooks
	Toys
U-V	Universities and Colleges

CURRICULUM SUBJECTS

Volume	Articles
A	Arithmetic
	Art
G	Geography

An extended list of curriculum-related articles appears after each main section: Kindergarten and Grades 1 through 3, Grades 4 through 6, and Grades 7 through 9.

▶ **HOME, HEALTH, RECREATION, AND FINANCE**

Does someone among your family or friends have a health problem that you would like to know more about? Are you looking for help in decorating your home or balancing the family budget? Or are you, perhaps, searching for ideas about where to go for vacation?

THE NEW BOOK OF KNOWLEDGE contains a wealth of articles relating to the home, health, finance, recreation, and other nonacademic topics. The article INTERIOR DECORATING, for example, reveals the secret of good interior design—how to choose the style, balance and scale, color, light, pattern, and texture that will work well together in a room.

In the article FAMILY BUDGETS, you can learn how a simple six-step plan will help you get the most from your money.

The article DISEASES provides information about more than 60 specific diseases, ranging from acne and bulimia to heart disease and sickle-cell anemia.

THE NEW BOOK OF KNOWLEDGE is also a wonderful resource for vacation planning. There are articles filled with important and fascinating facts about each of the 50 states in the United States, every country in the world, from Afghanistan to Zimbabwe, and many of the world's major cities. There are also many special articles such as NATIONAL PARK SYSTEM, which provides listings of more than 300 of our nation's scenic, historical, and scientific treasures, including parks, monuments, historic sites, recreational areas, nature preserves, and military parks and battlefield sites.

The following is just a small representative selection of the various nonacademic topics included in THE NEW BOOK OF KNOWLEDGE. As you browse through the list, you will undoubtedly find many articles of special interest to you, and those articles will lead you to many more.

THE HOME

Volume	Articles
A	Air Conditioning
	Antiques and Antique Collecting
B	Bread and Baking
	Building Construction
C	Clothing
	Computers
	Cooking
D	Decorative Arts
	Detergents and Soap
	Dry Cleaning
E	Electric Lights
	Electronics
F	Fashion
	Food Around the World
	Food Preservation and Processing
	Food Regulations and Laws
	Food Shopping
	Food Spoilage and Contamination
	Furniture
G	Gardens and Gardening
H	Heating Systems
	Homes
	Household Pests
	Houseplants

An extensive list of the articles about Hobbies and Leisure-Time Activities appears in the Appendix of this STUDY GUIDE.

THE HOME-SCHOOL PARTNERSHIP

From the moment of birth, a child begins to learn. Parents or other primary care givers are not only a child's first teachers, they may be the most important teachers a child will ever have. Children learn much in their first few years of life, and once they begin school, their home life strongly affects their school performance. A recent study found that parents make a significant difference in a child's school achievement.

Most adults feel that it is harder to be a parent today, and they consider it particularly difficult to find sufficient time to spend with their children. Nevertheless, parents want the best for their youngsters. They are concerned about preparing them for their school years, and they want to share in their day-to-day school experiences by providing support in the home for schoolwork.

▶ **THE HOME ENVIRONMENT**

When teachers across the nation were asked in a recent survey about what would help improve American education, their overwhelming response was that they could do their best job educating children who were sent to school in good physical condition and with positive mental attitudes toward learning.

Children need adequate food, clothing, and shelter to be physically fit to learn. It is equally important for children to develop a sense of self-worth. Children who feel good about themselves are better able to learn. Their self-esteem comes from knowing that they are valued members of the family and that they have the loving support and understanding of family members. Allowing children freedom and independence within consistent limits; providing just enough supervision and guidance for their protection; and rewarding their efforts with praise and encouragement are all ways by which children learn that they are loved and respected for who they are.

Given this kind of atmosphere in which to grow, children also need a few key learning experiences. There are at least two things parents can do that will help children be successful in school—Reading to them, daily if possible, and talking with them as you share time together.

Educational studies have shown that children who are read to on a regular basis come to school ready to learn to read and that they experience fewer difficulties mastering the art of reading. Fortunately, children's books are readily available. Inexpensive books for young children can be purchased at bookstore sales and in supermarket and discount stores. They can be picked up for nickels and dimes at tag sales. Local public libraries contain shelves full of wonderful fiction and nonfiction books for children of all ages, free to anyone with a library card. School-age children are able to buy books at discounted prices at school book fairs, and teachers often encourage book sharing by providing time for youngsters to trade favorite books with their classmates. Children of any age love to be read to, and they should be encouraged to participate actively in the reading experience.

Talk with children about what they are reading. Ask them about what is taking place in the story and what they think will happen next. Have them find things in the illustrations that are named in the story. Encourage them to ask questions. Praise them when they "read" to you from a favorite book they have heard many, many times. Demonstrate to children that you enjoy reading, too. Let them see you enjoying a book, magazine, or newspaper in your leisure moments. A few minutes a day spent with children and a book can make a substantial difference to their success in school.

Talking with children is another essential learning experience. Telling stories, explaining the steps you use in preparing a meal or fixing a faucet, playing word games, posing riddles, and singing songs are just a few meaningful ways to communicate with youngsters. Encourage your children to talk to you. Show your interest in the questions they raise. Help them work out solutions to problems verbally. Take the time to listen when they are eager to share an experience or a feeling. By learning how to use language to communicate with others, children build a speaking and listening vocabulary that will form the foundation for learning to read and write.

In addition to reading to and talking with children, parents should try to provide, as much as they are able, a wide variety of experiences for their children. Taking them for walks around the neighborhood and stopping in at local businesses, parks, playgrounds, and libraries are free activities that offer fruitful opportunities for talking and learning. Trips to museums, zoos, athletic events, and concerts have obvious benefits in broadening children's interests and knowledge.

By participating actively in your children's learning experiences, you will learn their preferences, interests, strengths, and weaknesses. You will then be better prepared to provide the successful experiences at home that will give them the confidence they need to meet the challenges of school.

▶ **PARENT INVOLVEMENT IN SCHOOL**

Once children are in school, they find that their learning becomes more regimented. Parents and care givers often discover that schools today are very different from the schools they attended. They are not sure about what the school expects or what actually goes on in the classroom. Some parents come to believe that their children's education is now out of their hands and should be left to the professionals.

Research, however, documents that children do best in school when parents view themselves as being in charge of their children's education. Parental involvement has proven to be more important to children's success in school than family income or level of education. Most educators realize that well-informed parents can be strong supporters and allies in the work they do. They are reaching out more frequently to involve parents in the school and its activities.

Parents demonstrate that they think education is valuable when they continually share their children's school experiences. Getting to know your youngster's teachers is of primary importance. What do they expect of their students? Do children in their classrooms spend some of their time at their desks listening and completing teacher-directed activities? Are students expected to take responsibility for their own learning for part of the day, moving around the room, choosing from a variety of activities to work on individually or cooperatively with other children? Are students required to learn facts for tests as well as solve problems requiring critical thinking? Do their teachers evaluate the progress of students by keeping a portfolio of their work? Knowing what is required of your children will enable you to offer the most effective support.

Schools recognize the need for good home-school communication and most schools use parent-teacher conferences and written reports as a means of reporting on children's progress. Because of working hours and other responsibilities, parents or other care givers sometimes find it difficult to keep in touch with teachers or to attend school functions. When that is the case, it is important that some other key family member make the contact or attend the meeting. When you miss teacher conferences or school functions, you are sending your children the message that school matters may not be important enough to take some of your time and concern. When the effort is made to be in regular contact with teachers and administrators, you signal your children that school and schoolwork are important and serious business for both of you.

Increasingly, schools welcome parents' participation in other school activities. Many moms and dads, and grandparents, too, perform valuable services as classroom assistants and volunteer tutors or become active in parent-advisory or PTO groups.

▶ HOW IMPORTANT IS HOMEWORK?

At the end of the school day, children returning home from school are often asked, "Do you have any homework?" The typical response is: "Oh, we finished it in school."

When children return to the classroom the next day and are asked to hand in the homework assignment, they can invent amazing excuses for the missing work. How important is it? What can parents do to help children get over the homework hurdle?

Studies show that doing homework regularly and conscientiously helps raise student achievement. Teachers recognize the importance of homework in helping students become independent learners. Talk to teachers early in the school year to find out what, in general, the homework requirements will be for your children.

Work together with your children to set up ground rules that will promote good study habits. First, agree on a regular time and place for study, one that accommodates the needs of each child and the availability of a family helper, and be firm in sticking to it. Be ready to handle distractions—telephone calls, a turned-on TV set, interference from brothers and sisters. Help your children get started each day by making sure they understand what they are supposed to do for their assignments and that they have the materials they need. Do not do the homework for your children, but be ready to assist when they ask for help. Many parents, especially when younger children are involved, check completed assignments to make sure a child has not misunderstood the work. This can prevent embarrassment for youngsters and will enable you to alert the teacher to possible problems they may be having in learning the material. The articles LEARNING and STUDY, How To, in THE NEW BOOK OF KNOWLEDGE include other useful homework and study tips.

Homework can help your children become better students with good study habits and keep you informed about their work in classes.

OVERVIEW OF MAJOR CURRICULUM AREAS

▶ **WHO DECIDES WHAT CHILDREN WILL LEARN?**

There is no national curriculum for American schools. There is a body of knowledge, however, that is taught in most school systems in kindergarten through grade 12 across the entire United States. Most state departments of education develop curriculum guidelines that recommend and sometimes mandate how this knowledge should be organized and sequenced through the grades in their state. It is usually the local school district, however, that makes the final decisions about what children in their schools will learn. These decisions, to some extent, reflect the values, attitudes, concerns, and cultures of the community in which the school district is located. Although regional influences may result in differences in emphasis or in the choice of specific topics to be covered, the curriculum requirements for the major subject areas are essentially the same for almost every school district in America.

▶ **WHAT ARE CHILDREN EXPECTED TO LEARN?**

Reading, writing, and arithmetic have been the focus of education in America ever since the first public schools were established by law in Massachusetts in 1647. More time is still spent on reading, language arts, and mathematics in today's elementary, middle, and junior-high schools than on any other subjects. Four subject areas—the language arts, mathematics, science, and social studies—do make up the core curriculum for all students from kindergarten through the ninth grade. However, because most educators agree that it is essential to build a strong foundation for reading and mathematics literacy in the primary grades, other subjects are often given much less attention at the primary levels. Although children in the primary grades are exposed in various ways to science and social studies topics, in reality, these subjects do not generally become part of the regular curriculum until the fourth grade.

Depending on budget and time constraints, the core curriculum will be rounded out with art, music, physical education, and health. Most elementary schools in the United States do not provide the opportunity for children to learn a foreign language, and the percentage of middle school and junior high school students taking a foreign language is low. In addition, students in grades 6 through 9 generally take a semester or a year of a home economics or industrial arts or technology course. Computer technology is not usually offered as a separate subject until high school, but most youngsters are exposed to computers at various grades before they reach senior high school.

▶ **READING, LANGUAGE, AND LITERATURE—THE LANGUAGE ARTS**

Reading and writing are the keystones of the school learning experience. Everything else that children learn in school depends on their success in learning to read and write. Together with listening and speaking, they are the means by which one person communicates with another, and they are essential skills for living and working in our society.

Two quite different approaches to teaching these important skills predominate in today's elementary and middle schools. The one familiar to most parents is the traditional model in which grammar and usage, reading, writing, spelling, penmanship, and oral language are treated as separate subjects, each given its own time and emphasis in the school day. A number of schools use a newer method in which listening, speaking, and the various reading, writing, and grammar and usage skills are taught together as an integrated whole. This method, usually referred to as the whole language or integrated language arts method, tends to use literature as the unifying element around which language arts activities are woven.

In the traditional reading program, teachers use a series of graded textbooks as their instructional base. The readers contain relatively short selections that may be excerpts from classic children's literature or may be selections written specifically for the textbook. Vocabulary and sentence length and structure are tightly controlled to conform to the reading level of the book. In the primary grades, the reading process is broken down into a number of decoding or phonics skills and comprehension skills that children learn in a sequenced pattern. At the end of the third grade, it is expected that the student has acquired a sizable sight vocabulary, is also able to sound out or decode new words, and can use the various subskills of reading in an integrated way to construct meaning from the text. The student should be well on the way to becoming an independent reader.

In the whole language or integrated language arts classroom, the student is more likely to learn to read from an assortment of fiction and nonfiction books, student-authored books, and other reading materials than from a traditional reader. At times the teacher may select a title for the whole class or a group within the class to read together. At other times, students make their own choices about what they will read. Reading and grammar and usage subskills are not taught in isolation or in a set sequence. Their presentation is based on the contents and the styles of the books students are reading. Listening, speaking, and writing activities also tend to be assigned to stimulate and produce student responses to what is being read. Many whole language teachers plan their instruction around theme-based units focusing on topics that touch on many of the curriculum areas.

In the middle grades, it is assumed that students have learned the basics of reading and are now ready to read to learn. They are taught more complex comprehension skills such as inferential and critical-thinking skills, and they increase their reading vocabulary. They should be ready to read content-area textbooks and reference materials for information.

Reading is not usually taught as a separate subject in grades 7 through 9, except for those students who have exhibited reading difficulties. Middle and junior high school students are, however, given opportunities to develop and apply more sophisticated and complex reading abilities in literature courses. Some curriculum specialists recommend that at these grade levels, reading instruction be incorporated into every subject, especially English, social studies, science, and mathematics.

Regardless of the type of reading program employed, students are asked to do more writing in today's classroom than in earlier times, and to spend less time practicing formal rules of English grammar and usage. Beginning in the primary grades, youngsters generally learn to write using a technique called the writing process rather than by concentrating on the mechanics of writing. They learn that there are several stages in the writing process:

- Prewriting—gathering ideas, planning, and deciding on content, purpose, audience, and style
- Drafting—focusing on content and writing style rather than on the mechanics of grammar and usage
- Revising—making changes and improvements in content and style
- Editing—making corrections in spelling, capitalization and punctuation, grammar, and usage
- Publishing—producing, either by writing down or typing, a final draft of the finished work, and sharing it with an audience

Teachers sometimes ask youngsters to spend some time every day writing in a journal on any topic they choose and often to write a longer story, report, or essay. Attempts are also made to be sure students transfer what they learn about the writing process to their assignments in each of the other curriculum areas. A goal of every school's reading, language, and literature program is to make students effective communicators so that they can read, understand, and appreciate what others have written and be able to express their own ideas and feelings effectively in writing and speaking.

▶ **MATHEMATICS**

Mathematics is, more than ever before, a fundamental and basic curriculum area. As advances in different technologies cause our world to change, today's students will find it important to understand how to use mathematics to cope with these changes. The mathematics curriculum has recently undergone comprehensive analysis, reorganization, and modification to ensure that this instructional area reflects these changes as much as possible.

Mathematics is generally taught in a sequential and cumulative manner. Understanding certain math concepts is often necessary before one can understand higher-order, more abstract concepts. The scope of mathematics for grades K through 9 incorporates a number of strands, including:

- numbers and number patterns
- arithmetic operations involving addition, subtraction, multiplication, and division of whole numbers, fractions, and decimals
- measurement, using both standard and metric units
- geometry

- estimation and mental arithmetic
- statistics
- probability
- integers
- pre-algebra concepts and algebra

Today more emphasis than ever before is put on teaching mathematics in the context of problem solving and its applications to real-world situations. There is also less emphasis on isolated computational proficiency. Many educators believe that, while it is necessary to learn computational skills, the use of hand-held calculators should be accepted as a legitimate method of computation. Many middle school and junior high school students, therefore, are using calculators to do basic operations, allowing them more time to concentrate on the important aspects of problem solving and mathematical reasoning.

Today's mathematics classroom is not always a place where children sit at their desks quietly doing only pencil-and-paper activities. It is also frequently a place containing diverse materials that young learners can take in their hands, manipulate, and explore. Especially in the early grades, math is becoming a hands-on subject. Younger children are not yet capable of understanding abstract mathematical concepts; they learn best by playing and experimenting with concrete materials that may include pattern blocks, an abacus, Cuisenaire rods, geoboards, counting and sorting materials, and measuring tools. Computers are often available to children of all ages to help them develop data bases of statistics, create geometric displays, construct graphs, or simulate real-life situations.

Throughout the grades, students are sometimes given experiences in which problems are solved using a group approach. This process brings individuals together to work as a problem-solving team that develops strate-gies and achieves solutions. Students also learn in these situations that there is often more than one way to solve mathematical problems and that sometimes such problems may have more than one right answer.

The goal of mathematics instruction is to help students achieve sufficient success in mathematics to have confidence in their ability to use it both in school and in the everyday world.

▶ SOCIAL STUDIES

The social studies program is an area of the school curriculum that focuses on people. Students in every grade, K through 9, study the diverse ways in which people work together to form societies and interact with one another in different environments and situations. In addition to history, government, civics, and geography, the social studies curriculum draws on some of the social sciences—anthropology, economics, political science, psychology, and sociology. Until junior high school, however, topics from these subject areas are not studied in any depth as separate disciplines.

Key goals for the social studies curriculum include:

- preparing young people to be informed citizens capable of fulfilling their responsibilities in a democratic society
- developing an understanding of the United States and the diversity of its political and social institutions, traditions, and values
- helping students understand and appreciate the history, diversity, and interdependence of world cultures
- involving students in identifying and analyzing local, national, and global problems and developing strategies needed to respond to them.

The tremendous scope of the social studies curriculum has led to different views about how this important subject area should be taught. Some schools focus on traditional history and geography, sometimes teaching them as separate core subjects. Other schools believe that the world has become so complex and full of critical social issues that history and geography alone are not enough to provide a basis for preparing young people for their adult roles in society. In these schools, additional subjects are integrated into the social studies curriculum. State curriculum guidelines generally reflect one or the other of these views.

There is a basic or core social studies curriculum covered in most American classrooms, however. The typical framework is sometimes called the "expanding environments" or "widening horizons" organization. Children first learn about how people live together in families, neighborhoods, and communities, and in their own towns, cities, and states. At grades 5 through 9 the curriculum broadens to include separate courses on the history of the United States and on the regions and nations of the world.

Young people cannot understand the past or the present without acquiring skills that enable them to do much more than memorize names, dates, and places. Students must understand historical events and their relationship to current events and issues. In the social studies classroom students are often encouraged to go beyond their textbooks and to use a variety of print and nonprint materials as resources for information that will advance their ability to understand historical events.

To do this they are taught the research and reference skills they need to become successful gatherers of information. They are also taught how to be good critical thinkers who can analyze and evaluate information and make sound judgments about how to use it.

Students are asked to read biographies and primary sources such as letters, diaries, journals, memoirs, and eyewitness accounts about real people and events. They also read secondary sources ranging from encyclopedias and atlases to historical essays and novels, journals, magazines, and newspapers that provide information and offer a variety of interpretations and points of view. Maps and globes enable students to locate places and estimate distances around the world and learn about the different physical features of world regions and how such differences influence historical events. An appreciation and understanding of the world's diversity is gained also through their experiences with the literature, art, and music of different cultures. The use of films, videotapes, and field trips often takes students beyond the classroom to gain insights into places and events not attainable with print materials alone.

Social studies homework frequently includes doing the research needed to write reports and essays, to prepare for debates, to conduct interviews or surveys, or to work on other special projects.

THE NEW BOOK OF KNOWLEDGE can be especially helpful to the social studies curriculum. It provides accurate and objective information about the people, places, and events associated with important periods in history. It provides youngsters with an excellent first source of information for each area of this curriculum they will study.

▶ SCIENCE AND TECHNOLOGY

Most children have a lively curiosity. Almost as soon as they can speak, youngsters start asking questions. The school science curriculum is committed to nurturing children's curiosity about the natural world in which they live.

In the elementary grades the science curriculum is usually broken into small units of study, each devoted to a topic from one of the scientific disciplines of life, earth, and physical science. The life science units in the early grades focus on plants, animals, human biology, and ecology. Life science expands in the middle grades to include studies of the cell, genetics, and evolution. Topics in astronomy, geology, the oceans, and weather make up the earth science units. Physical science concentrates on matter, on energy in its variety of forms (heat, light, sound, electricity, and magnetism), on physical forces and motion, on work and machines, and on chemistry. The study of technology, the science concerned with the ways in which we adapt our natural world to meet our needs, is included as it relates to specific units of study in each area.

Most students in grades 7 through 9 take separate year-long courses in life science, physical science, and earth science, although in some schools ninth graders take either a general science or a biology course.

Throughout the grades, scientific knowledge is sometimes taught within the context of major concepts and themes that help students understand connections and relationships across the different branches of science and technology. These concepts and themes may include energy and matter, scale and structure, cause and effect, patterns of change, systems and interaction, models and theories, and others.

The primary aim of the K through 9 science curriculum is to ensure that students will achieve scientific literacy. Goals often cited as important for scientific literacy include:

- knowledge of the facts, concepts, principles, laws, and theories that are used to explain the natural world
- development of a scientific habit of mind, i.e., the ability to think scien-

tifically when answering questions, solving problems, and making decisions
- understanding the possibilities and the limitations of science and technology in explaining the natural world and in solving human problems
- understanding how science, technology, and society influence one another and having the ability to use this knowledge in everyday decision making

In addition to textbooks, many schools use an open-ended, hands-on approach to teach science that calls for the active participation of students in conducting scientific inquiries and becoming familiar with the scientific process. The classroom becomes a laboratory containing plants, small animals, and a selection of scientific equipment. Small groups of children working together use these materials to learn the steps in the scientific method through their own explorations and investigations and by thinking and acting like real scientists:

- posing a question or a problem
- developing a hypothesis or a likely explanation
- designing and conducting an experiment to test the hypothesis
- making observations
- collecting, analyzing, and organizing data
- drawing conclusions

When it is not feasible for children to carry out their own experiments, teachers often conduct demonstrations. Classroom science experiences are extended through field trips to nature centers, parks, zoos, and science museums. Some schools have their own nature trails on school grounds with interesting signs and labels to stimulate children's learning. Some states and school districts have also invested in interactive multimedia programs produced on CD-ROM and other electronic technologies to take the place of traditional textbooks.

The middle school and junior high school are transitions between the elementary program, in which concepts from each of the scientific disciplines are taught each year, and the separate subject-area departments of high school. The science teachers for grades 7 through 9 are also more likely to be science specialists or to have had training in science. At these grade levels there is instructional emphasis on laboratory and field activities.

The science highlight of the year in many schools is the annual science fair, at which individuals or teams of students plan, construct, and explain original science projects. To assist students, information and tips for preparing outstanding science fair projects can be found in the article EXPERIMENTS AND OTHER SCIENCE ACTIVITIES in THE NEW BOOK OF KNOWLEDGE.

Students of all ages are also encouraged by their teachers to apply their interests in science to activities outside of school. Many simple experiments can be done using materials readily available in the home. Children enjoy collecting things and are often asked to make leaf, insect, shell, seed, rock, or other types of natural science collections as homework assignments. The article EXPERIMENTS AND OTHER SCIENCE ACTIVITIES describes the scientific process and gives directions for simple experiments from each of the scientific disciplines that youngsters can do at home. The many different science articles and biographies in THE NEW BOOK OF KNOWLEDGE include many other science activities and projects that can be done in or out of school. It is an excellent resource for school reports and science projects as well as for continuing one's interest in an area of science outside the classroom.

As they conduct their scientific studies throughout their school years, young people discover that reading and learning about science can be a rich and enjoyable lifelong experience.

▶ HEALTH AND SAFETY

Children's health and safety is an important concern of the school. Every school gives evidence of this concern by offering numerous health services, including providing a school nurse on the premises, maintaining cumulative health records for each student, and conducting screening tests to identify health and learning problems. There are also school district policies on emergency care, communicable disease control, and the administration of medication. Above all, schools attempt to provide safe and sanitary facilities for all students.

Although school personnel demonstrate their concern about students' health and safety in all these ways, not all children receive systematic, sequential instruction in health and safety as part of the standard K through 9 curriculum. Health education is usually cited as part of the curriculum in every school district. In some elementary schools, however, it may only be covered in one period a week or incidentally within the science or physical education curriculum. Many middle school and junior high school students, however, usually receive a one-semester health course that may be taught by the school nurse or by the physical education, science, or home economics teacher.

A comprehensive, up-to-date health program motivates and promotes the development of good, lifelong health habits and teaches the skills and strategies necessary to avoid risky behaviors. It encompasses physical, mental, emotional, and social health. These are usually integrated into the study of ten major health topics:

- human body systems
- prevention and control of disease
- substance use and abuse (drugs, alcohol, and tobacco)
- nutrition
- mental and emotional health
- accident prevention, safety, and first aid
- family life
- physical fitness and personal care
- consumer health
- community health, environmental health, and health care resources

In some school districts, sex education is considered part of the health program. It usually covers issues involving sexual development, as well as interpersonal relationships and gender roles. It tries to educate students about how to make responsible choices. In other school systems, special classes or one- or two-week sex education courses are offered at the middle school or junior high school level with parental permission required.

Health educators generally agree that, given today's social problems, students also need to learn and acquire decision-making and refusal skills. In many classrooms, the consequences of risky behavior are presented through role-playing, open discussion, and modeling strategies. Activities included in decision-making models, for example, help students make intelligent judgments about the course of action to take when confronted with a risky question, problem, or situation. Other models demonstrate how to resist negative peer pressure without losing good friends.

Health education is important. Good health programs produce knowledgeable students who possess the skills and motivation to become responsible individuals within families and communities.

▶ MUSIC

Music is not one of the core subjects in the school curriculum, but it is a significant element in the lives of students. All young people seem to have a natural affinity for music. Younger children sing, hum, and dance spontaneously. They enthusiastically repeat the recorded music they hear on audio systems and on radio and television. As children approach adolescence, they spend more time listening to music, often while doing some other activity, than they do watching television or reading.

Although it may not get the attention devoted to core subjects, music is, nevertheless, an integral factor in turning out well-rounded students. At the elementary level, some instruction in music is typically required for all students. In many elementary schools a music program is taught by a music specialist, who meets with each class or grade once or twice a week. The specialist strives for a balance between general musical knowledge and performance skills. If music instruction is the responsibility of the classroom teacher, it often consists primarily of listening activities.

Children in a music program in the primary grades sing, listen to different types of music, engage in rhythmic exercises and dramatic play, and play simple rhythm instruments. They begin to learn some of the basic musical elements, including tempo, pitch, melody, and rhythm.

Students in a music program in the middle grades learn musical symbols and notation and how to read music. They apply their knowledge as they perform vocally or on a simple instrument, such as a recorder, and as they improvise or compose music. By listening to live or recorded musical performances, youngsters learn to recognize different instruments and to appreciate various musical forms, styles, and periods. The history of music and the biographies of great composers and performers are often coordinated with listening experiences. There may be exposure to classical and contemporary masterworks as well as to the folk music of different cultures. Popular musical forms such as jazz, the blues, rock, and rap are often included in such courses.

Some schools offer instrumental lessons for middle grade students, who must usually be able to rent or purchase their own instrument. Instrumental lessons generally culminate in group performances.

In grades 7 through 9, students are usually offered as an elective one semester or one year of music taught by a music specialist. They also have opportunities to join a performing group, becoming active members of the school band, orchestra, or chorus or of an ensemble group for jazz, rock, or some other form of popular music. Even though rehearsals and performances occur outside regular class time, students are eager participants in these groups. They allow young people with special musical interests or talents to develop their full potential.

New technologies are appearing more frequently in general music classes. These may include computers, synthesizers, and electronic keyboards for composing and producing music.

Students who have gone through a music education program can be expected to:

- develop basic music skills that will enable them to establish a lifelong relationship to music
- understand music elements, vocabulary, and notation
- enjoy a wide variety of musical forms and styles that are part of our historical and cultural heritage
- perform and create music and respond to music through movement and dance

Youngsters who enjoy music will take pleasure in THE NEW BOOK OF KNOWL-EDGE articles on musical instruments, the history and forms of classical and popular music, the biographies of famous composers and performers, and the music of other countries around the world.

▶ ART

Not every child has artistic talent, but most children enjoy and can benefit from art activities and experiences. Students are provided with opportunities to study art in most elementary schools, even though some states do not require that art be taught at this level. Tightened budgets and crowded school days have resulted in less frequent art instruction by specialists. When there is no art specialist available, art may be taught by the classroom teacher or may be incorporated into other subject areas. Children may illustrate stories they have listened to in reading periods or written in language arts classes, make posters with science or health themes, or construct models of historically significant structures for social studies projects.

Most schools, at the minimum, encourage youngsters to express themselves creatively, using a wide variety of art media and techniques. Children commonly have experiences in drawing, painting, printmaking, collage, sculpture, constructions, and an assortment of crafts. In well-equipped schools, students even become involved with photography, video production, and computer art.

When an art specialist is on hand, students will also learn something about the elements and principles of art and design, such as color, line, texture, and perspective. They will become familiar with all the forms art can take, ranging from architecture to painting, sculpture, and the graphic and decorative arts. A specialist may also introduce students to basics of art history and art criticism and help them begin to develop an appreciation for artworks produced by different cultures around the world.

Art fairs are popular events at many schools. Students proudly display examples of their best efforts for parents and others from the school and surrounding communities.

Art education provides a means of personal satisfaction for young people. It should also enable them to:

- perceive and understand basic elements of art and design
- use art as a means of communicating their ideas and feelings
- express themselves creatively in a variety of media
- appreciate and evaluate artworks
- enjoy art as part of our historical and cultural heritage

For students with special abilities or interests in art, THE NEW BOOK OF KNOWLEDGE offers a wealth of art information. There are biographies of famous artists; articles presenting the history of art from prehistoric to modern times; articles describing different art forms, processes, and media, many of which include special "how to" sections; and articles about the art and architecture of major countries around the world. Beautiful full-color art reproductions illustrate most of these articles.

▶ PHYSICAL EDUCATION AND SPORTS

Largely because of new technologies and an increase in labor-saving devices, many Americans lead sedentary life-styles at home, in the workplace, and in their leisure activities. Consequently, many Americans are not physically fit. Although our children seem to be constantly on the move, they too have been influenced by our changing lifestyles, and numerous studies show that too many of our youngsters are out of shape and lack basic physical and athletic skills. One of the key aims of the school physical education program is to help students develop healthy patterns of activity and preferences for athletic pursuits that they will carry into their adult lives.

Only a handful of states include physical education as part of their curriculum requirements. Most elementary, middle, and junior-high schools, however, do have gym and playground facilities, even if they may not have trained physical education instructors. Much learning does take place in these facilities under the direction of the classroom teacher.

In schools with physical education specialists and regularly scheduled gym classes, the physical education program is often thorough. These schools recognize that many of their students have little opportunity for vigorous exercise and that a number of them have neither the ability nor the motivation to participate or excel in competitive team sports. The well-balanced physical education program, therefore, offers a variety of activities involving:

- physical fitness and conditioning
- movement skills, rhythmic activities, and dance
- stunts, tumbling, and gymnastics
- game skills
- individual and two-person sports
- team sports

In gym classes for younger children, the emphasis is on the coordination of large and small muscles and on the development and coordination of general motor skills through play, game, and dance experiences. Many primary-grade students also learn simple tumbling, stunt, and conditioning activities, as well as basic athletic skills they will apply in later grades to more sophisticated games and sports.

Youngsters in the middle and junior-high grades are offered activities that will help them develop agility, strength, endurance, power, flexibility, and speed. Although competitive team sports become important for many students at this level, there is equal emphasis on fitness training, individual and two-person games and sports, track and field, gymnastics, dance, and self-testing. In the middle grades, softball, basketball, soccer, and volleyball are commonly taught team sports. Football, wrestling, field hockey, racket and paddle games, and swimming, if a pool is available, are added to the program for grades 7 through 9.

Since the passage of Title IX as federal law, girls and young women must be given equal opportunity and equal treatment in all school physical education activities and programs.

In the physical education curriculum, students can experience the joy, exhilaration, and satisfaction that accompany successful physical performance. They can also develop:

- an acceptable level of fitness with a lasting desire to maintain it
- the physical and movement skills needed to participate successfully in leisure activities of their choice
- a positive self-concept
- appropriate social and emotional behaviors including sportsmanship, cooperation, self-control, and leadership
- an appreciation and understanding of specific sports

In THE NEW BOOK OF KNOWLEDGE, most team sports and games are discussed in articles written by notable athletes or other sports experts. Accurate rules, directions, and diagrams accompany these articles. In addition, enthusiasts will find information on individual sports such as skiing, golf, running, ice-skating, and many, many more.

KINDERGARTEN AND GRADES 1 THROUGH 3

▶ MEET THE EARLY SCHOOL CHILD

Even though each child grows and learns at an individual pace, nearly all children go through similar stages of development. Teachers in kindergarten and the early grades recognize these growth characteristics and take them into account when they plan a program for early childhood education.

Rapid growth and development is the primary characteristic of the child from ages 5 through 8. Most 5-year-olds are extremely active, physically and mentally. They seem to be in a state of perpetual motion and they are curious about everything. Large muscles develop more rapidly than small muscles and younger children need outdoor play with space to run, jump, and climb. Small muscle growth is aided by activities such as cutting, coloring, pasting, and drawing. Although 5-year-olds have fairly short attention spans, their eyes, ears, and other senses all come into play as they explore the world and the people around them. These youngsters are friendly, eager to please, and need interaction and secure relationships with family members, friends, and teachers. Thinking is stimulated by experiences with concrete objects and a need to relate their learning to their own personal experiences.

Kindergarten classrooms reflect the nature of the 5-year-old. Kindergarten rooms are usually large and open with movable tables and chairs and a variety of learning areas. Children select many of their own activities as they move from one corner to another. Among the activities may be building a block bridge; observing how plants grow from seeds they have planted; measuring and mixing in the cooking area; examining picture books; singing and listening to music; and fingerpainting or making clay animals. What seems like play to the casual observer is really young children's work. It is how they learn. The kindergarten teacher moves among groups and individuals, guiding, leading, facilitating their activities, and helping them develop social skills. Outdoor activity is also an important part of the typical kindergarten day.

Children from ages 6 through 8 exhibit many of the same traits as 5-year-olds, but as they grow physically and as their experiences expand, changes take place. Although they are still active, hands-on learners, primary-grade youngsters develop considerable verbal ability, are increasingly able to reason, and begin to acquire problem-solving skills. They are able to concentrate on tasks for longer periods of time. As they grow less self-centered, they become more tolerant and open-minded and they take more interest in other people. Eagerly seeking new experiences, these youngsters are constantly expanding their horizons and exploring the world beyond home, family, and school. Developing 8-year-olds become increasingly independent and they need guidance and clear limits. With many positive learning experiences behind them, as third graders they can be self-confident, enthusiastic learners.

Youngsters must make a big adjustment between kindergarten and the elementary classroom. In grades 1 through 3 learning takes place in a more serious and structured, less playful environment. Children are usually required to spend a large part of the day in quiet, small-group or whole-class activities. Teachers realize, however, that youngsters in these grade-level classrooms are still literal learners and thinkers, and they still need numerous opportunities for hands-on learning experiences.

The K through 3 years are wonderful years during which children are reaching out to a wide and exciting world. These students are still very young, however, and much is expected of them. They need support, understanding, and friendship. Above all they need to feel accepted and appreciated by family members and teachers.

Enjoyable activities you and your youngsters can do together to reinforce what they are learning in the core curriculum areas—Reading, Language, and Literature; Mathematics; Social Studies; and Science—are listed after each of those sections.

The lists of articles at the very end of this section for Kindergarten and grades 1 through 3 include many, but certainly not all, of the articles about each subject area that appear in THE NEW BOOK OF KNOWLEDGE. It is important that students look up the names of topics they want to read about in the Index or in the set itself to locate all of the information they may need or want.

▶ READING, LANGUAGE, AND LITERATURE

The overall objectives of the reading, language, and literature programs that begin in the primary grades are: mastering the mechanics of reading and writing; acquiring the ability to read with comprehension and to write with proficiency; and developing good, lifelong reading and writing habits.

In kindergarten the focus of the reading program is on readiness skills that prepare the child for reading and writing. These include auditory and visual discrimination skills and those motor and coordination skills that will enable the young child to hold a crayon or pencil, to color and draw, and eventually to print and write. Kindergarten youngsters are also given repeated opportunities to develop and practice listening and speaking skills. They learn to follow simple rules and directions, deliver messages, ask and answer questions about their various activities, and share their ideas, feelings, and experiences with others. Inviting picture books, with and without words, are readily available to look at and use for imagining and creating stories. Their teachers tell them stories, read books and poems aloud, and lead them in word games and songs. In kindergartens using a more academic approach, youngsters will also begin to learn the relationships between alphabet letters and the sounds they represent.

In grades 1 through 3, as much as half the day may be devoted to reading instruction. Children begin to read by learning word recognition and word-attack skills. There are simple words that they may learn to recognize on sight. Children learn how to decode other words by being shown how to associate phonetic sounds with a letter or group of letters. Later, children also learn to identify words by dividing them into their structural parts. Dividing words into syllables, finding common prefixes and word endings, and breaking compound words into smaller words are all techniques for unlocking longer, more difficult words encountered for the first time. Children also learn how to identify a new word and its meaning by its context in a sentence.

By the end of the third grade, young readers will usually have acquired a literal level of comprehension. They should be able to locate details, identify main ideas, arrange events in a logical sequence, predict outcomes, and draw conclusions. In addition, many children will be able to demonstrate some appreciation of literature and a grasp of several literary elements including character, author's purpose, figurative language, and the difference between realism and fantasy.

In a traditional reading program, the class is usually divided according to reading ability into three relatively homogeneous reading groups. While the teacher works on direct instruction with one group, the rest of the class completes reading-related assignments or participates in self-directed individual or group activities. In a whole language or integrated language arts program, grouping tends to be more flexible and informal.

Primary-grade teachers are particularly alert to signs of reading difficulties, and they try to take steps to eliminate problems before they block a child's progress. Most schools also provide special reading teachers who are trained to make diagnoses and provide corrective help for children with reading problems. If you feel that your child requires special help, it is important that you approach the teacher or principal who can recommend appropriate action.

At the same time that they are learning to read what others have written, primary-grade youngsters begin to express their own ideas and feelings in written language. Kindergarten children can usually print their own names and perhaps a few other well-known names and words. In first grade, children typically learn manuscript writing because it is easier to read and write and resembles the printed words in books. Toward the end of second grade or at the beginning of third grade, children are taught how to change over to connected cursive writing.

As they are taught the steps in the writing process—drafting, composing, revising, editing, and publishing—primary-grade students also learn about proper word usage, spelling, capitalization, and punctuation, as these skills are needed. Many teachers allow youngsters to use "invented spelling" at first, writing words as they would sound when spoken, so that spelling issues do not slow down the youngsters' learning how to write down their ideas. Lessons on spelling and language mechanics are offered at a time when they will not interfere with the natural flow of ideas onto paper. By the time they enter fourth grade, students usually have developed some proficiency in writing sentences, paragraphs, and short reports, and they should enjoy expressing themselves creatively in writing.

Home Activities for Reading, Language, and Literature

- Read aloud to your children, every day if you can. Discuss the people, places, and events you read about.

- Take your children to the local library and let them share with you choosing books to bring home.

- Make up and tell stories to one another. One of you might begin a story and the other finish it. Help your children make their own books by writing and illustrating stories.

- Encourage your children to read to you from school or library books. Help them pronounce difficult words. Praise their efforts. Make this an enjoyable shared experience.

- Teach your children to observe the world around them and provide opportunities for them to talk about their experiences.

- Encourage your children to speak clearly and to listen carefully.

- Listen to your children retell favorite stories they have heard or read.

- Play simple word games. "Give a word that means the same as. . . ." "Give a word that means the opposite of. . . ." "Give a word that rhymes with. . . ." As your children get older, urge them to do simple crossword puzzles.

- Help your children write letters, invitations, and thank-you notes to relatives and friends.

- Encourage your children to make a "New Words" dictionary, and try to add a special word to it at least once a week.

- Help your children enjoy educational television programs so that they have many opportunities to listen to how standard English is used and spoken.

▶ **MATHEMATICS**

Children in kindergarten and the primary grades work with a variety of materials to develop concepts, understandings, and skills in mathematics. Kindergarten youngsters often come to school knowing something about counting and numbers, but they must acquire math readiness skills before they will be able to work with numbers in meaningful ways.

In the kindergarten classroom, youngsters learn to sort by using simple objects such as buttons, and by comparing how objects are alike and different. They compare groups of objects to determine which group has less or more objects than another. They learn the concept of one-to-one correspondence by discovering that three oranges have the same number as three apples. They learn the concept of conservation by recognizing that three boxes are three boxes no matter how they are spread out or pulled together. Kindergarten children learn to count using cardinal (1, 2, 3) and ordinal (first, second, third) numbers. Simple geometry, measurement, money, time, and spatial relationships also have a place in the readiness curriculum. Students receive extensive practice using manipulative materials to solve math problems presented as stories that are based on real-life experiences.

Students in the primary grades are not yet abstract thinkers. They continue to use concrete objects as they learn the basic facts and techniques of computation with whole numbers. Frequent work with number lines and hands-on experiences to determine and understand place values are important activities for them. From the beginning, youngsters are also taught to estimate before making calculations as a way of judging the reasonableness of an answer. Primary students enjoy measuring length, volume, weight, time, and temperature using an assortment of measuring tools and expressing answers in both standard and metric units. They learn to identify common geometric shapes, to create and interpret simple pictorial, bar, and line graphs, and to predict outcomes and carry out simple activities involving probability. They conduct simple surveys and experiments and begin to learn how to organize and interpret statistical data. Seeing and understanding mathematical relationships and patterns is another important skill that may be introduced to them in the early grades. Helping students acquire skill in solving problems is an ongoing activity and is usually based on situations appropriate to the students' level of understanding, and experience. Students are given opportunities to try solutions using a variety of problem-solving strategies.

By the end of the third grade most youngsters will possess confidence in their ability to compute and to solve math problems in school and in their everyday lives. Many respond to the fascination of math and it becomes their favorite subject. A few will have difficulties with mathematics' abstract concepts and more complicated methods. These students may need special coaching at home as well as in school.

Home Activities for Mathematics

- Encourage your children to find and read numbers on common objects—cereal boxes, jar and can labels, calendars, newspaper ads, store signs, traffic signs.
- Ask your children to count common objects. "How many clouds are in the sky today?" "How many people are in the checkout line?"
- Ask your children to estimate quantities. "How many puffs are in your bowl of cereal?" "How much milk will this container hold?"
- Encourage your children to read the

time from analog and digital clocks. Ask time questions. "How long will it take before the cookies are done?" "What time do you have to leave to get to school on time?"
- Help your children follow simple cooking recipes. Let them measure the ingredients with appropriate measuring utensils.
- Plan a party or special event with your children. Let them work out how many invitations are needed, how many favors, how much food, and how much these things will cost.
- Help your children find books in the library that contain number puzzles and math games.
- Encourage your children to look for geometric shapes such as circles, squares, rectangles, triangles, and cones in common household objects.
- Discuss with your children how you use math at home or in your job. Help them understand how math is involved in many day-to-day activities.
- Play games together that use math and probability. "How many times will the coin come up heads in 10 tries? In 15 tries? In 20 tries?"

▶ SOCIAL STUDIES

One of the first social studies lessons children will have is learning that they belong to a family. Youngsters also learn that belonging to a family brings with it responsibility and that the people in family groups depend upon one another. Gradually youngsters learn that each family is part of a larger group, a community, and that there are many different kinds of communities. During the kindergarten and primary school years, the social studies curriculum concentrates initially on children's families, neighborhood, and community. Youngsters learn that there are basic needs families share and that there are many different kinds of family groups in our own country and in other nations. They examine how different families live, work, and play together. They soon discover that everyone must follow rules if people are to live and work together successfully. What youngsters know about family units is then applied to the school community.

In the second and third grades, the social studies curriculum expands to include the neighborhood, local village, town, or city. Short class trips to the local post office, bank, supermarket, or police station demonstrate in a very real way how social and business institutions work in a community. Classroom visits by community workers teach youngsters about the many services needed to keep a community running smoothly. Police officers may talk about traffic rules and the reasons for them. A mail carrier may explain how letters are delivered.

Through these firsthand experiences, children also discover basic economic principles about how goods and services are produced and used and how earning money allows people to buy the things they need and want.

Classroom teachers use books, posters, films, newspapers, postcards, and photographs to help children understand that all neighborhoods and cities have many similarities but also many differences, and each has its own special needs and problems.

Primary-grade youngsters are also introduced to some key facts about our country's history and cultural heritage. Many schools focus on Native Americans, the voyages of Columbus, and the early American colonies. Facts about our history and the people who played important roles in our development as a nation are taught along with the study of national symbols, such as the American flag and the Statue of Liberty, and the celebration of national holidays.

Learning about geography grows out of the study of communities and United States history. Students begin to work with simple maps and globes. Often they make maps of their neighborhoods, pinpointing the location of their own homes and schools. Later they might also work with map puzzles and trace, draw, and color maps of the United States and of the world.

As their social studies knowledge expands and as they become more adept readers and writers, students learn and use the research skills they need to gather information and to write reports. Among the commonly taught skills for this age-group are: locating information; using library resources; using tables of contents and glossaries in books; making and interpreting diagrams and graphs; and selecting and organizing information.

Home Activities for Social Studies
- Get your children started on a stamp, coin, or postcard collection. Help them find out more about the people and places shown.
- If you can, start bank accounts for your children. Help them fill out the necessary forms.
- Give your children opportunities to earn money for work done, and help them plan how to use it.
- Talk with your children about the significance of the different holidays. Include them in activities you pursue to make and do things to celebrate each holiday.
- Read together the folklore, legends, and myths of different cultures and communities. Libraries have excellent collections of these stories.
- Watch television programs about different regions and cultures of the world. Discuss the similarities and dif-

ferences between these groups and our own culture.

- When you take trips outside your community, help your children locate the destination on a map. Share with them how you have decided what direction you will take and calculate the distance. As time goes on they may be able to make such decisions, too. When you arrive, discuss any special geographical features.

▶ SCIENCE AND TECHNOLOGY

The chief task of the K through 3 science program is to nurture the natural curiosity young children have about themselves, about the living and nonliving things around them, and about the forces of nature. A good primary science program provides a balanced curriculum that includes the life, earth, and physical sciences. Throughout the science program, children are introduced to basic concepts about scientific facts and principles. They begin to learn how to ask questions, make observations and predictions, plan and do simple experiments, and come to conclusions—all aspects of the scientific method.

Beginning in kindergarten, students begin to learn about the needs, habits, and relationships of living things. Youngsters might plant seeds and observe growth patterns. They might learn the special traits of mammals, birds, reptiles, amphibians, and fish and observe the life cycles of butterflies and frogs. Dinosaur studies offer a favorite way to learn about things that lived long ago. Classroom terrariums and aquariums provide an authentic means of observing the interrelationships within an aquatic, desert, or woodlands habitat. Youngsters are eager to care for the plant and animal specimens these miniature environments contain.

Young children are fascinated by space and space exploration, and they enjoy accumulating information about the sun, moon, planets, and other objects such as stars and the constellations.

Changing weather patterns are often observed and charted with youngsters measuring temperature, wind, rainfall, and humidity, describing cloud formations, and competing with the weatherman in making predictions about future weather.

Rock, mineral, soil, and water samples are collected to learn about the earth and its resources. The dynamics of our planet are made understandable as youngsters make models and diagrams of volcanoes and earthquakes.

By manipulating levers, inclined planes, pulleys, gears, and other simple machines that may be in their classroom, children learn about how things move and how they work. The importance of energy in their everyday lives is shown with investigations into magnetism, electricity, light, and sound.

The K through 3 years are the years when children's natural curiosity is at its peak. They are the ideal years during which to start a child on the exciting path of scientific discovery.

Home Activities for Science and Technology
- Take your children into your yard or a neighborhood park on a spring day and see how many different forms of life can be found. Include flowers, trees, grasses, large and small land animals, insects, and birds. Repeat the activity in the summer, fall, and winter.
- If you can, encourage your children to keep and care for a small pet.
- Ask your children to help tend houseplants or plant a garden. Let them have a special plot of their own.
- Get your children started on collections of objects from nature—small

rocks, tree leaves, weeds, seeds. Borrow field guides from the library and help them identify and label the specimens.

• Help your children become sky watchers. Ask them to keep a record of the changing shape of the moon over the period of a month. Find out together what causes this phenomenon. Locate easily identifiable constellations like the Big Dipper.

• Watch science and nature programs on television together. Talk about the interesting things you learn.

• Let your children help take responsibility for household recycling of items such as paper and plastics or for plans you have made to conserve water and gas or electricity.

▶ **HEALTH AND SAFETY**

The early grades are a good time to help children begin to learn good health habits and attitudes that will last throughout their lives. The primary-grade curriculum introduces young children to the major body systems and organs. They also learn about some of the causes of disease and how to prevent some infections. Caring for the body so that it functions smoothly is often taught through simple units on nutrition, physical fitness, and personal care.

Like adults, children are not always happy. They, too, experience sadness, loneliness, anger, shame, jealousy, and other feelings that can be frightening. They learn that everyone has these feelings sometimes, and they begin to learn how to handle these emotions and how to get along well with others.

Primary-grade youngsters are vulnerable to many types of danger. They need to be taught safety rules that will help them avoid accidents at home, at school, and in other places. It is also important to stress that youngsters remember such safety rules when they are around strangers or in areas unfamiliar to them.

In today's society, even very young children are exposed to the dangers of drugs. A good health program teaches youngsters how to use medicines safely and encourages them to make healthy choices about alcohol, tobacco, and illegal drugs.

Young children have frequent contact with doctors, dentists, and nurses in health clinics or hospitals. The school health program helps them become familiar with the work of these people and institutions.

▶ **MUSIC**

Young children respond to music spontaneously. Even when music specialists are not available, kindergarten and primary-grade youngsters are offered a variety of musical activities. They sing, clap, listen to music, dance, and play simple rhythm and percussion instruments. The primary-grade teacher often knows how to play the piano or guitar and how to accompany and direct children's singing and dancing.

In a structured music program, students can learn to keep time to a beat, match pitch, identify high and low musical sounds, and sing a melody. By grades 2 and 3 they can begin to learn the basic elements of musical notation.

Youngsters are also sometimes taught how to identify different singing voices and musical instruments as they listen to recorded music. They listen and respond to marches, lullabies, American folk songs, and songs from other cultures.

The main goal of the primary music curriculum is to help and encourage youngsters to enjoy and appreciate music of all kinds and to feel comfortable expressing themselves musically.

ART

The primary-grade art program provides opportunities for children to express themselves creatively with freedom and satisfaction. In the primary grades children have access to a wide variety of art materials and tools. They use poster and finger paints, sand, clay, colored paper, string, papier-mâché, and fabrics of different textures. Even common objects such as buttons, pipe cleaners, and egg cartons are used in the collages, drawings, and paintings they create. Because it is known that large muscles develop first, children are encouraged to work with large sheets of paper, large brushes, and thick crayons. By experimenting and exploring freely, youngsters discover on their own how these tools and materials work.

Teachers understand that young children are not yet ready to represent the things they see in a realistic style and that adult standards should not yet be imposed on the youngsters' creations.

Reproductions and posters of the works of great artists are sometimes examined and discussed during the art period. Students can learn something about color, line, and design as they are encouraged to talk about a master painting or sculpture.

PHYSICAL EDUCATION AND SPORTS

The physical education program is designed to help children acquire physical and athletic skills, habits, and attitudes that will last beyond their school years. In many schools the regular classroom teacher is responsible for gym or physical education in-struction. In others, there is a special physical education teacher.

The emphasis of the primary physical education program is often on fitness, rhythmic movement, some gymnastic activities, games, and sports.

Fitness and conditioning activities often begin with running, walking, jumping rope, or dancing. They continue with muscle stretching and strengthening exercises including bending, toe touches, crab walks, rope climbing, push-ups, and sit-ups. By the second and third grades youngsters are ready for activities that improve muscle coordination, such as the standing broad jump.

Young children enjoy discovering all the different ways in which their bodies can move. In gymnastics they run, skip, slide, hop, and gallop. They move arms and legs, manipulate objects to a rhythmic beat, and learn simple dances. Gymnastic activities sometimes include walking a balance beam and doing forward and backward rolls.

Primary-grade youngsters are taught a number of game skills basic to sports they will play when they are older. By third grade girls and boys can bounce a ball with one hand, dribble soccer balls and basketballs, strike a ball off a stationary object, and pass a ball in various ways to a partner. They use these skills in chasing games, relays, and team games.

In a good physical education program it is recognized that children will have varying levels of physical and athletic ability, but every child is included and involved in every activity. Every child also learns the importance of cooperation and sportsmanship in games and sports.

CURRICULUM-RELATED ARTICLES

Some of the important articles in THE NEW BOOK OF KNOWLEDGE that relate to the K through 3 school curriculum are listed here. Many other articles you or your youngsters may want to read while they are studying topics in these curriculum areas can be found by looking them up in the Index or in the set itself.

READING, LANGUAGE, AND LITERATURE

Vol.	Reading, Writing, and Language
B	Book Reports and Reviews
D	Diaries and Journals
E	Encyclopedias
H	Handwriting
J	Jokes and Riddles
L	Language Arts Letter Writing Libraries
M	Magazines
P	Phonics
R	Reading
S	Spelling Storytelling Study, How to
T	Tests and Test Taking Textbooks
U-V	Vocabulary
W-X-Y-Z	Writing

Vol.	Literature
A	Arabian Nights
C	Caldecott, Randolph Children's Book Awards Children's Literature
F	Fables Fairy Tales Folklore
I	Illustration and Illustrators
J-K	Jokes and Riddles
N	Nonsense Rhymes Nursery Rhymes Newbery, John

Vol.	Author Biographies
A	Andersen, Hans Christian
B	Barrie, Sir James Matthew
F	Field, Eugene Frost, Robert
G	Grahame, Kenneth Greenaway, Kate Grimm, Jacob and Wilhelm
H	Hughes, Langston
J-K	Kipling, Rudyard
M	Milne, A. A.
P	Potter, Beatrix
S	Sendak, Maurice Seuss, Dr. Stevenson, Robert Louis Sandburg, Carl
T	Thurber, James
W-X-Y-Z	White, E. B.

Vol.	Selections from Literature
A	Andersen, Hans Christian—The Emperor's New Clothes Arabian Nights 　Aladdin and the Wonderful Lamp (excerpt) 　The Forty Thieves (excerpt)
B	Barrie, Sir James Matthew—Peter Pan (excerpt) Bible Stories 　Noah's Ark 　David and Goliath 　Jonah 　Daniel in the Lions' Den 　The Boy Jesus
C	Christmas Story (Gospel according to Luke)

F Fables
  The Lion and the Mouse (Aesop)
  The Ant and the Grasshopper
    (Aesop)
  The Four Oxen and the Lion (Aesop)
  The Tyrant Who Became a Just Ruler
    (Bidpai)
  The Blind Men and the Elephant
    (Saxe)
  The Moth and the Star (Thurber)

Fairy Tales
  The Enchanted Princess (German)
  The Princess on the Pea (Andersen)
  The Sleeping Beauty (Perrault)
  Little Red Riding-Hood (de la Mare)

Field, Eugene—A Dutch Lullaby

Figures of Speech
  Silver (de la Mare)
  The Toaster (Smith, W. J.)
  Dandelions (Frost, F. M.)
  The Little Rose Tree (Field, Rachel)
  Everyone Sang (Sassoon)
  The Night Will Never Stay (Farjeon)
  Brooms (Aldis, D.)
  No Shop Does the Bird Use
    (Coatsworth, E.)

Folklore
  Cinderella or The Little Glass Slipper
    (Perrault)
  John Henry (American)
  Johnny Appleseed (American)
  Pecos Bill (American)

Frost, Robert
  The Last Word of a Bluebird
  The Pasture
  Stopping by Woods on a Snowy
    Evening
  The Road Not Taken

G Grimm, Jacob and Wilhelm
  The Shoemaker and the Elves
  Rapunzel
  Hansel and Gretel

Grahame, Kenneth—The Wind in the
  Willows (excerpt)

J-K Kipling, Rudyard—The Elephant's
  Child

M Milne, A. A.—Missing

N Nonsense Rhymes
  I Went to Noke (Nursery)
  The Song of Milkanwatha (Strong)
  OIC (Anonymous)
  The Common Cormorant
    (Anonymous)

Jabberwocky (Carroll)
The Maiden of Passamaquoddy
  (DeMille)
The Reason for the Pelican (Ciardi)
The Yak (Belloc)
Habits of the Hippopotamus
  (Guiterman)
Eletelephony (Richards)
I Wish That My Room Had a Floor
  (Burgess)
Antigonish (Mearns)
The Walloping Window-blind (Carryl)
The Owl and the Pussy-Cat (Lear)
There Was an Old Man Who
  Supposed (Lear)
There Was a Young Lady of
  Woosester (Anonymous)
A Sleeper from the Amazon
  (Anonymous)

Nursery Rhymes
  Jack Sprat
  Georgie Porgie
  The Old Woman in a Shoe
  Jack and Jill
  Hey Diddle, Diddle
  Miss Muffet
  Mary's Lamb
  Lullaby
  Boy Blue
  Hickory, Dickory, Dock
  Baa, Baa, Black Sheep
  Pease Porridge Hot
  Humpty Dumpty
  Jack Horner

P Potter, Beatrix—The Tale of Jemima
  Puddle-Duck
Poetry
  The Water Babies (excerpt, Kingsley)
  Firefly (Roberts, E. M.)
  The Circus (Roberts)

S Stevenson, Robert Louis
  Requiem
  My Shadow
  Looking-Glass River
  The Swing
  The Gardener
  Bed in Summer
  Kidnapped (excerpt)

Sandburg, Carl
  Fog
  The Skyscraper to the Moon and
    How the Green Rat with the
    Rheumatism Ran a Thousand Miles
    Twice

F	Franklin, Benjamin Friedan, Betty Fulton, Robert
H	Henry, Patrick
J-K	Jackson, Andrew Jackson, Jesse Jefferson, Thomas Keller, Helen Kennedy, John F. King, Martin Luther
L	Lee, Robert E. Lincoln, Abraham
M	Madison, James
Q-R	Revere, Paul Roosevelt, Eleanor Roosevelt, Franklin D. Roosevelt, Theodore
S	Stowe, Harriet Beecher Stuyvesant, Peter
T	Tubman, Harriet
W-X- Y-Z	Washington, George Whitney, Eli Wright, Orville and Wilbur

Vol.	**Geography**
A	Agriculture Atlantic Ocean
B	Biomes
C	Cities Climate Continents
D	Deserts
E	Earth Equator
F	Forests and Forestry
I	Indian Ocean Islands
L	Lakes
M	Maps and Globes
N	National Park System Natural Resources North America
O	Oceans and Seas of the World
P	Pacific Ocean and Islands
Q-R	Rivers
S	Seasons
U-V	United States

W-X- Y-Z	Weather Wetlands World

THE NEW BOOK OF KNOWLEDGE contains articles on individual cities, states, countries, regions, and continents. Young readers will find information in these articles about the land, people, history, and government of places in which they are interested.

Vol.	**Holidays**
C	Christmas
E	Easter
H	Hanukkah Holidays
I	Independence Day
N	New Year Celebrations Around the World
P	Passover Purim
Q-R	Religious Holidays
T	Thanksgiving Day
U-V	Valentines

SCIENCE AND TECHNOLOGY

Vol.	**Plants, Animals, and the Human Body**
A	Animals Apes
B	Bats Birds Body, Human Butterflies and Moths
C	Cats
D	Dinosaurs Dogs
E	Endangered Species
F	Flowers and Seeds Frogs and Toads
H	Hibernation Horses and Their Relatives
I	Insects
L	Leaves Life

M	Medicine, Tools and Techniques of Monkeys and Their Relatives
N	Nature, Study of
P	Plants
Q-R	Rabbits and Hares
T	Trees Turkeys
W-X-Y-Z	Wild Flowers

Vol.	Earth and Space
A	Astronauts
C	Climate Clouds Constellations
E	Earth-Moving Machinery Earthquakes Electricity
I	Ice
J-K	Jupiter
M	Magnets and Magnetism Matter Milky Way Minerals Moon
O	Ores
Q-R	Rainbow Rocks
S	Space Exploration and Travel Sun
T	Telescopes Thunder and Lightning
U-V	Venus
W-X-Y-Z	Water Weather

HEALTH AND SAFETY

Vol.	Article
B	Baby
D	Digestive System Doctors
E	Ear Eggs and Embryos Eye
H	Health Hospitals
M	Mental Health
N	Nurses and Nursing
P	Physical Fitness
S	Safety Skeletal System
T	Teeth

MUSIC

Vol.	Article
A	Anderson, Marian
B	Ballet
C	Carols Country Music
D	Drum
F	Folk Dancing Folk Music
H	Handel, George Frederick
L	Lullabies
M	Mozart, Wolfgang Amadeus Musical Instruments
N	National Anthems and Patriotic Songs
O	Opera Orchestra
P	Piano
Q-R	Recorder
S	Schubert, Franz
T	Tchaikovsky, Peter Ilyich
U-V	United States, Music of the

ART

Vol.	Art and Artists
B	Bruegel, Pieter, the Elder
C	Cassatt, Mary Chagall, Marc Color
D	Drawing Dürer, Albrecht
G	Gainsborough, Thomas
H	Homer, Winslow
I	Illustration and Illustrators
J-K	Kandinsky, Wassily Klee, Paul

L	Leonardo da Vinci
M	Matisse, Henri
	Miró, Joan
	Moses, Grandma
	Museums
O	O'Keefe, Georgia
P	Picasso, Pablo
Q-R	Reynolds, Sir Joshua
	Rockwell, Norman
U-V	United States, Art and Architecture of the
U-V	Van Gogh,Vincent
	Vermeer, Jan
W-X-Y-Z	Whistler, James Abbott McNeill

Vol.	Arts and Crafts
C	Clay Modeling
D	Decoupage
F	Finger Painting
L	Linoleum-Block Printing
N	Needlecraft
O	Origami
P	Papier-mâché
	Posters
	Puppets and Marionettes
Q-R	Rubbings

PHYSICAL EDUCATION AND SPORTS

Vol.	Article
B	Badminton
	Ball
	Baseball
	Basketball
	Bicycling
	Bowling
C	Croquet
D	Darts
F	Field Hockey
	Fishing
	Football
G	Gymnastics
H	Hiking and Backpacking
	Horseshoe Pitching
I	Ice Hockey
	Ice-Skating
J-K	Jogging and Running
	Judo
	Juggling
J-K	Karate
L	Little League Baseball
O	Olympic Games
	Owens, Jesse
P	Paddle Tennis
	Pelé
	Physical Education
	Physical Fitness
Q-R	Racing
	Robinson, Jack Roosevelt (Jackie)
	Roller-Skating
S	Shuffleboard
	Skiing
	Soccer and Youth Soccer
	Softball
	Swimming
T	Table Tennis
	Thorpe, James Francis (Jim)
	Track and Field

GRADES 4 THROUGH 6

▶ **THE STUDENT IN THE MIDDLE GRADES**

In grades 4 through 6, young students experience an interval of relative balance, calm, and stability compared with their earlier period of transition from home to school during the primary years, or compared with the coming years of confusion and stress that usually characterize adolescence. Physical growth continues, but the body changes in less striking ways. The mind and emotions steadily mature, and young learners are expected to have more control over their feelings and to accept more responsibility for how and what they learn.

These youngsters cherish their sense of growing independence, yet they want and accept limits. They are eager to find their place in their own age-group and to develop close relationships with friends. Peers begin to have more influence over their behavior and thinking, but family ties are still strong. This is the age of belonging—to a team, a group, a club, or a clique. It is also an age when youngsters enjoy family togetherness. They love to help plan family projects, trips, hobbies, and outings.

Middle grade students are eager to know what things are, how they work, how they were discovered, and how they are used. Children of this age have a great need to understand meanings behind facts and to see connections. Although their ability to comprehend at an abstract level is growing, these youngsters still need to learn by doing. However, attention spans are longer and interests are more intense. Children of 9 or 10 can spend hours with a favorite activity. Nevertheless, they may pass from interest to interest as they go through the grades, always ready to open doors to new experiences and understandings.

Depending on the community in which they live, students in grades 4 through 6 may attend one of three different types of school configurations. Most middle graders attend an elementary school, although it may not be the same building they attended in the primary grades. Many sixth graders and some fifth graders go to a middle school. Some sixth graders move on to a junior high school.

Those students still in elementary schools will find their learning taking place in a familiar environment. They spend most of the day in a self-contained classroom, with one teacher for all the core curriculum subjects. In some middle schools, a team-teaching approach is used. Teams of two or more teachers will share teaching responsibilities for their classes. One may teach science and math; another may teach English and social studies. In other middle schools and most junior high schools, instruction is completely departmentalized, with a different teacher for each subject.

Whatever the type of school they attend, these youngsters continue to need parental or adult guidance and support during the middle grade years. Let them know you expect them to do well. Motivate them with encouragement and praise. Help them to feel good about themselves and their abilities. Provide assistance, as needed, with homework and other school activities. Keep the communication lines with your children and your children's teachers open and active. These are important years—years in which young people must acquire the confidence, the knowledge, and the skills they will need to do well in high school and in their adult years.

Enjoyable activities you and your youngsters can do together to reinforce what they are learning in the core curriculum areas— Reading, Language, and Literature; Mathematics; Social Studies; and Science—are listed after each of those sections.

The lists of articles at the very end of this section for grades 4 through 6 include many, but certainly not all, of the articles about each subject area that appear in THE NEW BOOK OF KNOWLEDGE. It is important that students look up the names of topics they want to read about in the Index or in the set itself to locate all of the information they may need or want. For example, in the Social Studies area, articles about each of the countries of the world are not listed in this section but can easily be located by looking each one up under its own name.

▶ READING, LANGUAGE, AND LITERATURE

The foundations of reading are taught in the primary grades. Students entering the middle grades should have sound word-attack and word-recognition skills, be able to comprehend what they read at least at a literal level, and begin to understand the elements of good literature. All these skills must be applied and expanded if students are to grow in ability. The reading curriculum in grades 4 through 6 is composed of a mix of developmental reading, content-area reading, and recreational reading.

Developmental reading instruction continues at grades 4, 5, and 6 so that middle grade students learn more advanced reading skills and strategies. Emphasis is on word analysis and higher-level comprehension and critical-thinking skills. Learning prefixes, suffixes, inflected endings, and root words teaches youngsters how to decipher most words, even difficult multisyllabic words. Vocabulary and dictionary skills are taught, usually also including the study of context clues, synonyms, antonyms, and words with multiple meanings, to give students the ability to learn how to unlock the meanings of words.

Reading is primarily a process of constructing meaning from written words, and students are also taught how to apply a variety of comprehension and critical-thinking skills and strategies to do it well. These skills range from making inferences, understanding cause and effect relationships, and summarizing main ideas and key facts to understanding a writer's point of view, recognizing various persuasive devices, and being able to distinguish between fact and opinion.

In the primary grades, youngsters learned the mechanics of reading and began to read simple essays, stories, and poems. In the middle grades, students need to know how to read to learn. They must use reading to get information from many different types of books, including content-area textbooks, reference books, nonfiction books such as biographies, and many other types of resources. Reading these many different texts for information requires the use of good study skills as well as advanced reading skills, so study skills are also emphasized at these levels. Students must also know how to use the various parts of a book—the table of contents, preface, copyright page, index, glossary—to find out where the information one needs in it may be located. They also learn how to skim or scan through a book to locate information quickly; how and when to use encyclopedias, atlases, almanacs, and other reference materials; how to locate resources by referring to a library card or electronic catalog; and how to use graphic sources of information, such as tables, lists, charts, graphs, time lines, pictures, diagrams, and maps and globes. In addition, youngsters are taught to adjust their method and rate of reading depending on the type of material and their purpose in reading it. As they read their social studies, science, and math textbooks, and as they consult the variety of other print materials they need to use, students are, in effect, applying their reading knowledge as well as their thinking, comprehension, and study skills throughout the school day.

Teachers in the middle grades also recognize the importance of nurturing their students' recreational reading interests and activities, and some classroom time is provided for reading for pure pleasure. Youngsters are motivated to explore many literary genres: traditional folktales, myths, fables, and epics; realistic fiction; fantasy and science fiction; suspense and mystery; historical fiction; poetry; biographies; and books about personal experiences and adventures. Class or group discussions revolve around students' reactions to and interpretations of what they have read and include discussions of the setting, plot, characters, mood, and the author's use of language. Knowing about the elements of good literature helps children make worthwhile reading choices and enhances their reading enjoyment.

Reading growth is a complex process. Middle grade teachers remember that each child is an individual with different needs and abilities. Whether they use a traditional or whole-language approach, they try to ensure that every child's needs are met.

Children are introduced to the basics of writing in the primary grades. In grades 4 through 6 more frequent writing opportunities help students hone their skills. Introducing them to the elements of writing as a craft during these years helps them become better users of written language.

Aware that most youngsters sometimes have difficulty selecting a topic to write about, many teachers conduct prewriting brainstorming sessions. Students and teacher join in discussion of a general theme, sharing ideas and suggestions for writing topics and approaches. Once topics have been selected, students are encouraged to write a first draft quickly, concentrating on key ideas and details. Many teachers ask students to review each other's drafts, either as partners or in small groups. Youngsters learn to make thoughtful, supportive comments and recommendations during this peer review, helping each other revise and improve their writing. Once revised drafts are completed, the editing process takes over. Teachers may conduct mini-lessons at this point, focusing on an aspect of spelling, grammar, usage, or capitalization and punctuation. Other teachers hold student-teacher conferences during the revising and editing steps. When all revisions and corrections have been made, students "publish" their final versions. This may mean simply writing their pieces in their best handwriting or turning them into booklets or books with illustrations and covers.

During the writing process, students are often encouraged to think of themselves as authors and to find a personal writing voice, incorporating humor, colorful language, or other characteristics that are natural to their own personality or use of words.

Middle grade writing assignments will usually include stories, poetry, reports, and essays. Some youngsters write articles for class or school newspapers. Direct connection to the reading curriculum is made by encouraging youngsters to use the literature they read in the classroom or at home as models for their own writing.

In schools with computers, middle graders may use simple word-processing programs. Many children find this a less cumbersome way of writing. They can edit and make changes, substitutions, and deletions quickly and easily without having to produce several handwritten copies.

English and spelling textbooks are used to provide the basic instruction children need in the conventions and mechanics of written language, and students also learn how to use a dictionary and a thesaurus. The proof of their learning, however, is their growing ability to communicate effectively in writing.

Children acquire their basic speech patterns from their parents and families, from their neighborhood friends, and from the speech of the region in which they live. Their speech patterns are largely formed by the time they start school. The school can do much, however, to improve and polish them as necessary by providing instruction in oral expression. Teachers offer many opportunities for youngsters to practice oral expression. These range from making simple announcements to taking part in group discussions. In the middle grades, students report on individual and group projects, tell about personal experiences, give and explain information and directions, tell stories, recite poetry, take part in dramatics and choral speaking, make introductions, conduct interviews, read aloud, and dramatize telephone conversations.

Students are also taught that good listening habits are important. They are shown how to be attentive and courteous while others are speaking and responsive to the thoughts and questions expressed by a speaker. Above all, students learn that listening is an important avenue for learning.

Home Activities for Reading, Language, and Literature

- Continue to read aloud to your youngsters as often as possible.
- Listen to your youngsters read to you from books, magazines, or from stories and reports they have written themselves.
- Discuss authors and types of books you enjoy reading together. Find more books by the same author in your local library. Ask the librarian to recommend other authors and types of books similar to your current favorites.
- Help your youngsters develop the habit of looking up information in encyclopedias and other reference

books. Encourage their enthusiasm and interests.

- Start a letter diary together. Each day, or once or twice a week, one of you write a letter to the other and ask the other person to write a response.
- As your youngsters come upon interesting new words in their reading or in other activities, encourage them to look up the meanings and usage of these words in a dictionary. Urge them to use these words in their own writing and conversation.
- Make dinner table conversation an enjoyable experience for the entire family. Tell riddles, jokes, and stories, and share with each other the day's special events and activities.
- This is a good age level for your youngsters to find regular pen pals. They may be friends or relatives who live some distance away. Many magazines for young people publish the names and addresses of Pen Pal Clubs or of youngsters who want to correspond with others having similar interests.

▶ **MATHEMATICS**

In grades 4 through 6, students consolidate and build on the mathematical skills they acquired in earlier grades. They are also taught how to develop their reasoning abilities further and use them to learn new, more complex and more advanced math concepts and strategies.

Middle grade youngsters apply their knowledge of addition, subtraction, multiplication, and division to larger numbers and to fractions and decimals. Their understanding of how to work with numbers is enhanced as they learn about the different properties of numbers. Concepts of prime and composite numbers, ratio, proportion, and percent are also introduced at this level. Their work is

not always done as paper-and-pencil activities. Students also learn estimation, mental arithmetic, and the use of calculators and computers.

Mathematical patterns and relationships are discovered as youngsters learn about equations, inequalities, ordered pairs, and coordinate graphs. Visual and concrete experiences help students also understand geometric concepts. Students create models and use rulers, compasses, and protractors as they explore two- and three-dimensional geometric figures, measure angles, and determine symmetry, congruency, and similarity in geometric forms.

Hands-on measuring tools, including yardsticks, meter sticks, gallon and liter containers, balance scales, and others, are often used to help students learn how to determine length and distance, weight and mass, volume and capacity, and area and perimeter. Youngsters learn to use both standard and metric units and to make conversions within both systems.

Experiences in collecting and interpreting numerical data are provided, and students present the results in the form of tables, charts, or graphs, or by calculating the mean, median, and mode of the statistical data they have collected. Experiments with coins, dice, playing cards, and other objects are often used as the basis for helping students learn the strategies they need to make probability predictions.

A key element in the middle grade mathematics curriculum is the problem-solving strand. All of the concepts and skills students learn in mathematics are applied in problem-solving situations. Students at this level learn how to use a logical sequence of steps and a variety of strategies for solving problems. Finding a pattern; using a picture, chart, or model; working backwards; making an organized list; and breaking a complex problem into two or more simple problems are among the strategies they learn to use in working out solutions to the problems they must solve.

By the time they finish the sixth grade, most students will have formed a lifelong attitude toward mathematics. Unfortunately, many youngsters lose interest in, and enjoyment of, math during the middle grade years. Many lack confidence in their ability to understand and use math in school and in everyday life. Parents also find that it becomes more difficult to help their youngsters in math as time goes on. It is important for parents to communicate with the teacher or principal if their children start to show negative attitudes toward the subject or seem to be having difficulty doing the work. Concerned parents and teachers will want to have every opportunity to ensure that math is a positive and pleasurable experience for every child.

Home Activities for Mathematics

- Help your youngsters become aware of how large numbers are used in news articles, books, and on television programs. Ask them to read a number and talk about how big a quantity it represents. Do the same with fractions and decimals.
- If your youngsters have a special interest in a sport, encourage them to collect statistics for the sport and its players. In baseball, for example, youngsters love to rattle off batting averages, runs batted in (RBI's), home runs, base hits, stolen bases, strikeouts, and many other statistics.
- Help your youngsters use mathematics in everyday activities. Encourage them to set up budgets that include money earned, an allowance, savings, and purchases. Help them figure out best buys when shopping together.
- Ask your youngsters to estimate measurements when you are on an excursion or trip. "How high do you think that building is?" "How far is it across the lake?" "How many people will fit in the elevator?" Follow up by trying to find the answer when you can.
- Encourage your youngsters to collect interesting number facts that appear in the media or in their reading. This activity may include the sales figures for the latest recording of a favorite entertainer or the distance between the Earth and the nearest star.
- Play games involving numbers with your youngster. Card and dice games call for computation and memory skills, and many board games call for the use of play money.
- Help your youngsters interpret and use the information in everyday schedules, graphs, and tables. You can use many items to do this, including television and movie schedules, arena and theater seating diagrams, train and bus timetables, and pie and line charts and graphs you find in newspaper and magazine articles.

▶SOCIAL STUDIES

Social studies in the middle grades includes history, geography, political science, economics, current affairs, and topics from the social science subjects such as anthropology, sociology, and psychology. Although the social studies curriculum varies from school to school, in general, students in grades 4 through 6 learn about their own city and state; the history and geography of the United States and other nations in the Western Hemisphere; North and South America's historical and cultural roots; and the diverse regions and nations of the world.

The study of the history of the United States usually concentrates on Native Americans, the age of the discovery and exploration of the North American continent, the colonial and revolutionary periods, and the Civil War. Major events from the late 1800's to the present may be covered, but not in depth. Emphasis on modern and contemporary history is usually given in grades 7 through 9 and in high school. Middle grade teachers try to help students understand the traditions and the political and cultural institutions of the United States and to appreciate the events and the people that most influenced our history and the development of our society.

Students learn about the geography of the United States by reading a variety of information sources and comparing and contrasting information about the different regions of the country. Physical and political maps, population tables, product maps, travel brochures, and other tools are also examined to determine how the land, the economy, the people, and the cultural traditions of one region vary from those of another. During the study of the United States, many schools include a companion study of one or more neighbors—Canada and Central and South America.

The study of world history and geography in the middle grades focuses on prehistoric, ancient, and medieval civilizations and on the cultural and social characteristics of other countries and regions. Students also learn to identify the geographic influences that affect the way people live.

Because the future of our nation and of the world depends upon intelligent and informed citizens, students also begin to study current affairs. Some classes subscribe to a daily local newspaper or to professionally prepared school newspapers designed for particular grade levels. Many schools use educational television or radio programs to present and stimulate interest in current events.

An important outcome of current-events studies is that youngsters become able to identify national and world issues. They enthusiastically take part in discussions and debates about such topics as the environment and conflicts between nations, as well as issues such as hunger, homelessness, and racism. Middle grade students sometimes debate serious matters that touch directly on their own lives and futures. Their increasing ability to empathize with others leads many youngsters at these age levels to begin to take seriously their rights and responsibilities as citizens in a democracy.

Teachers and school administrators commonly encourage activities that promote the development of citizenship skills. Many schools have student councils made up of elected class representatives. Parliamentary procedure is followed as students work on the council or on school committees. Youngsters also learn that there are many ways in which one person or group can be effective in bringing about change and resolving problems. They learn how to write letters and interview people. They collect and raise money for worthy causes. They campaign to save a local landmark, a stream, or an endangered species in their community and bring these issues to the attention of local, state, or federal government officials.

In the pursuit of social studies information, students also use research and problem-solving techniques. They discover that the study, research, and problem-solving skills they are acquiring in their reading, writing, and mathematics classes can be applied to their social studies projects. Working alone or in groups, youngsters use these skills when they consult an assortment of resources to locate, gather, interpret, evaluate, and organize information and then to prepare and deliver oral and written reports.

By the end of the sixth grade, youngsters will have made giant strides toward acquiring the abilities they will need to understand the complexities and the development of human societies around the world.

Home Activities for Social Studies

- Plan a trip with your youngsters. Show them how the scale and legends on a road map help you determine your route. As they develop an understanding of this kind of information, let them take charge of the road map and be responsible for directions to the driver.
- Discuss important news events at the family table. Help your youngsters distinguish between sensational gossip, unfounded rumor, and relevant facts that can be proven.
- Plan family outings or trips to include visits to museums and historical sites.
- Take your youngsters with you when you vote. Show them the ballot and voting machine. Talk about how you decide on the candidate you choose to vote for.
- Investigate and construct your family tree with your youngsters. Let them interview family members and fill in as many branches of the tree as possible. Talk about the family's origins.
- If you have a personal computer in your home, encourage your youngsters to use educational games, data bases, and simulations with social studies themes. Let them discover how much fun this can be.
- Help your youngsters find ways of taking action on local and national matters of concern to them. They may want to write a letter to the local newspaper or to a public official, or they may want to join a special interest youth club or other organization.
- Encourage and help your youngsters locate places in the news on a map or globe.

▶ **SCIENCE AND TECHNOLOGY**

The middle grade science program continues the balanced approach of the primary grades in which concepts from each of the scientific disciplines—life science, earth science, and physical science—are taught each year. The scope is much broader, however. Students are introduced to a wider range of topics—from atoms to the universe, from bacteria to elephants, from light bulbs to space telescopes. They study only a limited number of concepts and principles in depth, however, as they develop an appreciation of and the habit of scientific thinking.

Youngsters in grades 4 through 6 become familiar with plant and animal life. They learn the similarities and differences in the traits of the simplest living things, such as bacteria and protozoans, and in the traits of animals with and without backbones. They trace the growth and development of flowering plants and plants with seeds or spores. As they examine the many different forms that life takes, students arrive at several key understandings: what an ecosystem is; how plants and animals make adaptations to their environments and how they change or evolve over time; how living things interact; and how the relationships among all the members of an ecosystem are intertwined.

Studies about space expand to include not only our solar system but also the other stars, galaxies, and objects that make up the universe. The wonders and riches of our own planet are presented so that students can learn about rocks, minerals, soil, water, and natural forces. They learn how weather, plate tectonics, volcanoes, and earthquakes constantly build up and wear away the surface of the planet. Students weigh the benefits of advancements in science and technology against the costs and trade-offs to human society and to the environment as they investigate air, water, land, and energy resources.

Several of the most fundamental principles and laws of physical science are first taught in grades 4 through 6. In the study of matter and its properties, students learn about the laws of the conservation of matter, and about atoms, elements, the periodic table, and how substances interact with each other physically and chemically. Isaac Newton's three laws of motion are demonstrated as students acquire knowledge about work, energy, and forces. Experiments with heat, light, sound, electricity, and magnetism lead young scientists to the understanding that although energy can be transferred from one system to another, the total amount of energy remains constant.

Middle grade students are usually ready to understand quite sophisticated scientific and technological concepts. They do this best when they are given opportunities to experiment, to draw conclusions, and to work through problem-solving activities.

Home Activities for Science and Technology

- Encourage your youngsters to find books in the library that give instructions for easy-to-do science experiments and activities. Help them do some of these activities and talk about the results.
- Youngsters at this age level have an exceptional empathy with animals. If it is possible, this is a good time to encourage them to have a pet, such as a puppy, kitten, or fish, and learn how to be responsible and care for it.
- Help your youngsters keep track of weather forecasts in the newspaper or from a radio or television newscast for a three- to four-week period. Consider together how often the forecast was correct. Was there a difference in how often short-range forecasts (one to two days) were correct compared to longer-range forecasts (four to five days)? Decide whether or not you can

draw any conclusions about the accuracy of weather forecasting.
- Young people at this age are curious about how things work. Help your youngsters find instruction booklets, articles, and books written for their age level that explain how some of the electronic devices in your home work. These might include telephones, VCR's, microwave ovens, and calculators.
- Try some roadside or curbside geology investigations. Whenever you and your youngsters pass a building or park, visit a beach, or spot a fresh roadcut, examine the rocks you find. How many different samples can you find? Can you identify any? Can you find fossils in any? Examine together some books about rocks written for the age levels of your youngsters.
- Encourage your youngsters to keep a science diary or logbook. They may write about any interesting science observations or experiences they have, or they may focus their diary on one science topic such as bird-watching or stargazing.

▶ HEALTH AND SAFETY

The school health program for grades 4 through 6 continues to develop many of the topics begun in the primary grades, including the human body, nutrition, physical fitness, personal care, diseases, mental health, safety, and drug, alcohol, and tobacco use and abuse. Students now study these subjects in more depth.

When studying the human body, students examine its important systems in more detail. For example, as they study the structure of the circulatory system, they also learn how each of its components—heart, blood, and blood vessels—functions; how the circulatory system and the respiratory system work together; and how diet and exercise affect both systems. In addition, youngsters go beyond body systems to study simple aspects of more complex concepts such as heredity and genetics.

First aid is added to the concept of safety, and students learn the proper procedures to follow in various types of emergencies. Investigations into communicable and noncommunicable diseases expand to include heart disease, cancer, and other serious illnesses. In the area of mental health, youngsters continue to talk about effective ways of handling their feelings, and they also learn about how to improve their self-image and how to deal with stress. All children are encouraged to commit themselves to a regular exercise and fitness program and to maintain healthy attitudes toward the use of drugs, alcohol, and tobacco.

Students at this stage are ready to move beyond personal health and examine issues involved in consumer health and in community and environmental health. They learn how to use label and pricing information to make wise choices when shopping for food and health products, and they learn how to evaluate advertisements for these products. They become familiar with the various health services provided in their neighborhood: health departments, hospitals, health clinics, and emergency services.

Middle grade students often develop a keen sensitivity to environmental problems, and many youngsters become enthusiastic volunteers in environmental causes, working to reduce air, water, and garbage pollution in their homes and in their community.

Through the school health program, youngsters are provided with information and experiences that will help them maintain health-promoting attitudes and habits that are intended to last into adulthood.

▶ MUSIC

Music begins to become an important part of life for many children in the middle grades. At home they listen to music while working on hobbies, doing chores, or completing homework assignments. They enjoy watching music videos and often mimic popular entertainers. Many 10- and 11-year-olds eagerly pick up popular dance steps and dance at home or at parties with their friends.

In school most youngsters participate in singing activities, frequently learning songs related to themes in the social studies or literature curriculum, such as songs of pioneers and cowboys and folk songs from around the world. Music teachers encourage students to read music and to experiment with part singing and harmony.

As they are asked to listen to recorded or live music, youngsters become familiar with a variety of musical styles, periods, and forms, ranging from classical and baroque to jazz and rock. In a thorough curriculum, they examine the elements a composer uses to communicate a musical message, including tempo, rhythm, melody, timbre, and harmonics. Students also learn how to pay attention to the contributions of different types of instruments and voices in a musical work.

Many children of this age learn to play a musical instrument through private lessons or at school, where they often have an opportunity to play in a band or orchestra. Some take voice lessons or participate in a school choral group.

Through a variety of musical activities, students can expand their appreciation and enjoyment of music.

▶ ART

Art is a very enjoyable school experience for middle grade children. They paint, draw, model in clay, design posters, construct with wood, make puppets and models, and work with paper, fabric, and many other materials and tools. They are usually allowed to base much of their creative work on personal experiences, and they are also asked to create pieces for projects in other subject areas. For example, students learning about the Middle Ages in social studies may create their own stained-glass windows using colored cellophane and black construction paper. A science unit on the ecology of a wetland may prompt the painting of a classroom mural depicting the many life-forms found in a wetland habitat.

Youngsters in grades 4 through 6 increase their knowledge of the elements of design and are encouraged to experiment with color, line, shape, space, and texture in their own works. In some programs they learn how to compare the styles of different artists and different cultures or historical periods by viewing and discussing print reproductions, slides, or videotapes of a broad range of artworks.

The school art program for the middle grades motivates youngsters to express their own individual ideas and feelings through art activities and to appreciate art in many of its forms.

▶ PHYSICAL EDUCATION AND SPORTS

Physical fitness, rhythmic activities, gymnastics, and game skills constitute the core of the physical education program for grades 4 through 6. A wide variety of indoor and outdoor activities including walking, running, muscle stretching and strengthening, push-ups, pull-ups, and sit-ups help youngsters gain proficiency in agility, strength, endurance, power, flexibility, and speed.

The rhythmic and gymnastic part of the program calls for folk dancing, forward- and backward-roll variations, and various skills performed on the balance beam.

There is more emphasis for this age-group on games and sports skills. Students leaving the sixth grade usually have a basic knowledge of several popular games and their rules. These generally include softball, soccer, volleyball, and basketball. Most students should be able to throw, hit, and field a softball; kick, pass, and dribble a soccer ball; shoot, pass, catch, and dribble a basketball; serve and volley a volleyball; and catch, pass, and kick a football.

At this age, students are not pressured to become star performers in a physical activity or in a particular sport. They are encouraged to participate in these activities and games for their own well-being and enjoyment and to develop skills and abilities they can use all of their lives. The physical education program in grades 4 through 6 tries to promote a positive self-image in each child. The program helps middle school children acquire appropriate social and emotional behaviors toward others.

CURRICULUM-RELATED ARTICLES

Some of the important articles in THE NEW BOOK OF KNOWLEDGE that relate to the 4 through 6 school curriculum are listed here. Many other articles you or your youngsters may want to read while they are studying topics in these curriculum areas can be found by looking them up in the Index or in the set itself.

READING, LANGUAGE, AND LITERATURE

Vol.	Reading and Language
A	Alphabet
E	English Language
G	Grammar
L	Language Arts
P	Parts of Speech Phonics
Q-R	Reading
S	Slang Synonyms and Antonyms
W-X- Y-Z	Word Games Word Origins

Vol.	Writing
A	Abbreviations Address, Forms of
C	Compositions
D	Diaries and Journals
F	Figures of Speech
H	Handwriting Homonyms
L	Letter Writing
O	Outlines
P	Proofreading Punctuation
S	Spelling
U-V	Vocabulary
W-X- Y-Z	Writing

Vol.	Oral Language/Speech
D	Debates and Discussions
J-K	Jokes and Riddles

Vol.	
P	Plays Pronunciation Public Speaking
S	Speech Speech Disorders Storytelling
T	Tongue Twisters

Vol.	Reference, Research, and Study Skills
B	Book Reports and Reviews Books: From Author to Reader
D	Dictionaries
E	Encyclopedias
I	Indexes and Indexing
L	Libraries
M	Magazines Maps and Globes
N	Newspapers
P	Paperback Books
Q-R	Reference Books Research
S	Study, How to
T	Time Management Tests and Test Taking Textbooks

Vol.	Literature
A	Africa, Literature of American Literature Arabian Nights Arthur, King
B	Ballads Biography, Autobiography, and Biographical Novel

C	Caldecott, Randolph
	Children's Book Awards
	Children's Literature
D	Diaries and Journals
	Drama
E	Essays
F	Fables
	Fairy Tales
	Fiction
	Figures of Speech
	Folklore
G	Greek Mythology
H	Humor
I	Illustration and Illustrators
	Iliad
J-K	Jokes and Riddles
L	Literature
	Legends
M	Mystery, Detective, and Suspense Stories
	Mythology
N	Newbery, John
	Nonsense Rhymes
	Norse Mythology
O	Odyssey
P	Poetry
Q-R	Robin Hood
S	Science Fiction
	Short Stories

H	Hawthorne, Nathaniel
	Hemingway, Ernest
	Henry, O.
	Homer
	Hughes, Langston
I	Irving, Washington
J-K	Kipling, Rudyard
L	London, Jack
	Longfellow, Henry Wadsworth
P	Poe, Edgar Allan
Q-R	Rossetti Family
S	Sandburg, Carl
	Sendak, Maurice
	Stevenson, Robert Louis
	Shakespeare, William
	Steinbeck, John
	Swift, Jonathan
T	Thurber, James
	Tolkien, J. R. R.
	Twain, Mark
V	Verne, Jules
W-X-Y-Z	White, E. B.
	Whittier, John Greenleaf
	Wilde, Oscar

Vol. **Author Biographies**

A	Alcott, Louisa May
	Andersen, Hans Christian
B	Barrie, Sir James Matthew
	Blume, Judy
	Browning, Elizabeth Barrett and Robert
	Burns, Robert
C	Carroll, Lewis
D	Dickens, Charles
	Dickinson, Emily
	Doyle, Sir Arthur Conan
	Dunbar, Paul Laurence
E	Eliot, T. S.
F	Frost, Robert
G	Grahame, Kenneth
	Grimm, Jacob and Wilhelm

Vol. **Selections from Literature**

A	Andersen, Hans Christian—The Emperor's New Clothes
	Arabian Nights
	Aladdin and the Wonderful Lamp (excerpt)
	The Forty Thieves (excerpt)
	Alcott, Louisa May—Little Women (excerpt)
B	Barrie, Sir James Matthew—Peter Pan (excerpt)
	Bible Stories
	Noah's Ark
	David and Goliath
	Jonah
	Daniel in the Lions' Den
	The Boy Jesus
	Browning, Robert—Pied Piper of Hamelin (excerpt)
	Burns, Robert—A Red, Red Rose
C	Carroll, Lewis—Alice's Adventures in Wonderland (excerpt)
	Christmas Story (Gospel according to Luke)

D Diaries and Journals
The Diary of Anne Frank (excerpt)
Dickinson, Emily
A Bird Came Down the Walk
I'll Tell You How the Sun Rose
Doyle, Sir Arthur Conan—The Red-Headed League (excerpt)
Dunbar, Paul Laurence
Promise
Fulfilment

F Fables
The Lion and the Mouse (Aesop)
The Ant and the Grasshopper (Aesop)
The Four Oxen and the Lion (Aesop)
The Tyrant Who Became a Just Ruler (Bidpai)
The Blind Men and the Elephant (Saxe)
The Moth and the Star (Thurber)
Fairy Tales
The Enchanted Princess (German)
The Princess on the Pea (Andersen)
The Sleeping Beauty (Perrault)
Little Red Riding-Hood (de la Mare)
Field, Eugene—A Dutch Lullaby
Figures of Speech
Silver (de la Mare)
The Toaster (Smith, W. J.)
Dandelions (Frost, F. M.)
The Little Rose Tree (Field, Rachel)
Everyone Sang (Sassoon)
The Night Will Never Stay (Farjeon)
Brooms (Aldis, D.)
No Shop Does the Bird Use (Coatsworth, E.)
Folklore
Cinderella or The Little Glass Slipper (Perrault)
John Henry (American)
Johnny Appleseed (American)
Pecos Bill (American)
Frost, Robert
The Last Word of a Bluebird
The Pasture
Stopping by Woods on a Snowy Evening
The Road Not Taken

G Gettysburg Address
Grimm, Jacob and Wilhelm
The Shoemaker and the Elves
Rapunzel
Hansel and Gretel
Grahame, Kenneth—The Wind in the Willows (excerpt)

H Hawthorne, Nathaniel—Tanglewood Tales (excerpt)

I Irving, Washington—Rip Van Winkle (excerpt)

L Legends
Roland and Oliver (France)
The Legend of the Blue Plate (China)
Legend of the White Deer (Native American)
London, Jack—The Call of the Wild (excerpt)
Longfellow, Henry Wadsworth—The Arrow and the Song

N Nonsense Rhymes
I Went to Noke (Nursery)
The Song of Milkanwatha (Strong)
OIC (Anonymous)
The Common Cormorant (Anonymous)
Jabberwocky (Carroll)
The Maiden of Passamaquoddy (DeMille)
The Reason for the Pelican (Ciardi)
The Yak (Belloc)
Habits of the Hippopotamus (Guiterman)
Eletelephony (Richards)
I Wish That My Room Had a Floor (Burgess)
Antigonish (Mearns)
The Walloping Window-blind (Carryll)
The Owl and the Pussy-Cat (Lear)
There Was an Old Man Who Supposed (Lear)
There Was a Young Lady of Woosester (Anonymous)
A Sleeper from the Amazon (Anonymous)

P Poe—Eldorado
Poetry
The Water Babies (excerpt, Kingsley)
Firefly (Roberts, E. M.)
The Circus (Roberts)

Q-R Revolutionary War
The Story of Johnny Tremain (excerpt, Forbes)
Rossetti—Who Has Seen the Wind

S Sandburg, Carl
Fog
The Skyscraper to the Moon and How the Green Rat with the Rheumatism Ran a Thousand Miles Twice (Rootabaga Stories)

Science Fiction
  Twenty Thousand Leagues Under the
    Sea (excerpt, Verne)
Stevenson, Robert Louis—Kidnapped
  (excerpt)
Swift, Jonathan—Gulliver's Travels
  (excerpt)
T Thurber, James—The Great Quillon
  (excerpt)
Tolkien, J. R. R.—The Hobbit
  (excerpt)
Twain, Mark
  The Adventures of Tom Sawyer
    (excerpt)
  The Celebrated Jumping Frog of
    Calaveras County (excerpt)
W-X- White, E. B.—Charlotte's Web
Y-Z (excerpt)

MATHEMATICS

Vol.	Article
A	Abacus
	Algebra
	Arithmetic
B	Budgets, Family
C	Calendar
	Computer Graphics
	Computer Programming
	Computers
D	Decimal System
E	Einstein, Albert
F	Fractions
G	Geometry and Geometric Forms
	Graphs
I	Interest
M	Mathematics
	Mathematics, History of
	Money
N	Newton, Isaac
	Number Patterns
	Number Puzzles and Games
	Numbers and Number Systems
	Numerals and Numeration
P	Percentage
Q-R	Roman Numerals
S	Sets
	Statistics
T	Time
	Topology
W-X- **Y-Z**	Weights and Measures

SOCIAL STUDIES

**Vol.   Early and Medieval History and
        Culture**

Prehistoric Cultures

F	Fire and Early People
I	Ice Ages
L	Leakey Family
P	Prehistoric Art
	Prehistoric People
S	Stonehenge
T	Tools

Ancient Civilizations

A	Alphabet
	Alexander the Great
	Ancient Civilizations
	Ancient World, Art of the
	Ancient World, Music of the
	Antony, Mark
	Apostles
	Archaeology
	Aristotle
	Attila
B	Bible
	Bible Stories
	Buddha and Buddhism
	Byzantine Art and Architecture
	Byzantine Empire
C	Caesar, Gaius Julius
	Christianity, History of
	Cicero, Marcus Tullius
	Cleopatra
	Confucius
	Constantine the Great
E	Egyptian Art and Architecture
G	Greece, Ancient
	Greece, Art and Architecture of
	Greece, Language and Literature of
	Greek Mythology
H	Hannibal
	Hinduism
	Homer
I	Iliad
J-K	Jesus Christ
	Jews
	Judaism
L	Latin Language and Literature

M	Moses
N	Nero
O	Odyssey
	Olympic Games
	Oriental Art and Architecture
P	Peloponnesian War
	Pericles
	Persia, Ancient
	Plato
	Punic Wars
Q-R	Rome
	Rome, Ancient
	Rome, Art and Architecture of
S	Socrates
T	Ten Commandments
	Trojan War
W-X-Y-Z	Wonders of the World

Middle Ages

A	Armor
B	Bacon, Roger
C	Castles
	Cathedrals
	Charlemagne
	Crusades
F	Feudalism
G	Gothic Art and Architecture
	Guilds
H	Heraldry
	Holy Roman Empire
	Hundred Years' War
I	Illuminated Manuscripts
	Islam
	Islamic Art and Architecture
J-K	Joan of Arc
J-K	Knights, Knighthood, and Chivalry
	Koran
M	Magna Carta
	Mecca
	Middle Ages
	Middle Ages, Music of the
	Mohammed
Q-R	Romanesque Art and Architecture
S	Stained-Glass Windows
W-X-Y-Z	William the Conqueror

(See also the history section of articles on England, France, Portugal, and Spain.)

Vol.	**United States History**

(Note: You will find additional listings for U.S. History on pages 69–72.)

Age of Discovery and Exploration

A	Aztecs
B	Balboa, Vasco Núñez De
C	Cabot, John
	Cartier, Jacques
	Champlain, Samuel De
	Columbus, Christopher
	Coronado, Francisco
	Cortes, Hernando
D	Drake, Sir Francis
E	Eric the Red
	Ericson, Leif
	Exploration and Discovery
F	Ferdinand and Isabella
G	Gama, Vasco Da
H	Herbs, Spices, and Condiments
	Hudson, Henry
I	Incas
	Indians, American
J-K	Jolliet, Louis, and Jacques Marquette
L	La Salle, Robert Cavelier, Sieur de
M	Magellan, Ferdinand
	Maya
N	Navigation
	Northwest Passage
P	Pizarro, Francisco
	Ponce De León
U-V	Verrazano, Giovanni Da
	Vespucci, Amerigo
	Vikings

Colonial and Revolutionary Periods

A	Adams, John
	Adams, Samuel
	African Americans
	Allen, Ethan
	Arnold, Benedict
B	Bill of Rights
	Boone, Daniel
	Brant, Joseph
C	Colonial Life in America
	Colonial Sites You Can Visit Today
D	Declaration of Independence

F	Federalist, The Founders of the United States Franklin, Benjamin French and Indian War	**C**	Carson, Kit Carver, George Washington Child Labor Civil War, United States Clay, Henry Compromise of 1850 Confederate States of America Cowboys Crockett, David (Davy)
H	Hale, Nathan Hamilton, Alexander Hancock, John Henry, Patrick	**D**	Davis, Jefferson Dix, Dorothea Douglass, Frederick Dred Scott Decision DuBois, W. E. B.
I	Independence Hall		
J-K	Jamestown Jay, John Jefferson, Thomas Jones, John Paul	**E**	Emancipation Proclamation Erie Canal Ethnic Groups
L	Lafayette, Marquis De Lewis and Clark Expedition Liberty Bell Louisiana Purchase	**F**	Farragut, David Frémont, John Charles Fulton, Robert Fur Trade in North America
M	Madison, James	**G**	Gettysburg Address Gold, Discoveries of Grant, Ulysses S.
O	Oglethorpe, James Overland Trails	**H**	Houston, Samuel
P	Paine, Thomas Penn, William Perry, Oliver Hazard Plymouth Colony	**I**	Immigration Indians, American Industrial Revolution
Q-R	Quakers	**J-K**	Jackson, Andrew Jackson, Thomas Jonathon ("Stonewall")
Q-R	Raleigh, Sir Walter Revere, Paul Revolutionary War	**J-K**	Kansas-Nebraska Act
S	Smith, John Stuyvesant, Peter	**L**	Labor Movement Lee, Robert E. Liberty, Statue of Lincoln, Abraham
T	Tecumseh Thirteen American Colonies	**M**	Mexican War Monroe Doctrine Monroe, James Mormons
U-V	United States, Constitution of the		
W-X- **Y-Z**	War of 1812 Washington, George Westward Movement Williams, Roger	**P**	Pioneer Life Pony Express
		Q-R	Ranch Life Reconstruction Period
	Civil War and an Expanding America	**S**	Sherman, William Tecumseh Slavery Stowe, Harriet Beecher
A	Abolition Movement Addams, Jane African Americans Anthony, Susan B.	**T**	Territorial Expansion of the United States Tubman, Harriet
B	Barton, Clara Boone, Daniel Booth, John Wilkes Bowie, James Brown, John	**U-V**	Underground Railroad

W-X-	Washington, Booker T.		**I**	Idaho
Y-Z	Whitney, Eli			Illinois
	Women's Rights Movement			Indiana
W-X-	Young, Brigham			Iowa
Y-Z			**J-K**	Kansas
				Kentucky
			L	Louisiana
The Twentieth Century			**M**	Maine
B	Bush, George			Maryland
C	Civil Rights			Massachusetts
	Clinton, William			Michigan
	Communism			Minnesota
D	Depressions and Recessions			Mississippi
	Disarmament			Missouri
				Montana
F	Fascism		**N**	Nebraska
H	Holocaust			Nevada
J-K	Kennedy, John F.			New Hampshire
	King, Martin Luther			New Jersey
	Korean War			New Mexico
L	League of Nations			New York
M	Malcom X			North Carolina
N	Nazism			North Dakota
	Nixon, Richard M.		**O**	Ohio
P	Panama Canal			Oklahoma
Q-R	Racism			Oregon
	Reagan, Ronald W.		**P**	Pennsylvania
S	Spanish-American War		**Q-R**	Rhode Island
T	Terrorism		**S**	South Carolina
U-V	United Nations			South Dakota
U-V	Vietnam War		**T**	Tennessee
W-X-	Women's Rights Movement			Texas
Y-Z	World War I		**U-V**	Utah
	World War II		**U-V**	Vermont
				Virginia
			W-X-	Washington
Vol.	**The Fifty States of the United States**		**Y-Z**	West Virginia
A	Alabama			Wisconsin
	Alaska			Wyoming
	Arizona			
	Arkansas			
C	California		**Vol.**	**Government**
	Colorado		**B**	Bill of Rights
	Connecticut		**C**	Cabinet of the United States
D	Delaware			Capitol, United States
F	Florida			Citizenship
G	Georgia			Civil Rights
H	Hawaii		**D**	Declaration of Independence
				Democracy
			E	Elections

F	First Ladies
	Freedom of Religion, Speech, and Press
G	Government, Forms of
	Greece, Ancient
L	Law and Law Enforcement
	Locke, John
M	Magna Carta
	Municipal Government
N	Naturalization
P	Presidency of the United States
Q-R	Rome, Ancient
S	State Governments
	Supreme Court of the United States
U-V	United Nations
	United States, Congress of
	United States, Constitution of the
	United States, Government of the
W-X-Y-Z	Washington, D.C.
	White House
	(See also names of presidents and individual departments of the United States government.)

Vol.   Geography

A	Atlantic Ocean
B	Biomes
C	Cities
	Climate
	Continents
D	Deserts
E	Earth
	Earthquakes
	Equator
	Erosion
F	Forests and Forestry
G	Geography
	Glaciers
	Greenwich Observatory
I	Indian Ocean
	International Date Line
	Islands
L	Lakes
	Latitude and Longitude
M	Maps and Globes
	Mountains
N	Natural Resources

O	Ocean
	Oceans and Seas of the World
P	Pacific Ocean and Islands
	Population
	Prairies
Q-R	Rain Forest
	Rivers
S	Seasons
T	Tides
	Time
	Tropics
U-V	Volcanoes
W-X-Y-Z	Weather
	Wetlands
	World
W-X-Y-Z	Zones

Vol.   World Regions and Cultures

United States and Canada

A	American Literature
C	Canada
	Canadian History
	Canadian Government
G	Great Lakes
M	Mississippi River
	Missouri River
N	North America
Q-R	Rocky Mountains
S	Saint Lawrence River and Seaway
U-V	United States, Art and Architecture of the
	United States, Government of the
	United States, History of the
	United States, Music of the
	(See also articles on individual states and Canadian provinces, and major cities.)

Latin America and the Caribbean

A	Amazon River
	Andes
C	Caribbean Sea and Islands
	Central America

L	Latin America
	Latin America, Art and Architecture of
	Latin America, Literature of
	Latin America, Music of
P	Panama Canal
S	South America
	(See also articles on individual countries.)

Europe and the Commonwealth of Independent States

A	Alps
B	Balkans
C	Commonwealth of Independent States
	Commonwealth of Nations
E	English Art and Architecture
	English Language
	English Literature
	English Music
	Europe
	European Community
F	France, Art and Architecture of
	France, Language of
	France, Literature of
	France, Music of
G	Germany, Art and Architecture of
	Germany, Language of
	Germany, Literature of
	Germany, Music of
	Greece, Art and Architecture of
	Greece, Language and Literature of
I	Ireland, Literature of
	Italy, Art and Architecture of
	Italy, Language and Literature of
	Italy, Music of
M	Mediterranean Sea
Q-R	Russia
	Russia, Art and Architecture of
	Russia, Language and Literature of
	Russia, Music of
S	Scandinavia
	Scandinavian Literature
	Spain, Art and Architecture of
	Spain, Language and Literature of
	Spain, Music of
U-V	Union of Soviet Socialist Republics
	United Kingdom
	(See also articles on individual countries.)

Middle East and Africa

| **A** | Africa |
| | Africa, Art and Architecture of |

	Africa, Literature of
	Africa, Music of
	Arabs
C	Congo River
E	Egyptian Art and Architecture
I	Islam
J-K	Jews
	Judaism
M	Middle East
N	Nile River
P	Palestine
S	Sahara
	Suez Canal
	(See also articles on individual countries.)

Asia

A	Asia
B	Buddha and Buddhism
C	Chinese Art
	Chinese Literature
E	Everest, Mount
G	Ganges River
H	Himalayas
	Hinduism
I	India, Art and Architecture of
	India, Literature of
	India, Music of
J-K	Japanese Art and Architecture
	Japanese Literature
O	Oriental Art and Architecture
	Oriental Music
S	Siberia
W-X-	Yangtze River
Y-Z	(See also articles on individual countries.)

Southeast Asia and the Pacific

A	Aborigines, Australian
	Australia
N	New Zealand
P	Pacific Ocean and Islands
S	Southeast Asia

SCIENCE

Vol.	Life Science
A	Algae
	Amphibians
	Animals
	Apes
	Arachnids
	Audubon, John James
B	Bacteria
	Biomes
	Birds
	Body, Human
	Burbank, Luther
C	Carson, Rachel
	Carver, George Washington
	Cells
	Crustaceans
D	Darwin, Charles Robert
	Dinosaurs
E	Earthworms
	Ecology
	Endangered Species
	Evolution
	Experiments and Other Science Activities
F	Ferns
	Fish
	Flowers and Seeds
	Fossey, Dian
	Frogs and Toads
G	Goodall, Jane
H	Hibernation
I	Insects
J-K	Jellyfishes and Other Coelenterates
L	Leeuwenhoek, Anton Van
	Life
M	Mammals
	Metamorphosis
	Monkeys and Their Relatives
	Mosses
	Muir, John
	Mushrooms
N	Nature, Study of
O	Oysters, Octopuses, and Other Mollusks
P	Photosynthesis
	Plants
	Prehistoric Animals
	Protozoans
Q-R	Reptiles
S	Shells
	Spiders
	Starfishes and Their Relatives
T	Trees

Vol.	
W-X-	Weeds
Y-Z	Wild Flowers
	Worms

Vol.	Physical and Chemical Science
A	Archimedes
	Atoms
C	Carbon
	Color
	Curie, Marie and Pierre
E	Edison, Thomas Alva
	Electric Lights
	Electricity
	Energy
	Experiments and Other Science Activities
F	Faraday, Michael
	Fire and Combustion
	Fission
	Floating
G	Galileo
	Gases
	Gravity and Gravitation
H	Heat
	Hydrogen
L	Lenses
	Light
	Liquids
M	Magnets and Magnetism
	Matter
	Motion
N	Newton, Isaac
	Noise
	Nuclear Energy
O	Oxygen and Oxidation
S	Solids
	Sound and Ultrasonics
T	Thermometers and Thermostats
	Thompson, Benjamin
W-X-	Weights and Measures
Y-Z	Wheels
	Work, Power, and Machines

Vol.	Technology
A	Airplanes
	Automobiles
	Aviation

B	Bell, Alexander Graham
	Bridges
	Building Construction
C	Communication
D	Daguerre, Louis
E	Earhart, Amelia
	Earth-Moving Machinery
	Eastman, George
F	Fulton, Robert
G	Gyroscope
H	Helicopters
	Howe, Elias
I	Inventions
J-K	Jet Propulsion
L	Locomotives
M	Medicine, Tools and Techniques of
	Microscopes
	Morse, Samuel F. B.
N	Navigation
P	Photography
Q-R	Radar, Sonar, Loran, and Shoran
	Radio
	Roads and Highways
	Robots
	Rockets
S	Ships and Shipping
	Space Exploration and Travel
	Space Probes
	Space Research and Technology
	Space Satellites and Shuttles
	Space Telescopes
	Submarines
T	Telecommunications
	Telegraph
	Telephone
	Telescopes
	Tools
	Transportation
	Trucks and Trucking
	Tunnels
W-X-Y-Z	Watt, James
	Wheels
	Whitney, Eli
	Wright, Wilbur and Orville

HEALTH AND SAFETY

Vol.	Article
A	AIDS
	Alcoholism
	Antibiotics
B	Baby
	Barnard, Christiaan
	Blindness
	Blood
	Body, Human
	Brain
C	Cancer
	Circulatory System
	Consumerism
D	Deafness
	Digestive System
	Diseases
	Doctors
	Drew, Charles Richard
	Drug Abuse
	Drugs
E	Ear
	Eggs and Embryos
	Eye
F	First Aid
	Fleming, Sir Alexander
	Food Preservation and Processing
	Food Regulations and Laws
	Food Shopping
	Food Spoilage and Contamination
G	Genealogy
	Glands
H	Hair and Hairstyling
	Health
	Heart
	Hospitals
I	Immune System
J-K	Jenner, Edward
M	Mental Health
	Muscular System
N	Nurses and Nursing
	Nutrition
P	Pasteur, Louis
	Physical Fitness
	Poisons and Antidotes
Q-R	Reproduction
S	Safety
	Skeletal System
	Sleep
	Smoking
T	Teeth
U-V	Vaccination and Immunization
	Vitamins and Minerals

MUSIC

Vol.	Music and Musical Instruments
B	Ballads Ballet Bands and Band Music Bells and Carillons
C	Carols Choral Music Clarinet Country Music
D	Dance Dance Music Drum
G	Guitar
H	Harmonica Hymns
J-K	Jazz
J-K	Keyboard Instruments
L	Lullabies
M	Music Musical Comedy Musical Instruments
N	National Anthems and Patriotic Songs
O	Opera Operetta Orchestra Orchestra Conducting
P	Percussion Instruments Piano
Q-R	Recorder Records and Record Collecting Rock Music
S	Stringed Instruments
U-V	Violin Voice Training and Singing
W-X-Y-Z	Wind Instruments

Vol.	Music History and Biographies
A	Ancient World, Music of the Anderson, Marian
B	Bach, Johann Sebastian Beethoven, Ludwig Van
C	Chopin, Frederic Classical Age in Music Copland, Aaron
D	Debussy, Claude
F	Foster, Stephen
G	Gershwin, George Gilbert and Sullivan Operettas Grieg, Edvard
H	Handel, George Frederick
M	Mendelssohn, Felix Middle Ages, Music of the Mozart, Wolfgang Amadeus
O	Offenbach, Jacques
P	Prokofiev, Sergei
Q-R	Renaissance Music
S	Schubert, Franz Strauss, Johann, Jr.
T	Tchaikovsky, Peter Ilyich
U-V	Verdi, Giuseppe

Vol.	Music Around the World
A	Africa, Music of
E	English Music
F	Folk Dancing Folk Music
L	Latin America, Music of
O	Oriental Music
U-V	United States, Music of the

ART

Vol.	Art
A	Architecture Art
C	Cathedrals Color
D	Design Drawing
I	Illuminated Manuscripts Illustration and Illustrators
L	Louvre
M	Metropolitan Museum of Art Museums
N	National Gallery (London) National Gallery of Art (Washington, D.C.) National Gallery of Canada
O	Obelisks

P	Painting
	Photography
	Prado
S	Sculpture
U-V	Uffizi Gallery
W-X-	Watercolor
Y-Z	

Vol.	**Art History and Biographies**
A	Ancient World, Art of the
B	Benton, Thomas Hart
	Botticelli, Sandro
	Bruegel, Pieter, the Elder
C	Cassatt, Mary
	Cezanne, Paul
	Chagall, Marc
D	Dali, Salvador
	Degas, Edgar
	Drawing, History of
	Dürer, Albrecht
E	Egyptian Art and Architecture
F	Folk Art
G	Gainsborough, Thomas
	Gothic Art and Architecture
	Greece, Art and Architecture of
H	Homer, Winslow
J-K	Klee, Paul
L	Leonardo da Vinci
M	Michelangelo
	Miro, Joan
	Moses, Grandma
O	O'Keeffe, Georgia
	Oriental Art and Architecture
P	Peale Family
	Picasso, Pablo
	Prehistoric Art
Q-R	Raphael
	Rembrandt
	Renaissance Art and Architecture
	Renoir, Pierre Auguste
	Reynolds, Sir Joshua
	Rockwell, Norman
	Roman Art and Architecture
	Romanesque Art and Architecture
U-V	Van Gogh, Vincent
	Vermeer, Jan
W-X-	Whistler, James Abbott McNeill
Y-Z	Wood, Grant
	Wyeth Family

Vol.	**Art Around the World**
A	Africa, Art and Architecture of
C	Canadian Art and Architecture
	Chinese Art
D	Dutch and Flemish Art
E	English Art and Architecture
F	France, Art and Architecture of
G	Germany, Art and Architecture of
I	India, Art and Architecture of
	Islamic Art and Architecture
	Italy, Art and Architecture of
J-K	Japanese Art and Architecture
L	Latin America, Art and Architecture of
Q-R	Russia, Art and Architecture of
S	Spain, Art and Architecture of
U-V	United States, Art and Architecture of

Vol.	**Decorative Arts and Crafts**
C	Ceramics
	Clay Modeling
	Collage
D	Decorative Arts
	Decoupage
F	Finger Painting
L	Linoleum-Block Printing
M	Macramé
	Mosaic
N	Needlecraft
O	Origami
P	Papier-mâché
	Posters
	Pottery
	Puppets and Marionettes
Q-R	Rubbings
S	Silk-Screen Printing
	Stained-Glass Windows
T	Tapestry
W-X-	Weaving
Y-Z	Wood Carving
	Woodcut Printing

PHYSICAL EDUCATION AND SPORTS

Vol.	**Article**
A	Archery

B	Badminton	**L**	Lacrosse
	Ball		Little League Baseball
	Baseball	**O**	Olympic Games
	Basketball		Owens, Jesse
	Bicycling	**P**	Paddle Tennis
	Bodybuilding		Pelé
	Bowling		Physical Education
	Boxing		Physical Fitness
C	Canoeing	**Q-R**	Racing
	Cheerleading		Racket Sports
	Croquet		Robinson, Jack Roosevelt (Jackie)
D	Darts		Roller-Skating
	Diving		Rugby
F	Field Hockey		Ruth, George Herman (Babe)
	Fishing	**S**	Sailing
	Football		Shuffleboard
G	Gibson, Althea		Skateboarding
	Gymnastics		Skiing
H	Handball		Skin Diving
	Hiking and Backpacking		Soap Box Derby
	Horseback Riding		Soccer and Youth Soccer
	Horseshoe Pitching		Softball
	Hunting		Swimming
I	Ice Hockey	**T**	Table Tennis
	Ice-Skating		Tennis
J-K	Jogging and Running		Thorpe, James Francis (Jim)
	Judo		Track and Field
	Juggling	**U-V**	Volleyball
J-K	Karate	**W-X-**	Water Polo
	Karting	**Y-Z**	Waterskiing
			Wrestling

GRADES 7 THROUGH 9

▶ THE YOUNG ADOLESCENT

There are moments when the parents of an early teen feel that, without warning, their child has become a stranger. The son or daughter they have known since birth suddenly looks very different and behaves in unaccustomed ways. Their youngster is caring and responsible one minute and sullen and uncooperative the next. These changes are all part of the normal pattern of transition and turmoil that characterize the young adolescent.

It is a time of considerable and often abrupt physical, emotional, social, and intellectual growth and development. No longer a child but not yet an adult, the teenager may exhibit the behavior and characteristics of both. It is a stage that is often as difficult for parents and teachers as it is for the teenager.

The young adolescent's problems usually start with bodily changes. They make rapid gains in height and weight. Their arms and legs, hands and feet, seem to outgrow the rest of their body, frequently resulting in clumsy, uncoordinated actions. There are wide variations in the size and maturity of individuals of the same age or grade level, and girls often become heavier and taller and mature earlier than boys their age. Along with rapid growth may come new problems with skin conditions or body odor. Sexual development and the onset of puberty are embarrassing for some, mystifying or exciting for others.

Many youngsters accept these startling changes gracefully. Others are made anxious and worry excessively about their health and their bodies. They may translate their worries into aggressive or withdrawn behavior and may experience many mood swings. Adults can help young adolescents accept their new growth by helping them understand that what is happening to them is a perfectly natural part of growing up.

Physical and hormonal changes have an impact on the emotional and social behaviors of early teens. Strong, often conflicting, needs dominate their personalities. They are redefining their relationships with adults and are frequently inconsistent in their need for independence from adult authority and their desire for guidance and regulation. They want respect and they want to be treated fairly and reasonably. They need to be able to place their trust in adult family members and teachers.

The need to conform to the code of their peers is all-important to the young adolescent. Because they are very afraid of being ridiculed, their friends' values and beliefs about right and wrong behavior, religion, drugs, sexuality, and education may conflict or seem to take precedence over the values of their family. Many inner-city youngsters face the additional pressures caused by youth gangs. Finding a place in a group takes on urgent importance at this stage, and adults should help channel this urge by helping their teenagers find appropriate clubs and other organizations to join.

Young teens are in the process of learning how to form friendships with members of their own sex and how to behave with persons of the opposite sex. At the same time they are struggling to develop a unique personal identity, and they may experiment with many roles before they find the personality that is their own. Craving success and recognition, they look to parents and teachers for guidance, understanding, and acceptance.

Along with their changing bodies, feelings, and social behaviors, early adolescents are developing intellectual sophistication. They are capable of abstract reasoning and reflective thinking. They are fascinated by concepts such as justice, democracy, friendship, and the obligations of freedom. A natural curiosity motivates their learning, and they are always ready to question and challenge the ideas and actions of others. Topics related to their own personal concerns and goals are more apt to arouse their enthusiasm and active involvement as learners.

Most students in grades 7 and 8 attend a middle school or junior high school. Ninth graders may already be in a senior high school. Most young teens will experience a more structured, departmentalized school program and will have to deal with many more teachers than they did in their earlier school years. Their school day usually consists of six periods, and each subject is given paramount importance by the instructor who teaches it.

All students study English, mathematics, social studies, and science each year in grades 7 through 9. Many begin a foreign language, usually French or Spanish. Depending on the school's facilities, physical education may be offered each year as well. In addition, students generally take at least one course in music, art, health, and home economics or industrial arts (technology education in some schools).

There is homework assigned for most subjects, and the work requires substantial time and effort on the part of the student. Tests and grades are taken very seriously and school can become yet another anxiety-producing factor in the young adolescent's life. On the other hand, many of the young person's social activities center on the school's extracurricular groups, clubs, and teams, and the school can serve as a conduit for social and emotional development as well as for intellectual growth.

For most teenagers the years of young adolescence are as scary, thrilling, and invigorating as a rollercoaster ride. Parents of young teens experience their own highs and lows, too. You can help make it a smoother ride by listening carefully to your teenagers. Pay close attention to what they tell you verbally and by their actions. Try to be patient and understanding. Let them know you are ready to take their concerns seriously, and try to help them find satisfactory solutions to their problems. They may not always admit it, but young adolescents need caring, supportive parents and adults more than ever to guide them on their quest for adulthood.

▶SUCCESS IN SCHOOL

Young adolescents are very busy people. They spend most of their weekdays going to school, participating in after-school activities, doing homework, visiting with friends, and doing things on their own. For some teenagers the only interaction with family members takes place around the table at mealtimes. Even on weekends, young teens often want to follow their own recreational agendas and can be drawn into family activities only with reluctance. Parents and teens can lose touch at this turning point in young people's lives.

Concerned parents and care givers need to penetrate these barriers and continue to provide the support, direction, and encouragement that will help their youngsters achieve success in middle school or junior high school. The teenager who drops out of high school is often the youngster who falls behind scholastically in grades 7 through 9. It is also a fact that youngsters who do not perform to their full potential in these important years will not be sufficiently prepared to tackle the high school courses that make entry into a college or a job after graduation easier.

Parents can continue to exercise influence on their teenager's school performance in a number of direct, and sometimes subtle, ways:

- With the exception of real illness, make sure your teenagers attend classes every day. If it is absolutely necessary for them to be absent, make sure the schoolwork for all subjects is made up. If the absence has been longer than one or two days, talk to teachers yourself to get their help in making up what was missed in lectures or classroom activities.
- Most young teens lack organization skills and have difficulty setting up a homework or study plan. Refer to page 3 of this STUDY GUIDE for helpful homework suggestions. Make sure each student has a quiet, relatively private spot for study.
- Keep a regular household routine that accommodates the needs and schedules of all family members. There should be definite times set for meals, study periods, household chores, and family recreation.
- Set aside time each day for a one-on-one conversation with your teenagers. If your youngsters are reluctant to talk about school, try asking questions that require more than a simple "yes" or "no" answer. "What's your favorite subject this semester?" "What do you like about it?" "Why do you think you did so well (or so poorly) on that last test?" "How can you do even better next time?" Talk about out-of-school interests and activities, too. Listen objectively. Try to be helpful and reassuring rather than judgmental.
- Create a home atmosphere that encourages learning. Books and newspapers should be visible—library books are fine. Try to have a good dictionary, thesaurus, and other reference books on hand—inexpensive paperbacks or second-hand books will do the job. Let young people see adults reading for pleasure as well as for information. Make a habit of watching some educa-

tional documentaries and cultural programs on television. Try to talk about current events and local issues with your teenagers.

- Include books as gifts on birthdays and holidays. Find out who the teenager's favorite authors are and what type of books are preferred. Historical? Mystery? Fantasy? Sports? Realistic? Good nonfiction books can start new interests and can support learning taking place in the classroom.

- Continue to do things as a family group. Play games together. Have a picnic. Go to athletic events, concerts, museums, plays, or art shows. In many communities there are many free cultural and sporting events. High school and local college performances and sports events can be particularly enjoyable because you will probably know some of the players or performers in them.

- Try to carry on the family reading-aloud activities that were part of your teenager's everyday life during his or her preschool and elementary school years. You probably will not get a young teen to sit still for this on a regular basis. When you have come across an especially good book, or magazine or newspaper article, however, capture a few minutes to read a particularly interesting passage and you may hook the youngster into wanting to read it, too.

- Many middle schools and junior high schools use a tracking system in which students are assigned to classes and subjects on the basis of test scores and past performance. If any of your youngsters are in a low-track group, speak with teachers, the guidance counselor, and the principal to find ways of helping them to do well and, if

it seems possible, improve enough to be moved into a higher track.

- If your teenagers have problems in school, try to pinpoint specific reasons and work with your youngsters and school personnel to create an action plan that will lead to a successful turnaround.

Above all, know your youngsters, keep informed about the expectations and requirements of their school and teachers, and provide the guidance and support they need.

The lists of articles at the very end of this section for grades 7 through 9 include many, but certainly not all, of the articles about each subject area that appear in THE NEW BOOK OF KNOWLEDGE. It is important that students look up the names of topics they want to read about in the Index or in the set itself to locate all of the information they may need or want. For example, in the Social Studies area, articles about each of the countries of the world are not listed in this section but can easily be located by looking each one up under its own name.

▶ LANGUAGE AND LITERATURE

The emphasis of the English curriculum for grades 7 through 9 is on reading, understanding, and appreciating literature; writing in a grammatical, well-organized, and coherent manner; and speaking effectively in a variety of situations. Unless a youngster exhibits major deficiencies in reading, most students in middle school or junior high school do not have a period in which reading skills are taught. Students will take several semesters of literature and grammar and composition courses and sometimes a course in speech or communication.

Literature courses are usually organized so that students learn the distinguishing characteristics of short stories, novels, poetry, drama, and nonfiction. Students are exposed to a broad spectrum of classic and contemporary works by well-known American authors and by writers from other countries and cultures. Students learn how to analyze literary works and to become knowledgeable about the elements writers use to communicate their ideas and feelings: plot, character, setting, theme, mood, tone, language, symbolism, and imagery. Students are asked to think, write, and talk about their reading. By learning how to communicate their interpretations and evaluations, young people also learn how to read with greater insight and deeper understanding.

In their grammar and composition course, students learn how to apply the writing process to four main types of composition: narration, description, exposition, and persuasion. They study the intricacies of grammar, mechanics, and usage and learn how to construct coherent and effective sentences, paragraphs, and themes. In their compositions students are expected to demonstrate clear and logical thinking in the support and development of a central idea. Writing assignments are often assigned for homework and may include writing a character sketch, explaining a process, writing an essay to answer a question, or writing a poem, an editorial, or an autobiography. By ninth grade most youngsters have also learned how to do a research report.

Vocabulary study is an important component of both the literature and the grammar and composition course. Youngsters encounter many new and exciting words as they read, and they are encouraged to use the dictionary and word analysis techniques to learn the meanings of words not made clear by the text. Reviewing what they know or need to learn about affixes, common roots, synonyms, antonyms, and analogies also helps them determine word meanings.

The speech course promotes self-confidence in oral communication and involves students in public speaking, group discussion, debate, and dramatic reading activities. The importance of responding courteously and appropriately to a presenter is also stressed.

▶ MATHEMATICS

There is variation from school to school in the types of math courses offered in grades 7 through 9. Not all students in the same grade in a particular school will take the same courses. Students with more background and ability will usually take more advanced courses than the average or weaker student. For some youngsters, middle school or junior high mathematics will consist primarily of the review, extension, and application of familiar math skills and concepts. For others, the math curriculum will consist of preparation for the more rigorous courses in algebra, geometry, and trigonometry of high school.

All students will be offered at least one course in which previously taught skills—those involving numbers, measurement, geometry, patterns and functions, statistics, probability, and logical reasoning—are strengthened and taught in greater depth. Some youngsters will take a pre-algebra class. Some will take a transition course that combines applied mathematics with pre-algebra and pre-geometry topics and concepts. Others will undertake a course made up of a combination of consumer and business applications for a variety of real-life topics and situations: earning and spending money, budgeting, banking, taxes, insurance, housing, and transportation. The more able eighth graders will be offered an algebra course.

The college-bound ninth grade student studies high school level algebra or occasionally formal geometry. Algebra is also an option for non-college-bound students, or they may study general mathematics or business math.

For a large number of young people, the ninth grade course is the culmination of their experience with school mathematics, and they may never proceed beyond this level. These students should be given special encouragement to make the most of their math studies during the junior high school years.

▶ SOCIAL STUDIES

American and world history and geography constitute the core of the social studies curriculum for grades 7 through 9. There are wide variations, however, in the specific courses offered at each of the grade levels by different school districts.

The study of American history may be a one-year or two-year course. It usually consists of a chronological presentation of political, cultural, social, economic, and geographic influences on the development of the United States as a nation, spanning the years from pre-colonial times to the present. More time and emphasis are assigned to the post-Civil War and contemporary eras than in earlier grades. As they survey and study important events and assess the contributions of key figures, students also learn about many of the major ideas and movements that influenced our country's past and present history. These will include abstract concepts such as democracy, freedom, responsibility, equality, and parity, as well as specific movements and processes such as the evolution of political and social institutions, slavery, immigration, the rise of industry, the impact of technology, the spread of cities and urban areas, and the role of women and diverse racial and ethnic groups.

The vast scope of world history and geography is presented in a number of different courses in different schools. These courses vary widely in their structure and emphasis. Some students study the history of Europe, Asia, Africa, and the Americas chronologically from ancient civilizations to early modern times. Other students will make in-depth investigations into selected world regions or world cultures. Still others will focus on key historical and contemporary trends, problems, and issues in a Global Studies course.

Along with their studies of America and the world, many youngsters have the opportunity to take separate courses in state history, civics, economics, or geography.

As they gather information on social studies topics, middle school and junior high school students are urged to use original primary and secondary sources; to apply critical and creative thinking to the analysis and evaluation of research data and its source; and to synthesize this information in order to make rational decisions about local, national, and international problems and issues.

▶ SCIENCE AND TECHNOLOGY

When they enter the seventh grade, most students have their first experience with science courses taught according to specific disciplines. In grades 7 through 9 science is offered in a three-year sequence by discipline: life science, physical science, and earth science, not necessarily in that order. All three courses incorporate information about technology, emphasizing its applications and its impact on society.

The life science course provides a survey of the five kingdoms into which living things are classified, according to their characteristics and relationships: the Monera (bacteria); the Protista (single-celled organisms); Fungi; Plants; and Animals. Students also conduct in-depth investigations into the structure and function of cells; genetics and the role of DNA; the evolutionary process; the structure and functions of the organ systems of humans and other animals; and the major ecosystems of the world. In many classrooms students use a microscope and do simple dissections for the first time.

In the physical science course, many topics introduced in earlier grades are extended. These include motion, forces, energy in all its forms, the properties of matter, atomic structure, and the periodic table. Students are usually ready at this age to begin new studies into the principles of chemistry. They learn about compounds, mixtures, chemical bonding, chemical interactions and reactions, and acids, bases, and salts. Demonstrations and experiments help them understand the more complex concepts of basic physics and chemistry.

Most ninth graders are offered the earth science course or a high school biology course. In earth science classes, students delve into the geology of the earth, its history, and the forces that shape it, emphasizing the role of plate tectonics. They also study the oceans of the earth, the earth's atmosphere, meteorology, and astronomy. The biology course covers the traditional life-science topics mentioned above, but with heavier concentration on the cell, microbiology, genetics, evolution, reproduction, and body chemistry.

Some ninth graders complete their science education with a general science course.

At present there is a need for people to understand the growing number of important problems in our society that require scientific and technological solutions and an equally important need for more young people to embark on science-based careers. For these reasons educators are urging students to continue their science studies through high school, and many states are mandating additional science courses as requirements for graduation. It is also important for youngsters in the middle school or junior high

school to be better prepared for the more rigorous requirements of high school science.

▶ HEALTH EDUCATION

The study of health is especially important for the young adolescent who is experiencing physical, emotional, social, and intellectual changes. The comprehensive health program for grades 7 through 9 usually provides information about ten major health topics: human body systems; prevention and control of disease; substance use and abuse; nutrition; mental and emotional health; accident prevention, safety, and first aid; family life; physical fitness and personal care; consumer health; and community and environmental health and health care resources. It is important for students to take this opportunity to use the knowledge presented in the course they take to learn how to make healthy choices in their daily lives and to adopt positive behaviors and attitudes that will last a lifetime.

Important subtopics of particular interest to the young teen usually include: grooming and skin care; fitness programs; stress management; eating disorders and weight control; alcohol and drugs; the human life cycle; human reproduction; safe and effective cosmetic and health care products; emergency care; and sexually transmitted diseases. Understanding how to cope with these concerns helps adolescent youngsters become more comfortable with the changes they are experiencing in their own lives. It also gives them confidence in their ability to deal with the day-to-day problems and situations that may affect their well-being.

▶ FOREIGN LANGUAGE

Most elementary schools do not provide instruction in a foreign language. Many youngsters have their first contact with another language in the seventh, eighth, or ninth grades. French and Spanish are the languages most frequently offered and students are usually given their choice between the two. Ninth graders often have more of a selection from which to choose. Depending upon the composition and interests of the local community, students may have the opportunity to learn German, Italian, or Latin as well as French or Spanish.

Foreign language courses for grades 7 through 9 usually employ a cultural and conversational approach. Students learn to listen, speak, read, and write the language. Emphasis is on modeling the dialogue of everyday situations—visiting friends, going to school, shopping, attending sports and cultural events, or taking a bus or train ride. These dialogue situations are used as a basis for learning about the culture, geography, customs, and traditions of the country or the countries in which the language predominates.

Although students learn the basic elements of the grammar of the language, more structured grammar study is reserved for high school.

▶ MUSIC

In grades 7 through 9 music is usually taught by a music specialist, and students have many opportunities to participate in a variety of musical experiences and activities.

A one-semester or one-year course in music appreciation is generally offered to all students as an elective. Youngsters are introduced to the major periods and developments in classical and popular music history and to the biographies of major composers and performers. They study musical elements such as rhythm, melody, harmony, and counterpoint and learn to recognize a variety of musical forms, including the symphony, sonata, opera, and operetta. These topics are coordinated with experiences in listening to recorded or live performances.

Some youngsters may participate in school choral or dance groups or may play an instrument in the school band or in the orchestra.

All young adolescents enjoy listening to music. Many take private voice, instrument, or dance lessons; some even begin to form their own musical groups outside of school. Certain youngsters exhibit exceptional talent in music at this age, and they should be challenged to develop it to their full potential. All students, regardless of their musical ability, should be encouraged to develop a thoughtful response to music and to continue to participate in musical activities.

▶ ART

Art instruction in grades 7 through 9 provides young teenagers with a variety of art experiences in a one-semester or one-year art course often offered as an elective.

Students experiment with an assortment of art media, tools, processes, and techniques. They may delve into poster making, lettering, painting, drawing and illustration, clay modeling, costume design, advertising design, and interior and stage decoration. They explore the use of color, perspective, proportion, dimension, line, and other elements and principles of visual composition and design.

Students become familiar with the history of art as they examine and analyze major works from different historical periods. They learn how to identify and compare stylistic differences in the works of significant artists. The role of artists in the media is also probed as students investigate the work of photographers, illustrators, costume and set designers, cartoonists, computer-graphics artists, and artists in television, video, and film production.

In some schools, students with a special ability or interest in art may be able to take additional art courses or may participate in an after-school art club.

For young adolescents, activities in art and music can provide a positive and productive avenue for releasing emotions and for expressing thoughts and ideas.

▶ PHYSICAL EDUCATION AND SPORTS

Almost all youngsters enjoy participating in sports and physical activities during their elementary school years. Enthusiasm for these activities begins to decline at about age 10. Some early teens lose all interest in keeping their bodies fit and no longer take part in games and sports on their own. The school physical education program for grades 7 through 9 plays an important role in keeping all young adolescents involved in fitness and sports activities during this crucial period of physical change and growth.

As in the earlier grades, the physical education curriculum is a combination of fitness, gymnastic activities, and games and sports. There is more emphasis on team sports at this level, although individual sports are preferred by many youngsters, and some schools add table tennis, wrestling, badminton, and paddle and racket games to their sports program. In team sports, football, basketball, baseball, and track and field are popular with boys; basketball, track and field, softball, and volleyball are generally favored by girls.

Students are usually asked to demonstrate proficiency in skills involving balance, endurance, strength, flexibility, and agility. Social attitudes and skills such as responsibility, leadership, tolerance, and a positive self-image are also stressed.

Recognizing that not all youngsters are athletes, the school physical education program is geared to helping teenagers acquire attitudes and skills that will help them maintain physical fitness in later years and remain actively involved in worthwhile recreational activities.

▶ HOME ECONOMICS AND INDUSTRIAL ARTS

Students in middle school or junior high school usually have the opportunity to study home economics or industrial arts. In some schools, industrial arts is called technology education. These courses are unique compared to the rest of the curriculum in that they help students learn and use practical skills.

The home economics course focuses on the skills of day-to-day living. Topics studied usually include family life and home management; food and nutrition; clothing; home furnishings; and how to be a smart consumer. During the course, students are required to complete a number of hands-on projects, which may include planning a menu and preparing a meal, planning a room and making a three-dimensional model, or sewing a simple garment. Role playing and dramatization are used to clarify the complexities of home and community relationships and family living.

In the industrial arts or technology education course, students are introduced to hand and power tools and their applications to the basic elements of mechanical drawing or drafting. They also learn about common industrial materials such as metal, plastics, and ceramics and about the tools and processes used in electricity, electronics, printing and graphic arts, photography, and other general crafts. Students are required to complete several projects that demonstrate what they have learned about materials and processes and what level of skill they have reached with basic tools, techniques, and procedures.

CURRICULUM-RELATED ARTICLES

Some of the important articles in THE NEW BOOK OF KNOWLEDGE that relate to the 7 through 9 school curriculum are listed here. Many other articles you or your youngsters may want to read while they are studying topics in these curriculum areas can be found by looking them up in the Index or in the set itself.

LANGUAGE AND LITERATURE

Vol.	Language
A	Alphabet
E	English Language
G	Grammar
H	Homonyms
L	Language Arts
P	Parts of Speech
Q-R	Reading
S	Semantics
	Slang
	Synonyms and Antonyms
W-X-Y-Z	Word Games
	Word Origins

Vol.	Writing
A	Abbreviations
	Address, Forms of
C	Compositions
D	Diaries and Journals
E	Essays
F	Figures of Speech
H	Handwriting
	Humor
J-K	Journalism
L	Letter Writing
O	Outlines
P	Proofreading
	Punctuation
S	Spelling
U-V	Vocabulary
W-X-Y-Z	Writing

Vol.	Oral Language/Speech
D	Debates and Discussions
J	Jokes and Riddles
O	Oratory
P	Parliamentary Procedure
	Plays
	Pronunciation
	Public Speaking
S	Speech
	Speech Disorders
	Storytelling
T	Tongue Twisters

Vol.	Reference, Research, and Study Skills
B	Book Reports and Reviews
	Books: From Author to Reader
D	Dictionaries
E	Encyclopedias
I	Indexes and Indexing
L	Libraries
M	Magazines
N	Newspapers
P	Paperback Books
Q-R	Reference Books
	Research
S	Study, How to
T	Tests and Test Taking
	Time Management

Vol.	Literature
A	Aeneid
	Africa, Literature of
	American Literature
	Arthur, King

B	Ballads
	Beowulf
	Biography, Autobiography, and
	Biographical Novel
C	Canadian Literature
	Chinese Literature
D	Diaries and Journals
	Drama
E	English Literature
	Essays
F	Faust Legends
	Fiction
	Figures of Speech
	Folklore
G	Germany, Literature of
	Greece, Language and Literature of
H	Hebrew Language and Literature
	Humor
I	Illustration and Illustrators
	Iliad
	India, Literature of
	Ireland, Literature of
	Italy, Language and Literature of
J-K	Japanese Literature
L	Literature
	Latin America, Literature of
	Latin Language and Literature
	Legends
M	Mystery, Detective, and Suspense
	Stories
	Mythology
N	Newbery, John
	Nobel Prizes: Literature
	Nonsense Rhymes
	Norse Mythology
	Novels
O	Odes
	Odyssey
P	Poetry
	Pulitzer Prizes
R	Russia, Language and Literature of
S	Scandinavian Literature
	Science Fiction
	Short Stories
	Spain, Language and Literature of

Vol.	**Author Biographies**
A	Adams, Henry
	Austen, Jane

B	Baldwin, James
	Balzac, Honoré de
	Bellow, Saul
	Blake, William
	Brontë Sisters
	Browning, Elizabeth Barrett and Robert
	Bryant, William Cullen
	Buck, Pearl
	Burns, Robert
	Byron, George Gordon, Lord
C	Cervantes Saavedra, Miguel de
	Chaucer, Geoffrey
	Chekhov, Anton
	Conrad, Joseph
	Cooper, James Fenimore
	Crane, Stephen
D	Dante Alighieri
	Defoe, Daniel
	Dickens, Charles
	Dickinson, Emily
	Donne, John
	Dos Passos, John
	Dostoevski, Fëdor
	Doyle, Sir Arthur Conan
	Dreiser, Theodore
	Dryden, John
	Dumas, Alexandre *Père* and Alexandre
	Fils
	Dunbar, Paul Laurence
E	Eliot, George
	Eliot, T. S.
	Emerson, Ralph Waldo
F	Faulkner, William
	Fitzgerald, F. Scott
	Frost, Robert
G	Goethe, Johann Wolfgang von
H	Hardy, Thomas
	Hawthorne, Nathaniel
	Heine, Heinrich
	Hemingway, Ernest
	Henry, O.
	Holmes, Oliver Wendell
	Homer
	Horace
	Hughes, Langston
	Hugo, Victor
I	Ibsen, Henrik
	Irving, Washington
J-K	James, Henry
	Johnson, James Weldon
	Johnson, Samuel
J-K	Keats, John
	Kipling, Rudyard

		Vol.	**Selections from Literature**

L Lewis, Sinclair
London, Jack
Lowell, Robert

M Marlowe, Christopher
Melville, Herman
Milton, John
Molière
Morrison, Toni

O O'Neill, Eugene
Orwell, George
Ovid

P Poe, Edgar Allan
Pope, Alexander

Q-R Racine, Jean Baptiste
Rossetti Family

S Sandburg, Carl
Scott, Sir Walter
Shakespeare, William
Shaw, George Bernard
Shelley, Percy Bysshe
Spenser, Edmund
Stein, Gertrude
Steinbeck, John
Stevens, Wallace
Stevenson, Robert Louis
Strindberg, August
Swift, Jonathan

T Tennyson, Alfred, Lord
Thackeray, William Makepeace
Thomas, Dylan
Thoreau, Henry David
Thurber, James
Tolkien, J. R. R.
Tolstoi, Leo
Twain, Mark

U-V Verne, Jules
Voltaire

W-X-
Y-Z Warren, Robert Penn
Wells, H. G.
Wharton, Edith
White, E. B.
Whitman, Walt
Whittier, John Greenleaf
Wilde, Oscar
Williams, Tennessee
Wordsworth, William
Wright, Richard

W-X-
Y-Z Yeats, William Butler

W-X-
Y-Z Zola, Emile

Vol.   Selections from Literature

A Africa, Literature of—African proverbs
and riddles
Alcott—Little Women (excerpt)

B Bible Stories
Browning, Elizabeth Barrett—How Do I
Love Thee (from Sonnets from the
Portuguese)
Browning, Robert—Pied Piper of
Hamelin (excerpt)
Buck, Pearl—The Good Earth (excerpt)
Burns, Robert—A Red, Red Rose
Byron, George Gordon, Lord
Childe Harold's Pilgrimage (excerpt)
The Prisoner of Chillon (excerpt)

C Cooper, James Fenimore—The Last of
the Mohicans (excerpt)

D Defoe, Daniel—Robinson Crusoe
(excerpt)
Dickens, Charles
David Copperfield (excerpt)
Oliver Twist (excerpt)
Dickinson, Emily
A Bird Came Down the Walk
I'll Tell You How the Sun Rose
Doyle, Sir Arthur Conan—The Red-
Headed League (excerpt)
Dumas, Alexandre *Fils*—The Three
Musketeers (excerpt)
Dunbar, Paul Laurence
Promise
Fulfilment

E Emerson, Ralph Waldo—The Concord
Hymn

F Frost, Robert
The Last Word of a Bluebird
The Pasture
Stopping by Woods on a Snowy
Evening
The Road Not Taken

G Gettysburg Address

H Hawthorne, Nathaniel—Tanglewood
Tales (excerpt)
Hugo, Victor—Les Misérables (excerpt)

I Irving, Washington—Rip Van Winkle
(excerpt)

J-K Keats, John
I Had a Dove
Endymion (excerpt)
When I Have Fears . . .

L Latin America, Literature of
The Heights of Machu Picchu
(excerpt, Neruda)

MATHEMATICS

SOCIAL STUDIES

C	Calhoun, John C.
	Civil War, United States
	Clay, Henry
	Colonial Life in America
	Colonial Sites You Can Visit Today
	Columbus, Christopher
	Compromise of 1850
	Confederate States of America
	Cooper, Peter
D	Declaration of Independence
	Douglas, Stephen A.
	Douglass, Frederick
	Dred Scott Decision
E	Emancipation Proclamation
	Exploration and Discovery
F	Federalist, The
	Fillmore, Millard
	Founders of the United States
	French and Indian War
G	Grant, Ulysses S.
H	Harrison, William Henry
I	Immigration
	Impeachment
	Incas
	Indians, American
	Industrial Revolution
J-K	Jackson, Andrew
	Jamestown
	Jay, John
	Jefferson, Thomas
	Johnson, Andrew
J-K	Kansas-Nebraska Act
L	Latin America
	Lee, Robert E.
	Lincoln, Abraham
	Lincoln-Douglas Debates
	Louisiana Purchase
M	Magna Carta
	Mann, Horace
	Marion, Francis
	Marshall, John
	Maya
	Mexican War
	Missouri Compromise
	Monroe Doctrine
	Monroe, James
	Morris, Gouverneur
N	Navigation
	Northwest Passage
O	Osceola
	Overland Trails

P	Pirates and Piracy
	Plymouth Colony
	Pontiac
	Public Lands
Q-R	Reconstruction Period
	Revolutionary War
S	Slavery
T	Territorial Expansion of the United States
	Thirteen American Colonies
	Tyler, John
U-V	Underground Railroad
	United States, Constitution of the
U-V	Vikings
W-X-Y-Z	War of 1812
	Washington, George
	Webster, Daniel
	Westward Movement
	Women's Rights Movement
W-X-Y-Z	Zenger, John Peter

Modern America Takes Shape (1865–1900)

A	Addams, Jane
	African Americans
B	Barton, Clara
	Blackwell, Elizabeth
	Bryan, William Jennings
	Buffalo Bill (William F. Cody)
C	Carnegie, Andrew
	Child Labor
	Civil Rights
	Civil Service
	Cowboys
D	Department Stores
	DuBois, W. E. B.
E	Ethnic Groups
F	Field, Cyrus
G	Geronimo
	Gold, Discoveries of
	Gompers, Samuel
H	Hayes, Rutherford B.
I	Immigration
	Indian Wars of North America
L	Labor Movement
	Liberty, Statue of
M	Manufacturing
	Morgan, John Pierpont

P	Petroleum and Petroleum Refining Pioneer Life	L	Labor-Management Relations League of Nations Lindbergh, Charles
Q-R	Ranch Life Red Cross Rockefeller, John D.	M	MacArthur, Douglas Malcolm X Marshall, George C. McKinley, William Mexico Middle East Missiles Mussolini, Benito
W-X- Y-Z	Washington, Booker T. Westinghouse, George Women's Rights Movement		

Twentieth Century America (1900–present)

A	Arabs Automobiles	N	Nazism New Deal Nixon, Richard M. North Atlantic Treaty Organization (NATO) Nuclear Weapons
B	Bethune, Mary McLeod Bunche, Ralph Bush, George		
C	Central America China Churchill, Sir Winston Civil Rights Civil Rights Movement Clinton, William Commonwealth of Independent States Coolidge, Calvin Cuba	O	Organization of American States Organization of Petroleum Exporting Countries (OPEC)
		P	Panama Canal Peace Corps Peace Movements Perry, Matthew C. Pershing, John J. Persian Gulf War Prohibition
D	DeGaulle, Charles Depressions and Recessions Disarmament Douglas, William O. Draft, or Conscription	Q-R	Racism Reagan, Ronald W. Reed, Walter Refugees Roosevelt, Eleanor Roosevelt, Franklin D. Roosevelt, Theodore
E	Eisenhower, Dwight D.		
F	Fascism Ferraro, Geraldine Ford, Henry Foreign Aid Programs Friedan, Betty	S	Segregation Social Security South Africa Spanish-American War Stalin, Joseph Steinem, Gloria Stevenson, Adlai E.
G	Germany Gorbachev, Mikhail		
H	Hispanic Americans Hitler, Adolf Haiti Holocaust Hooks, Benjamin L. Hoover, Herbert Hughes, Charles Evans	T	Taft, William H. Tanks Terrorism Treaties Truman, Harry S.
		U-V	Underground Movements Union of Soviet Socialist Republics United Nations Unknown Soldier Vietnam War
I	Imperialism International Relations International Trade		
J-K	Jackson, Jesse Johnson, Lyndon Baines	W-X- Y-Z	Warren Report Wilson, Woodrow Women's Rights Movement World War I World War II
J-K	Kennedy, John F. King, Martin Luther Kissinger, Henry Korean War		

Q-R	Rembrandt
	Revolutionary War (United States)
	Richelieu, Cardinal
	Rousseau, Jean Jacques
S	San Martín, José de
	Shakespeare, William
	Socialism
U-V	Voltaire
W-X-	Wellington, Duke of
Y-Z	Wren, Christopher

Nationalism, Imperialism, and the Modern Age (1800's through 1900's)

A	Africa
	Arabs
	Asia
	Australia
B	Begin, Menahem
	Ben-Gurion, David
	Bismarck, Otto Von
	Boer War
	Bush, George
C	Castro, Fidel
	Central America
	Chiang Kai-Shek
	Churchill, Sir Winston
	Civil Rights
	Clinton, William
	Commonwealth of Independent States
	Communism
	Conservation
	Crimean War
D	DeGaulle, Charles
	Dewey, John
	Disarmament
	Disraeli, Benjamin
	Dreyfus, Alfred
E	East India Company
	Einstein, Albert
	Environment
	Europe
	European Community
	Expressionism
F	Fascism
	Foreign Aid Programs
	Franco, Francisco
	Friedan, Betty
G	Gandhi, Mohandas
	Garibaldi, Giuseppe
	Gladstone, William
	Gorbachev, Mikhail

H	Hitler, Adolf
	Holocaust
I	Imperialism
	International Relations
	International Trade
	Islam
J-K	Kennedy, John F.
	Khruschev, Nikita
	King, Martin Luther
	Korean War
L	League of Nations
	Lenin, Vladimir Ilich
	Lloyd George, David
M	Mao Zedong
	Mazzini, Giuseppe
	Meir, Golda
	Middle East
	Missiles
	Modern Art
	Modern Music
	Mussolini, Benito
N	Napoleon III
	Nasser, Gamal Abdel
	Nazism
	Nehru, Jawaharlal
	Nixon, Richard M.
	North America
	North Atlantic Treaty Organization (NATO)
	Novels
	Nuclear Weapons
O	Organization of American States (OAS)
	Ottoman Empire
P	Palestine
	Peace Movements
	Population
	Poverty
Q-R	Reagan, Ronald W.
	Refugees
	Rhodes, Cecil
	Roosevelt, Franklin D.
S	Sadat, Anwar El-
	Schweitzer, Albert
	South America
	Southeast Asia
	Stalin, Joseph
	Suez Canal
	Sun Yat-Sen
T	Terrorism
	Thatcher, Margaret
	Tito
U-V	United Nations
	United States
	Union of Soviet Socialist Republics

U-V	Vatican City
	Victor Emmanuel
	Victoria, Queen
	Vietnam War
W-X-	Walesa, Lech
Y-Z	Wilson, Woodrow
	Women's Rights Movement
	World
	World War I
	World War II
W-X-	Yeltsin, Boris
Y-Z	
W-X-	Zionism
Y-Z	

Vol. Government

B	Bill of Rights
C	Cabinet of the United States
	Capitol, United States
	Census
	Central Intelligence Agency
	Citizenship
	Civil Rights
	Civil Service
	Courts
	Crime and Criminology
D	Declaration of Independence
	Democracy
E	Elections
	Electoral College
F	Federal Bureau of Investigation
	First Ladies
	Foreign Aid Programs
	Foreign Service
	Freedom of Religion, Speech, and Press
G	Government, Forms of
	Greece, Ancient
I	Impeachment
	International Relations
	International Trade
J-K	Jury
	Juvenile Crime
L	Law and Law Enforcement
	Lawyers
	Legislatures
	Locke, John
M	Magna Carta
	Municipal Government
N	Naturalization

O	Opinion Surveys
P	Parliamentary Procedure
	Parliaments
	Police
	Political Parties
	Presidency of the United States
	Prisons
	Propaganda
Q-R	Rome, Ancient
S	State Governments
	Supreme Court of the United States
T	Taxation
U-V	United Nations
	United States, Armed Forces of the
	United States, Congress of the
	United States, Constitution of the
	United States, Government of the
U-V	Vice Presidency of the United States
W-X-	Washington, D.C.
Y-Z	White House
	(See also the names of the presidents and of the individual departments of the United States government.)

Vol. Economics

A	Agriculture
	Agriculture, United States Department of
	Automation
B	Banks and Banking
	Budgets, Family
	Business
C	Capitalism
	Child Labor
	Communism
	Consumerism
	Credit Cards
D	Depressions and Recessions
	Dollar
E	Economics
	European Community
I	Income Tax
	Industry
	Inflation and Deflation
	Insurance
	Interest
	International Trade
L	Labor Movement
	Labor, United States Department of
	Labor-Management Relations

M	Manufacturing Marx, Karl Mass Production Money
N	Natural Resources
O	Occupational Health and Safety Old Age Organization of Petroleum Exporting Countries (OPEC)
P	Poverty Public Utilities
Q-R	Retail Stores
S	Sales and Marketing Social Security Socialism Stocks and Bonds
T	Tariff Taxation Trade and Commerce Trust Fund
U-V	Unemployment and Unemployment Insurance
W-X- **Y-Z**	Welfare, Public Workers' Compensation

Vol.	**Physical Geography**
A	Antarctica Arctic Atlantic Ocean Atmosphere
B	Biomes
C	Cities Climate
E	Earth Earthquakes Equator Erosion
G	Geography Glaciers Greenwich Observatory Gulf Stream
I	Indian Ocean International Date Line Islands
J-K	Jet Streams Jungles
L	Lakes Latitude and Longitude

M	Maps and Globes Mountains
N	Natural Resources
O	Ocean Oceanography Oceans and Seas of the World
P	Pacific Ocean and Islands Population Prairies
Q-R	Rain Forest Rivers
S	Seasons Surveying
T	Tides Time Trade Winds Tropics Tundra
U-V	Volcanoes
W-X- **Y-Z**	Water Weather Wetlands Winds and Weather World
W-X- **Y-Z**	Zones

SCIENCE AND TECHNOLOGY

Vol.	**Astronomy**
A	Astronomy
B	Black Holes Brahe, Tycho
C	Comets, Meteorites, and Asteroids Constellations Copernicus, Nicolaus Cosmic Rays
E	Eclipses
G	Galileo
H	Hawking, Stephen
J-K	Jupiter
J-K	Kepler, Johannes
M	Mars Mercury Milky Way Moon
N	Nebulas Neptune
O	Observatories

HEALTH AND SAFETY

F Family
First Aid
Food Preservation and Processing
Food Regulations and Laws
Food Shopping
Food Spoilage and Contamination
Freud, Sigmund

G Glands
Guidance Counseling

H Hair and Hairstyling
Harvey, William
Health
Health Foods
Heart
Hospitals

I Immune System

L Lenses
Lister, Joseph

M Medicine, History of
Menstruation
Mental Health
Mental Illness
Muscular System

N Narcotics
Nervous System
Nurses and Nursing
Nutrition

O Occupational Health and Safety
Old Age
Orthodontics
Osler, Sir William

P Physical Fitness
Poisons and Antidotes
Psychology
Public Health

Q-R Reed, Walter
Reproduction

S Safety
Skeletal System
Sleep
Smoking
Stomach

T Teeth
Transfusion, Blood

U-V Vaccination and Immunization
Vectors
Vitamins and Minerals

FOREIGN LANGUAGE

Vol. **Article**

F France, Language of

G Germany, Language of
Greece, Language and Literature of

H Hebrew Language and Literature

I Italy, Language and Literature of

L Languages
Latin Language and Literature

Q-R Russia, Language and Literature of

S Spain, Language and Literature of

MUSIC

Vol. **Music and Musical Instruments**

B Ballads
Ballet
Bands and Band Music
Bells and Carillons

C Carols
Chamber Music
Choral Music
Clarinet
Country Music

D Dance
Drum

E Electronic Music

F Folk Music Instruments

G Guitar

H Harmonica
Harp
Hymns

J-K Jazz

J-K Keyboard Instruments

L Lincoln Center for the Performing Arts

M Music
Musical Comedy
Musical Instruments
Music Festivals

N National Anthems and Patriotic Songs

O Opera
Operetta
Orchestra
Orchestra Conducting
Organ

P Percussion Instruments
Piano

Q-R Recorder
Records and Record Collecting
Rock Music

S	Stringed Instruments
U-V	Violin
	Voice Training and Singing
W-X-Y-Z	Wind Instruments

Vol.	**Music History and Biographies**
A	Ancient World, Music of the
	Anderson, Marian
B	Bach, Johann Sebastian
	Baroque Music
	Bartok, Bela
	Beatles, The
	Beethoven, Ludwig Van
	Berg, Alban
	Berlin, Irving
	Berlioz, Hector
	Brahms, Johannes
C	Chopin, Frederic
	Classical Age in Music
	Copland, Aaron
D	Dance Music
	Debussy, Claude
	Donizetti, Gaetano
	Dvořák, Antonin
E	Elgar, Sir Edward
F	Foster, Stephen
	Franck, César
G	Gershwin, George
	Gilbert and Sullivan Operettas
	Gluck, Christoph Willibald
	Grieg, Edvard
H	Handel, George Frederick
	Haydn, Joseph
I	Ives, Charles
L	Liszt, Franz
M	Macdowell, Edward
	Mahler, Gustav
	Mendelssohn, Felix
	Middle Ages, Music of the
	Modern Music
	Mozart, Wolfgang Amadeus
O	Offenbach, Jacques
P	Palestrina
	Prokofiev, Sergei
	Puccini, Giacomo
Q-R	Renaissance Music
	Romanticism

S	Schoenberg, Arnold
	Schubert, Franz
	Schumann, Robert
	Sibelius, Jean
	Strauss, Johann, Jr.
	Strauss, Richard
	Stravinsky, Igor
T	Tchaikovsky, Peter Ilyich
	Toscanini, Arturo
U-V	Verdi, Giuseppe
W-X-Y-Z	Wagner, Richard

Vol.	**Music Around the World**
A	Africa, Music of
	The *Mbira*
	The Talking Drum
D	Dutch and Flemish Music
E	English Music
F	Folk Dancing
	Folk Music
	France, Music of
G	Germany, Music of
I	India, Music of
	Italy, Music of
L	Latin America, Music of
O	Oriental Music
R	Russia, Music of
S	Spain, Music of
U-V	United States, Music of the

ART

Vol.	**Article**
A	Architecture
	Art
C	Cathedrals
	Color
	Computer Graphics
D	Design
	Drawing
E	Engraving
	Etching
G	Graphic Arts
H	Hermitage Museum
I	Illuminated Manuscripts
	Illustration and Illustrators
L	Louvre

M	Metropolitan Museum of Art Museums	**H**	Hals, Frans Holbein, Hans, the Younger Homer, Winslow
N	National Gallery (London) National Gallery of Art (Washington, D.C.)	**I**	Impressionism
		J-K	Kandinsky, Wassily Klee, Paul
O	Obelisks	**L**	Le Corbusier Leonardo da Vinci
P	Painting Photography Prado	**M**	Manet, Édouard Matisse, Henri Michelangelo
S	Sculpture		Mies Van Der Rohe, Ludwig Miro, Joan
U-V	Uffizi Gallery		Modern Art Modigliani, Amedeo
W-X- Y-Z	Watercolor		Mondrian, Piet Monet, Claude Moses, Grandma
		N	Nevelson, Louise
Vol.	**Art History and Biographies**	**O**	O'Keeffe, Georgia Oriental Art and Architecture
A	Ancient World, Art of the Angelico, Fra	**P**	Peale Family Pei, I. M. Picasso, Pablo
B	Baroque Art and Architecture Bellini Family Benton, Thomas Hart		Pollock, Jackson Prehistoric Art
	Bernini, Giovanni Lorenzo Botticelli, Sandro Brancusi, Constantin	**Q-R**	Raphael Rembrandt Renaissance Art and Architecture
	Braque, Georges Bruegel, Pieter, the Elder Byzantine Art and Architecture		Renoir, Pierre Auguste Reynolds, Sir Joshua Rockwell, Norman
C	Caravaggio, Michelangelo Merisi da Cassatt, Mary Cezanne, Paul		Rodin, Auguste Roman Art and Architecture Romanesque Art and Architecture
	Chagall, Marc		Romanticism Rubens, Peter Paul
D	Dali, Salvador Daumier, Honoré Degas, Edgar	**S**	Sargent, John Singer Sullivan, Louis Surrealism
	Delacroix, Eugène Donatello Doré, Gustave	**T**	Tintoretto Titian Toulouse-Lautrec, Henri de
	Drawing, History of Durer, Albrecht		Turner, Joseph Mallord William
E	Eakins, Thomas Egyptian Art and Architecture Expressionism	**U-V**	Utrillo, Maurice
		U-V	Van Dyck, Anthony Van Gogh, Vincent Velásquez, Diego
F	Folk Art Fragonard, Jean Honoré Francesca, Piero della		Vermeer, Jan
		W-X- Y-Z	Warhol, Andy Whistler, James Abbott McNeill
G	Gainsborough, Thomas Gauguin, Paul Gothic Art and Architecture		Wood, Grant Wren, Christopher Wright, Frank Lloyd
	Greece, Art and Architecture of Giotto Di Bondone Goya, Francisco Greco, El		Wyeth Family

PHYSICAL EDUCATION AND SPORTS

Q-R   Racing
Racket Sports
Rifle Marksmanship
Robinson, Jack Roosevelt (Jackie)
Roller-Skating
Rowing
Rugby
Ruth, George Herman (Babe)

S   Sailing
Shuffleboard
Skateboarding
Skiing
Skin Diving
Skydiving
Soap Box Derby
Soccer and Youth Soccer
Softball
Surfing
Swimming

T   Table Tennis
Tennis
Thorpe, James Francis (Jim)
Track and Field

U-V   Volleyball

W-X-
Y-Z   Water Polo
Waterskiing
Weight Lifting
Wrestling

HOME ECONOMICS AND INDUSTRIAL ARTS (TECHNOLOGY EDUCATION)

Vol.   **Home Economics**

A   Adolescence
Air Conditioning

B   Bread and Baking
Budgets, Family

C   Candy and Candy Making
Child Development
Clothing
Consumerism
Cooking
Cotton
Crocheting

D   Dairying and Dairy Products
Decorative Arts
Design
Detergents and Soap
Dry Cleaning
Dyes and Dyeing

F   Family
Fashion
Fibers
First Aid
Fish Farming
Fishing Industry
Food Around the World
Food Preservation and Processing
Food Regulations and Laws
Food Shopping
Food Spoilage and Contamination
Fruitgrowing
Furniture

G   Grain and Grain Products

H   Health
Health Foods
Heating Systems
Herbs, Spices, and Condiments
Home Economics
Homes

I   Interior Decorating

J-K   Knitting

L   Laundry
Leather
Lighting

M   Macramé
Meat and Meat Packing

N   Needlecraft
Nutrition
Nylon and Other Synthetic Fibers

O   Outdoor Cooking and Picnics

P   Poultry

Q-R   Recipes
Refrigeration
Rugs and Carpets

S   Safety
Sewing
Silk

T   Textiles

U-V   Vegetables
Vitamins and Minerals

W-X-
Y-Z   Weaving
Wool

Vol.   **Industrial Arts (Technology Education)**

C   Ceramics

D   Dies and Molds

E	Electricity	**M**	Materials Science
	Electric Motors		Mechanical Drawing
	Electronics		Metals and Metallurgy
	Electroplating	**N**	Nails, Screws, and Rivets
	Engraving	**P**	Photography
G	Graphic Arts		Plastics
	Grinding and Polishing		Printing
I	Industrial Arts	**T**	Tools
	Industrial Design	**W-X-**	Wood and Wood Products
L	Locks and Keys	**Y-Z**	Woodworking

APPENDIX

HOBBIES AND OTHER LEISURE-TIME ACTIVITIES IN THE NEW BOOK OF KNOWLEDGE

The favorite leisure-time activities of American families include hobbies, arts and crafts, sports, and games. Your youngsters may share their hobbies and other recreational activities with family members or with their friends, or they may choose to pursue an interest by themselves.

THE NEW BOOK OF KNOWLEDGE is an especially valuable resource for the hobbyist or the arts and crafts, sports, or games enthusiast. It contains numerous articles that describe and provide simple directions for a variety of leisure-time pursuits.

HOBBIES AND LEISURE-TIME ACTIVITIES

Vol.	Making Collections
A	Antiques and Antique Collecting
	Autographs
B	Buttons
C	Coins and Coin Collecting
D	Dolls
L	Leaves

Q-R	Records and Record Collecting
	Rocks
S	Shells
	Stamps and Stamp Collecting

Vol.	Model Making
A	Airplane Models
	Automobile Models

Q-R	Railroad Models		B	Badminton
				Baseball
Vol.	**Arts and Crafts**			Basketball
C	Clay Modeling			Bicycling
	Collage			Boardsailing
	Crocheting			Boats and Boating
				Bobsledding
D	Découpage			Bowling
	Dollhouses			Boxing
	Drawing		C	Camping
E	Enameling			Canoeing
F	Finger painting			Cheerleading
	Flower arranging			Croquet
J-K	Knitting		D	Diving
L	Linoleum-Block Printing		F	Fencing
M	Macramé			Field Hockey
N	Needlecraft			Fishing
O	Origami			Football
P	Papier-mâché		G	Golf
	Photography			Gymnastics
	Puppets and Marionettes		H	Handball
Q-R	Rubbings			Hiking and Backpacking
S	Sewing			Horse Racing
W-X-	Weaving			Horseback Riding
Y-Z	Wire Sculpture			Horseshoe Pitching
	Woodworking			Hostels and Hosteling
				Hunting
Vol.	**Raising Plants and Animals**		I	Iceboating
A	Aquariums			Ice Hockey
B	Birds as Pets			Ice-skating
C	Cats, Domestic		J-K	Jogging and Running
D	Dogs			Juggling (Learning the Cascade)
F	Fish As Pets		J-K	Karting
G	Gardens and Gardening			Kites
	Guinea Pigs, Hamsters, and Gerbils		L	Lacrosse
H	Houseplants			Little League Baseball
P	Pets		M	Marbles
T	Terrariums			Mountain Climbing
			P	Paddle Tennis
Vol.	**Sports and Outdoor Games**			Polo
A	Archery		Q-R	Racing
	Automobile Racing			Racket Sports
				Rifle Marksmanship
				Roller-skating
				Roping
				Rowing
				Rugby

S	Sailing	**C**	Card Games
	Shuffleboard		Charades
	Skateboarding		Checkers
	Skiing		Chess
	Skin Diving		Crossword Puzzles
	Skydiving	**D**	Darts
	Soapbox Derby		Dominoes
	Soccer	**F**	Folk Dancing
	Softball	**J-K**	Jacks
	Spelunking	**M**	Magic
	Surfing	**N**	Number Puzzles and Games
	Swimming	**P**	Plays
T	Tennis	**Q-R**	Radio, Amateur
	Track and Field	**T**	Table Tennis
U-V	Volleyball		Tricks and Puzzles
W-X-	Water Polo	**U-V**	Ventriloquism
Y-Z	Waterskiing		Video Production at Home
	Wrestling	**W-X-**	Word Games
		Y-Z	
Vol.	**Indoor Activities and Games**		
B	Backgammon		
	Billiards		

LITERATURE IN
THE NEW BOOK OF KNOWLEDGE

As children browse through THE NEW BOOK OF KNOWLEDGE, they are often captivated by the many literary selections they come upon, sometimes returning to their favorites again and again. Parents, too, spend many pleasurable moments reading selections to youngsters not yet able to read to themselves.

The literary selections in the set include fiction, nonfiction, and poetry—classics, short stories, legends, fairy tales, fables, myths, essays, poems and excerpts from novels and poems. Some selections accompany the biography of a famous writer. Others appear in articles that discuss a particular type of literature.

Below is a list of the literary selections contained in the encyclopedia. You will find information about selections that are particularly appropriate for your youngster's age-group in the grade-level sections of this STUDY GUIDE.

Vol.	Article	Literary Selections
A	Africa, Literature of	African proverbs and riddles
	Andersen, Hans Christian	The Emperor's New Clothes
	Arabian Nights	Aladdin and the Wonderful Lamp (excerpt)
		The Forty Thieves (excerpt)
	Alcott, Louisa May	Little Women (excerpt)
B	Barrie, Sir James Matthew	Peter Pan (excerpt)
	Bible Stories	Noah's Ark
		David and Goliath
		Jonah

		Daniel in the Lions' Den
		The Boy Jesus
	Browning, Elizabeth Barrett and Robert	How Do I Love Thee (from Sonnets from the Portuguese)
		Pied Piper of Hamelin (excerpt)
	Buck, Pearl	The Good Earth (excerpt)
	Burns, Robert	A Red, Red Rose
	Byron, George Gordon, Lord	Childe Harold's Pilgrimage (excerpt)
		The Prisoner of Chillon (excerpt)
C	Carroll, Lewis	Alice's Adventures in Wonderland (excerpt)
	Christmas Story	Gospel according to Luke
	Civil Rights Movement	I Have a Dream (excerpts)
	Cooper, James Fenimore	The Last of the Mohicans (excerpt)
D	Defoe, Daniel	Robinson Crusoe (excerpt)
	Diaries and Journals	Anne Frank's Diary (excerpt)
	Dickens, Charles	David Copperfield (excerpt)
		Oliver Twist (excerpt)
	Dickinson, Emily	A Bird Came Down the Walk
		I'll Tell You How the Sun Rose
	Doyle, Sir Arthur Conan	The Red-Headed League (excerpt)
	Dumas, Alexandre *Père* and Alexandre *Fils*	The Three Musketeers (excerpt)

	Dunbar, Paul Laurence	Promise
		Fulfilment
E	Emerson, Ralph Waldo	The Concord Hymn
	Essays	The Fight (Hazlitt: excerpt)
F	Fables	The Lion and the Mouse (Aesop)
		The Ant and the Grasshopper (Aesop)
		The Four Oxen and the Lion (Aesop)
		The Tyrant Who Became a Just Ruler (Bidpai)
		The Blind Men and the Elephant (Saxe)
		The Moth and the Star (Thurber)
	Fairy Tales	The Enchanted Princess (German)
		The Princess on the Pea (Andersen)
		The Sleeping Beauty (Perrault)
		Little Red Riding-Hood (de la Mare)
	Field, Eugene	A Dutch Lullaby
	Figures of Speech	Silver (de la Mare)
		The Toaster (Smith, W. J.)
		Dandelions (Frost, F. M.)
		The Little Rose Tree (Field)
		Everyone Sang (Sassoon)

		The Night Will Never Stay (Farjeon)
		Brooms (Aldis)
		No Shop Does the Bird Use (Coatsworth)
	Folklore	Cinderella or The Little Glass Slipper (Perrault)
		John Henry (American)
		Johnny Appleseed (American)
		Pecos Bill (American)
	Frost, Robert	The Last Word of a Bluebird
		The Pasture
		Stopping by Woods on a Snowy Evening
		The Road Not Taken
G	Gettysburg Address	Gettysburg Address
	Grahame, Kenneth	The Wind in the Willows (excerpt)
	Grimm, Jacob and Wilhelm	The Shoemaker and the Elves
		Rapunzel
		Hansel and Gretel
H	Hawthorne, Nathaniel	Tanglewood Tales (excerpt)
	Hugo, Victor	Les Misérables (excerpt)
I	Irving, Washington	Rip Van Winkle (excerpt)
J-K	Keats, John	I Had a Dove
		Endymion (excerpt)
		When I Have Fears . . .
	Kipling, Rudyard	The Elephant's Child

L	Latin America, Literature of	The Heights of Machu Picchu (Neruda: excerpt)
	Legends	Roland and Oliver (France)
		The Legend of the Blue Plate (China)
		Legend of the White Deer (Native American)
		The Legend of Robin Hood (England)
	London, Jack	The Call of the Wild (excerpt)
	Longfellow, Henry Wadsworth	The Arrow and the Song
		The Village Blacksmith
M	Melville, Herman	Moby Dick (excerpt)
	Milne, A. A.	Missing
	Milton, John	L'Allegro (excerpt)
N	Nonsense Rhymes	I Went to Noke (Nursery)
		The Song of Milkanwatha (Strong)
		OIC (Anonymous)
		The Common Cormorant (Anonymous)
		Jabberwocky (Carroll)
		The Maiden of Passamaquoddy (DeMille)
		The Reason for the Pelican (Ciardi)
		The Yak (Belloc)
		Habits of the Hippopotamus (Guiterman)
		Eletelephony (Richards)

T	Tennyson, Alfred, Lord	Crossing the Bar (from The Lady of Shalott)	
	Thackeray, William Makepeace	Vanity Fair (excerpt)	
	Thoreau, Henry David	Walden (excerpt)	
	Thurber, James	The Great Quillo (excerpt)	
	Tolkien, J. R. R.	The Hobbit (excerpt)	
	Twain, Mark	The Adventures of Tom Sawyer (excerpt)
		The Celebrated Jumping Frog of Calaveras County (except)

W-X-Y-Z	White, E. B.	Charlotte's Web (excerpt)	
	Whitman, Walt	O Captain! My Captain!	
		When Lilacs Last in the Dooryard Bloom'd	
	Wordsworth, William	Daffodils	
		My Heart Leaps Up When I Behold	
W-X-Y-Z	Yeats, William Butler	Under Ben Bulben (excerpt)	
		The Lake Isle of Innisfree	

PROJECTS AND EXPERIMENTS IN THE NEW BOOK OF KNOWLEDGE

Many articles in THE NEW BOOK OF KNOWLEDGE include useful and enjoyable projects or experiments. These excellent activities help students improve their understanding of basic concepts by giving them hands-on experiences with ideas or processes they have just read about. In addition, these activities provide many choices and ideas students can use for school projects and fairs in science, mathematics, language and literature, art, music, home economics, and personal hobbies and crafts.

Vol.	Article	Projects and Experiments
A	Abacus	The Chinese abacus
	Antibiotics	Growing penicillium molds
	Apple	How to sprout apple seeds
	Aquariums	How to set up a home aquarium
	Arithmetic	Using an addition table
		Using a multiplication table
		Using estimation strategies
B	Balloons and Ballooning	What makes a balloon rise?
	Birds	Bird-watching
	Birds as Pets	Choosing a bird

			Numbers in boxes
			Cards in order
			Pennies at home
			How tall will you grow?
			Another weigh
			Letter play
			Number play
			A corn-y story
			Clockworks
			I know your number
			A dice trick
			Which door?
			Which pill?
			Where are those signs?
			Digits everywhere
			Number pyramids
			Pig
			A number board
	Numbers and Number Systems		Recognizing numbers in everyday situations
	Numerals and Numeration Systems		Can you read and write Egyptian numerals?
O	Optical Illusions		Illustration: Making a miniature "movie"
	Osmosis		An experiment to show osmosis
	Outlines		Preparing an outline for a talk or composition
P	Parties		Planning a party
	Peanuts and Peanut Products		How to make your own peanut butter
	Pets		How to care for pets
	Photography		Developing the film
			Printing the photographs
	Plankton		Collecting plankton

Plant Pests		The gall maker and its home
Plants		Growing potato plants
		Growth movements
Plays		How to put on a play
Psychology		Testing the way people think and remember
		Do you remember everything you perceive?
Public Speaking		Preparing a speech
Puppets and Marionettes		How to make a puppet
		How to make a marionette
Q-R	Radio, Amateur	How to become a ham radio operator
	Recipes	Dinner for four; sweets and snacks
	Recorder	How to play the recorder
	Records and Record Collecting	Record collecting as a hobby
	Rubbings	The wax method
		The graphite method
S	Shells	Collecting shells
	Soils	Soil demonstrations: Can changes in temperature break up rocks?
		Do growing plants break up rocks?
		Why should topsoil be conserved?

		Observing the differences in soil particles		Tests and Test Taking	General strategies
		Testing to see if soil is acid		Ticks	How to safely remove a tick
	Solar System	Creating a model of the solar system		Tongue Twisters	Five tough tongue twisters
				Topology	Problems in topology
	Sound and Ultrasonics	Demonstrations you can do with sound	**U-V**	Valentines	How to make valentines
	Stamps and Stamp Collecting	Collecting stamps	**W-X-** **Y-Z**	Water	Conserving water at home
					Purifying dirty water
	Sun	Observing sunspots		Weaving	Learning to weave
				Winds and weather	Demonstration of Coriolis force
T	Teeth	Caring for teeth		Woodworking	Woodworking projects
	Telegraph	Make your own telegraph set		Worms	How to make an earthworm farm
	Terrariums	How to make a terrarium			

WONDER QUESTIONS IN THE NEW BOOK OF KNOWLEDGE

Wonder Questions have been an integral part of the encyclopedia since the original 1911 edition of THE BOOK OF KNOWLEDGE. They have always been a source of pleasure and adventure for those of us who are in constant search of interesting bits of information about everything.

Vol.	Article	Wonder Questions
A	Abolition Movement	What were the Gag Rules?
	Aerodynamics	What keeps a plane up in the air?
	Africa	What are the Mountains of the Moon?
	African Americans	What is Kwanzaa?
	Asia	What and where is Asia Minor?
	Astronauts	Why are astronauts weightless?
	Astronomy	How do astronomers measure distances in space?
	Atmosphere	Is the Earth's atmosphere warming?
	Atoms	How big is an atom?
		What holds matter together?
		What is the difference between nuclear energy and atomic energy?

	Automation	What is automation? What is feedback?
B	Bacteria	Are bacteria plants or animals?
	Badminton	What makes a champion?
	Balloons and Ballooning	What makes a balloon rise?
	Bats	How do bats find their way in the dark?
	Bees	Are there really "killer" bees?
	Bermuda	What is the Bermuda Triangle?
	Birds as Pets	Can people get parrot fever?
	Blindness	What is a talking book?
	Blood	What is blood made of?
	Body, Human	What is the largest organ of your body?
	Books	What information is on a copyright page?
	Brain	Does a larger brain mean greater intelligence?
	Bridges	Why were some of the early bridges in America covered?
	Building Construction	Why is a tree or an American flag sometimes placed on the highest part of a building under construction? Why don't tall buildings blow down in a strong wind?
	Bullfighting	How did bullfighting begin?
	Business	What are gross income and net income?
	Butterflies and Moths	How can you tell a butterfly from a moth?
C	Calendar	Why are the abbreviations "B.C." and "A.D." used with dates?
	Candles	Why do we put lighted candles on a birthday cake and then blow them out?
	Card Games	What is the origin of the suits in a deck of cards? Why are there three face cards in each suit?
	Cement and Concrete	How is cement made?
	Census	How is the U.S. population census taken?
	Checkers	How old is checkers?
	Clowns	Why don't most clowns speak?
	Coins and Coin Collecting	Why are some coins grooved around the edge?
	Colonial Life in America	What did the colonists eat?
	Columbus, Christopher	Where did Columbus really land on his first voyage to the New World? What were the consequences of Columbus' voyage in 1492?
	Computers	What are bits and bytes?

	Cosmic Rays	Why are cosmic rays important?	
D	Dairying and Dairy Products	What is a dairy farm?	
	Debates and Discussions	What is the difference between a debate and a discussion?	
	Delaware	What was Rodney's Ride?	
	Deserts	How did Death Valley get its name?	
	Dinosaurs	What were dinosaurs?	
		What was the deadliest dinosaur that ever walked the earth?	
	Doctors	Is the Surgeon General really a surgeon?	
	Dogs	What are the dog days?	
	Dollar	How can you tell if a bill is counterfeit?	
	Dyes and Dyeing	What makes dyes fade?	
E	Earth	How do earthquakes help scientists learn about the Earth's interior?	
	Earth, History of	How do geologists learn about the history of the planet Earth?	
	Economics	What is the amazing "invisible hand"?	
	Ecuador	What were the enchanted islands?	
	Electric Motors	What makes electric motors run?	

	Elevators and Escalators	How fast can the fastest elevators climb?	
	England, History of	What happened to the Princes in the tower?	
	Europe	Where and what are the Low Countries?	
	Exploration and Discovery	Why was the New World named "America"?	
	Explosives	What is an explosive?	
F	Fairy Tales	Where did fairy tales come from?	
	Fallout	How soon does fallout fall?	
		How long does fallout last?	
	Fibers	What is a fiber?	
		Why do fibers differ?	
	Fillmore, Millard	What was the Know-Nothing Party?	
	Fire and Combustion	What makes a fire?	
	Fire Fighting and Prevention	What happens when you pull the fire alarm?	
	First Aid	What is a "Good Samaritan"?	
	Fish	How big do fish grow?	
		What fish's "mother" is really its father?	
		Do fish sleep?	
	Fishing	When was the fishing reel invented?	
	Floating	Why do boats float?	
		Why do balloons float?	
	Fog and Smog	Why is it difficult to see through fog?	

	Journalism	What are tabloids?
	Jupiter	What is the Great Red Spot on Jupiter?
J-K	Karate	What is the difference between karate and judo?
	Kennedy, John F.	Who was Lee Harvey Oswald?
	Kingdoms of Living Things	What is a backbone?
	Kites	Why does a kite fly?
L	Lawyers	What is meant by "Possession is nine points of the law"?
	Lead	What is the "lead" in a lead pencil?
	Learning	Did ancient Egyptians understand the importance of the brain?
		What is an IQ test?
	Leather	How is leather made?
	Leaves	Why do leaves change color?
		Why do trees lose their leaves in the fall?
	Life	How well can machines imitate the activities of human beings?
	Light	What causes the delicate colors of soap bubbles?
	Lobsters	Why must lobsters be cooked alive?
	Locomotives	How did the cowcatcher get its name?
M	Mammals	What is a mammal?

	Mars	Is there life on Mars?
	Mathematics, History of	Who invented mathematical signs?
	Medicine, Tools and Techniques of	Why must a fever thermometer be shaken?
	Microscopes	How much magnification can a microscope give?
	Microwaves	Why do foods cook faster in a microwave oven?
	Milky Way	How far away is the nearest galaxy?
	Moon	What is earthshine?
	Moss	When is a moss not a moss?
	Mountains	What is the longest mountain chain in the world?
	Muscular System	What is the levator labii superioris alaeque nasi?
	Museums	Who works in a museum?
	Music	What is the origin of clef signs?
		Why are so many musical terms written in Italian?
	Musical Instruments	How do musical instruments make sounds?
N	National Cemetery System	Who may be buried in national cemeteries?
	National Park System	How are national park system areas established?

Neptune	What is the outermost planet in the solar system?	
Newspapers	Is the news truth? What is a press release?	
Noise	How does noise affect hearing?	
Numbers and Number Systems	What is infinity?	
Numerals and Numeration Systems	Who invented zero?	
Nursery Rhymes	Was Mother Goose a real person?	
Nylon and Other Synthetic Fibers	How are synthetic fibers named?	

O Old Age — What are the problems of old age?

Onion — Why do most people "cry" when chopping onions?

Opinion Surveys — How is an opinion survey done?

P Pacific Ocean and Islands — What is the Great Barrier Reef?

Paper — How is paper made?

Peace Movements — What is a pacifist?

Pearls — What makes a pearl valuable? How are artificial pearls made?

Perfumes — What are toilet water and cologne?

Photosynthesis — How do plants get energy from sunlight? How can plants produce more food?

Plants — How big can a plant grow?

Plastics — Why do leaves change color in the autumn? Which plant has the biggest seed? What is cellophane?

Pluto — Is Pluto really a planet?

Poetry — How did poetry begin? What is poetry?

Population — Will population growth stop?

Psychology — What is personality? Do you remember everything you perceive? What is instinct?

Public Relations — What is the difference between public relations and advertising?

Pumps — How do pumps work?

Q-R Rabbits and Hares — What is the difference between a rabbit and a hare?

Radio — Why can you hear radio stations from farther away at night? What is static?

Radio and Radar Astronomy — Does life as we know it on Earth exist anywhere else in the universe?

Railroads — How did 4 feet 8½ inches come to be picked for the width of track?

Rain, Snow, Sleet, and Hail — What is the shape of a falling raindrop?

		Is there such a thing as red snow?
Rain Forest		Where are the rain forests?
Revolutionary War		Who was Molly Pitcher?
Roman Catholic Church		What are holy days? Why is it called the Roman Catholic Church? What are sacramentals?

S Salt — How do we get salt?

Saturn — Where did Saturn's rings come from?

Seasons — Why is it hotter in summer than it is in winter?

Sharks, Skates, and Rays — How do sharks find their prey?

Ships and Shipping — Why are the left and right sides of a ship called port and starboard? Why are ships christened with champagne?

Silver — Why the name "sterling"?

Slavery — Where was slavery abolished first?

Sleep — What happens during sleep?

Soils — Can changes in temperature break up rocks? Do growing plants break up rocks? Why should topsoil be conserved?

Sound and Ultrasonics — Why do you hear a roaring sound, like the sound of the sea, when you hold a large snail or conch shell over your ear?

Suppose a tree crashes to the ground in a forest where there is no one to hear it. Does the sound exist?

Spiders — What is the largest spider?

Spies — What are some types of espionage agents?

Starfishes and Their Relatives — How does a starfish move?

Stars — What are stars made of? Why do stars twinkle?

Stocks and Bonds — What are blue chip stocks? What is "cornering the market"?

Stomach — What makes a stomach growl?

Stonehenge — Who built Stonehenge?

Submarines — How is a submarine navigated underwater?

Sun — Does sunspot activity affect the Earth's climate?

T Tea — How is tea made?

Technology — What is high technology?

Television — What are television ratings?

Textbooks — Who writes textbooks?

Thunder and Lightning — What is thunder? How can you tell how close a thunderstorm is to you?